RESEARCH SERIES, NO. 38

SOCIALISM
IN
SUB-SAHARAN AFRICA

A NEW ASSESSMENT

EDITED BY

CARL G. ROSBERG &
THOMAS M. CALLAGHY

INSTITUTE OF INTERNATIONAL STUDIES
University of California
Berkeley

International Standard Book Number 0-87725-138-X

Library of Congress Card Number 79-84635

© 1979 by the Regents of the University of California

CONTENTS

CONTENTS

PREFACE

In 1964 *African Socialism* was published as an initial multi-disciplinary effort to explore the themes and meaning of an ideology born of the African independence movement. African socialism tended to be identified with a new African future and few African leaders ignored it. This new volume, appearing fifteen years later, seeks to supplement that effort and to provide a new evaluation of socialism in Africa and an explanation for the continued attractiveness of socialist ideology to many African leaders and peoples. The first part of the volume undertakes an assessment of the efforts to implement African socialism in the early 1960's; the second part focuses upon the use (and abuse) of socialism as a developmental ideology in Africa; the third part is a preliminary analysis of the nature and problems of the "second wave" of socialism in sub-Saharan Africa.

We would like to thank the Institute of International Studies and the Committee on Research of the University of California, Berkeley, for the generous support they have provided. We wish to extend our appreciation to the contributors of this symposium whose cooperation made this volume possible. Each author, of course, is responsible for the views and opinions expressed in his or her own contribution.

We are also very grateful to John Ravenhill for his many helpful comments. The editorial assistance of Paul Gilchrist of IIS has been invaluable in the preparation of this symposium for publication. The expert composer typing of the text in final form for publication was by Christine Egan.

C.G.R.
T.M.C.

Berkeley, California
February 1979

NOTES ON CONTRIBUTORS

CARL G. ROSBERG is Professor of Political Science and Director, Institute of International Studies, University of California, Berkeley.

THOMAS M. CALLAGHY teaches political science at the Pennsylvania State University.

LADIPO ADAMOLEKUN is Professor and Head, Department of Public Administration, University of Ife (Nigeria).

EDWARD A. ALPERS is Associate Professor of History, University of California, Los Angeles.

KEVIN BROWN is a staff member of the Food Policy Center, Washington, D.C.

SAMUEL DECALO is Professor and Head, Department of Political and Administrative Studies, University of Botswana and Swaziland (Botswana).

JOHN W. HARBESON is Associate Professor of Political Science and Chairperson, Division of Social Sciences, University of Wisconsin-Parkside.

KENNETH JOWITT is Associate Professor of Political Science, University of California, Berkeley.

DAVID D. LAITIN is Assistant Professor of Political Science, University of California, San Diego.

JAMES A. McCAIN is Associate Professor of African and Afro-American Studies, State University of New York at Brockport.

NOTES ON CONTRIBUTORS

DEAN E. McHENRY, JR. is Assistant Professor of Political Science, University of Illinois at Urbana-Champaign.

STEPHEN A. QUICK is Assistant Professor of Political Science, College of the Holy Cross (Massachusetts).

LARS RUDEBECK is Associate Professor of Political Science and member of the Working Group for the Study of Development Strategies, University of Uppsala (Sweden).

ANN SEIDMAN is Nancy Duke Lewis Professor and Visiting Professor in Sociology, Brown University.

INTRODUCTION

Socialism in Africa is no longer in its infancy. Two decades or more have elapsed since African leaders began advocating an African socialism in which concerns for rapid economic growth are linked to an equitable distribution of wealth and an avoidance of class structure. In a few countries serious efforts were embarked upon to implement socialist policies. Despite the initial optimism of African leaders, the task has proved to be herculean; the results often appear meager,* and most goals remain unfulfilled "unanalyzed abstractions."† Rhetoric has clashed with harsh realities, bringing to an end (as Thomas Callaghy explains in a succeeding chapter) the socialist experiments of the Nkrumah regime in Ghana and Keita regime in Mali. Elsewhere the passage of time has not led to a precise definition of African socialism. A general consensus of its nature has not emerged, and little systematization of its tenets has taken place. The initial vaunted distinctiveness of African socialism has receded as more Marxist-Leninist sounding views of socialism have come to dominate the scene in the "second wave" of African aspirations to implement socialism. The current trend is toward versions of scientific socialism. But in both the earlier and the more recent efforts, pragmatism in the face of severe obstacles is the salient characteristic of African efforts at socialist transformation.

The use of African socialism to underscore the distinctiveness of the continent has declined. It is no longer a special badge of continental identity. The African situation did not prove to be as distinctive as many had believed it to be, and African states have not been exempt from general laws of social and political change. The communalism of pre-colonial Africa did not, as hoped, make for an easy or rapid transition to socialism. Political and economic legacies

*In *The Arusha Declaration, Ten Years After* (Dar es Salaam: Government Printer, 1977), President Nyerere states that "Tanzania is neither socialist, nor self-reliant" (p. 1). However, he believes the Tanzanian people "have taken some very important steps towards our goal" (p. 2) and are following the correct path: "We have many problems to overcome, and many mistakes to correct; but we are moving in the right direction" (p. 48).

†See "Introduction" in William H. Friedland and Carl G. Rosberg, Jr., eds., *African Socialism* (Stanford: Stanford University Press, 1964), p. 2.

1

were serious obstacles to change—particularly the nature of the in-herited colonial state and the dependent role of African states in the world economic system. It became apparent that socialism was not "natural" to Africa. The roots of African socialism in indigenous society proved to be very shallow. As the nature of societal relations and the structures of domination became appreciated in the post-independence period, some African thinkers and rulers such as Sékou Touré began to move back to older notions of socialism that stressed struggle and class conflict.

Instead of being able to cut ties to the outside world and in-crease local autarky, African leaders have been forced to come to terms with the dependent position of their states in the world eco-nomic system. While the degree of their dependency varies, African states are generally at the mercy of fluctuations in the international economic situation—worldwide inflation, recession, oil crises, declining aid revenues, changing commodity prices and demands, trade problems, and debt. Ann Seidman addresses an array of these dependency relations in the initial essay in this volume.

Let us now consider some of the political, social, and economic problems which have inhibited the implementation of socialism.

POLITICAL AND SOCIETAL ISSUES OF IMPLEMENTATION

African socialist leaders have made "tactical" concessions or, in the terminology used by Kenneth Jowitt in his analysis of the role of ideology in African politics, there are self-imposed ideological constraints on socialist leaders in acting in conformance with their proclaimed political identity. These concessions have been made at the expense of advancing socialism in order to assure political survival or the maintenance of political order. They are necessary because party/state power is inadequate, which usually forces com-promise with both internal and external groups and often results in unwanted and costly commitments that jeopardize socialist pro-grams. "Touré's struggle for personal survival," says Ladipo Adamo-lekun, "became the major determinant of how he should seek to transform Guinea into a socialist state." For example, Touré abol-ished some state enterprises in order to encourage trade and relaxed exclusive state control of trade and commerce because of group resistance. When a socialist program meets too much resistance, proves too costly, or is too difficult to implement (as Stephen Quick indicates has occurred in Zambia in the case of the cooperative

program), it may be abandoned. The political costs of continuance may be too high. African leaders must maintain themselves in power first; only then can they devote their attention to the development and implementation of socialist programs. President Agosthino Neto of Angola, for example—as Kevin Brown shows—has had to cope with both internal party challenges to his authority and a continuing civil war.

For socialist leaders such as Touré, Nkrumah, and Keita, neo-colonialism and/or imperialism was seen as a more significant enemy to the establishment of socialism than any internal opposition. However, resistance by domestic elements has been much stronger than expected. Thus Quick argues that the abandonment of experiments in rural socialism in Zambia was a combination of weak political will by the political elite and the resistance of parastatal bureaucrats, local entrepreneurs, African communal farmers, and various foreign groups. Similarly, Touré has been subjected to strong pressure from internal capitalist-oriented groups, both traders and bureaucrats. And John Harbeson's analysis suggests that Ethiopian military leaders have been confronted with resistance from both the right and the left—from local notables and elites, regional rebels, and bureaucrats to radical students and urban workers. The establishment of control by the new socialist elites in both Ethiopia and Angola has proved to be an enormous task requiring massive outside military and technical assistance, and both efforts have been characterized by intense factionalism and struggles for the control of the socialist polity.

The argument frequently advanced by proponents of African socialism that traditional African culture was a ready foundation for socialist programs was greatly overstated. The belief that there existed a traditional African socialism has proved to be largely a myth, and reliance on traditional African values to support socialist policies has been a key weakness in the African version of socialism. Many appeared to believe that the collectivization of agriculture would be easily accomplished because of traditional communalism; however, as Dean McHenry reports, rural populations in Tanzania (for example) did not voluntarily submit to villagization in large numbers—much less to consistent and effective communal production. And in Zambia, an important factor in the breakdown of the attempt to establish a viable cooperative program was intense conflict among rural participants.

The hope remains that the essence of socialism can somehow be effectively translated into the African context without having to

3

take an antagonistic stance toward traditional values and structures, but it would appear that the second wave attempts at socialism are likely to pursue a confrontational course toward the traditional culture. Despite the emphasis by Amilcar Cabral on identifying the Africanness of scientific socialism, efforts in the former Portuguese territories of Mozambique, Angola, and Guinea-Bissau are focused on the creation of a "new socialist man" who is free of colonial, capitalist, racist, and tribalist "complexes," and bringing to an end—as Lars Rudebeck puts it—"once and for all 'the exploitation of man by man.' " The adoption of scientific socialism in these countries appears to strengthen this attitude of confrontation toward traditional social structures. Post-imperial Ethiopia has also opted for a confrontational stance with respect to many elements of the *ancien regime* sociopolitical and economic structure. Here there is little glorification of traditional values; one exception, of course, is *Ethiopia Tikdem*—the centrality of national unity.

There has been a reluctance in the past to employ extensive coercion to implement socialist policies—as a matter of principle. Perhaps the foremost of this disposition has been President Julius Nyerere of Tanzania. Despite much obfuscation, however, he finally permitted the use of coercion (the *threat* of coercion was usually sufficient) to advance Tanzania's villagization program, but according to McHenry, he has not allowed coercion to be used to institute collective production. The elites of the second wave of socialism appear more inclined to attempt the employment of coercion as an instrument of policy implementation. However, the coercive potential of most African states is quite limited, and is often restricted to the maintenance of basic order. As noted, a pervasive weakness in the pursuit of the socialist option in Africa is the low level of state/party power. Ruling political parties are organizationally weak and are not (or are only very poor) mobilizational structures. The weakness of the party as a whole, however, may not be as important as a lack of consensus among the leadership regarding the desirability of socialism. Where ideology becomes part of the power struggle, socialism tends to be identified with the present head of state, and power contenders may seek to promote alternatives to it. An additional weakness of the African party/state is that it has very few dedicated and trained cadre. Its technical capabilities are thin; inefficiency and corruption are often rampant; hierarchical control is uncertain. It has not been a Marxist-Leninist "organizational weapon" capable of bringing about major socioeconomic and behavioral change even if the political will may have existed.

INTRODUCTION

The "first wave" of African expressions of socialism in the early 1960's was largely devoid of class analysis. Many African leaders asserted that there were no classes in Africa—that socio-economic stratification and conflicting group interests did not exist there. An element of this attitude was a hesitancy to identify *internal* enemies of socialism in African states, with the result that political parties have been inclusionary rather than exclusionary. By being a citizen one is normally a member of the ruling party; hence one is a socialist. Thus the doctrine of African socialism purported to provide leadership with a unifying and legitimatizing ideology, and party organization was open rather than vanguard in design. While Sékou Touré, an early proponent of African socialism, belatedly came to accept a class analysis of Guinea's polity, he continues to identify the ruling Parti Democratique as both a vanguard and a "mass" party. Members of Guinea's "exploiting class"—i.e., traders and industrialists—can be party members, but Touré has stipulated that they "cannot direct the party." Tanzania's leadership code includes a similar prohibition for its "exploiting class." The adoption of scientific socialism by the second wave of the mid-1970's has tended to favor a vanguard party and to foster class analysis to identify the internal enemies of the revolution.

The tasks confronting African leaders in building socialist economies have been formidable, and the cores of most preexisting economic structures have remained practically untouched. All African economies, whether socialist or capitalist-oriented, are fundamentally mixed and export-oriented. The capabilities of the state in capital accumulation, planning, control, and implementation have proved to be extremely limited. Planning capabilities, in particular, have not been up to early expectations. Expectations of pan-African socialism and hopes for intensive inter-African economic cooperation have not been realized. Despite their oft-expressed determination to achieve self-reliance, the fact remains that African states are still heavily dependent on the capitalist trade system and in some cases are more extensively integrated into the capitalist-dominated world economy than before independence.

While state intervention and participation in the various sectors of the economy have increased, these are not necessarily indications of the fostering of socialism in these sectors or in the country as a whole. Such state activities are as likely to represent some form of state capitalism as socialism. Possessing mixed economies, African states permit—even actively encourage—outside private or state foreign investment. In some cases there are sizable parastatal sectors,

5

as in Tanzania, but comprehensive economic control by the state is not necessarily the result. Many nationalizations have taken place, but direct state operation control is still rare. Some of these nationalizations have occurred more by default than by design, leaving the parastatal sector burdened with weak and even failing economic enterprises which are not allowed to die. In Tanzania, and to some degree in Guinea, private domestic investment has been officially discouraged, but some form of private domestic economy continues there. Touré has even had to back down and reverse socialist control measures in Guinea's trading and commercial sectors. In other countries, capitalism thrives despite professed socialist orientations. Pragmatism has clearly ruled the day, as it has—so far—in the second wave attempts in Angola and Mozambique. The nature of economic relations makes major structural change practically impossible if economic collapse is to be avoided.

As noted earlier, the economies of African socialist states remain dependent on and integrated into the world capitalist economy —subject to its crises and fluctuations, to its inflation, recessions, and technological changes. Economic autarky is not a viable option. Heavily dependent on commodity trade, they are also dependent on outside sources for capital accumulation, technical assistance, and investment plans. The relations between socialist states and multinational corporations appear to be little different from those in non-socialist states. Despite the ideological ties and orientation of scientific socialist African states with external socialist powers, no dramatic economic alternatives have become available. While offering considerable military aid, the socialist powers have not (with one or two exceptions) provided critical economic or technological aid. Because of the high costs of development plans and economic crises, the debt levels of African socialist states have risen dramatically, further tying them to the world capitalist economy and, more important, occasionally leading to attempts by international financial organizations to impose economic restrictions and policies on them. Devaluations, austerity measures, import regulations, and other restrictions have made large-scale economic planning even more difficult than in the past. Moreover, basic economic resources are often quite scarce. Such scarcity often leads to heightened internal conflict over the distribution of resources, which may well test a regime's capability to manage conflict. Where this capability does not exist, planning efforts become even more chaotic. In his essay on Zambia, Quick shows how the 1967 financial crisis there adversely affected planning and the development of rural

6

socialism. The Kaunda government did not possess enough power or resources to force through tough sector decisions which would have protected the socialist rural experiments from the effects of the crisis, but powerful interests in other sectors were able to protect their shares of the budget.

The parastatal sectors in African socialist states have proved difficult to govern. The necessary technical cadre are not available in many cases, investments are often poorly planned, and policy decisions are *ad hoc*. Coordination with government planners is frequently poor, goals of different sectors often conflict, and the priorities of profit and social criteria are not adequately defined. In addition, parastatal sectors tend to promote capitalist attitudes, values, and life styles within ostensibly socialist societies, often with detrimental effects. Some writers claim that this fosters the consolidation of a "bureaucratic bourgeoisie" whose interests are antithetical to those of socialist development. In short, parastatal sectors often help maintain—even reinforce—close linkages with the world capitalist economy.

IDEOLOGY AND COMMITMENT

African socialism as the ideology of the first wave was often a confusing, even contradictory set of principles which was not integrated into a coherent doctrine. Little effort was made to systematize it, and African socialism remained a set of ideas supposedly particularly adapted to the environment of the African continent. Its largely vague abstractions were never developed into a clearly defined programmatic guide to action. The problem of vagueness and incoherence has been ameliorated in part by the adoption of scientific socialism by the second wave elites, but even with the committed efforts of the second wave, the tendencies toward eclecticism, pragmatism, and adaptation to African conditions are threats to the coherence and power of the ideology.

A powerful ideology is of little value if there is only a weak commitment by leaders and cadres to make it work. The commitments to socialism of a number of African leaders have proven to be largely opportunistic in their attempts to secure and maintain power. Thus the commitments of the military rulers in Benin and Congo/Brazzaville seem to be primarily pragmatic and formalistic. In both countries, as Samuel Decalo points out, the gap between political rhetoric and action is immense. Scientific socialism is the *lingua franca* through which various political struggles are acted out: it

7

is a means of attempting to create legitimacy with powerful and radical urban groups, of conducting factional infighting, managing ethnic tensions, and conducting purges. The changes are purely formalistic, however, and there is no prospect, in terms of resources and cadres, of the pursuit of integrated socialist options in the immediate future.

If the various forms of socialist ideology have not brought major socioeconomic transformation to Africa, they may have other important functions. One of the most important of these may be to introduce new symbols and meanings into the African political arena which redefine political thinking and thereby political reality. Their function then is to introduce a counter-reality which can help to reshape existing values and structures, and by altering the political consciousness, lead to change. David Laitin suggests that when socialist ideology is translated into the vernacular it can bring to life new ideas which give the Marxist alternative vision meanings easily understood within the traditional milieu. When this is done it makes possible sociopolitical speculation by the masses for whom social changes are ostensibly carried out. Of major concern here is to what degree the content of socialist ideology is changed when translated. Is it really the same ideology with the same meanings, or in being translated into another language rooted in a very different worldview, is its content significantly altered? For example, does translating socialist thought into Somali, which is permeated by Islamic and nomadic culture, alter the content in ways that tend to protect key cultural/religious components of Somali society that may be antithetical to socialism? Also, what happens if the sociopolitical speculations of the masses come to conclusions that are inconsistent with the socialist policies of the regime in power?

One approach to answering the latter question is to examine a situation where socialist ideas were propagated vigorously for some years to see what impact, if any, they had. Ghana provides such an opportunity. How did Nkrumah's vigorous (if not always consistent) exposition of socialist views affect Ghanaian political culture? Did his efforts redefine the political world in a specifically socialist way that was lasting? Which ideas took root and which did not? If some ideas have had some impact, do they have any effect on current policies? While James McCain's findings are only preliminary, they indicate that "mass" (in contrast to "elite") belief in Ghana is distinctly pragmatic, and not specifically socialist to any significant degree. No particular interest is expressed in state ownership of the means of production. Some value is placed both on individualistic

8

and materialistic notions and on the notion of community. There is significant appreciation of stratification differences, but the "mass" respondents do not see themselves as part of an international revolutionary proletariat, and they are willing to accept ties and involvement with capitalist countries. The "mass" respondents blame Ghana's ills less on the colonial past than do the "elite" respondents, and while they believe that economic sacrifice is necessary for economic advance, they feel that it must be equitably distributed and that the masses ought to be consulted. Only about 50 percent believe that Africa has a natural bent toward socialism and democracy, but above all the "mass" respondents have very basic, non-ideological needs—jobs, lower cost of living, better housing and roads, less corruption—and they are not necessarily committed to socialism as the way to obtain them.

THE "SECOND WAVE"

Socialism in sub-Saharan Africa appears to have entered a new phase with the emergence of new experiments in Somalia, Congo/Brazzaville, and Benin and, even more significant, in Angola, Mozambique, Guinea-Bissau, and Ethiopia. The appearance of this second wave—particularly in the latter four countries—is an indication of the continued vitality of the socialist ideology in the search for a new and distinct polity. Unlike the countries of the first wave, who came to independence as constitutional nationalist movements or parties, the three ex-Portuguese territories—Mozambique, Angola, Guinea-Bissau—became independent as revolutionary movement regimes. The first three came to power in the mid-1970's after many years of liberation struggle, while in Ethiopia a revolutionary socialist movement led by the military has followed the overthrow of Haile Selassie's regime in 1974.

These new efforts have some distinctive characteristics which differentiate them from the first wave attempts. Perhaps the three most important differences are the adoption of scientific socialism, the attempt to create effective Marxist-Leninist vanguard parties, and a greater willingness to use coercion. In these countries scientific socialism, rather than some form of "African socialism," has been adopted. The distinctiveness of the African situation is being downplayed, although the necessity for adaptation to local conditions is still acknowledged. The use of scientific socialism leads the rulers of these states to put more emphasis on class analysis and the identification and exclusion of internal enemies. The type

9

of socialist ideology of FRELIMO in Mozambique, for example, is distinctly different from the first wave variety. Edward Alpers shows how FRELIMO's socialist ideology developed through a protracted internal political struggle while it was waging a military and political struggle for liberation. This different socialist ideology was developed before coming to power; FRELIMO did not have to muddle through to a radical socialist position after taking power as Castro did. This different type of socialist ideology for Africa is exclusionary rather than inclusionary, stresses struggle and conflict (both within the party and the country as well as without), has an internationalist framework, and postulates the existence of a vanguard party. It is not at all clear how firmly entrenched these new characteristics are or how much difference they will make in the final outcome. The combined result of the protracted and violent struggle for power and the commitment to scientific socialism may mean that the new socialist elites have better organized and more militant and dedicated organizational and military apparatuses at their disposal, but this is not yet clear. The successful conversion of the movement-regimes into effective Marxist-Leninist vanguard parties remains to be accomplished; the task is a difficult one, and the outcome uncertain. Finally, these regimes appear much more willing to use coercion to accomplish their goals, but the availability of effective coercive instruments remains problematic.

These second wave countries are clearly identified with external socialist powers, and in Ethiopia and Angola outside assistance of major proportions has been required to establish political control and consolidate the positions of the new socialist rulers, who have been threatened by civil war and/or secessionist movements. Success in these second wave efforts will be dependent upon the consolidation of internal control and the continued availability of external assistance—military, economic, and technical. But no matter how high the level of external socialist assistance, dependence on the world capitalist economy will remain a major constraining factor.

It should be emphasized that while the tasks faced by African socialist countries are formidable, they are not unique. Other regimes aspiring to socialist transformation have faced a similar array of problems—civil wars, foreign intervention, and factionalism—but on the whole they have had better bases upon which to build. In the case of the Soviets there were the beginnings of an industrial economy, and in China there was a military/party organization capable of mobilizing and controlling the population. Established

Communist countries have also been able to employ tenets of nationalism in the building of national unity. Moreover, the Soviet Union did not have to look outward because it had a large internal market. It could practice autarky because it had substantial resources. The building of socialism in African countries will remain far more problematical and uncertain than it has been for the established Communist powers.

PART I

AFRICAN SOCIALISM &

PROBLEMS OF IMPLEMENTATION

AFRICAN SOCIALISM AND THE WORLD SYSTEM: DEPENDENCY, TRANSNATIONAL CORPORATIONS, AND INTERNATIONAL DEBT

Ann Seidman

INTRODUCTION

In the little more than a quarter-century since the end of World War II, extensive changes in Africa have significantly altered its role in the world political-economic system. More than forty new nations have attained political independence and embarked on different paths of nation-building. Several characterize their approaches as "socialist," but only a handful have begun to make the institutional changes necessary to initiate an effective transition toward socialist reconstruction of their political economies.

The world economic system within which the new African states are striving for development has also changed since World War II. On the one hand, a third of the world's population—in widely differing countries ranging from the Soviet Union and China to Vietnam and Cuba—have proclaimed the building of socialism as their goal. There is no one socialist model for the Africans (or any others) to follow: each socialist state is working out its own approach. Serious disagreements have developed concerning the essential steps to be taken and the institutional changes required. However, the widespread adoption of the socialist perspective—especially in developing nations—has provided ideological and even material support for African countries seeking to break out of the capitalist commercial system and reconstruct their political economies along socialist lines.

On the other hand, the capitalist commercial system has changed. The old model, in which colonial governments and companies divided up the third world, including Africa, into separate spheres of influence and economic exploitation, has all but disappeared. In its place, giant transnational corporations have emerged—sometimes collaborating, sometimes bitterly competing, to maintain and extend their penetration in the newly independent nations.

15

In this chapter we will first examine the nature of the changing capitalist world system into which the new states of Africa were born, and then outline the efforts of some African states to reduce their dependence on that system and initiate a transition to socialism in order to provide productive employment opportunities and raise the living standards of the masses of people in all sectors.

NEW AFRICAN STATES VS. THE CHANGING CAPITALIST WORLD SYSTEM

Several factors shape the new methods by which transnational corporations seek to achieve their old goals in the post-World War II world.[1] These impact on the development perspectives of particular African countries in different ways.

First, technological changes have led to a basic shift in the capitalist international division of labor.[2] The demand for some raw materials—cotton, sisal, even basic minerals like copper—has been reduced, relative to growing output, by the introduction of synthetics, substitutes, and the recycling of used materials in the core industrialized economies. Those African countries whose export enclaves had been geared by decades of colonialism primarily to the export of one or two of these commodities have been very adversely affected.*[3] In contrast, countries producing raw materials for which technological developments have created new and expanding demand —oil, uranium, bauxite—have, at least temporarily, "lucked out." Especially those with the research facilities, technical capacity, and financial resources needed to realize new technological possibilities can take advantage of the competition between transnational corporations.†

Second, the transnational corporations have entered into fierce competition to sell their excess manufactured goods in African markets.[4] Some had previously been excluded by the French-British colonial hegemony; now they each seek to secure a foothold by building last-stage assembly and processing plants behind tariff barriers erected by the African governments. This involves the initial import of capital-intensive machinery and equipment and the continuing import of parts and materials, but it only marginally affects the pattern of external dependence of the typical African economy. Only under the umbrella of the South African racist regime have the transnationals contributed to building up an integrated industrial

*E.g., Tanzania (sisal), Zambia (copper), Ghana (cocoa).

†E.g., oil countries like Algeria, Nigeria, Libya, Gabon.

base, and South Africa is the only country in Africa listed by statisticians among the "developed" nations of the world.[5]

Third, the heavy capital investments required to utilize large-scale capital-intensive technologies to extract the mineral resources of the periphery have fostered the emergence of globally competing transnational financial institutions to facilitate the expansion of their nationally based transnational industrial corporate associates.[6] The efforts of national center governments to employ Keynesian-type monetary controls has led to the ballooning of the essentially unregulated Eurodollar market, where the largest banks sometimes collaborate, sometimes compete, to capture the lucrative corporate business.

Confronting these transnational corporate giants, many African governments have adopted state interventionist policies which they have proclaimed as variants of "African socialism." In reality they are typically little more than thinly disguised state capitalist measures which have led to increased dependence on transnational corporate and financial institutions. The governments have made few changes in the inherited sets of institutions which gear their political economies to the export of raw materials. On the contrary, they have pursued measures to expand the export of agricultural and mineral produce in keeping with conventional wisdom, hoping to earn foreign exchange to finance their rapidly multiplying administrative and infrastructural costs.[7] Their competitive efforts to sell their crude products to the core industrial nations, where relative demand was in many cases declining, contributed significantly to falling prices and worsened terms of trade. African farmers who owned their own farms (such as cocoa farmers in Ghana and Western Nigeria, coffee farmers in Tanzania, Kenya, Uganda, and Ivory Coast, cotton farmers in Sudan, Egypt, Uganda, and Tanzania) were seriously affected by the fall of world prices for their exports.* Government acquisition of shares of ownership of export industries—for example, the purchase of 51 percent and 100 percent, respectively, of the copper mines in Zambia and Zaire—did little to alter the outcome.[8] The governments were forced to shoulder the burden of direct profit losses in addition to the loss of tax revenues.

Government measures to stimulate import-substitution manufacturing industries, including government ownership of shares through state corporations, served primarily to encourage transnational corporations to establish last-stage assembly and processing

---

*In Ghana, by 1966 the real per capita income of the farmers had dropped below the levels of the Great Depression of the 1930's.

plants. They typically produced the wrong kinds of commodities—mainly luxury and semi-luxury items for those who could afford to buy them. (Beer and cigarettes became increasingly important segments of local manufacturing industry.) They tended to be relatively capital-intensive and based on the import of transnational corporate technologies rather than providing jobs for growing numbers of urban unemployed. They continued to import parts and materials rather than contribute to the development of domestic resources. They were located in and fostered the further growth of the export enclaves rather than spreading productive employment opportunities in neglected rural areas.[9]

Despite innumerable government proclamations of the necessity of "rural development," extensive areas outside the export enclave continue to stagnate. Inherited market structures and credit and farm inputs are too frequently directed to existing export-oriented agriculture,[10] often dominated by large estates or "progressive" African farmers. Class stratification has steadily deepened in expanding cash-crop regions. Food production, mostly carried on by women given little option but to continue to use outmoded techniques on less fertile lands, has tended to decline. The drought of the 1970's, with its associated widespread famine, exposed the inadequacy of food production as nation after nation was forced to spend precious foreign exchange to buy grain on the world market.[11] The migration of tens of thousands of rural poor into overcrowded urban slums has been accelerated across the continent.

In most African countries, state intervention, far from initiating a transition to a socialist political economy, fostered the burgeoning of what has become widely known as the "bureaucratic bourgeoisie."[12] Parastatal managers, together with key government administrators and politicians, used their legally obtained high salaries (not infrequently along with not-so-legally obtained additions)[13] and funds borrowed from the banks to invest in large farms, speculative real estate, retail and wholesale trade, and, in some cases, shares in local subsidiaries of transnational corporations. They utilized their influence at national and local levels to direct a variety of state actions to foster their private sector entrepreneurial activities.

Widespread official criticism of the growing "urban-rural gap" typically focuses on holding down the wages of low-paid urban workers. There is seldom serious intent to develop effective redistributive income policies or to capture and direct investable surpluses to the planned restructuring of the productive sectors so as to spread employment opportunities throughout the countryside. Rather,

policies are commonly designed to ensure the continued profitability of factories, mines, and estates in which the "bureaucratic bourgeoisie" now holds a personal stake.

Pursuing a variety of essentially state capitalist policies, by the 1970's most of the newly independent African countries had become, in short, increasingly externally dependent, their fragile economies increasingly characterized by instability and a growing gap between the "haves" and "have-nots."[14] In many, the attempt to maintain a democratic facade gave way to military rule in a pattern all too reminiscent of Latin America.

Although throughout the 1960's all the newly independent African countries competed eagerly to attract overseas capital, transnational corporations and financial institutions expanded their investments most rapidly in the state capitalist economy of South Africa. Some $20 billion in foreign funds were poured into that country, exceeding the total foreign investment (excluding that in pumping oil) in the rest of the African continent combined.[15] Foreign funds today provide a fourth of South Africa's total investment and about 40 percent of the capital in its manufacturing industry.

West German- and United States-based transnational corporations in particular expanded their capital and technological contributions in South African manufacturing industry during the 1960's. In this they frequently collaborated closely with South African parastatals—sometimes supplementing British capital, sometimes squeezing it out. Four of five U.S. dollars invested in manufacturing in the entire African continent, for example, are concentrated in South Africa.[16] Transnational corporations and, in some cases, their home governments apparently viewed South Africa's police state as a "stable" regional sub-core from which to conduct their operations throughout the southern continental periphery.*

Transnational corporations' affiliates and subsidiaries have expanded their profitable operations throughout the southern African periphery from their bases in South Africa. They participate in various kinds of ventures with South African capital to

---

*Contradicting U.S. Ambassador to the United Nations Andrew Young, who had characterized the South African government as at least "morally illegitimate" after the 1976 Soweto uprising, President Carter, in a report buried at the bottom of a news story, asserted that South Africa "has a legally constituted government and is a stabilizing influence in the southern part of that continent" (New York Times, April 19, 1977).

obtain minerals and agricultural raw materials: iron ore, pineapples, and timber from Swaziland; copper, nickel, and diamonds from Botswana; copper, zinc, uranium, and fish from Namibia; chrome and coal from Zimbabwe; copper and other minerals from Zaire and Zambia. They have also established distribution networks through which they sell the goods they produce or import into South Africa throughout the southern third of the continent.

In the 1970's, Africa, along with the rest of the Western world, was deeply affected by international monetary and economic crises. In fact, the deepening and prolongation of the boom-depression cycle characteristic of the capitalist world was rooted in part in the rapid post-World War II extension of transnational corporate penetration in the newly independent countries of Africa and the rest of the third world. The corporations accumulated and reinvested vast amounts of capital in expanding, technologically advanced production in the core industrial countries; this was accompanied by intensified competition to extract greater investable surpluses from the periphery. They mined increasing amounts of crude materials produced by low-paid labor in third world countries, while they expanded their sales of high-priced capital-intensive technologies (as well as luxury and semi-luxury items) for the benefit of the limited high-income groups in these countries. They drained capital from the lopsided third world economies in the form of profits, interest, and dividends, and (in recent years) licensing fees and high salaries for their managerial personnel. These activities further narrowed the potential markets for their growing surpluses of manufactured goods.

Throughout the 1950's and to an even greater extent in the 1960's (in a pattern reminiscent of the 1920's), worsening terms of trade caused country after country in Africa—and elsewhere in the third world—to seek to reduce its imports and expand its exports.[17] In the 1960's, rising domestic expenditures for infrastructure, worsened terms of trade, and mounting balance-of-payments deficits caused many African states to expand both their internal and external debt. In the late 1960's and 1970's, spurred by International Monetary Fund (IMF) advice and prodding by transnational banks, many devalued currencies and introduced "austerity programs." Taxes, especially on middle- and lower-income groups, were raised. Government spending was slashed. Such monetary and fiscal measures tended to squeeze credit and cause unemployment, especially among smaller firms, and devaluation led to higher prices for the imported items on which the African economies had become increasingly dependent, contributing to rising prices throughout the

domestic economy. All these measures tended to shift the burden of the economic crises in the African countries onto the shoulders of the lower-income groups.

By the late 1960's the Western nations also began to suffer balance-of-payments difficulties. These culminated in the U.S. devaluation of the dollar and the emergence of an international monetary crisis. Within a few short years, a euphemistically designated "recession" had spread throughout the advanced Western economies of the United States, Western Europe, and Japan.

The "oil crisis" of the early 1970's was an aggravating factor, but by no means the underlying cause of the deepening and prolongation of the economic crisis. Rather, it reflected the growing importance of oil as a consequence of profound technological changes which had altered the relative importance of particular resources and the countries in which they were located. The manipulation of oil prices by OPEC countries together with the transnational oil companies raised the profits of *both*. This made the terms of trade even worse for those third world countries which had to import high-priced petroleum products as well as manufactured goods produced in the core industrial countries.

As the African countries exhausted their traditional sources of credit, they began to turn to the Eurodollar market for funds.[18] The largest borrowers were not the "low-income" African countries, but the "middle-" and "high-income" countries with visible resources which the international bankers assumed could be exploited to ensure repayment.[19]

Zaire, with its large copper and cobalt reserves, borrowed about $431 million between 1971 and 1974.[20] As copper prices plummeted and import costs rose, Zaire's mismanaged economy was faced with bankruptcy by 1977. Its inability to repay its transnational banking creditors was a major factor accelerating the latter's efforts to utilize the IMF facilities to "discipline" defaulting countries to ensure that they would pay their debts.*[21]

---

*While the attention of Western financial circles focused on Zaire, South Africa—confronting mounting unemployment and unrest among its African population, rising import costs, and growing military expenditures—borrowed far more heavily. It devalued its currency twice, aggravating internal inflationary pressures, which led to cumulative price increases of over 30 percent in 1975-76. By March 1977, it was reported to have borrowed around $9 billion, about a third of it provided by U.S. banks—especially Chase Manhattan, Citicorp, Manufacturers' Hanover, and Morgan Guaranty (Bank for International Settlements report in *Financial Times* [London], June 18, 1977, and *Financial Mail* [Johannesburg], esp. July 2, 1976).

In short, the transnational corporations' competitive penetration of Africa, spurred by rapid technological advance, aggravated the underlying contradictions which led to the deepened and prolonged economic crises of the 1970's. In many of the politically independent African nations, the new "bureaucratic bourgeoisies" used state power to strengthen their own political and economic status. The countries made little or no effort to restructure the inherited institutions which linked their peripheral export-oriented economies to the Western commercial world system; instead, they competed with each other to create "attractive investment climates," seeking to obtain further transnational corporate penetration. However, the expansion of their low-cost crude exports, combined with worsening terms of trade and the drain of profits, interest, dividends, and high salaries to transnational corporations, narrowed their markets for the mounting manufactured goods surpluses produced by accelerated investments in the industrial core nations. Thus the development of the international "monetary crisis," aggravated by the "oil crisis," reflected a deepening of the general crisis throughout the capitalist world.

INITIATING THE TRANSITION TO SOCIALISM

Many, if not most, African governments have proclaimed their goals to be "socialist." In only a few countries, however, have the governing political parties sought to implement the institutional changes required to reduce external dependence and initiate a transition to socialism. A transition to socialism requires the implementation of measures to create the necessary institutions to achieve socialized ownership of the means of production, and their development to meet the needs of the masses of the working people in both urban and rural areas. Inevitably, given the differences in their histories and inherited institutional structures, their leadership, and the particular obstacles confronting them, each African country must trace this path in its own way. In a brief overview of this type, it is possible only to illustrate the range of widely differing efforts with a few examples.

Examination of the experience of African countries embarking on the transition to socialism suggests that in the early phases of that process two kinds of institutional change are essential. First, it is necessary to create a political base, uniting urban wage earners, peasants, and committed "petit bourgeois" elements behind the institutional changes needed to build a socialist economy.[22] In

Africa, creation of this kind of base is difficult because of the small size of the urban working class and its lack of "worker" consciousness,[23] the difficulties of communicating with scattered rural peasants, and the institutionalized isolation of the intellectuals. In Algeria and the former Portuguese territories, years of guerrilla struggle helped to forge a degree of unity among the national liberation forces. Nevertheless, the coup which made Boumédienne the president of Algeria and the civil war (and subsequent coup attempt) in Angola suggest the many continuing difficulties encountered in efforts to cement the essential mass base for building socialism.

The second kind of institutional change necessary in the transition to socialism involves utilizing state machinery to control the "commanding heights": basic industries, export-import and internal wholesale trade, the banks and financial institutions. Experience indicates this is critical for the implementation of a long-term strategy to restructure the externally dependent political economy to achieve an integrated, balanced structure capable of providing productive employment and higher standards of living for the masses of the population.[24] The process of transition necessitates the formulation and implementation of a series of plans in the context of, say, a twenty-year perspective program to restructure the political economy. National plans should include measures to: (1) strengthen national control over the "commanding heights" and reduce transnational corporate and financial influence over the critical sectors of the economy; (2) allocate physical resources to build appropriate kinds of industries specifically linked to increase agricultural productivity, provide productive employment opportunities, and produce goods to meet the needs of the people in all sectors of the economy; (3) implement financial plans to achieve a more equitable pattern of income distribution and to direct investable surpluses to the critical productive sectors; (4) formulate educational and training programs to ensure a supply of qualified men and women needed to staff industrial and agricultural projects as they are developed.

The African countries attempting the transition to socialism have not been equally successful in achieving these two critical kinds of institutional change. In the brief space available here, it is possible to review the contrasting experiences of only a few: Tanzania, Algeria, and the former Portuguese colonies.

A. *Tanzania*. Tanzania is the only former British colony whose government is still explicitly dedicated to the attainment of socialism in the sense being discussed in this chapter. At independence (1961),

President Nyerere devoted a year to organizing the Tanganyika African National Union (TANU)—a national political party—to build a mass base. Over the years, a large proportion of the population has been brought together into ten-house party cells, designed as the vehicle for two-way communication between the people and the leadership. The extent to which TANU members are imbued with a socialist perspective is not clear.[25] President Nyerere is an avowed pragmatist, and some claim that the leadership of the party is not really devoted to the cause of building socialism. They argue that "petit bourgeois" elements seek to advance their own interests rather than implement the transition to a fully socialized political economy.[26] (The consequences of uniting TANU with the Zanzibar party are as yet unknown.)

In 1967, following the fall in world prices for Tanzania's major export crops, TANU initiated measures through the government to assert direct control over the "commanding heights."[27] The foreign-owned banks and insurance firms were taken over in toto, and over the years integrated into a single financial system increasingly capable of directing credit to the key productive sectors. The major export-import and internal wholesale houses were placed in the state sector. These have begun to regulate the flow of imports and distribution of goods throughout the nation, more or less within the framework of planned perspectives, but not without severe difficulties and several reorganizations. The government acquired a majority of the shares of ownership of the largest existing industries and placed them within a parastatal sector, but most of the top-level managers remained those provided by the transnational corporate "partners" operating within the framework of controls established through the state-owned financial and trade sectors, as well as state participation on local boards of directors.[28]

Serious problems have been encountered in reshaping old institutions and creating new ones to ensure that the efforts to assert state control over the critical sectors of the economy have been conducted to enhance the welfare of the masses of the population. These may be illustrated by examining two aspects of the parastatals' (state corporations') role in the industrial sector.

First, as is true in all former British colonies, Tanzania's main instrument of control over its newly acquired shares in industry was the parastatal. The parastatal was initially conceived as an autonomous body, outside the controls of the civil service: this would enable it to operate flexibly like a profit-maximizing private enterprise. In Tanzania the daily operations of the parastatals were left in

24

the hands of the managers supplied by the foreign partners, who continued to own important blocks of shares. Ministerial control could be exercised only indirectly through board meetings, but the ministers were typically so overburdened with responsibilities that they were unable to do more than provide cursory supervision. As a result, it was difficult to ensure that the factories contributed effectively to Tanzanian development. What they produced and how they produced it tended to be determined by transnational corporate aims rather than Tanzanian development perspectives in many cases. Many of the plants were dependent on imported parts and materials, and control over decisions concerning what to import and how much to pay for imports sometimes gave managers a means of shipping out investable surpluses through overinvoicing.[29] In addition, there was the danger that Africans who entered the managerial ranks dominated by the foreign partners might be coopted into the transnational corporate sphere, seeking to take advantage of high salaries and perquisites to advance themselves.

Tanzania attempted to devise protections against these dangers. Tanzania's governmental authorities required the parastatals to operate through the nationalized banking system. This provided them with additional information about financial conditions, enabling them to require firms to carry out their financing activities in accord with national plans. In addition, the chairman of the National Development Corporation—the umbrella organization responsible for all firms in which the government holds shares—was made chairman of each parastatal company in the group, and National Development Corporation department heads responsible for particular companies sat on their boards of directors. A management information system was created to monitor the performance of the Corporation's departments, and the management executive committee regularly reviewed operating problems and current progress.[30]

In an effort to replace transnational corporate managers, Tanzania channelled university graduates into state corporations until localization there equalled that in the civil service.[31] At the same time, the Presidential Standing Committee on Parastatal Organizations (instituted following the Arusha Declaration) froze parastatal salaries[32] and curtailed other perquisites such as housing and car allowances.[33] Rental housing was nationalized to reduce the opportunity for parastatal managers to speculate in real estate— a common form of enrichment in other countries.

In line with its declared socialist perspectives, Tanzania insti-

tuted a program of workers' councils in an effort to develop workers' control of parastatals from below,[34] with the aim of increasing both managerial responsibility for national development and worker productivity; in reality, however, these councils remained essentially advisory bodies.[35] As might be expected, they were primarily concerned with working conditions and wages. It is difficult for workers who have little or no knowledge of possible conflicts between national and transnational corporate goals and of methods of operation (particularly bookkeeping skills) to participate effectively in directing management along nationally desirable paths. Institutionalization of effective workers' control takes time and requires worker education and ideological leadership relating particular factories to the need for national economic reconstruction.

Another aspect of the problems encountered by Tanzania in its efforts to assert national control over development through government ownership of shares in industrial projects is that of ensuring that new investments contribute to building a balanced industrial and agricultural economy capable of providing increased employment opportunities for the broad masses of the population in all sectors. On the one hand, the institutional mechanisms for ensuring that new investments are appropriate take time to establish. The National Development Corporation, initially supposed to behave like a private firm, had to be reorganized to give it greater control over its newly acquired subsidiaries; at the same time, it had to work closely with the government planning agencies and the banks, as well as TANU, to direct new investments to the production of essential consumer goods and the appropriate machinery and equipment. But the criteria for new investments remained vague: "short-term opportunity and accident" tended to dictate choices between projects.[36] The Second Five-Year Plan, while attempting to list several social criteria, left the task of formulating a long-term industrial strategy for the future. Tanzanian ministers on the boards of directors had little direct influence on the National Development Corporation investment policy; already busy, they received papers for directors' meetings only shortly before they took place. The NDC board made decisions about major industrial investments like the Mwanza textile mill and the sisal pulp mill after only a week's notice.[37]

Foreign investors initiated most of these projects, hoping to obtain 51 percent or more government financing; they made their profits in the initial sale of machinery and equipment and —in some instances—an ongoing supply of parts and materials. French inter-

ests, for example, promoted the Mwanza textile mill, and the NHC staff lacked time to consider any issues beyond the proposal's overall economic viability. The Mwanza textile mill was relatively capital-intensive and required the import of expensive machinery, parts, and materials. The Mwanza factory cost about three times as much as the Friendship textile mill, built near Dar es Salaam with Chinese assistance, but achieved the same output with only about a third as many workers. Given Tanzania's scarce capital and need for employment opportunities, the Mwanza plant appears to have been built without regard to the social criteria formulated in the Five-Year Plan. However, the social criteria delineated in the Plan[38] could be construed to conflict with "overall profitability"—also an explicitly formulated goal.[39] In 1972 the General Manager of the NDC reported that "in several cases in the past we have been blamed for misinterpreting Government and Party policies."[40]

Unless the government and party can decide on an appropriate long-term strategy for the physical development of industry, linked closely with careful financial planning, the potential for restructuring the economy is unlikely to be realized. It is expected that such a long-term strategy will be incorporated in the next five-year plan, but whether it will be, and to what extent it will be successfully implemented, remains to be seen.

To date, the primary emphasis in Tanzania has been on the creation of ujamaa villages, proclaimed as an effort to create agricultural production units to avoid increasing rural stratification as cash crop production expands.[41] This effort was accelerated in the 1970's, but not without difficulties.

The reallocation and development of agricultural resources is a time-consuming process. It takes a year to plow, sow, and harvest one perennial crop, and peasants must continue to produce foodstuffs if they are to remain self-sufficient—at least during the transition to greater [planned] participation in the increasing national division of labor. Unfortunately, in the Tanzania case the accelerated villagization program coincided with the drought of the early 1970's, which reduced crop output in widespread areas of the countryside as well as throughout the rest of the continent. As a result, Tanzania's food output declined, and it was forced to import enormous amounts of grain. This, together with the rising costs of oil and manufactured goods imports, contributed to serious balance-of-payments deficits. To cover these, Tanzania—like many other African countries—was forced to borrow funds abroad.[42]

This heavy borrowing may seriously endanger Tanzania's

efforts to implement its transition to socialism if the government is
forced by its creditors to adopt typical IMF-type remedies. The
IMF's role in pressuring governments to implement policies which
throw the burden of economic crisis on the working people of the
third world countries has been well documented.[43] In Africa, the
first post-independence African government to experience this kind
of pressure was Ghana under President Nkrumah. As cocoa prices
plummeted in the early 1960's, Ghana was confronted with a serious
economic crisis. Critics have argued that the Nkrumah administration
was wasteful and corrupt, but it has been pointed out elsewhere
that the failure to institute effective plans to alter the inherited
institutional structure in order to build a balanced, integrated economy directed to meeting the needs of the Ghanaian population was
far more significant.[44] Ghana's increasing dependence on cocoa
exports inevitably led to an economic crisis when cocoa prices fell
from about 725 cedis per ton in 1954-55 to 338 cedis per ton in
1964-65. (They dropped 22 percent in 1965 alone, drastically
reducing foreign exchange earnings and government revenues.) To
cover its mounting social expenditures, the government borrowed
heavily overseas. As the difficulty in paying off its debts increased,
the government sought IMF assistance. The price for that assistance,
the Nkrumah government was informed, was the implementation
of several measures that included a cut in the price paid to cocoa
farmers, manifestation of a "liberal attitude toward foreign investment," sharp reductions in government spending and a halt
to the launching of new industrial projects, and an end to bilateral
and barter arrangements with socialist countries.*[45]

The Ghana government immediately cut the cocoa price paid
to the farmers. It announced it was making efforts to comply with
other IMF requests, but that some were inconsistent with its efforts
to restructure its political economy.[46] Within weeks of this announcement, the Nkrumah government was overthrown. There is
little doubt that the reduction of the price paid to the cocoa farmers
was a factor contributing to public support for the coup in the
cocoa belt.

The post-coup government, which included civil servants who
had previously negotiated with the IMF, set about implementing
the IMF proposals in full. It devalued Ghana's currency, which

---

*The Soviet Union had agreed to purchase about a third of Ghana's cocoa
crop at a price almost double that prevailing in the world market in exchange
for capital goods and equipment required by Ghana to implement its industrial
expansion program.

increased the cost of the foreign debt in cedi terms,* and contributed to further domestic inflation. The new military government ended all trade agreements with the socialist countries, sold off state enterprises to foreign firms at exceptionally low prices, and slashed government expenditures by laying off hundreds of workers. Unemployment mounted. Domestic prices soared.

The rest of the story is well-known: the military government was replaced by a civilian administration which in turn was overthrown. Ghana's increasingly externally dependent economy steadily deteriorated. The new military government, initially announcing efforts to achieve effective economic reconstruction, was quickly persuaded to pursue the IMF-charted path. The "debt trap" had clamped its jaws on the first newly independent African victim.

What IMF "advice" was given to the Tanzanian government a decade later has not been published. The government has, however, taken steps to reduce state employment and devalue its currency. Domestic inflation remains a serious problem. The government has not sold off state shares of ownership of industries or other critical sectors of the economy. Whether it will be able to continue to pursue its socialist perspectives will depend in part on whether it can return to its self-reliant policies or obtain assistance from OPEC or socialist countries.

Tanzania would appear to be in a better position than Ghana was to return to its self-reliant posture. Whereas Ghana under Nkrumah never attained effective control of the "commanding heights,"† Tanzania has made significant steps in this direction.[47] Its nationalized banks can provide the means of implementing an effective financial plan to direct domestic surpluses to well-planned industrial projects in the context of a long-range strategy for building a balanced industrial structure integrated with agricultural growth. This should be facilitated by the Tanzanian government's serious efforts to implement a meaningful incomes policy. Tanzania's control of its export-import and internal wholesale trade should help it to

---

*The IMF insisted that even those debts which had been contracted as a result of bribes paid by foreign firms must be paid off.

†The banks remained entirely in foreign hands: the state-owned commercial bank was never very significant. The Ghana National Trading Corporation, managed by a former manager of the United Africa Company, handled only part of the national trade. Basic industries remained predominantly in the private sector—except for the new ones which began to be established in the last years of the Nkrumah administration.

develop the domestic market for goods produced by its growing industrial sector.

In the final analysis, however, in Tanzania—as in Ghana[48]—the achievement of a socialist transformation depends fundamentally on the ability of the party and government to mobilize the working people and the peasantry to carry through the institutional changes required for a long-term industrial strategy to build a socialist state.

Tanzania's experience underlines the difficulties facing any country with small investable surpluses which seeks through increased socialization of the means of production to achieve self-reliant, integrated, balanced development which will expand productive employment and raise the living standards of its population. The education and involvement of the masses of the people in the complex process of restructuring critical national and local institutions is an imposing task, and freeing those institutions from domination by transnational corporate interests is by no means simple. In the midst of these difficulties, it is essential to focus careful attention on the details of physical and financial plans to ensure the allocation of resources in the directions most likely to lead to integrated development.

B. *Algeria*. Algeria's national liberation movement won independence from France after years of guerrilla warfare. Many of the French settlers left after the cessation of hostilities, simply deserting estates and small-scale manufacturing establishments.[49] Various types of workers' management schemes were established, some of which were successful, but it is difficult for a newly independent people to take over and manage a national economy—especially when during more than a century of colonialism the majority of the working people have been denied rudimentary education and skills.

The Algerian government has initiated institutional changes to exert control over the commanding heights: the major banks have been nationalized; export-import and internal wholesale trade is firmly in the hands of the state; and the control of basic industries, oil, iron and steel, and petro-chemicals is in the state sector. Some small-scale consumer goods industries remain in private hands.

By the early 1970's, Algeria had formulated a long-term industrial strategy focusing on the massive construction of basic industries in an effort to transform the entire national political economy by establishing high levels of productivity in every sector.[50] Whereas rising oil prices have contributed to serious balance-

of-payments problems for countries like Tanzania, for Algeria—one of the leading OPEC nations—they have provided most of the necessary investable surpluses for the planned transformation of its economy. The remainder has been borrowed from the socialist and capitalist countries, but high oil prices have facilitated repayment of the debts on time.[51] About 40 percent of Algeria's national product is invested annually—a major share of it in basic manufacturing industries, with a smaller amount directed to stimulate the lagging agricultural sector. The new industries are relatively capital-intensive, but efforts are being made to integrate them into the rest of the national economy to increase productivity in other sectors. The planners apparently intend that by the time Algeria's limited oil reserves give out and/or the world's energy users have developed lower-priced energy sources, Algeria will have created a relatively self-reliant industrialized economy free of its former dependence on the Western capitalist nations. Meanwhile, however, the relative complexity of the capital-intensive industries makes it more difficult to achieve increased worker control.

Algeria confronts serious problems in its agricultural sector which differ from those of Tanzania. It inherited a profoundly dualistic agricultural economy: major export crops were produced by large settler-owned estates, while the majority of Algerian peasants scraped a bare subsistence from fragmented, infertile plots in the hinterland. The estates have been turned into state farms, with a degree of worker participation in their management, and the government has sought to organize the peasants in the less developed regions into producer cooperatives, providing them with the necessary inputs and marketing facilities.[52] This has been a prolonged endeavor, and many of the peasants have drifted from the rural areas into the cities, adding to problems of urban unemployment. A major drawback of the creation of a capital-intensive industrial sector is that it is as yet incapable of absorbing the labor displaced in the agricultural sectors. Over time it is anticipated that increasing productivity in the rural sectors will contribute to higher living standards and reduce the urban drift, but the achievement of socialized development in the agricultural sectors—even in countries with significant investable surpluses—clearly takes time.

C. *The Former Portuguese Colonies.* Mozambique, Angola, and Guinea-Bissau all attained political independence in 1975, after years of coordinated guerrilla warfare which contributed to the downfall of the dictatorship in Portugal. Unlike the leaders of the

first wave of African states seeking to make the transition to socialism, the political leadership of the former Portuguese colonies immediately focused attention on the critical institutional changes needed to mobilize the masses of the peasantry and workers while asserting direct control over the commanding heights of the national economy. All have declared their aim of following the Marxist-Leninist road to socialism. Mozambique explicitly reorganized Frelimo as a vanguard party with the aim of giving leadership to the working people, peasantry, and committed petit bourgeois elements.[53] Angola, facing the complex task of rebuilding its economy after the destruction caused by a two-pronged invasion after it gained independence, and threatened by renewed invasions from north and south, took a little longer to announce such a step.[54] Meanwhile, the national party—MPLA [Popular Movement for the Liberation of Angola]—continued to organize the population into ten-cell groups to mobilize and educate them for participation in the transition process.

Both Angola and Mozambique had fully nationalized the banks by early 1978. Both exercise state control over export-import and internal wholesale trade. They have not attempted to take over management of basic industries like the Cabora Bassa hydroelectric project in Mozambique or the Cabinda oil wells (owned by Gulf Oil) in Angola; they have, however, begun to negotiate new contracts to define their long-term interests and presumably their ultimate control, while ensuring continuation of the current inflow of government revenues. As their government spokespersons have emphasized, laying the groundwork to gain control of the "commanding heights" has to be approached much like preparing to capture an enemy stronghold in a military campaign.[55] It is necessary to prepare the groundwork and ensure that the necessary cadres and backup material are in place before the final push.

On this foundation, in both Angola and Mozambique, the governments plan to move on to socialize the means of production in agriculture and industry over time. They seek immediately to mobilize to restore and increase agricultural productivity in order to ensure that their populations have enough to eat without spending precious foreign exchange to import foodstuffs.* As soon as possible, agriculture will be stimulated to produce many of the necessary raw materials for a growing industrial sector. Mozambique

*In both countries the departing Portuguese settlers destroyed machinery and transport equipment, and in Angola agricultural productivity was further hampered by the invasion by South African and Zaire-backed forces.

is moving rapidly toward collectivization of agricultural production, building on forms of cooperation which began during the years of producing foodstuffs for the guerrilla army.[56] Many large-scale estates abandoned by Portuguese settlers have been turned into state farms with worker participation in their management, while peasants in the subsistence sector are being mobilized into communal villages centered around collective productive activities and the increase of collectively provided services to raise their living standards.[57]

In Angola the government initially concluded that the peasants, having been given the right to use their own labor on their own land since the end of Portuguese rule, preferred to increase productivity on their own land.[58] The government's main contribution will be to provide necessary inputs credit and markets through an expanding network of cooperatives, leading to more socialistic forms of production as the potential for larger-scale production grows and peasant consciousness changes.

Neither Angola nor Mozambique has had time to formulate a long-term industrial strategy. At most, they have used their few skilled workers to repair and continue production with existing manufacturing machinery and equipment, much of which was badly damaged by the departing Portuguese. Meanwhile, they are beginning to take stock of available resources and industrial potential, as well as necessary industrial and agricultural linkages. Mozambique ministers have already met with Tanzanian planners to discuss future possibilities of coordinating and linking industrial developments between the two countries to take advantage of potential economies of scale, especially for basic industries.[59] Perhaps this will lay the groundwork for a regional hydroelectric power grid built around Cabora Bassa and existing electrical capacity, as well as the vast potential which may ultimately be harnessed by developing Stigler's Gorge in Tanzania. Eventually, they may be able to share their capital and resources to build basic industries like iron and steel, machinery, fertilizers, and chemicals. Obviously, however, the gathering of essential information and the implementation of key institutional changes to formulate and carry out an effective regional industrial strategy will take time.

It is evident that the transnational corporations do not welcome these efforts to achieve a thoroughgoing social transformation in the new nations in southern Africa. It is difficult to specify the transnational corporate initiatives directed at undermining the new Mozambique and Angolan governments; for self-evident reasons, these are covert. However, many efforts have been made to destabi-

lize the governments. Departing Portuguese employees tried either to take essential machinery and equipment required for transport with them (or destroy it) or to ruin existing industries and agricultural estates. Shipments of machinery, equipment, and spare parts for factories previously owned by transnational interests reportedly have arrived damaged or containing fewer goods than had been paid for. Counterfeit money has been introduced to undermine the national money and banking systems. It is difficult to determine to the full extent the activities which have been directly fostered or financed by Western, including U.S., interests.* Obviously destructive have been the Rhodesian invasions of Mozambique and the South African and other foreign support for the attempts of UNITA to undermine the Angolan government, as well as the second full-scale attack on Namibian refugee camps in 1978, in which hundreds of women and children were killed 150 miles inside southern Angola.

It is essential to realize that the transnational corporations have long perceived of southern Africa as an integrated region, the exploitation of which would be possible through the industrial (and military) buildup of South Africa.[60] In attempting to assess the role of transnational corporations vis-à-vis Mozambique and Angola, therefore, it is necessary to review their overall role in southern Africa, particularly South Africa. Transnational corporations based in South Africa have long violated the UN boycott of Southern Rhodesia (Zimbabwe).[61] Their rapidly expanding investments in South Africa's manufacturing industry have built up that country's military-industrial base so that it is the most powerful (in modern technological terms) on the continent.[†] Transnational corporate banks have loaned almost as much money to help the South African government overcome its political-economic crisis (in part stemming from the independence of Mozambique and Angola)[62] as they have loaned to all the rest of the independent African countries combined.[63] They have continued to build up South Africa as the military-industrial base for their operations throughout the region. The U.S.. along with Britain and France, by

---

*Such activities in the recent past have been fully exposed by John Stockwell in *In Search of Enemies* (New York: Norton, 1978).

†This military buildup has led Andrew Young, U.S. Ambassador to the United Nations, to argue that it is necessary to find a "neo-colonial" solution in South Africa. By contrast, the liberation movements—especially the African National Congress of South Africa—backed by the "front line" presidents (including those of Mozambique and Angola) maintain that armed struggle by guerrilla armies is the only way to achieve political-economic independence.

their triple veto of the UN Security Council resolutions to halt further investment, loans, or trade with South Africa ensured the continuation of these investments and loans.[64]

Furthermore, the home governments of the transnational corporations, led by the U.S. administration, are making every effort to ensure that Zimbabwe and Namibia install "moderate" governments to forestall the kind of fundamental restructuring of their political economies being carried through in Mozambique and Angola. President Carter has maintained that continued transnational corporate investment in South Africa is essential to ensure cooperation of the South African regime in achievement of this goal.[65]

Whether Mozambique and Angola can break out of the circle of dependency created over the years by transnational corporations based in South Africa remains to be seen. Steeled by a decade of guerrilla warfare and aware of the pitfalls encountered by the socialist-oriented states to the north, their political leadership is clearly committed to a continuing effort to achieve a socialist transformation which will influence the shape of future development in southern Africa. Their success has already contributed vitally to the struggles of the liberation movements of Namibia and Zimbabwe; their continued success is crucial to the fundamental political-economic reconstruction required to realize the vast regional potential for development geared to providing productive employment opportunities and higher living standards for the masses of the region's populations.

SUMMARY AND CONCLUSION

Africa's role in the world capitalist commercial system has changed substantially in the few short years since more than forty African states have attained independence. On the other hand, the transnational corporations have intensified their competitive efforts and devised new techniques to penetrate the externally dependent African political economies. Many African states, demagogically declaring as their aim the building of socialism, have instead created a bureaucratic bourgeoisie—an emergent class which has used state power to advance the power and privileges of its limited numbers. While some of these states have experienced a kind of growth, their policies have opened the door to the increased domination of the national political economies by the transnational corporations and further impoverishment of the majority of the people.

Only a few states have sought to initiate effective transitions toward building self-reliant, integrated socialist economies. Their historical backgrounds and resource endowments differ significantly. Tanzania, with one of the lowest per capita incomes on the continent, has taken significant steps to restructure the political-economic institutions inherited from the colonial past, with a view to building rural socialism. In recent years it has encountered serious problems which, aggravated by drought, have necessitated heavy overseas borrowing. This brings with it the danger of increased external dependency. Algeria, endowed with valuable oil wealth, has introduced critical institutional changes and embarked on construction of heavy industry in expectation of rapid transformation of the national economy. Serious political problems remain, including those of integrating the rural population into the development process, cementing a mass base among the peasants and workers, and creating the conditions necessary to enable them to participate at every level of national political-economic decisionmaking.

The efforts of Mozambique and Angola to initiate a transition to socialism have been too brief to permit meaningful evaluation. However, the new political institutions built in the course of a decade of guerrilla warfare appear to have laid a solid foundation for implementing proposed socialist-oriented programs. In addition, their planners undoubtedly have learned of steps to be taken and pitfalls to be avoided from the experiences of other African nations. Most important of all, they have begun to take the needed steps to build a united movement of urban workers and peasantry to participate in formulating and implementing the measures necessary to achieve the proposed socialist transformation.

Their cooperation with the neighboring states and the liberation movements still struggling to free Namibia, Zimbabwe, and ultimately South Africa is an important feature of this ongoing process. If the fully liberated countries of southern Africa can unite to prepare and carry out joint plans for regional development, vast opportunities exist for building basic industries to provide productive employment and raise the living standards of the peoples through a socialist transformation of the entire region.

THE STRUGGLE FOR RURAL SOCIALISM IN TANZANIA

Dean E. McHenry, Jr.

INTRODUCTION

The optimism of those who advocated African socialisms in the early 1960's has turned to pessimism. Kwame Nkrumah's efforts to bring socialism to Ghana were blocked by his overthrow in 1966; Mali's drive toward socialism was thwarted by Modibo Keita's deposition in 1968; Léopold Senghor's commitments to socialism in Senegal have diminished; Sékou Touré's goals for a socialist Guinea have been warped by repeated frustration. Even in Tanzania, the country celebrated more than any other for the clarity of its socialist vision and the sincerity with which its leaders sought to realize that vision, most goals remain unfulfilled. Early in 1977 President Julius Nyerere observed:

> In 1956 I was asked how long it would take Tanganyika to become independent. I thought 10 to 12 years. We became independent 6 years later! In 1967 a group of the Youth who were marching in support of the Arusha Declaration asked me how long it would take Tanzania to become socialist. I thought 30 years. I was wrong again: I am now sure that it will take us much longer![1]

What has obstructed rapid progress toward a socialist society in Tanzania? The answer can be found in the rural areas. It is there that the major struggle for socialism has been waged. This struggle has revolved around efforts to implement what is known as the Ujamaa village policy. Although administrative and technical difficulties have seemed paramount, the principal factor affecting its implementation has been political conflict over whose interests are to be served. The policy, the attempts to implement it, and the sources of resistance to it will be evaluated in this article.

DEAN E. McHENRY, JR.

UJAMAA: TANZANIA'S AFRICAN SOCIALISM

The ideology of a country can be defined as the set of ideas which reflects the values of those who are politically and/or economically dominant in the country. In the late 1950's and early 1960's, at about the time their countries were achieving independence, several African leaders put forward views which they referred to as African Socialism. These views reflected widespread resentment of the behavior of their colonial overlords during the preceding decades of colonial rule and an absence of significant societal differentiation—a result of the African people's common struggle against foreign domination. Over time, however, the bitter memories of colonialism were largely forgotten, and the unity fostered by the anti-colonial struggle diminished. The effect upon African socialist leaders varied from country to country. Some leaders were overthrown, and African Socialism died with their ouster; some were never able to convince the other members of the politically dominant group to accept socialism; some used socialist ideology to camouflage the growth of privilege. But some leaders convinced enough members of the dominant group to accept African Socialist ideology to enable them to use the state in an attempt to realize their ideological goals; President Nyerere was one of these.

UJAMAA AS IDEAS

Without any question Nyerere has been the most influential political figure in Tanzania for the last quarter century. From the early 1950's he was the principal strategist and leader in the struggle for independence, and since the early 1960's he has played a similar role in the struggle for African socialism. His ideas on the latter were first presented in a 1962 paper entitled "Ujamaa—The Basis of African Socialism."[2] He adopted the Swahili term *Ujamaa*, which means "familyhood," because of its connotations of a sharing community. Nyerere envisioned a society where people possessed what in his view was the "attitude of mind" characteristic of traditional family life, including beliefs in the value of equality, democracy, self-reliance, sharing, and the obligation to work. Collective ownership and production were inherent in traditional family life. He distinguished Ujamaa from capitalism ("which seeks to build a happy society on the basis of the exploitation of man by man") and from "doctrinaire" socialism ("which seeks to build its happy society on a philosophy of inevitable conflict between man and man").[3] He

38

believed that family attitudes and practices could be extended beyond the family unit to incorporate everyone in the country. These ideas were adopted as guiding principles by the dominant political party—the Tanganyika African National Union (TANU) —and although they have been expanded and refined, they remain the core of Tanzania's ideology.

However, the retention of what Nyerere considered traditional Ujamaa values and their extension to relations outside the family proved extremely difficult.* There was a trend away from such values. In 1963 Fred Burke observed that "a growing number of young Tanganyikans are rejecting communal values . . . and are extolling an individualistic set of values."[4] Four years later Cranford Pratt observed that "communal values were being rapidly eroded under the impact of an acquisitive individualism."[5] This movement away from Ujamaa has been attributed to the spread of a cash economy and the desire to emulate wealthier countries. It manifested itself in an army mutiny in 1964 and student protests against "national service" in 1966. It continued even after the union with Zanzibar—a country espousing more radical socialist ideas—in 1964 and the establishment of a one-party state under the party advocating Ujamaa—TANU—in 1965. And it was not halted by the rural policies that Burke has suggested were very expressive of Ujamaa principles. Work on self-help activities declined; the cooperative movement increasingly facilitated the growth of inequality; villagization in the form of the village settlement scheme became such a distortion of Ujamaa that it was discontinued; and the de jure abolition of freehold ownership did little to eliminate the inequalities in African land holdings. Alarmed by this situation, Nyerere prepared what became known as the Arusha Declaration.

---

*There is a dispute about the validity of Nyerere's identification of Ujamaa values with traditional life in Tanzania. The basis of disagreement appears related to different perspectives of (a) time, (b) samples, and (c) units of analysis. When Nyerere suggests that Ujamaa values characterized traditional family units, he may be accurately representing the modal situation many years ago, but inaccurately representing the situation in more recent times. Similarly, he may be accurately representing the situation in some parts of the country, but inaccurately representing it in other areas. Or he may be reflecting the relationships within a family unit accurately, but not among different families in a community. At some time, however, for many families in most ethnic groups, Nyerere's characterization is probably accurate.

UJAMAA AS POLICY

Early in 1967 Nyerere submitted a policy proposal to the TANU National Executive Committee (NEC) meeting in Arusha; it was approved with minor changes. The Arusha Declaration, as it came to be known, is the most important of Tanzania's socialist documents.[6] Its importance lies less in the theory it propounds than in the practices it initiated. It called for nationalization of the major means of production and exchange, for adoption by national and local leaders of a socialist code of conduct, and for focusing attention on rural as opposed to urban development. Both nationalization and the leadership code were rapidly implemented. Tanzania's success in implementing these steps has been explained in terms of the self-interest of the dominant group, the skilled "packaging" of the two actions, and unique factors characterizing the Tanzanian polity. Issa Shivji, an articulate Tanzanian Marxist, suggests that the nationalizations were sought by the dominant class—the "bureaucratic bourgeoisie"—in order to gain firmer control of the economy, and that the leadership code was accepted as an "act of class self-restraint imposed on the individual members of this class in the long-term interests of the class as a whole."[7] Pratt takes issue with Shivji's assertion that "the Arusha Declaration . . . was a selfish, class-motivated intervention manipulated into being by the bureaucratic bourgeoisie."[8] He identifies a number of features of the Tanzanian polity as the basis for the acceptance of the Declaration, including the broad acceptance of traditional values basic to Ujamaa by both leaders and followers, the prior commitment to socialism of several important ministers and political leaders, the absence of a significant class of African entrepreneurs or wealthy farmers, the loyalty of the army after the reorganization and reforms following the 1964 mutiny, and the fear among leaders of popular discontent with the continuing drift toward the growth of a privileged class.[9] Shivji and Pratt agree that while the bureaucracy in Tanzania accepted nationalization readily, it adopted the leadership code with reluctance, but they disagree concerning the role of self-interest in the acceptance of the Declaration.

In contrast to the prompt implementation of the nationalization and leadership code portions of the Declaration, efforts to focus attention on socialist rural development awaited suggestions made by the President a few months later. "Socialism and Rural Development" was a kind of addendum to the Arusha Declaration, but its impact on the people of Tanzania rivaled that of the Declara-

tion itself.[10] (Its Swahili title "Ujamaa Vijijini," literally translated "Socialism in the Villages" or "Socialism in Rural Areas," more accurately conveys its content than does the English title.) The primary objective was to make rural areas socialist through getting the people "to live and work together for the good of all." Communities based on this principle were not unknown in Tanzania. The TANU Youth League had been instrumental in starting several in various parts of the country. Among the best known was one at Litowa in Songea district started by the Peramiho branch of the TYL in late 1960. Soon other communal farming villages were started in the Litowa area, and they united to form what became known as the Ruvuma Development Association (RDA).[11] The local initiative and self-reliance of these settlements influenced Nyerere's ideas about what should be done. The President recognized that there was such diversity in population densities, means of livelihood, and customs of people in different areas that no one blueprint would apply everywhere, but for most areas he suggested a three-step process that would lead to what he called an "Ujamaa village."

The first step was to persuade people to move their houses into a single village and plant food crops in the surrounding area.[12] (In 1967 it was estimated that over 86 percent of the population lived in scattered homesteads.)[13] As might be expected, villagization was not a new idea. The colonial government had required it in many tsetse fly-infested areas as a preventive measure against sleeping sickness, for example, and Nyerere had called for villagization in his 1962 inaugural speech, arguing that it was a necessity for such things as the provision of tractors, construction of schools, building of hospitals, development of sources of clean drinking water, and creation of small village industries.[14] The village settlement scheme was a response to this call. As we shall see, the President later sought to dissociate this first step from the Ujamaa village program.

The second step was to persuade people "to start a small communal plot (or some other communal activity) on which they work cooperatively, sharing the proceeds at harvest time according to the work they each have done."[15] The methods of persuasion used were crucial. Inducements were considered inappropriate both because of limited resources and because of previous unfortunate experiences. They had been used to attract people into settlements under the village settlement scheme at great expense, producing significant inequalities and reducing motivations to work. Although Nyerere deemed force appropriate in certain situations, such as where a few

people did not contribute their fair share in self-help projects or in efforts to increase agricultural production, he emphatically rejected its use in building Ujamaa villages. As we shall see, this rejection would produce confusion when compulsion was later used for villagization.

The third step was for the villagers to devote virtually all their productive efforts to communal work. The centrality of communal production to an Ujamaa village is evident in both the second and third steps. Two years later Nyerere *equated* Ujamaa villages with "cooperative production for the benefit of the community."[16] As we shall see, communal production was extremely difficult to sustain.

Each of these steps was an integral part of Nyerere's model for the creation of an Ujamaa village. The government was to keep "hands off." The President was caught in a dilemma: he wanted the government to help the villages, but he feared that such help might undermine the villagers' self-reliance. Partly as a result, he tried to enlist everyone who was interested in the program to initiate the building of an Ujamaa village. Once again Nyerere's ideas were endorsed by TANU and the task of implementation began.

THE UJAMAA VILLAGE: POLICY IMPLEMENTATION

The Ujamaa village policy required two major actions for its implementation: (1) people had to move together and (2) they had to work together. Although these actions were part of a single overall policy, their implementation can best be examined by considering them separately.

GENERAL SUCCESS OF MOVEMENT INTO VILLAGES

In the decade following the initiation of the policy in 1967, the rural population grew from about eleven to about fourteen million. At the same time, the proportion living in what were popularly known as Ujamaa villages rose from 0 to over 90 percent (see Table 1). The tremendous success suggested by the figures in Table 1 is illusory: few of the villages conformed with the ideal described in "Socialism and Rural Development." As a result, the government temporarily stopped using the designation "Ujamaa village" in 1975, but most peasants continued to use it. The confusion over what constituted an Ujamaa village was to a large extent a consequence of changes in the methods used to promote "villagization."

PERCENT OF RURAL POPULATION IN TANZANIA
ESTIMATED TO BE IN UJAMAA VILLAGES: 1969-1976

Year	Percent
1967	0.0%
1968	0.7
1969	1.7
1970	4.4
1971	12.5
1972	15.6
1973	15.5
1974	19.1
1975	66.6
1976	91.3

For sources of estimates, see footnote 17.

Note: The term "Ujamaa village" is used in the popular rather than the legal sense.

This history of the efforts to implement the Ujamaa village policy can be divided into three phases, each of which is related to the use of a new technique for gaining the compliance of the rural population. During the first, from about 1967 to about 1969, persuasion dominated; during the second, from about 1969 to 1973, inducement was added; and during the third, from 1973 to 1976, compulsion was added. This meant that methods less and less acceptable to the President were being employed. However, because of changes in the terminology used to describe the settlements, Nyerere could maintain that no force was being used to create Ujamaa villages. How was this possible?

During the first phase of policy implementation, Nyerere's strictures against the use of compulsion and the bad experiences with inducement in the village settlement scheme led to primary reliance on persuasion. The use of the technique was straightforward. The President's remarks on Ujamaa villages were widely distributed, leadership seminars were held throughout the country, and the President, the second vice-president, ministers, regional and area commissioners, TANU leaders, and many others toured rural areas exhorting people to join together to form Ujamaa villages. Govern-

43

ment and party officials relied mainly on the argument that living and working together would make the battle against poverty, ignorance, and disease easier to win, but sometimes they suggested that TANU or the government might provide water or other amenities to the peasants if they lived in Ujamaa villages. In general there was a tendency to exaggerate the benefits to be derived from compliance —a practice which the President frequently warned might undermine TANU and government credibility. In addition to persuasion, some aid which served as an inducement was provided to villages, and as a reaction to emergency situations, the first "operations" took place. "Operations" involved the concentrated use of persuasion, inducements, and compulsion to move large numbers of people into villages. The first occurred in Handeni district, because of drought, and in the Rufiji River valley, because of flooding. Except for such emergency cases, the use of force was limited, and when it was used, those who employed it were usually rebuked by the President.* By 1969, despite these efforts, only about 2 percent of the rural population had joined Ujamaa villages. As a result, attention was given to supplemental techniques—i.e., inducements and compulsion.

During the second phase, government resources were more effectively applied to the promotion of Ujamaa villages than during the first phase. Presidential Circular No. 1 of 1969 required that

> all Government policies and the activities and decisions of all Government officials, must . . . be geared towards emphasising the advantages of living together and working together for the good of all; they should be angled at discouraging the continuation of private individual farming; and should attempt to dampen down the urge for private expenditure . . . in favour of communal expenditure.[18]

To rationalize the use of inducements, the claim was made that aid was being given to help people once they were in the villages—not to lure them there. In effect, there was no difference: inducements "sweetened" the act of compliance. Efforts at persuasion were continued, and additional "operations" in special problem areas were undertaken. Operation Dodoma was initiated in 1971 because of famine, and Operation Kigoma in 1972 because of persistent poverty. These "operations" were on a larger scale than those previ-

---

*A case in point is the removal of the regional commissioner from West Lake region during this period for employing force to get people to move into Ujamaa villages.

ously undertaken and continued for several years. An intensification of party and government leaders' efforts was obtained through threats of sanctions and offers of rewards. Those who sought to be candidates for election to the National Assembly in 1970, for example, were threatened with rejection by TANU if they were not working closely with villages; TANU executive committees threatened party leaders with dismissal if they refused to join nearby villages; active officials were publicly praised by the President and other top leaders; and the prospects for promotion were enhanced by diligent work in support of the Ujamaa village policy. Yet by 1973 only about 15.5 percent of the rural population had been brought into Ujamaa villages—a decline from the previous year. At this point the approach was radically altered.

During the third phase, the "operation" became the principal mechanism for gaining peasant compliance. The President signaled what he intended to do at the NEC meeting in mid-1972. He distributed copies of his 1962 inaugural address in which he argued that villagization was necessary for rural development; he then asked for approval of a separation between the "Ujamaa" concept and the "village" concept so that the villagization program might be more rapidly carried out. "Ujamaa" had been so closely associated with the use of methods of persuasion (and the avoidance of compulsion) that separation of the two concepts was a necessary prelude to the use of force to get people to move into villages. According to the former executive secretary of TANU, the President argued that once people "live together they will themselves see the benefits of cooperation for their common good."[19] The NEC approved Nyerere's request, but there was little change in the rate of policy implementation, and a year later Nyerere brought the issue before the delegates at the 16th biennial conference of TANU (1973). Carefully distinguishing between the process of villagization and the building of Ujamaa, he made a strong plea for a concerted effort to achieve villagization everywhere in the country.[20] Then, in November 1973, while on tour in Mbulu district, he announced that all people in rural areas would have to move into villages at the end of 1976.[21] In none of these instances—at the NEC meeting, at the biennial TANU conference, or at village meetings—did he explicitly call for the use of force in villagization, but the implication that it was appropriate became progressively clearer. Its use in the villagization policy became confused with its use in the Ujamaa village policy, however. The confusion was enhanced by the party's Swahili newspaper, which reported the President's announcement of a 1976

deadline for movement into villages as a deadline for movement into *Ujamaa* villages and declared, in a subsequent editorial, that "the issue of living in Ujamaa villages is now an ORDER of the Party."[22] Nyerere tried once again to clarify the distinction between villagization and the Ujamaa village policy at the 17th biennial conference of TANU (1975); he argued that "you can compel people to live in villages, but a decision to work in cooperation with others must be made entirely voluntarily."[23] But confusion between a "village" (i.e., the result of villagization) and an "Ujamaa village" (i.e., the result of the Ujamaa village policy) continued for good reason. Moving together to establish a village is the first *step* in building an Ujamaa village, as outlined in "Socialism and Rural Development." The separation of the two allowed party and government officials to claim that there had been no change in the Ujamaa village policy's prohibition against compulsion, while using force to achieve the first step in building an Ujamaa village.

"Operations" became a test of the regional administrations, which had been enlarged in 1972 during a period of a major decentralization of political responsibility. Nyerere concluded that "the majority of our leaders came out of it well—some of them very well indeed."[24] Since no national guidelines were given for operations, regions and districts drew up their own plans. To obtain ideas, some leaders sent delegations to other regions that had already carried out operations. A diversity of plans emerged, but timetables similar to the one given in Table 2 were usually established:

Table 2

SHINYANGA DISTRICT OPERATION TIMETABLE: 1974

Time Period	Action
February - April	Politicization and Ward Development Committee selection of sites
April	Approval of site locations
May - July	Plots assigned to individuals and building started
August	Seminar for leaders on mechanics of movement
17 August - 22 September	Movement of the people

Source: Juma Volter Mwapachu, "Operation Planned Villages in Rural Tanzania: A Revolutionary Strategy for Development," *Mbioni* 7, 11 (1975): 17-21.

Some lives were lost, houses were destroyed, and police, militia, and army personnel were involved, but the direct application of force to a large proportion of the population was unnecessary because the determination of the government soon became widely known. Wherever possible, trucks were used to carry people and belongings to the sites selected. By 1976 about 91 percent of the rural population had moved into villages—a significant accomplishment; in the process, however, there was increasing confusion concerning what was a socialist village.

CONFUSION CONCERNING WHAT CONSTITUTES AN UJAMAA VILLAGE

Even the Ujamaa villages formed shortly after the publication of "Socialism and Rural Development" differed from the vision outlined by Nyerere. In the late 1960's it was estimated that only about 10 percent of them had significant communal work.[25] Virtually all villages that had been formed were considered embryo Ujamaa villages. In order to make some kind of differentiation among them, some administrators began to apply systems of ranking predicated on the stage of development achieved. Nyerere's three-stage system based on the degree of work done communally was most frequently employed, but there were considerable differences among the systems used. Kondoa employed a set of stages based primarily on degrees of political consciousness,[26] for example, while Iringa used stages based on organizational criteria.[27] Some administrators balked at the whole notion of stages because it implied a kind of differentiation socialism sought to eliminate. Meanwhile, few peasants were aware of the administrative designation of an Ujamaa village as "stage one" or "stage three." There was, then, a diversity of interpretations of the nature of Ujamaa among both villagers and administrators.[28]

In an effort to promote a uniform standard of classification, the central government defined registration as a multi-purpose cooperative as the highest stage of Ujamaa village development. According to the *Economic Survey and Annual Plan* for 1970/71: "The ultimate aim of the Ujamaa village programme is that the village should become a fully collectivized unit, i.e., a production and marketing cooperative. Most Ujamaa villages are still a long way from this level."[29] As a result of this equation of successful implementation of the Ujamaa village policy with registration as a cooperative society, the number of Ujamaa villages thus registered increased significantly (see Table 3). However, registration as coop-

Table 3

ESTIMATED PERCENTAGE OF UJAMAA VILLAGES
REGISTERED AS COOPERATIVE SOCIETIES: 1967-1974

Year	Percent
1967	—
1968	—
1969	0.9%
1970	0.5
1971	1.8
1972	5.8
1973	6.1
1974	7.8

Source: Calculated from Sehemu ya Mipango na Utafiti Kikundi cha Takwimu, Ofisi ya Waziri Mkuu na Makamu wa Pili wa Rais, *Maendeleo ya Vijiji vya Ujamaa* (Dar es Salaam: National Printing Co., 1974), Tables 1.1 and 3.0.

eratives frequently did not mean full achievement of Nyerere's third stage of village development. For example, many of the villages registered in Iringa district in the early 1970's became legal cooperatives simply to get loans. In other areas, two or more villages were combined on paper for the purpose of meeting the minimum membership requirements for cooperatives. The result was even greater confusion about what Ujamaa in the villages meant. Furthermore, the whole cooperative movement was coming under strong attack from the peasants (particularly for its lack of democracy) and from the party/government (particularly for its inefficiency). This situation reached its climax in 1975 with the passage of the Villages and Ujamaa Villages Act, which formally disbanded all the multi-purpose cooperative societies which had been established for Ujamaa villages.[30]

Meanwhile, the villages formed through "operations" had introduced additional confusion. Those created by the early operations in such places as Rufiji, Dodoma, and Kigoma were called Ujamaa villages, while those created in later operations frequently were not so designated. Officials began to apply such terms as "development villages" or "permanent villages" to them, even though they had been formed in essentially the same manner as

those established in earlier operations. The character of some Ujamaa villages which had previously established communal farms had been changed by the influx of people who had not previously participated in such activities. The net result was further confusion about what constituted an Ujamaa village.

In the Villages and Ujamaa Villages Act of 1975, an effort was made to establish a uniform nomenclature. The act distinguished two categories of settlement: "villages" and "Ujamaa villages." The distinction was not clear-cut. Both would have the same form of organization, both would be cooperatives (though not registered under the old Cooperative Societies Act), both would seek equality, self-reliance, and increases in income, and both would aim at "the full realization of socialist ideals."[31] But a "village" could be designated an "Ujamaa village" by the responsible minister only if it had a recommendation from a regional executive committee of the party stating that the committee "is satisfied that a substantial portion of the economic activities of the village are being undertaken and carried out on a communal basis."[32] In essence, the distinction was based on the same criterion Nyerere had emphasized in "Socialism and Rural Development," but the determination of the appropriate designation was now formalized and centralized. Since registration of existing settlements as villages continued through 1977, the problems involved in determining whether the activities of the villages are sufficiently communal to warrant promotion to Ujamaa village status have not yet been faced. Needless to say, the diversity of popular conceptions of what constitutes an Ujamaa village has not been eliminated by the passage of the Villages Act.

LIMITED SUCCESS OF UJAMAA IN THE VILLAGES

The villagization policy was popularly associated with the Ujamaa village policy despite repeated party/government attempts to make it clear that settlement in villages was not the same as creation of Ujamaa villages. As early as 1971 the party noted in its newspaper (Nationalist) that "merely living in Ujamaa villages without the peasants working together . . . is as good as not having moved into the Ujamaa villages at all."[33] Four years later the President emphasized to delegates at the 17th biennial conference of TANU that "living in villages is only a beginning. The people in the villages have to work together to get the benefits of living together."[34] These statements were in response to major problems experienced in the effort to build Ujamaa within the villages.

As we have seen, the heart of Nyerere's vision of an Ujamaa village was communal production; yet its introduction has been the most difficult of all tasks in implementing the policy. Many villages have either made no attempt to start communal production activities or have given up on what they started, rates of participation have been low, and income has been low. The results of a four-region survey conducted in 1975 are shown in Table 4.

Reasons for the limited success of communal production are many and varied. A circular pattern developed: expectations of low production resulted in low participation, which resulted in low production, which perpetuated low expectations. In many villages a substantial proportion of the production was reserved for the village and/or village leaders and not returned to the participants; thus work on the communal plot became a form of taxation, while work on an individual plot was exempt. As a result, even those who participated in communal farming tended to work harder on private farms than on the communal farms; in addition, there was a tendency for the

Table 4

ESTIMATES OF EXTENT OF COMMUNAL PRODUCTION ACTIVITY, INCOME, AND PARTICIPATION IN UJAMAA VILLAGES FOR THE 1973/74 CROP YEAR

Region	Ujamaa Villages with Communal Production Activity (percent)	Average Annual Participation per Adult in Ujamaa Villages (days)	Average Income per Day in the Most Productive Quarter of the Villages with Communal Production Activity (in cents)
Dodoma	37%	3.5	8
Iringa	52	26.4	18
Kigoma	7	5.3	3
Kilimanjaro[a]	56	58.6	49

Source: D.E. McHenry, Jr., "Peasant Participation in Communal Farming: The Tanzanian Experience," African Studies Review 20, 3 (December 1977): tables B, 1, and 6.

[a]Since only 0.4% of the population of Kilimanjaro region lived in Ujamaa villages (the lowest proportion for any region in the country), these figures do not mean that the number of participants in or the income derived from communal production was substantial.

villagers to allocate better lands for private than for communal production. Restrictions on access to the communal crop (or on income from the communal crop) bred discontent. For example, just before the regular harvest, when food supplies were short, the participants were unable to consume what they were producing communally. In fact, often many months or even years passed before villagers were able to get anything from communal production because various officials had to deduct outstanding debts of the village and approve the amount to be distributed to individuals. Although part of the crop was usually distributed in kind, most was sold to marketing boards for much less than the boards sold them for. Communal production outside the family unit was a new institution to many, and there were suspicions—especially among those brought into villages by "operations"—that it would work to their disadvantage. These factors, along with a serious drought in many parts of the country in the early 1970's, were responsible for the limited success of communal production. Improvements in production were sought through such means as tying income more closely to work contributed, increasing penalties for non-participation, and more rapid distribution of products and/or proceeds, but they were largely unsuccessful. By the mid-1970's there was a deemphasis on communal production in many parts of the country.*

The difficulties with communal farming have not resulted in a shift away from all forms of communal work. Indeed many activities continue to be done collectively, such as school-related construction, road work, construction of water-supply systems, housing, health facilities and shops, and brickmaking. By the mid-1970's many leaders felt that working together at such activities was the best way to gain experience which could lead eventually to communal production. The shift of emphasis from communal production to other communal activities was clearly manifested in the effort to create village shops. To facilitate this process, officials in Dodma district banned all private shops outside Dodoma town in 1974; the ban was extended to neighboring Mpwapwa the following year. Then early in February 1976 the prime minister (while on tour in Kilosa district) ordered the closure of all private shops by the end of the month as

*This has been evidenced most generally in a tendency to create block farms where private plots are contiguous and similar crops are grown. According to officials in regions such as Kigoma, this is only a temporary retreat from communal production. In the future there could be a gradual transition to communal farming through the introduction of communal plowing and/or spraying and/or harvesting.

part of what he called Operation Maduka (Operation Shops).[35] The move caught nearly everyone off guard, including most government officials. In Lindi and Mwanza regions the party executive committees demanded that such shops be closed,[36] but the rush created problems. Some villages had no alternative sources of necessities, so that the closure of private shops meant considerable hardship. Other villages opened shops only to experience losses because of a lack of commercial skills or theft. By May the government newspaper editorialized: "To close a private shop does not in any way constitute a step toward socialism. In fact it may constitute a denial of service to the people."[37] The President then halted the program to abolish all private shops.[38] Thus, even with respect to non-productive communal activities, efforts to move toward Ujamaa involved problems.

While communal work was at the core of the vision of an Ujamaa village, democratic control was perhaps even more basic. There has been an implicit assumption that if democratic control exists, communal activities will follow eventually. Popular control of village organization and governance has been promoted with mixed results. The most common form of popular control has been one in which the villagers choose some form of council and a chairman and secretary to run the village; the council establishes functional committees to assist it. (Two models are given in Table 5.)

Table 5

TWO MODEL STRUCTURES OF UJAMAA VILLAGES

Cooperative College Model (1972)	Villages and Ujamaa Villages Act Model (1975)
General Meeting	Village Assembly
Executive Committee (incl. chairman and secretary)	Village Council (incl. chairman and secretary)
Committees:	Committees:
Education and Culture	Education, Culture and Social
Defense and Conciliation	Welfare
Planning and Development	Security and Defense
Finance and Loans	Finance and Planning
Works	Production and Marketing
Shop	Others where necessary
Health	

Sources: Chuo cha Elimu ya Ushirika Moshi, *Vijiji vya Ujamaa, Mafunzo Maalum Kwa Vikundi vya Kujifunza* (Moshi: Chuo cha Ushirika, 1972), p. 12; and Government Notice No. 162, 22 August 1975, Sec. 8.

Until regularized by the Villages and Ujamaa Villages Act in 1975, there was some variation from village to village. For example, there were different sets of committees, which might include a women's committee, a cooperative committee, or a labor committee, and there were different sets of officers, which might include a vice chairman, assistant secretary, or treasurer. But the general form was basically the same everywhere.[39] It made popular control possible, but it did not ensure it. Chairmen and secretaries sometimes came to play the old role of headmen, and sometimes they made decisions which should have been referred to the village as a whole. By institutionalizing democratic control, the governance structures made it easier for villagers to prevent gross inequalities, promote activities which contribute to the general welfare, and move toward communal settlement at a pace determined by the people.

RESISTANCE TO UJAMAA VILLAGE POLICY IMPLEMENTATION

Why did so many problems arise in bringing people together into villages and in getting them to work together? Here we will consider three frequently cited sources of resistance: that from the bureaucracy, that from abroad, and that from the peasantry. Resistance came in two forms: rejection and distortion. The latter is often too subtle to be easily recognized either by those engaged in it or by outside observers. The claim is made that both of these forms of resistance are but reflections of the struggle among groups for political domination of Tanzania.

BUREAUCRATIC RESISTANCE

The group within Tanzania generally considered to be consolidating its position of dominance of the state consists of high party and government officials, identified by some as a "bureaucratic bourgeoisie" because of its association with the bureaucracy.[40] While important differences exist between the upper and lower levels of the bureaucracy and between political and functional administrators, they have similar positions in the state and many interests in common. The decentralization of 1972 reduced the distinctions between those employed in the central ministries and the field agents. Thus it is not unreasonable to follow the practice of most observers in treating the bureaucracy as a kind of unit in its reaction to the Ujamaa village policy. The relationship between the party and the "bureaucratic bourgeoisie" has been ambiguous. On the one hand,

many see the party as the principal hope for thwarting a consolidation of power by the bureaucracy; on the other hand, others note that the party's leaders are already members of the bureaucracy. Nyerere, as head of both party and government, has sought to bridge the gap between the party/state bureaucracy and the bulk of the population through his role as populist spokesman.[41]

By means of the Ujamaa village policy, the President sought to bring the peasantry into the political arena where they might serve as a counterweight to the growing power of the bureaucracy. Because the members of the bureaucracy recognized the possibility of such a consequence (some argue), they resisted implementation of the policy. Such a view appears to explain many of the developments during the implementation process. For example, the President's early efforts to involve non-official agents in policy implementation may have been due to a fear of bureaucratic subversion of the policy. His circular early in 1969 calling for greater government assistance and attention to Ujamaa villages may have been a reaction to a bureaucratic tendency to assist private more than Ujamaa development; his split of villagization from the Ujamaa village policy may have been a result of continuing frustration with the pace of bureaucratic implementation; and the relatively long delay before widespread "operations" were undertaken may be an indication of further bureaucratic resistance.* The use of the term "Ujamaa village" for any village may have been a subtle effort by the bureaucracy to distort the policy, and communal efforts within the villages may have been subverted by the bureaucracy in a variety of ways, such as failing to assign teachers after school rooms were built, failing to provide for quick distribution of communal farming products, permitting corruption of village leaders, or providing special help for richer peasants. All these things would have undermined Ujamaa villages and thus made them less likely to provide a vehicle for peasant challenges to bureaucratic domination.

Critics of those who assert that bureaucratic subversion has been primarily responsible for the slow movement toward socialism argue that most of the actions suggestive of bureaucratic resistance were not attempts to thwart the rise of the peasantry. For example, Phil Raikes, an expert on Tanzanian development, contends that

*The great energy with which the operations were eventually undertaken can perhaps be explained by the bureaucracy's conclusion that villagization would increase its control over the peasantry (and not the reverse), or the realization by individual officials that their employment and promotion depended on successful implementation of the village policy.

those who see villagization as "a deliberate attempt to distort policy and to wreck socialism as represented by ujamaa" are wrong:

> In the first place, it is not entirely clear that [villagization] distorts official policy as presently expressed from the highest levels. More importantly, any socialist aspects of ujamaa (initially utopian socialist or populist rather than marxist) had already been effectively eliminated some years ago. What remains can hardly be considered threatening to the bureaucracy since it involves the steady accretion of bureaucratic controls over most aspects of the economy and society. At a more subjective level, this supposedly clear and self-interested attitude seems not to portray accurately the opinions of most bureaucrats on villagization. These appear to range between a militaristic enthusiasm which enjoys the display of power involved in the move to villages and a resigned pessimism which considers that "politics" is the ultimate cause of all problems.[42]

Further, the seeds of confusion over what an Ujamaa village is were planted not by the bureaucracy, but by Nyerere's initial formulation, which villagers interpreted to mean that general commitment to build socialism qualified a village as an Ujamaa village. And the deep involvement of the bureaucracy in running the village, requiring it to do such things as prevent corruption, might have done more to subvert self-reliance and democracy in the village than the corruption itself would have. Thus there is good reason to question many of the claims of those who argue that the bureaucracy resisted the implementation of the Ujamaa village policy because it felt threatened.

Indeed most of those who attack the bureaucracy for thwarting movement toward Ujamaa lump together deliberate and inadvertent actions which have delayed implementation of the Ujamaa village policy as indications of policy opposition. Since few of these actions can clearly be identified as "deliberate," their case is based primarily on "inadvertent" actions. This is unfair. Almost of necessity the bureaucracy was required to take the lead in the implementation of the policy; inevitably, the administration would receive credit for success or blame for failure. The bureaucracy had limited manpower, limited resources, limited time, and a limited number of skilled personnel. Even a bureaucracy fully committed to socialism would be expected to make mistakes on the order of those "inadvertent" errors which occurred. Undoubtedly there was some bureaucratic resistance based on fear of the peasantry, but the evidence does not

support the contention that the bureaucracy played (or sought to play) the principal role in slowing implementation of the Ujamaa village policy in order to prevent the rise of a peasant opposition.

FOREIGN RESISTANCE

The argument that foreign resistance has been responsible for the slow progress toward socialism is derived most often, though not always, from tenets of dependency theory. It is assumed that the locally dominant group possesses only delegated power—real power being retained by those dominant in the metropole. Because the interests of the latter are not furthered by the development of socialism in the periphery, they work against policies which lead toward it. Thus there would be foreign resistance to the Ujamaa village policy.

In subtle ways contacts between members of the Tanzanian bureaucracy and representatives of metropole countries may have reinforced the individualistic values of the bureaucrats and decreased their enthusiasm for socialist policies. The high salaries and comfortable life styles of aid personnel in Tanzania, trips abroad by Tanzanian officials, the affluence reflected in the Western mass media reaching Tanzania and by the businessmen and trade representatives from the West who visited Tanzania—all these may have led some officials to see non-socialist policies as more beneficial to them. Villagization was attacked in the Western press,[43] and some aid donors appeared to favor private over communal farming. Poor results of International Development Association assistance to tobacco farmers was attributed by foreign aid officials in part to "premature introduction of collective cultivation under the ujamaa system," and the International Bank for Reconstruction and Development (IBRD) agreed to support Ujamaa villages in Kigoma region only after most communal farms had been transformed into block farms.* Nevertheless, large amounts of aid from Western countries continued to flow into Tanzania throughout the period of active Ujamaa policy implementation. Western skepticism concerning the communal production aspect of the policy does not appear to have been translated into active opposition.

In fact, the absence of significant foreign resistance to Ujamaa may reflect the self-interest of metropole countries. Shivji, who

*The IBRD project was called the "Kigoma Rural Development Project."

argues that the bureaucracy was a major cause of the policy's failure, maintains that Ujamaa could never lead to real socialism:[44] all it could do is integrate the rural areas into the world capitalist system. Such a development would be in accord with the interests of the metropole. Whatever the effects of the policy on the metropole, foreign resistance does not appear to have been a significant factor in slowing implementation of the Ujamaa village policy.

PEASANT RESISTANCE

That peasant resistance to the Ujamaa policy has slowed the movement toward socialism is beyond dispute. For the most part, peasants were slow to respond to the villagization aspect of the policy, and they have been less than enthusiastic about communal farming, but their reaction has not been uniform.

The principal—and most salient—division within the peasantry is between a small group of very wealthy peasants (generally referred to in Tanzania as "kulaks") and the large mass of relatively poor peasants. During the 1950's the colonial government adopted an agricultural policy that focused resources and attention on what it called the "progressive farmers"—i.e., those it considered most receptive to advice. With the spread of cash crops, this group of "kulak" farmers began to grow both in size and in wealth. Since a principal objective of the Ujamaa village policy was to halt the development of such a class, kulak resistance to the policy was expected. Perhaps as a consequence, most of the earliest operations— e.g., those in Handeni, Dodoma, and Kigoma—were initiated in areas where there were very few wealthy peasants. When the policy was extended to areas where kulaks were more numerous, the response was slow (e.g., Rungwe and Kilimanjaro), and there were scattered cases of open resistance. The most notable involved the killing of the Iringa regional commissioner (Klerruu) by a kulak farmer (Mwamwindi) during an argument at an Ujamaa village in the Ismani area of Iringa district on Christmas Day, 1971. The incident became a symbol of kulak resistance.[45]

The more common form of kulak reaction was a kind of formal acceptance but subtle resistance which Raikes refers to as "Kulak Ujamaa."[46] Shivji noted that "in . . . areas like Hanang, Kilimanjaro, and Mbulu Districts and the Usambaras, rich peasants have formed ujamaa villages on their own initiative as a method of getting more land and access to credit and other facilities provided by the government." In other areas, he observed, "the rich peasants have managed

to occupy leadership positions in the ujamaa village committees or forge links with the local bureaucracies, thereby using ujamaa in their own interest."[47] The assumption of leadership positions by kulaks did not always result in the distortion of Ujamaa. In the four-region study of Kigoma, Dodoma, Iringa, and Kilimanjaro previously referred to, it was found that the most active participants in communal farming and fishing were more likely to have "kulak" characteristics than were the least active ones.[48] In other words, the more wealthy peasants appeared to be more active than the less wealthy in the important socialist aspects of village life.

The differences between the more and less wealthy peasants are blurred by many shared interests, such as the desire for government extension services, dispensaries, schools, drinking water systems, and so on. The reluctance of most peasants to comply fully with the demands of the Ujamaa village policy was a fairly rational response.* In some areas the quality of the land to be used by the resettled peasants was inferior to that which they were abandoning; in other cases peasants had to abandon permanent crops in order to move into the new villages. Previous experiments with settlement during the colonial and early post-independence periods had not resulted in a long-range improvement of living standards. Customs which had given some order and security to peasant life were likely to be lost in the new village structures. The factors which motivated individuals in a family to work hard on a common plot of land did not operate with the same force among people from a number of families working on a village communal farm. Perhaps most important of all, though, was the peasants' fear that life in an Ujamaa village would increase their vulnerability to demands from the outside. While Ujamaa villages might increase the voice of the peasants in the affairs of the state, they might also increase the interference of the state in the lives of the peasants. In colonial times, concentrated settlement had meant demands for peasants to serve as porters, participate in European wars, pay taxes, and contribute labor for road-building and anti-tsetse fly work. More recently, settlement members had been more or less required to enter into a market system increasingly controlled by the state. Most of the

---

*Nyerere has argued that the peasants were not acting rationally when they resisted villagization (Interview by Hilary Ng'weno, *Daily News* [Dar es Salaam], 2 March 1976, p. 4); a similar view was expressed by the editors of the government newspaper in mid-1977 (*Daily News* [Dar es Salaam], 23 June 1977, p. 1). Both held that the "irrational" behavior of the peasants justified the use of force by the government.

production of communal farming was sold to state agencies at prices fixed by the state—prices which were much lower than those at which the crop could be bought in the stores or those others were willing to pay. The cumulative effect of all these considerations was a peasant resistance to the Ujamaa village policy which was probably much more significant than bureaucratic or foreign resistance in slowing the movement toward rural socialism.*

CONCLUSIONS

In the mid-1970's there was a pause in Tanzania's efforts to build rural socialism after a two-year period of massive movement of people into villages. (Between mid-1974 and mid-1975, 47.5 percent of the rural population was moved into villages, and between mid-1975 and mid-1976, another 24.7 percent.) The pause was reflected in the publication of a 1975 election manifesto which identified the 1970-1975 National Assembly as the "Implementation Parliament" and the 1975-1980 National Assembly as the "Consolidation Parliament."[49] It was also reflected in the fact that the President mentioned Ujamaa villages only once in his 1977 review of the ten-year effort to build socialism—and that was a reference to their general failure to pay back government loans.[50]

Interruptions have occurred in all major efforts to introduce rural socialism. In the People's Republic of China, for example, there have been shifts from phases of vigorous action (often referred to as "red" phases) to phases of consolidation ("expert" phases). The crucial question is whether the pause will turn into retreat—as happened in Mexico during the early 1940's. There both the proportion of communally farmed land within each collective entity (ejido) and the proportion of ejido land to the total cultivated land in the country began to decline. The principal factor in determining whether a pause is followed by a new advance or a retreat appears to be the character of those who control the state.[51] In China the commitment to communal production has persisted; in Mexico it waned. In Tanzania the struggle for control of the state has not yet been resolved.

In the formulation of the Ujamaa village policy, communal production was seen as the central economic feature of an Ujamaa

*Michael Lofchie has argued that the kulaks were particularly threatened and demoralized (see M.F. Lofchie, "Agrarian Socialism in the Third World: The Tanzanian Case," Comparative Politics 8 [April 1976]: 479-99).

village. However, as we have noted, most of the product of communal agriculture enters the state market system, while most of the product of subsistence agriculture does not. Thus communal production makes the peasants more vulnerable to those who control the state. Should those who control the state seek to extract even more from the villagers through pricing by marketing boards or taxing of consumer items, it seems likely that the peasantry will retreat further to family subsistence production. At present the dominance of Nyerere and others committed to broad popular welfare, helped by large infusions of foreign aid, has limited elite or bureaucratic demands for the extraction of a greater surplus from the rural areas. But should state control shift further toward a bureaucratic bourgeoisie which seeks to extract more wealth from the peasantry, it is unlikely that many peasants will voluntarily enter into communal agricultural production arrangements.

Although communal production was seen as the key to the achievement of the Ujamaa policy goals, the villagization aspect of the policy has brought a number of benefits by itself. Health and educational facilities have been improved, better water supply systems have been installed, emergency help has become easier to obtain, entry of peasants into the national political system has been facilitated, and it has become easier to introduce new ideas and methods of production. Thus Tanzania has moved closer to the achievement of many of the goals embodied in its version of African Socialism. But there is a paradox: the more steps taken toward realizing the vision of Ujamaa village life, the less confidence there is that it can ever be *fully* realized.

THE SOCIALIST EXPERIENCE IN GUINEA

Ladipo Adamolekun

The basic assumption of this analysis is that since 1967 the regime in Guinea led by President Ahmed Sékou Touré has been engaged in the task of transforming the country into a socialist state.* The aim is to assess what has been achieved to date: Which aspects of life in the Guinean society are socialist? What problems have hindered the transition to socialism? What are the prospects for the future? It is hoped that the answers to these questions will provide a fairly comprehensive assessment of Guinea's socialist experience. Before attempting to answer these questions, however, it will be helpful to review briefly the evolution of socialist thought in Guinea.

I. THE EVOLUTION OF SOCIALIST THOUGHT IN GUINEA

The history of modern political thought in Guinea dates back to the late 1940's. After World War II, the French colonial power allowed the emergence of formal political movements, groups, and parties in its West African colonies. The major political movement

---

*The hestitations of the Touré-led regime to make a full commitment to socialism in the years immediately following Guinea's independence (1958) are discussed below.

For this assessment I have drawn heavily on my book *Sékou Touré's Guinea: An Experiment in Nation Building* (London: Methuen, 1976). The analysis of the Guinean socialist experience in that book is based on extensive use of documentary sources that are generally not available outside Guinea, as well as on material obtained during visits in 1968 and 1970-71. Because I have not been able to visit Guinea since 1971, I have had to rely on secondary sources for post-1971 developments. I have benefitted tremendously from the much greater openness of the Touré regime to foreign observers (especially French) since 1977.—*L. A.*

that emerged was the Rassemblement Démocratique Africain (RDA). It was launched in Bamako (capital of present-day Mali) in 1946, and among its founding members were a few Guineans—including Sékou Touré. Because the political life of the West African territories was intimately linked to that of the metropolitan country, every West African party was allied or associated with one or another metropolitan party. The RDA allied itself with the French Communist Party (Parti Communiste Francais—PCF) until 1951. Thus between 1946 and 1951 the Guinean members of the RDA (who in 1947 established the Parti Démocratique de Guinée [PDG] as the Guinean branch of the RDA) were exposed in varying degrees to the political ideology of the PCF.

It is not easy to determine the extent of the penetration of French Communist ideology inside Guinea during this period. Perhaps the major instrument of Communist penetration was the trade union organization. In 1945 Touré created the first Guinean trade union—Syndicat du Personnel des Postes, Télégraphes et Télécommunication—and between 1945 and 1958, when he became the first President of the independent Republic of Guinea, he was intimately involved in trade union activities at the national, regional (French West Africa),* and international levels. During this period he was indoctrinated in several aspects of orthodox Marxist-Leninist ideology. Although a number of other aspiring leaders of post-1945 Guinea professed commitment to some forms of "socialist" ideas—most notably the leaders of the Parti Socialiste Guinéen, which was affiliated with the metropolitan French Socialist Party—the emergence of the PDG as the dominant Guinean party in the mid-1950's created a situation in which political thought in Guinea became virtually synonymous with that of the PDG. The chief articulator of PDG ideology has been Touré.

In spite of Touré's exposure to orthodox Marxist-Leninist thought, he did not express a formal commitment to socialism until almost a decade after the country gained its independence. The closest he got to the concept of socialism in the 1950's was in the importance he attached to African communal life. In 1959 he expressed this view as follows:

*By 1950 he had become the leader of all the trade unions in French West Africa affiliated with the French Communist-oriented trade union—Confederation Général du Travail (CGT). His most notable achievement at the national level was a 72-day strike (21 September to 30 November 1953) he organized to obtain improvements in the conditions of service of Guinean workers.

Africa is essentially communaucratic. . . . Collective life, social solidarity, give to African habits a basic humanism which many people would envy. It is . . . because of these human qualities that no individual in Africa can conceive of the organization of his life outside that of the family, village, or clan group.[1]

Touré believed that the traditional communal living in Africa would make the peasants accept the establishment of agricultural cooperatives, which would gradually develop into collective farms, but he found that Guinean peasants were unprepared to transfer their loyalties to "family," "village," and "clan" to an artificial group such as an agricultural cooperative. The cooperative system which was established collapsed, and most Guinean peasant farmers continued their subsistence farming.

There was a small group of PDG militants who advocated that the party should be formally committed to transforming Guinea into a socialist society along orthodox Marxist lines. Touré was strongly opposed to this idea, as the following excerpts from speeches he made in 1960 at the peak of the controversy clearly demonstrate:

We are told that we must necessarily choose between capitalism and socialism, but I regret and—let it be said between us—we are practically unable, all of us, to define what capitalism is, what socialism is. Why are we not asked, on the religious plane, to choose between Hinduism and Islam, Buddhism and Christianity?*[2]

People speak of socialism, of capitalism, and incidentally establish antagonisms where there are none. Socialism and capitalism are objective states; they exist or they do not exist; as objective states, practice consolidates or destroys one or the other. . . . *There is no question of knowing what system we shall permanently adopt; the question is to know perfectly our concrete realities and, within the framework of a revolutionary action, to find the best means which will allow us to achieve our economic, social, moral and intellectual objectives.*[3]

The act of opposing the notion of capitalism to that of socialism constitutes for us a negative affirmation because it does not solve our specific problems.[4]

Touré went on to assert that concern with "theories which are

*The speeches and other writings of President Touré are published as books, and they now comprise twenty-one volumes. The references in this study are made to the volume title, volume number, and relevant pages.

strange to us" had little or nothing to do with the crucial tasks facing the country: *"If we shut up ourselves in purely ideological speculations, we shall not achieve anything; we shall remain for perhaps ten or twenty years incapable of modifying qualitatively our present conditions."*[5]

Seven years after making these statements, Touré told the PDG's Eighth National Congress that "the fundamental option of the Democratic Party of Guinea is to construct a socialist society where the collective interests of the masses must prevail over those of a class or of a privileged minority."[6] Touré later explained the radical change in his position as follows:

> During the phase that is now coming to an end, the People, its Party, and its State experienced ambiguous situations and tolerated uncertain conditions. Today such a state of things is no more possible. We must be clear: we are committed to socialism. That is an irreversible fact.[7]

Touré's claim that there was a general uncertainty on the part of "the People, its Party, and its State" concerning whether or not to accept a commitment to socialism was a clever cover for his own ideological uncertainty. As already noted, there was a faction within the PDG which tried unsuccessfully to commit the party to socialism in the years immediately after independence. An account of the evolution of internal politics within Guinea in the years following independence helps to explain the resolution of Touré's uncertainty.

After successfully resisting the pressure from the left wing of the PDG to adopt socialism in the years immediately after independence, Touré found that the right-wing members of the party were out to enrich themselves and were prepared to overthrow the regime if it stood in their way. The climax of the right-wing challenge was reached in 1965 when a plot to overthrow the regime and establish a capitalist system that would be more in accord with the rightists' personal interests was uncovered.[8] It seems probable that this abortive plot helped to remove Touré's doubts about the desirability of a commitment to socialism. In any case, he could no longer claim, as he had in 1960, that "the act of opposing the notion of capitalism to that of socialism constitutes for us a negative affirmation." On the contrary, he had become convinced that "between socialism and capitalism, when the two regimes effectively assume all their presuppositions, the difference is not of degree, it is of essence."[9]

Touré then summed up his concept of socialism as follows: "Socialism in Guinea is not and cannot be different from socialism in other countries. Socialism is one, meaning scientific socialism. . . . Socialism is without nationality and cannot be the property of a single country."[10] The definitions of socialism offered by Touré show clearly that what he understands socialism to be accords generally with the orthodox definition of scientific socialism:

Socialism is a combination of states: mental, material, social, economic, political, cultural; socialism, then, supposes a complete transformation of the relationships linking man to man and man to nature.[11]

Socialism is intensive and conscientious work; it is the production of goods by the people and for the sovereign people; it is the mastery of all the techniques by the people.[12]

Socialism . . . is expressed by the effective exercise of political, economic and cultural power by the working people.[13]

It is only in his ideas about how socialism can be achieved in Guinea that Touré shows some originality. The major emphasis in these ideas, as set forth in *The Road to Socialism*,[14] is on education: "We have entrusted to the Guinean School the mission to be the foundation, the root, the growth cell of the new society to which our history invites us—the Socialist Society."

The Road to Socialism specifies that all children shall have nine years of education: the first six are the First Cycle and the remaining three the Second Cycle. First Cycle education is provided at the village or quarter level; Second Cycle education is provided within the arrondissements (administrative units comprised of several villages or quarters). The Second Cycle programs consist of two parts: (1) academic courses (40 percent of the training time of the pupils) and (2) productive activities, such as agriculture and livestock, industry, crafts, woodworking, and fishing (60 percent of the pupils' training time). The pupils with the best academic records complete secondary education in Third Cycle institutions, while the others remain in residence to constitute the nucleus of a socialist community. Some of those who complete the Third Cycle advance to the Fourth Cycle (higher education),* from where they go on to serve the state, while

---

*At the beginning of the 1977/78 academic year, there was a faculty of the University of Guinea in twenty-eight of the thirty-three administrative regions of Guinea. By 1982 it is estimated that Guinea will have produced sixteen thousand university graduates. (For details, see *Horoya*, 4-10 December 1977, pp. 11-35.)

others return to the socialist communities that have developed from the Second Cycle institutions. As each of these socialist communities expands, it is expected to integrate the surrounding village, which is already organized within the party structure as a local revolutionary authority (PRL).*

In *The Road to Socialism* Touré presents a kind of blueprint for the transformation of rural Guinea into full socialism—in theory. What has happened in practice is discussed below.

II. SOCIALIST TRENDS IN GUINEA

Party and State. Touré has been profoundly influenced by Marxist-Leninist ideology in his definition of the roles of the state and the party in the establishment of an appropriate institutional framework for translating socialist ideas into practice. Whoever has read Lenin's *The State and Revolution* will readily recognize Touré's indebtedness to Lenin's ideas.

Prior to 1958, Touré was essentially concerned with articulating ideas to guide the actions of the PDG under colonial rule. With the achievement of independence, the PDG became a ruling party, and it became necessary to define the respective roles of the party and the state. Within a few weeks of Guinean independence, a Western-style constitution was adopted, according to which state powers are shared between an executive (the President of the Republic and the government), a parliament, and a judiciary. The President of the Republic appoints the members of his government and is responsible to parliament for the government's policies. The President and the parliament alone can initiate laws, whose constitutionality is determined by the judiciary; the judiciary is an independent authority with responsibility to act as the "guardian of individual liberty." Without formally amending the constitutional provisions, Touré has articulated a concept of the state which subordinates the constitutional institutions to the country's ruling (and only) party—the PDG. Touré has explained the subordination of the state to the party as follows:

> The State does not possess the omnipotence which characterizes certain regimes, nor the absolute powers which the State holds in certain Nations, where the notion of the reasons of State in reality only covers the reasons of interest for the protection of the man or group of men who hold all or part of the State powers. We in-

*See p. 73 below.

tend that the reason of State, the State interest, should be determined in a constant manner by the interests of the people of Guinea. Thus the organs of the State and the nature of their powers are constantly conditioned by the interests and aspirations of the People, whose initiatives and capacities are promoted by a freedom which is expressed and translated through the intermediary activities of the Democratic Party of Guinea.[15]

The role of the party is more specifically defined as follows: "The Party assumes the directing role in the life of the nation: the political, judicial, administrative, economic and technical powers are in the hands of the Democratic Party of Guinea."[16] This concentration of all state powers in the hands of the party amounts to an unequivocal rejection of the principle of the separation of powers implicit in the country's Western-style constitution. The practical consequences of this "doctrine of party supremacy" are summed up by Touré as follows:

In order that the power of the Party should not exist only in the domain of theory, *the Guinean State structures have been modeled on, and harmoniously adapted to, the structures of the PDG*, and this concretely confers on the village committee, the steering committee of the section, the federation bureau, and the National Political Bureau the power to stimulate and control respectively the administrative authorities of the village, of the arrondissement, of the region, and of the Nation.[17]

It is pertinent at this juncture to say that the word *party* is not mentioned in the Guinean constitution. When in 1963 some PDG leaders suggested that one-party rule should be written into the constitution, Touré rejected the idea for the following reason: "To give a juridical character to the action of the PDG would, by subordinating it to the law, not only result in depriving our party of the preeminence which it exercises in all the activities of the nation, but also undermine its popular function and its practical effectiveness."[18]

In practice, the institutional framework of post-independence politics in Guinea faithfully reflects Touré's ideas of the respective roles of the state and the party. With regard to organizational structure, the party organization parallels that of the state (see diagram). As for the functioning of these institutions, Touré's emphasis on the supremacy of the party is reflected in his assertion that "if the Party does not function well, the State of Guinea cannot function well."[19] In reality there is no clear-cut division between the func-

PARTY AND ADMINISTRATIVE STRUCTURES IN GUINEA:
JANUARY 1978

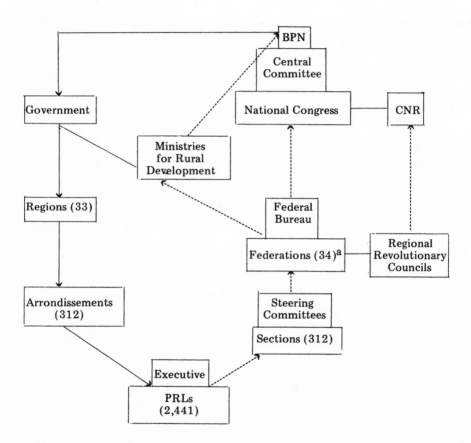

STATE   *PARTY*

aThe region of Conakry, the national capital, is divided into two federations;
hence there are 34 federations for the 33 regions.

⟶ Administrative hierarchy

·······⟶ Party hierarchy

tions of the party and those of the state because of the personnel overlap between the two.

At the national level, for example, the President of the Republic (who is also head of state) is the secretary-general of the party, as well as the leading member of the Bureau Politique National (BPN)—the seven-member executive of the Central Committee, the supreme authority of the party structure. The executive work of government is shared among the seven members of the BPN, who also constitute the cabinet of the government. Thus the critical posts in the government are held by the leading members of the party.

Although the party has its own permanent officials at the regional level—the federal secretaries—these officials are in most cases career civil servants who have been "detached" from the civil service and could return to the service at the end of their mandates with their seniority and pension rights intact. The secretaries of steering committees are *not* permanent party employees, however, and most of them are career civil servants who perform party functions without any remuneration.* Finally, at the level of the local revolutionary authorities (PRLs), the members of the elected executive serve as the agents of the state, but they are not members of the civil service and receive no pay from the state.

As a result of this personnel arrangement, the party institutions cannot "control" the state authorities, of which they are an integral part. In this case, then, there is a clear inconsistency between Touré's ideal and the reality. On the other hand, the overlapping of personnel between the party and state institutions makes valid Touré's claim that the party "determines and directs the action of the nation."[20] The personnel of the party structure which is responsible for formulating national policies dominates the state bureaucracy which implements these policies. In this connection, it should be noted that state officials occupying major posts are required to be "tested militants." Regional governors are an example: "I have never appointed a governor on the basis of his diplomas," says Touré; "the governors have always been chosen from among the tested militants."[21]

In practice, the Touré regime has found that many so-called "tested militants" are not genuinely committed to the party ideol-

---

*For example, by late 1977 about 70 percent of party officials at the section and federation levels were civil servants (mostly teachers); see *Horoya*, 13-19 November 1977, p. 20.

ogy. Thus, following an abortive Portuguese-led invasion in November 1970, it became evident that many senior party and state officials inside Guinea belonged to the "fifth column" that was in close touch with the Guinean exiles involved in planning the invasion.[22] Another problem faced by the Touré regime in applying the criterion of party militancy to appointments of senior state officials is that party militants do not always have the necessary technical competence. The Touré regime seeks to resolve this problem by providing ideological training for future state officials while ensuring that party militants receive appropriate technical and professional education. The experience of other societies has shown that it is not easy to produce individuals who are both politically militant and technically competent.[23]

The Mass Line and Class Struggle. While the Touré regime has heavily relied on Leninist ideas concerning the respective roles of the party and state, its attitude toward the critically important concept of class struggle—a concept to which most Marxist-Leninists attach the utmost importance—has been characterized by considerable vagueness and apparent inconsistencies.

While competing with other party groups inside Guinea in the late 1940's, the PDG leadership resolved at its first congress in 1947 to rely on mass mobilization as the surest means of dominating the Guinean political scene. The congress resolved to "go to the masses and take them into confidence." By 1957 the mass mobilization campaign resulted in the party's winning 75 percent of the total votes cast in a legislative election based on universal adult suffrage. When the PDG became the single ruling party in 1958, it was decided that it should continue as a mass party—a decision which led to the formulation of the doctrine of the mass line. This doctrine refers in part to the membership of the PDG, which is defined by Touré as "the entire people of Guinea."[24] As extracts from speeches made by Touré at various times since 1958 show, the option for a mass party implies a conscious rejection of the other alternatives known to him:

> Revolution can only be the act of the people. . . . It is not only those who have been to school who can accomplish it, nor the wage earners alone, nor traders alone, but the whole of the people. [1959][25]

> No, the PDG is not a communist party; it is not a class party; it is the party of all the people of Guinea, in which one will find, side by side, workers, peasants, craftsmen, civil servants and intellec-

tuals; it is a popular party whose program of action is based exclusively on the national interests of the Republic of Guinea. [1960] [26]

The PDG has refused to be the party of a class or of a social group in order to confuse itself really and intimately with the Guinean people in its totality. . . . Thus every dictatorship of class or of interest groups is rejected. [1966] [27]

Considering Touré's familiarity with orthodox Marxism, it is significant that he categorically rejected the idea of a class party right up to 1967. Touré underlined this rejection when, at the PDG's Sixth Congress in December 1962, he said:

If circumstances independent of our will impose a return to classical forms in order not to accept a base of compromise between the true and false, freedom and slavery, justice and exploitation, we will then choose the break up of its [the party's] organs in order to continue its fight with the clarity which is the attribute of class parties. [28]

In these circumstances, Touré's view is that the internal contradictions within the society should be played down in order to have a concerted national effort not only for the struggle against imperialism, colonialism, and neo-colonialism, but also to promote social and economic development. With respect to development, Touré says: "Whatever the differentiations which characterize the principal social groups of the society, each of them is directly interested in the problems which concern the edification of the nation and its development." [29]

At the PDG's Eighth Congress, held toward the end of 1967, Touré announced some significant changes in the doctrine of the mass line. The most important was the acceptance of the concept of class struggle as compatible with the doctrine of the mass line. According to Touré, his rejection of the concept of class struggle prior to 1967 was dictated by "tactical necessity." As he put it: "Cooperation between antagonistic social classes can only be envisaged from a tactical point of view . . . when the survival of the people is tied to the elimination of a major contradiction and when it therefore has to momentarily silence its internal contradictions described as minor." [30]

By 1967 he was of the opinion that "this tactical necessity had become precarious." This was because two clearly distinct antagonistic classes had emerged within Guinean society. On the one hand, there was the class of "the laboring masses"—"the working class, the

peasants, and the truly progressive elements"—and on the other hand, there was the class of "the reactionary elements of the bourgeoisie, the bureaucracy, and capitalism." He refers to the first as "the people's class" and the second as "the exploiting class."

However, despite his acknowledgment of the presence of these two antagonistic classes within Guinean society, Touré continued to insist that the PDG should be a mass party—a party for all the people of Guinea. The only distinction to be maintained between the two classes was that the members of the people's class were limited to nominal membership in the party while the members of the exploiting class exercised the party's powers of orientation, decision, and control:

> All the people are members of the party, but it is only the dynamic part, faithful to the people [that is, the people's class] that directs the party. The trader can be a member of the party, the industrialist can be a member of the party [both are considered members of the exploiting class], but he cannot direct the party.[31]

It should be noted that Touré's ideas about the membership of the PDG have been translated into practice. Every adult Guinean is a member of the PDG by virtue of the fact that his party dues are an integral part of his state tax. Since annual party dues are only 20 silys (about $1.00), it is unlikely that Touré's insistence on mass membership of the PDG has been based on financial considerations.

It is possible that Touré genuinely believes in the idea of the PDG representing all the people of Guinea and would rather tolerate a division with the PDG (e.g., the people's class and the exploiting class) than exclude some people from it. In terms of practical politics, he is able to use the mass character of the PDG to justify categoric opposition to the formation of an opposition party in Guinea.

An important consequence of Touré's strong attachment to the mass party concept is that it has led to the evolution of a party structure which allows for a fairly high degree of public participation in the political process. The party structure operates according to the principle of "democratic centralism," which requires a clearly defined line of communication from the base to the summit. The lower levels of the party structure are subordinate to the higher levels, but the higher levels must take into account the opinions expressed at the lower levels before arriving at decisions that are binding on the whole party. In addition to the main structure, the party has youth, women, and trade union wings—officially referred

to as "parallel institutions" of the party. All together, the party institutions had about 300,000 officials in 1970, or an average of one party official for every fourteen Guineans (not counting children).*

Special mention should be made of the 104,000 party officials who administer the affairs of the local revolutionary authorities (PRLs). They have responsibility for a wider range of activities, including the keeping of a civil register (births, deaths, marriages), some aspects of the administration of justice, the maintenance of law and order, and the mobilization of the citizens for locally initiated projects for promoting social and economic development. Touré sums this up as follows:

> The PRL constitutes in each base committee in the rural zone the government of the village, allowing to the village the exercise, on the local plane, of all the attributes of national sovereignty: to resolve all the problems conditioning the harmonious development of the village in all domains . . . political, economic, social, and cultural.[32]

So far no empirical study has been made (at least to the knowledge of this writer) concerning the nature of the class struggle in Guinea and the extent to which it is consistent with the doctrine of the mass line. However, available information suggests that while the notion of class consciousness à la Karl Marx or the idea of a class as a status group à la Weber is not yet fully developed inside Guinea, it is indisputable that there are distinct groups in terms of economic conditions and access to political power. The emerging pattern of social differentiation is clearly different from Touré's distinction between "the people's class" and "the exploiting class."[33] In reality, what exists in Guinea is a "middle class elite," on the one hand, and the peasants and working class, on the other. The middle class elite is divided into the "insiders" and the "outsiders." The "insiders" are those who constitute the leadership of the PDG (henceforth referred to as "the people's elite"), while the "outsiders" are those who are formally excluded from holding party posts because it is believed that they exploit their fellow citizens (henceforth referred to as "the bourgeois elite").

There is a sense in which there is serious competition between the people's elite and the bourgeois elite. Indeed the so-called "permanent plot" which President Touré claims to have been combatting

---

*Guinea's population in 1970 was estimated at about 4,000,000. (The latest population census carried out in September 1977 put the figure at 5,500,000; see *Horoya-hebdo*, No. 2311, 29 January-4 February 1978.)

since Guinea's independence in 1958 is to a large extent a struggle by the bourgeois elite to wrest economic advantages and political power from the people's elite. Although the bourgeois elite claim to reject the socialist option of the PDG leadership, and to be interested in the preservation of such basic human rights as "the right to elect and to be elected," "freedom of speech, of the press, of meeting, of association, of procession and of demonstration," in reality their main objective is the acquisition of economic and political power. In other words, there is competition between two elite groups rather than class struggle in the classical sense.[34]

The Touré regime has consciously prevented the development of class consciousness among the working class and the peasants. The peasants are not encouraged to see themselves as a spontaneous revolutionary force à la Fanon, nor is the working class allowed to entertain the hope of an eventual "dictatorship of the proletariat." The Touré regime simply proclaims that all peasants and all members of the working class belong to "the people's class." They occupy a subordinate position vis-à-vis the people's elite.[35]

Economic and Social Development. Following the accession of Guinea to independent status in 1958, the leadership of the ruling PDG proclaimed a commitment to a "non-capitalist way to development." From 1967 onward the expression "socialist approach" began to be used as a synonym for "non-capitalist way." Both terms are used to refer to a development policy which attaches great importance to a state-controlled economy and some form of collectivist organization in the rural areas. The major reason advanced by the Guinean leadership to justify this choice of a "non-capitalist way to development" is that it is "the only one [way] which safeguards the interests of the community while freeing every individual from the injustice which characterizes all relations of exploitation of man by man."[36] The critical point here is that developmental activities are to be closely tied to the social relations within Guinean society. The political will necessary for this linking of economic policy to social relations is provided in the Guinean leadership's assertion that they consider the economic domain to be an aspect of politics. As President Touré puts it: "We shall . . . have the economy of our politics and not the politics of our economy,"[37] indicating the supremacy of politics over economics.

A major feature of the Guinean socialist development strategy is commitment to a planned economy in which the emphasis is on the creation of a large public sector, while the private sector is kept to a minimum. There have been three plans since 1960: the Three-

Year Plan 1960-1962, the Seven-Year Plan 1964-1970, and the Five-Year Plan 1973-1977. A fourth plan is now in preparation.

Foreign experts were involved in both the preparation and implementation of the first plan, but the second and third plans suffered from the regime's determination to entrust both their formulation and execution to an inadequate and poorly trained corps of national planners. The second plan suffered most from this political domination: instead of a plan, there was only a shopping list of projects, of which only a small proportion were implemented. The third plan was a slight improvement over the second because of an increase in the number of trained national planners, but on the whole the attempts of the Guinean regime to formulate and implement development plans without the guidance of trained and experienced specialists have been unsuccessful. In this regard, the Guinean leadership has failed to learn from the Soviet experience.[38]

In all three plans the emphasis has been on the creation of a large public sector, with a deemphasis on private enterprise. Foreign private investment is tolerated, but indigenous private enterprise is positively discouraged. In 1960 President Touré stated his regime's position as follows: "We have never excluded cooperation with capital; we have only rejected capitalism as a form of social organization which does not correspond to our stage of development."[39] In practice the Touré regime has not merely *tolerated* foreign private investment; it has *encouraged* it. For several years after Guinea achieved independence, the Fria Bauxite complex, which accounted for more than 60 percent of the country's foreign exchange, was essentially a foreign capitalist enclave within a "socialist" economy. By the early 1970's, in addition to a fairly large number of public enterprises (about seventy-one by 1970), the regime had established several mixed-enterprise companies in partnership with foreign investors from both the Western capitalist and Eastern socialist blocs—especially in the mining sector.*

Opposition to indigenous private enterprise in Guinea has continued, however. The Guinean leadership believes that indigenous private enterprise will lead to the exploitation of man by man and the emergence of antagonistic classes of the "exploiters" and the "exploited." By 1970 the entire private sector of the Guinean econo-

*The Fria Bauxite Mining Complex became a mixed-enterprise company in 1973. Guinea's partners in mixed-enterprise companies include the USSR, the U. S., France, West Germany, Italy, Nigeria, Yugoslavia, Japan, and the People's Republic of China.

my consisted of 41 commercial enterprises, 499 retail trades, and 770 specialized traders (petrol, cinema, bars, etc.).[40]

In the sociocultural sector of development, the Guinean regime has maintained a complete monopoly.[41] In 1961 the private educational institutions in the country, which were attended by about 13,000 pupils, were nationalized, and since then education has remained the exclusive concern of the state. Similarly, all health facilities are state-owned. Private enterprise is not allowed in the fields of sports and cultural expression: culture is considered an excellent means of preaching mass commitment to socialist ideology. Religious activities have been discouraged in emphasizing the secular nature of the state.* No religious schools are allowed, and in 1967 the Catholic clergy was Africanized. A successful campaign was waged in the 1960's against some fanatical practices associated with Islam (the religion of about 85 percent of the population) and against some rituals associated with tribal beliefs—magic and human sacrifice, for example.

Perhaps the most critical test of socialism for the regime has been its commitment to reorganize rural life in terms of the modes of production, distribution, and exchange and of social relations. The regime's stated objective is to reorganize the rural areas in order to improve agricultural production (in both quantity and quality) by establishing new social structures which emphasize communal rather than individual or family production—i.e., cooperatives. It is believed that communal effort is conducive to the development of the kinds of social relations desired by the regime, while individual or family production might lead to the exploitation of man by man and the emergence of a rural bourgeoisie from among the more successful individual producers.

Starting with a colonial heritage of pseudo-cooperatives called *sociétés indigènes de prévoyance*, the post-independence regime in Guinea tried, between 1958 and 1968, to establish genuine cooperatives to transform life in the rural areas. By 1968 the various experiments of the regime had yielded very limited results. Tractors introduced to increase agricultural production had been confiscated by what became a "tractor bourgeoisie,"[42] and the production of both export crops and food crops fell dramatically. For example, the production of bananas in 1963 was 50,000 tons instead of a targeted 160,000; of a target of 25,000 tons of groundnuts in 1963, only

---

*A recent development that extends special consideration to the Islamic religion while maintaining the secular state is discussed below (pp. 79-80).

7,000 tons were produced; instead of 43,000 tons of coffee targeted for 1968, only 8,000 tons were produced. As for food crops, the Guinea which had been the "granary of French West Africa" [for rice] in the 1950's became an importer of rice in the late 1960's— importing approximately 60,000 tons of rice annually, in addition to a substantial quantity supplied under the American PL480 program. As for crops for industrial processing, of an estimated need of 2,000 tons of tomatoes for the cannery at Mamou, only 285 tons and 308 tons were produced in 1966 and 1967 respectively.

In addition, the cooperative arrangements for the marketing of agricultural produce and consumer goods failed to function properly, which fueled the black market system. There is also considerable smuggling of both food and export crops across Guinea's unguarded borders.[43]

In summary, it seems fair to conclude that the Touré regime is genuinely committed to transforming Guinea into a socialist society, but it is clear that the regime's intensions have not yet been translated into reality. In the concluding section of this paper, we shall review the prospects for a complete transition to socialism in Guinea.

III. CONCLUSIONS AND PROSPECTS FOR THE FUTURE

It now appears that the commitment of the Touré-led regime to transform Guinea into a socialist state is irreversible. Guinea's option is for "scientific socialism," which means the social ownership of the means of production, distribution, and exchange and the establishment of a society where all citizens are assured of minimum requirements of food, shelter, and clothing, equal access to essential social services (such as education, medical care, transportation, and recreation), and political freedom. It is clear that present-day Guinea cannot be described as a full-fledged socialist state. In this concluding section, attention will be focused on the two critical factors in determining the prospects for socialism in Guinea: (1) the leadership of the incumbent regime and (2) the disposition of the Guinean citizenry.

The Leadership. Without entering into the age-old debate concerning the role of leadership in the transformation of a society, we take the position that leadership is a critical factor in determining the orientations of all societies. The leadership factor is particularly crucial in a post-colonial state like Guinea, which at its accession to independent status in 1958 was no more than a "juridically constituted State without historical identity."[44] In addition, the fact that

colonial Guinea was administered as an outpost of a capitalist metropolitan country [France] imposes an even greater challenge on the post-independence leadership to transform it into a socialist society.

To what extent is Guinea's failure to achieve full-fledged socialism attributable to the leadership? Can the leadership do better in the near future? Is there a promise of more fully committed socialists to lead successor regimes?

President Touré is clearly the dominant figure in the current leadership team of Guinea, and whatever progress toward socialism has been made since 1958 can be largely attributed to him. While there are some who consider Touré a committed Marxist, there are others who claim that he is not a Marxist and is not really interested in transforming Guinea into a socialist society.[45] This writer's position is that President Touré understands what "scientific socialism" means and genuinely believes that the application of its principles to Guinea is much more desirable than the maintenance of the capitalist order inherited from France. However, three important factors have deterred him from single-minded pursuit of this objective. The first is the solidity of the capitalist arrangements established by the colonial powers, the second is the unfavorable international environment within which he has had to operate, and the third is his determination to survive as the supreme leader of Guinea.

With the advantage of hindsight, it can now be seen that Touré's unwillingness to declare an unequivocal commitment to scientific socialism until 1967 was the result of a combination of these three factors. At independence in 1958, more than 76 percent of Guinea's total trade was with France, and until 1960 the Guinean franc belonged to the French franc zone. Until about 1962, key services like water and electricity were run by French capitalist interests, but most important of all, the major industrial unit in Guinea until the late 1960's—the Fria consortium, responsible for over 60 percent of Guinea's total exports—was a French-dominated economic "enclave" over which the Guinean government had very little control. An attempt by the Touré-led post-independence regime to transform Guinea into a socialist state at that time would have met with stiff resistance from the French capitalist interests. In addition, the countries that surround Guinea (with the exception of the late Modibo Keita's Mali [1960-68]) had capitalist systems which fueled the development of smuggling and a black market system that seriously undermined the socialist measures that Touré began to introduce from around 1960 onward.

In these circumstances, Touré's struggle for personal survival became the major determinant of how he should seek to transform Guinea into a socialist state. From 1958 until 1967 he considered it a "tactical necessity" to blow hot and cold about socialism. The formation of a Leninist party organization, the breakaway from the franc zone, the state ownership of land (since October 1959), and the establishment of several state enterprises (including the nationalization of some French capitalist enterprises) were all socialist steps, but he also allowed the Fria industrial enclave to thrive, and periodically encouraged private trade by abolishing some state enterprises. At the same time that Touré was declaring an unconditional commitment to socialism in 1967, he considered it essential for the survival of his regime to pursue the path of mixed-economy enterprises for achieving industrialization rather than relying exclusively on state enterprises. The mixed-economy enterprises were established in partnership with both Western and Eastern bloc countries.

This industrialization strategy somewhat strengthened the economy of the country and reduced the problem posed by the surrounding capitalist states, but it also had the effect of forcing the capitalist-oriented elements inside Guinea into making desperate attempts to overthrow the Touré regime and establish a capitalist system. Most of the Guinean citizens who combined with the Portuguese in the abortive invasion of November 1970 were motivated by capitalist objectives.

Since 1970 President Touré has been engaged in a struggle to deal a finishing blow to the capitalist-oriented Guineans, on the one hand,* and to build socialism through the program of rural reorganization based on the PRLs and a socialist-oriented educational system, on the other. The struggle against capitalist-oriented elements assumed an ethnic dimension in 1976 (the "Diallo Telli Plot"), and in late 1977 the failure of the rural transformation program (production and distribution of goods and services, in particular) led to a minor revolt by market women in several cities. While still asserting a commitment to full socialism, Touré recently began to emphasize the "socialist" and "revolutionary" content of Islam.[46]

---

*Touré's counter-measures against his real and imaginary opponents since 1958 have become the subject of heated controversy in recent years, culminating in formal protests by both the International League for Human Rights and Amnesty International. By February 1978 it was estimated that about one thousand people were still in prison. For a first-hand account of the fate of political prisoners in Guinea, see J-P. Alata, *Prison d'Afrique* (Paris, 1976).

Without doubt the instinct for survival lies at the root of this new "tactical" move: the Foulah ethnic group (whose leaders were accused in 1976 of leading opposition to the regime) is almost entirely Muslim, while the appeal to religion can serve as an "opiate" to the discontented citizenry. It is not clear how long this new tactical phase will last, but past experience suggests that it will last as long as Touré sees it as the surest means of guaranteeing his survival as leader. Other recent measures such as the reestablishment of important trade links with France, the appeal to Guinean exiles to return to Guinea with the promise of freedom to practice their professions,[47] and the "reconciliation" with capitalist-oriented Ivory Coast and Senegal (including an agreement on free movement of persons and goods) suggest that the current tactical phase constitutes a strong deemphasis on the pursuit of the socialist objective.

Judging by past experience, the current trends are fully supported by most—if not all—of the members of the incumbent leadership. Therefore the prospect of a more socialist-inclined group carrying out a palace coup in defense of socialism does not appear to be a possibility. As for the possible successor leadership, the abortive invasion of 1970 revealed the heterogeneous character of the anti-Touré elements aspiring to national leadership. While there are some committed socialists among them, the majority favor a return to the capitalist arrangements established by the French colonial power. This writer's assessment is that an anti-Touré succession is very unlikely and that after Touré there will be a PDG-regime "Phase Two," which could modify the existing Touréan arrangements by introducing either more socialism or more capitalism, depending on the dynamics of both domestic and external politics.[48]

The Guinean Citizenry. In one of the few socioanthropological studies of post-independence Guinea, the American anthropologist W. Derman observes that "the transformation of peasants into socialists will be far more difficult than the transformation of serfs into peasants or the transformation of Guinea from colony to independent nation."[49] Derman acknowledges that the Touré-led regime successfully mobilized the masses to support the struggle for independence, and that it won the support of the mass of the Guinean citizens in the Foutah-Djallon area (Middle Guinea, inhabited by the Foulahs) when it destroyed the feudal order in which a few traditional leaders held the mass of the citizens as serfs. But granting these two important achievements by the Touré regime, Derman opines that the transforming of peasants into socialists will be very difficult.

In another context, Friedrich Engels asserts that "anyone who says that a socialist revolution can be carried out in a country which has no proletariat or bourgeoisie proves by this statement that he still has to learn the A, B, C of socialism."[50] Touré clearly rejects Engels's assertion. He does not see the Guinean working class as a "proletariat" and would rather distinguish between a "people's class" and an "exploiting class." The people's class consists of the peasants, the working class, and progressive intellectuals, while the exploiting class is made up of traders, industrialists, and all others who *employ* labor. It is on the people's class that he relies to transform Guinea into a socialist state.

The reactions of the ordinary citizen of Guinea to the socialist measures introduced by the Touré regime have depended on whether or not they bring about improvements in his standard of living (or at least do not deprive him of goods and services that he has previously enjoyed). Thus when serfdom was abolished in Middle Guinea, those newly freed enthusiastically welcomed the change. The emancipation of women (including the abolition of polygamy) was welcomed by most of the women. Similarly, the recognition given to youths by entrusting them with responsibilities (especially within the party militia) has been welcomed by them and given them a sense of pride. As for the workers, the systematic co-option of their leaders into key posts in the party and the state has made them see themselves as part of the vanguard of the revolution. All these steps taken by the party and state on behalf of groups of the citizenry are given wide publicity within the parallel organizations for the workers, youth, and women. It is from the ranks of all these organizations that the 300,000 party leaders (1970 figure) at the various levels are drawn. These individuals constitute the party "elite," and they enjoy, in varying degrees, better living standards than the rest of the citizenry.

The vast majority of Guineans have been affected for better *and* for worse by the varying fortunes of Touréan socialism since 1958. In the early 1960's, when private trade was allowed, the capitalist elements engaged in a "no holds barred" exploitation of their fellow citizens. This led to the abolition of private trade in 1964 and a total commitment to a socialist arrangement for production, distribution, and exchange in the rural areas beginning in the late 1960's. Because the socialist arrangements in the rural areas failed, the majority of peasants continued to produce privately for their personal needs. The peasants tolerated the introduction of the PRLs, with their brigades of production and the state-controlled

81

marketing system, but these socialist institutions have not really replaced the traditional peasant arrangements for production, distribution, and exchange. Faced with the malfunctioning of the PRLs and the state marketing system, the peasants have been in collusion with the black market system and the smuggling activities of the capitalist elements in the rural areas. On two occasions when the state has tried to strengthen its rural production and marketing systems (1970 and 1977) by clamping down on the black marketeers and the smugglers, the ineffectiveness of the state institutions has forced the peasants and others into revolt.*

The recent Touréan idea of preaching socialism via Islam appears to be an attempt to maintain the basic commitment of the citizenry to socialism, but it is doubtful that this Islamic "revolution" can aid in the transformation of the PRLs into genuine socialist units. The best hope for socialism in Guinea appears to be through the inculcation of socialist ideals in the children in the schools. The success of the Touré regime in expanding educational facilities at all levels, and the location of these facilities (including higher educational institutions) throughout the country, holds out the promise that, with greater commitment to socialist ideology and fewer "tactical" diversions motivated by the desire to stay in power, a socialist society can be established in the Republic of Guinea. But the "ifs" are many, which suggests that the abandonment of the socialist goal by a future regime cannot be ruled out.

*The 1970 "peasant unrest" (*malaise paysanne*) was contained by the free distribution of American PL480 rice to the rural farmers. The 1977 incident was led by market women in several cities demonstrating against the abolition of private trade; the government immediately reacted by describing the demonstration as the work of saboteurs and counterrevolutionaries, but by early 1978 there were reports that the regime had relaxed the 1975 charter of exclusive state-control of trade and commerce.

SOCIALISM IN ONE SECTOR: RURAL DEVELOPMENT IN ZAMBIA

Stephen A. Quick

What does it take to create a socialist society in Africa? In order to pose such a question, we need an understanding of what constitutes "socialist development," and this can come only from a comparative analysis of the socialist experience in general. If we had a model of the process of socialist development, we would be in a much better position to provide a critical analysis of the development programs carried out by African socialist regimes. While the utility of such a model is obvious, the task of constructing it is fraught with difficulties. On the theoretical level there is great disagreement about the meaning of the term "socialism," and on the practical level there are substantial differences between the development strategies of the main socialist countries.

This article will begin with a brief exposition of what I see as the main features of the socialist development model as abstracted from the theoretical writings of Marx and neo-Marxists and as exemplified in the historical experience of Russia and China. This exposition will focus on the crucial problem areas which must be confronted in the process of socialist development and must, because of space limitations, be extremely brief and simplistic. The remainder of the article will be an attempt to use this model to illuminate Zambia's brief flirtation with a socialist program of rural development.

THE MODEL

Socialism has long represented the desire for a classless, non-exploitative form of human society in which all people have a basic sense of dignity, share equally in the material wealth of society, and participate equally in the making of crucial social decisions.[1] While this vision encompasses virtually all aspects of human life, it is generally acknowledged that economics is the key. A socialist society is based fundamentally on a particular form of economic organization, and the process of transforming a society in the direction of

socialism involves primarily a reorientation of economic relationships. For convenience' sake, economic relationships can be divided into four general categories: (1) industrial organization, (2) agricultural organization, (3) mechanisms for coordinating economic activity, and (4) linkages between the domestic and international economies.

Early socialist theorists tended to assume that developed capitalist societies would be the first to undergo the transition to socialism, but the historical experience of the twentieth century has been that socialist revolutions have most often occurred in countries without a developed system of capitalist production. Most recent discussions of socialist development have recognized that noneconomic factors play a crucial role in the transition process, and that elements of what Marxists call the "superstructure" (laws, ideologies, political parties, etc.) have an important role in determining the kinds of changes which take place in the economic base.[2] The transition to socialism in poor countries may be critically dependent upon a particular form of state and a particular type of ideology, and this superstructural variable must therefore be added to the list of four "economic" areas to be altered in the transition to socialism. Let us examine each of these five areas in greater detail.

1. Industrial Organization. The dynamic center of a capitalist economy is the industrial sector, and the owners of industrial property are the group which is likely to provide the greatest resistance to the creation of socialism. The replacement of private ownership of industrial property by some form of collective ownership is therefore a crucial step in the building of socialism. The elimination of private ownership must be combined with a new kind of relationship between "owners" and workers in industry, for only by transforming these relations can a country create a working class which is willing to support the creation of socialism.

Early socialist thinkers believed that a militant, self-conscious working class would inevitably be created by capitalism. Capitalism would proletarianize and politicize the masses through progressive exploitation and immiseration, and the working class would then challenge the capitalist system of production. The historical reality of Russia and China challenged this view, however. In poor and backward countries, the masses are peasants, not proletarians, and the urban working class often enjoys a much higher standard of living than the majority. This complicates the task of building socialism by creating a working class which is torn between capital-

ism and socialism or even supportive of the capitalist mode of production. In such circumstances, the orientation of the workers needs to be shifted from the existing emphasis on hierarchy, non-participation in decision-making, and material rewards toward an emphasis on equality, participation, and non-material incentives,[3] and the small working class must be encouraged to identify with and accept responsibility for the peasant masses.[4]

2. Agricultural Organization. The existence of a large mass of landowning peasants has usually been seen as an obstacle to the creation of socialism because private production encourages an individualistic and competitive mentality, as well as providing a material basis for the development of classes. In addition, the isolated nature of peasant production makes it difficult for peasants to participate in collective forms of political action.[5] Finally, an agricultural system based on individual smallholders must be co-ordinated through the mechanism of market prices because non-market controls are either impossible to administer or are resisted by independent producers.[6]

For these reasons, and because it is virtually impossible to sub-stitute plan for market systems of coordination (see section 3 below) in a predominantly peasant economy, some form of collectivization is required in the agricultural sector. Agricultural collectivization can take a variety of forms—cooperatives, state farms, communes, ujamaa villages—but whatever the form, the basic intent is to orga-nize the peasantry, overcome their isolation, give them experience in working with others, and change their individualistic and competitive orientation to a cooperative orientation. Collectivization also makes it possible to turn idle labor into physical capital and to release needed manpower for industry.[7] Finally, collectivization makes possible the substitution of plan for market as the basic control system for the economy, and allows for the rapid extraction of investment surpluses from the rural sector without inflicting undue hardship on the rural masses.

3. Mechanisms for Coordinating Economic Activity. The basic device for coordinating economic activity in a capitalist society is the market system, in which individual producers are dominated by impersonal "laws of the market" which require them to produce things which "sell" rather than the things which are most needed by the society.[8] The transition to socialism involves a substitution of a plan-oriented system of coordination for the anarchy of the market,

85

which allows for the incorporation of a wide variety of social values in economic decision-making rather than the single value of profitability. The task of managing a planned system is complex, and beyond the resources of poor countries (as the Soviet experience of "war communism" clearly indicates),[9] but the substitution of plan for market is essential to the creation of socialism.

4. Linkages Between the Domestic and International Economies. Capitalism is a worldwide system of production, and it is generally agreed that the establishment of full socialism is possible only on a world scale.[10] Russia and China possessed the resources and population to undertake socialist development without substantial interaction with the capitalist world economy, but even for them the existence of strong capitalist nations made the creation of socialism difficult. Most third world countries are not in a position to follow the Russian and Chinese path of relative autarky: their economies are small, resource-poor, and linked in a multitude of ways to the international capitalist economy. These linkages not only distort the productive structure of third world economies, but also constitute major obstacles to the transition of socialism.

In most poor countries, foreign capitalist firms are responsible for a significant share of the investment in the extractive and manufacturing sectors. Such firms have a vested interest in the maintenance of capitalist production in these countries, and they are able to exert a powerful influence because of their wealth and power. In some cases, multinational firms have been known to sabotage socialist governments,[11] but their opposition to socialism usually takes more subtle forms. They generally resist those kinds of state planning which might decrease the profitability of their subsidiaries, and lobby for programs of national development which will maximize their profits. In pressing for their interests, multinational firms have the powerful weapon of investment, and many regimes have been persuaded to abandon socialist experiments because they might jeopardize their country's "favorable investment climate." This emphasis on capitalist criteria for evaluating national development plans leads to the erosion of elite commitments to socialism. Multinational firms press for patterns of import-substituting industrialization oriented toward the small, high-income consumer market, further deepening social inequalities; they encourage poor countries to accept advisors and experts from developed capitalist countries, who are naturally more favorable to capitalist programs for development than socialist ones; finally, they resist proposals to alter

owner-working relations in a more egalitarian and participatory direction.[12]

Given their limited capabilities, the most poor countries have been able to do in their attempts to control international capitalist firms is to require state co-participation in investment. Parastatal organizations have been seen as a way of disciplining multinational firms and of interjecting socialist values into their decision-making, but some recent literature suggests that the process might work the other way round—that the multinationals are able to use the parastatals to introduce capitalist values and evaluative criteria into the state's economic calculations.[13] All this suggests that continued close relationships with international capitalism and multinational firms are likely to prove inimical to the creation of socialism, but the severe resource limitations of most third world countries limit their options. Perhaps the best they can do is find more effective ways of controlling these relationships, or seek to reorient their external dependence toward countries more sympathetic to socialism.

5. *The Sociopolitical "Superstructure."* The class structures of most poor countries are simple and relatively undifferentiated, and consequently the state is generally free from obligations to powerful class interests.[14] This relative autonomy of the state creates the possibility for political and ideological factors to play a major role in defining the development of society.

In order to move a society toward socialism, it is crucial that socialist ideals, values, and analyses be articulated and widely disseminated. In addition to general socialist goals, an ideology for the transition period must include an accurate analysis of the society and of the social forces operating both for and against socialist development. A widespread understanding of the meaning of socialism and of the need for conflict and struggle in its creation is required of both the masses and the political elite. Ideological unity, especially among the elite, is of crucial importance during the early stages of the transition process.

At the level of organization, the transition to socialism requires a large and well-disciplined party/state apparatus. This apparatus must be large enough to extend through the whole of society, but flexible and responsive to local needs to assist in penetrating the basic units of social organization (family, village, neighborhood, etc.).[15] The optimum structure for such an apparatus appears to be a large number of cadres, recruited from the local population,

educated and disciplined in the needs of the transition process, and then returned to the masses to mobilize them for the task of transition. Discipline is particularly important for organization at the elite level. Because of the power the state wields in the transition process, corruption and elitism are a constant danger, and some mechanism is required to prevent these tendencies from dominating the state elite. In Tanzania, for example, some progress toward controlling elitist tendencies has been made through the imposition of a strict "leadership code."[16] Whatever the mechanism, something must be done to prevent the state elite from emerging as a new ruling class.

Thus socialism appears to require massive, simultaneous efforts to transform all of society. If all this is required to build socialism, it is hardly surprising that so few African governments can be called "socialist." But is all this *really* essential for the building of socialism in poor countries? Could it be that some of the features of the model are more essential than others, and that it is possible to move ahead in some directions while temporarily ignoring others? Must all of these things be done at the same time, or is it possible to tackle the transition to socialism incrementally or on an "experimental" basis?

The incremental approach has a good deal to recommend it—especially to positivistic social scientists who have become accustomed to dividing reality into discrete units for study. This intellectual orientation is reinforced by the resource limitations of poor countries, which make a small-scale, experimental approach to development (socialist or otherwise) seem attractive. From such a viewpoint, it would be seen as sheer folly for a poor African country to attempt to move simultaneously in all five areas.[17]

A Marxist, on the other hand, would see the incremental approach as likely to prove fatal to an attempt to create socialism. Marxists view society as a set of closely interrelated social forces so intimately connected with one another that change in one sector only is likely to be completely ineffective. They believe this is especially true with regard to the creation of socialism in poor countries. Such countries have usually been launched on the road to capitalist development by colonialism—especially by their economic integration into the international capitalist economy. Thus they have internal classes and social forces pushing them in the direction of capitalism. An incrementalist approach would involve efforts to develop socialism in one area while ignoring capitalist development in others. If the Marxist, integrated view of social

reality is correct, the capitalist sectors would almost certainly overwhelm the socialist experiments because capitalist relations are deeply rooted in the history of such countries. From the Marxist viewpoint, a transition to socialism in poor countries requires that attention be paid to transforming all five areas *simultaneously*. It may be possible to shift emphasis from one sector to another, but it is disastrous to ignore *any* sector because this means strengthening the anti-socialist forces in that sector.

In many ways this debate concerning incremental vs. integrated approaches to the transition to socialism parallels the debate between Trotsky and Stalin over the issue of "socialism in one country."[18] Trotsky argued that capitalism was an international phenomenon and that it would never be possible to create genuine socialism in the Soviet Union until the entire world was converted to socialism, while Stalin argued that it would be possible to create some form of socialism in one country which would provide a base from which to convert the world to socialism. This debate about socialism at the level of the nation-state has never been fully resolved, and the incrementalist/integrationist controversy reproduces it at the level of sectors within a single economy. The debate about "socialism in one sector" is thus a direct descendant of the earlier debate about "socialism in one country." To explore this issue, we will examine the case of Zambia—an illustrative, perhaps even classic example of the "socialism in one sector" approach.

THE ZAMBIAN POLITICAL ECONOMY

Zambia achieved independence in 1964 under circumstances which seemed to be very unfavorable to socialist development. The educated stratum of the country was tiny and largely ignorant of socialist theory, and the nationalist movement had concentrated almost entirely on liberation from colonial rule, with little thought about the regime which would follow liberation. Moreover, the British government granted independence so readily that there was no protracted struggle which might have "radicalized" the nationalists.[19] Despite these unfavorable conditions, an ideology emerged in Zambia following independence which rather closely resembled the "African Socialism" of other, more conspicuously militant African nations.

The key to the emergence of this ideology was Kenneth Kaunda, leader of the United National Independence Party (UNIP) and first President of the new state. A philosopher as well as statesman,

Kaunda recognized the need for a national ideology to guide development. He drew on a number of sources for his ideology of Zambian "Humanism": radical Christianity, existentialist humanism, Fabian socialism, and the Ujamaa socialism of his close friend President Julius Nyerere.[20]

For Kaunda the moral foundation of Zambian society lay in the traditions of the village: equality between members of society, mutual support, participation in collective work and decision-making, an absence of exploitation, and self-reliance. These values could and should be extended to all of society. He advocated the elimination of social classes and economic exploitation, equalization of the distribution of social rewards between elites and masses and between rural and urban sectors, the creation of an urban working class which was conscious of its responsibilities to the less-favored rural masses, the encouragement of collective and cooperative forms of production in agriculture, state ownership of a significant portion of the means of production, national social and economic planning, and the progressive elimination of the nation's dependence on foreign firms and foreign transportation routes.

In a number of respects, Kaunda's ideology of "Humanism" diverged from "classical" socialism. It tended to reflect an idealized traditional society. The class structure of Zambian society was not recognized; as a consequence there was a failure to anticipate the struggle which would be required to transform that society in the direction of socialism. Humanism defined the process of social development in moral and spiritual terms and was vague about the specific kinds of economic relationships required to create the good society. Finally, Humanism was primarily a utopia—a vision of what might be rather than an analysis of what was—giving it an abstract and amorphous quality.[21] While Humanism provided an impetus for Zambian decision-makers to think about socialist policies for development, when it came to practical policymaking, it quickly became clear that conditions were not conducive to socialist development in most areas of Zambia.

Industrial Sector. The industrial sector of Zambia was completely dominated by the foreign-owned copper industry. This industry was essential to the Zambian economy, and it could not be nationalized because there were virtually no Zambians with the managerial or technical expertise to keep the mines in operation. The copper companies had prevented Africans from being anything but laborers, and had reserved managerial and technical positions entirely for

Europeans.[22] In addition to making nationalization impossible, this policy established significant income differentials between European and African personnel. These differentials were the main target of the African mineworkers union which emerged in the 1950's.[23] The emphasis on European/African income differentials, by focusing the attention of the African labor movement on the distribution of income within the mining sector, drew attention away from the inequalities in income throughout the country. The copper industry workers in Zambia came to possess many of the characteristics of a "labor aristocracy," interested in their own economic well-being rather than in the creation of egalitarian socialism. Throughout the post-independence period, they continually opposed government policies for equalizing the distribution of income within Zambia, and eventually became major critics of the regime's policy of encouraging rapid rural development through large government investments in the agricultural sector.

In addition to the copper industry, the industrial sector of Zambia had a small but active domestic entrepreneurial class. This indigenous bourgeoisie was concentrated mainly in trade and small-scale consumer manufacturing industry. The political power of this class was limited because many of the entrepreneurs were Asian, but they helped to determine the nature of goods marketed in the society and provided a model for emulation by upwardly mobile Africans.* The continued existence of this petit-bourgeois sector contributed to the formation of economically based social classes in post-independence Zambia, and it became a focal point of resistance to the creation of socialism.

Economic Coordination. The new state lacked the personnel and data needed for effective economic planning. Statistical data on the Zambian economy were scarce, and educated manpower was virtually nonexistent. At the time of independence, there were less than one hundred African university graduates in all of Zambia and only one thousand African secondary school graduates.[24] The colonial policy of minimal educational development left Zambia heavily dependent on foreign manpower to run the economy. Much of this foreign manpower was in the private, multinational-controlled

---

*It is significant that the most popular of the government's economic reforms was a measure which allowed Zambians to take over Asian-owned businesses (see Andrew Beveridge, "Economic Independence, Indigenization and the African Businessman: Some Effects of Zambia's Economic Reforms," *African Studies Review* 17, 3 [December 1974]: 477-90).

sectors of banking, insurance, mining, and manufacturing, and as such naturally had an interest in maintaining the market as the basic mechanism for coordinating economic activity. The European civil servants in the various economic ministries and departments were also generally committed to the market as the mechanism of economic coordination, and used the lack of manpower and data as an effective argument against government planning. Since planning without planners is impossible, the new state was forced to employ a kind of development planning which merely specified aggregate output and state investment targets, and relied largely on the price mechanism and the market for communication between producers.[25]

Linkages with International Economy. As already noted, Zambia had to rely on international companies to run its copper industry, but new arrangements were worked out to reduce the amount of capital which left the country each year in the form of royalties, dividends, and interest.[26] The banking sector remained firmly under international control, as did much of the manufacturing sector. The close linkages between Zambia and the international capitalist system limited the freedom of maneuver of the new state, and were conducive to the penetration of the state by capitalist ideas and values. At the urging of the multinational companies, Zambia repeatedly requested foreign advisors from the aid agencies of major capitalist countries. These requests were usually honored, and much of Zambia's economic policy in the post-independence era was thus shaped by capitalist-oriented technical missions and foreign advisors. (Significantly, there were very few advisors from socialist countries.)

Zambia made one major attempt to control the operations of international firms in her economy. Soon after independence, several parastatal development companies were established to encourage and control future foreign investment, and in 1968 a series of reforms was announced which placed these parastatals firmly at the center of the economic life of the country.[27] Much of the activity of these institutions involved cooperation with multinational firms in new investment, negotiating the takeover of existing enterprises with such firms, or seeking managerial and technical advice about the running of state economic organizations from these firms. This inevitably resulted in close integration between the parastatals and multinationals, which led to the development of a similarity in their outlook. This outlook tended to reflect the views of the companies more strongly than the views of the Zambian government.[28]

Political/Ideological Superstructure. In the realm of ideology and organization, the newly independent Zambian state was extremely weak. "Humanism" was not fully articulated as the national ideology until 1968, and even then it was perceived by most Zambians as only a vague set of moral principles and not a meaningful guide to action. No attempt was made to systematize and publicize the ideology, and most Zambians had no idea how it might relate to their daily lives.* It also appears that most UNIP leaders either did not understand or did not accept the basic premises of Humanism, and that therefore there was a great deal of ideological conflict at the elite level.[29]

In terms of organization, the UNIP began to decline rapidly following independence. Given the shortage of skilled manpower, party activists were quickly recruited for positions in the central government, stripping the lower ranks of the party of their trained leaders.[30] Their places were taken by new party members, many of whom had joined the party after victory in the liberation struggle was certain, and whose commitment to the national interest was compromised by their concern for advancing their own careers. Furthermore, the party was based primarily in the urban centers, with little effective organization in the rural areas, which limited its ability to mobilize the masses. Party discipline was largely ineffective, especially in controlling elitism, and as a result many national leaders used their offices to enrich themselves to such an extent that political office soon came to be associated with economic prosperity—a development which further weakened any interest in socialism.[31]

Agricultural Organization. In the four areas of industry, economic coordination, international linkages, and politics and ideology, powerful forces were operating against any move toward socialism in Zambia. But what about agriculture? There were relatively few obstacles to socialist development in the agricultural sector, and it rapidly became clear that this sector would be the primary target for Kaunda's transformational efforts.

Zambian agriculture was essentially a three-tiered system, with a small number of large-scale European commercial farmers at the top, a substantial number of medium-scale African com-

*It has recently been suggested that the main problem is not that people do not understand Humanism, but that important groups perceive that their interests would be threatened by a precise definition of it (see "Conclusion," in Tordoff and Molteno, eds., pp. 393-99).

mercial farmers in the middle, and a very large number of small-scale and subsistence cultivators at the bottom. The colonial regime had relied heavily on the European commercial farmers for basic food supplies, but a number of experimental programs demonstrated that the productive potential of African farmers could be mobilized on a large enough scale to provide for the subsistence needs of the country.[32] The European farmers were not as essential to the Zambian economy as were the European copper producers, and they were not particularly well-connected with the UNIP; as a result, major concessions would not have to be made to them. A rural development program which stressed collectivization would doubtless antagonize the European farmers, especially since their estates would be likely targets for takeover, but their opposition would carry little weight.

A similar situation obtained with regard to the African commercial farmers. These farmers were concentrated in the Southern and Central Provinces, along the line of rail leading to the Copperbelt. For a variety of historical reasons, they tended to support the UNIP's major rival—the African National Congress—which was the country's first political party, but which had rapidly lost ground to the more militant UNIP.[33] The African commercial farmers were thus not closely associated with the new government, but they were of substantial importance to the economy, and policymakers did not want to antagonize them to the point where they might sabotage production. A comprehensive program of collectivization would certainly have antagonized these farmers, which acted as a major constraint on government action.

The rural masses had benefitted very little from the policies of the colonial regime with regard to agricultural prices, credit, transportation, marketing facilities, and extension assistance. At independence, the vast majority of Zambia's rural citizens participated only marginally in the agricultural economy. Their main source of income was seasonal labor in the urban areas or on European commercial farms. This work experience gave them a glimpse of a higher standard of living, and made them feel even more frustrated by the lack of income-earning opportunities in agriculture. The rural masses were the main political support of the UNIP in the rural areas, and much of this support was rooted in a belief that political independence would lead to a dramatic improvement in rural life.[34] The expectations of this group probably focused on increased opportunities for profitable individual farming, since this was the mode of agriculture with which they were familiar.

They had never engaged in collective farming, but national leaders believed that they would accept collectivization readily if it promised a rapid rise in their standard of living.

Thus the opposition to collectivization in the rural areas was likely to come primarily from groups which were of marginal importance to the new government, which opened the way for a socialist program of agricultural development. The absence of constraints was combined with an ideological vision which assigned priority to rural life. Kaunda's Humanism was based on a traditional African communalism which supposedly existed in the village, and it was important from an ideological perspective that the socialist rural development program be built upon this tradition. The Humanist assumptions about traditional communalism led naturally to the conclusion that collectivization in the rural areas would be relatively easy because the population was already accustomed to cooperative modes of production.

One of the first policies Kaunda outlined for the new Zambian government was a massive program to collectivize agriculture through a network of farming cooperatives. Cooperatives rather than state farms or communes were chosen because they appeared to fit better with the traditional social unit of the village, and because they offered the hope of collectivization without the bureaucratic incompetence and alienation of the masses which Kaunda saw as growing out of a state farm system.[35]

While this "socialist approach" was shaping up in the agricultural sector, decisions were being made not to pursue a socialist path of development in the other four sectors. In the industrial sector, multinationals were allowed to remain dominant, private ownership was accepted in the small-scale manufacturing and trading sector, and massive wage increases were granted to African mineworkers; comprehensive economic planning was abandoned as an impossible goal; investments and advisors continued to be sought from capitalist firms and countries; and in the realm of ideology and politics, Humanism remained abstract and incomprehensible to most Zambians, the UNIP was allowed to collapse, and government officials were not constrained in their pursuit of personal enrichment. Agriculture was the only area in which Zambia was preparing to follow a socialist model, and if we examine what happened in this "experiment," we may be able to shed some light on the problems of building "socialism in one sector."

RURAL SOCIALISM IN ZAMBIA

The cooperative movement was central to President Kaunda's vision of Zambian rural society, but he had difficulty persuading the nation's political elite to accept his view. On several occasions the President tried to mobilize the UNIP for the task of cooperative development; each time he received rhetorical support, but no firm commitment to action.[36] The reasons for the party's refusal were complex. Some politicians doubtless felt politically obligated to private cash-crop farmers and were reluctant to endorse a program of which their constituents disapproved. Others were themselves commercial farmers: the purchase of farms was one of the main methods used by the new political elite to secure positions of economic privilege. Many party leaders were obligated wholly to urban constituencies and were largely unconcerned about rural development; they saw rural development only in terms of possible reductions in the cost of food in the urban areas. Since collectivization involved the investment of resources with no assurance of future return, it was not the most desirable program from the point of view of the urban politician. Finally, there were a number of party leaders who believed that the party was not up to the task of mobilizing a major rural development program: the party apparatus in the rural areas was weak, and had become even weaker following independence, when many trained activists were transferred out of the countryside and into the Copperbelt or Lusaka.

Despite the party's unwillingness to back Kaunda's call for cooperatives, the President remained convinced of their importance, and concluded that he would have to go around the party if he were to get anything done. Accordingly, in January 1965 Kaunda made a major speech in which he called on the people of Zambia to form cooperative societies.[37] This "Chifubu Declaration" was enthusiastically received by the rural masses, who perceived it as the government's answer to the problem of rural stagnation.

Kaunda was able to mobilize mass enthusiasm for his cooperative ideal through exhortation, but he was experienced enough to recognize that enthusiasm was not enough to make a successful movement. The enthusiasm had to be tempered with organization, and since the UNIP had abdicated organizational responsibility, the President turned to the civil service for help in disciplining and supervising the drive for cooperatives.

The logical agency to assign organizational responsibility was the Department of Cooperatives, and it was to this department that

the President turned following the Chifubu Declaration. This choice was an unfortunate one: the Department of Cooperatives was completely unsuited for the task. Formed during the colonial era as an accounting advisory service to marketing cooperatives, the department in 1965 consisted of a small staff of accountants and bookkeepers supervised by Europeans, with operations confined to a small part of the countryside. The staff had no experience with farming and no training in organization-building, and yet they were being asked to assist in the formation of hundreds of small farming societies in remote parts of rural Zambia.[38]

This task, which was next to impossible for an agency with so little relevant experience, was rendered even more difficult by the ambiguous nature of elite commitment to rural socialism. Both within the civil service and within the party there was substantial disagreement about whether the formation of cooperatives was the best way to attempt to modernize rural Zambia. Various other alternatives were being given active consideration, of which the most significant were proposals for developing small-scale family farms and proposals for large-scale, capital-intensive settlement schemes. Proponents of these alternative strategies found support in various reports from international experts, which helped to block the development of a consensus. As a result of this conflict concerning the different approaches, it was decided that all three modes of agricultural production—cooperatives, settlement schemes, and individual farming—would be encouraged and supported by the government.[39] Thus both rural capitalism and rural socialism were to be explored as alternatives for Zambian agriculture.

Kaunda himself did not want to push for a total commitment to collectivization. His orientation toward problem-solving was eclectic and pragmatic, and he saw nothing wrong with experimentation and competition between programs. He strongly rejected coercion, which led him to prefer voluntary to mandatory collectivization. As a result of all these factors, collectivization through cooperatives never became the regime's *only* rural development policy. This decision for partial rather than complete collectivization, which is very different from the approach to rural organization adopted in both the Soviet Union and China,[40] was to be a source of considerable trouble for the cooperative movement.

The decision to develop several different approaches to rural development at the same time immediately created problems for the Department of Cooperatives. It meant that different agencies within the government were in direct competition with one another

97

for personnel and budget and loan funds. In this competition the department came off less well than other agencies.

The department's problems were particularly acute in the area of personnel. Given the extremely limited educational system left by colonialism, educated manpower was probably the country's scarcest resource, and competition for staff was keen—both within the government and between government and the private sector. Because of the continued existence of a private manufacturing and trading sector which offered profitable job opportunities for men trained in accounting and bookkeeping, many of the skilled accountants of the Department of Cooperatives left the agency for work in industry.[41] Within the state bureaucracy, because of the central importance of the industrial sector of the economy, appointments to state agencies active in the industrial area were more prestigious than appointments to agriculture-related departments; thus when given a choice, civil servants preferred to move to Treasury or Commerce and Industry (or to the parastatals) rather than stay in Cooperatives. And even within the agricultural ministries, promotion opportunities in departments concerned with improving small-scale private farming or the development of settlement schemes were more attractive than those in the Department of Cooperatives. These bureaucratic preferences, combined with a weak elite commitment to cooperatives, meant that the Department of Cooperatives had more vacancies and a higher rate of staff turnover than other departments.* These staffing problems forced the department to abdicate all responsibility for screening new societies and supervising their operations, creating serious difficulties for the movement from the outset.†

The personnel situation gives the clearest picture of the precarious status of cooperatives in the national development program, but there were also financial complications. The re-negotiation of

---

*In 1963 the Department of Agriculture had a 6 percent vacancy rate in junior-level field positions while the Department of Cooperatives had a 74 percent vacancy rate (see Northern Rhodesia, Ministry of African Agriculture, *Annual Report for 1963* [Lusaka: Government Printer, 1964], p. 11).

†The abdication was broadcast to all Provincial Cooperative Officers in the following terms: "We are not qualified to pass on technical advice. . . . It is not for officers of this department to decide whether or not the society is likely to be a success. Members of a proposed cooperative may have no knowledge of the business they intend forming, but if they wish to form the society, then it is their business and we cannot refuse to register them for that reason" (see "Circular Letter to All Provincial Cooperative Officers from the Registrar of Cooperatives, 3 February, 1965" [in File 24/12/1, Department of Cooperatives, Eastern Province Files, Chipata]).

royalty arrangements with the copper companies and the ready availability of foreign aid meant that the new regime was not seriously constrained by a lack of foreign exchange or government revenue. There was a great deal of money available for development projects, and the President's favored rural development program received authorization to disburse huge amounts of this money to help create cooperatives. According to the Humanist ideology, cooperation is the natural and traditional form of production in the villages; from this it follows that the rural people already know how to run cooperatives and that all they need to make a success is sufficient capital. This ideology dovetailed nicely with the desires of rural UNIP politicians to acquire new forms of patronage, and as a result the Department of Cooperatives was under a great deal of political pressure to distribute grants, short-term loans, and long-term loans to local cooperatives as quickly as possible and without much supervision.[42]

There were two major problems with this approach to loan-making. First, the multiplicity of rural development programs being pursued by the government gave rise to a multiplicity of agencies to administer loans. Loans for cooperatives became the province of three different agencies: the Department itself, the Credit Organization of Zambia (COZ), and the Land and Agricultural Bank. Each agency had a different primary purpose: the Department to develop cooperatives; the COZ to make loans to all types of small farmers, cooperative and private; and the Land and Agricultural Bank to make secured loans to large commercial farms. These differences in orientation led to substantial confusion, with the result that in many instances cooperative loans were never received, were received too late to affect planting, or were obtained in a form which invited misuse by local elites.

The second major problem with the loans program was that it was based on a faulty premise about village life. By 1965 the market economy had so effectively penetrated rural Zambia that there were few vestiges of cooperative agricultural production.[43] Collective effort was therefore a *radically new* form of economic activity, and the basic problem was not how to provide poor but cooperative farmers with capital, but how to persuade highly individualistic farmers to engage in cooperative activity. What was needed were education, assistance, and supervision—not money—but money was available and supervisory personnel were not, so the cooperatives got money.

The massive inflow of government funds immediately created

problems in local cooperative societies. Members of cooperatives tended to regard these funds as their wages for working on a government project, and used them for personal consumption instead of investing them. Quarrels broke out over the distribution of the government monies, rapidly destroying the unity of the societies. Within a year or two of their establishment, virtually all the societies had splintered into ten-member mini-societies. (Ten was the statutory minimum number of members for a society to be eligible for government monies.) Needless to say, ten-member societies were not the most efficient for purposes of agricultural production.

The conflicts which caused larger societies to split up did not end once the statutory minimum was reached, and tensions divided most societies into warring factions. Cooperative activity was almost impossible with these conflicts, and most societies were forced to live on loans rather than on the output of their farm. This situation caused many members to leave the cooperatives—departures facilitated by employment opportunities in the cities and alternative possibilities in farming. A study of several farming societies in the Eastern Province revealed that those who left in disgust were generally the more dynamic and efficient members, who quickly found employment in the urban areas, in private farming, on settlement schemes, or in the retail trade.* The availability of these other employment possibilities (all in areas receiving government support) helped to strip the cooperatives of their most talented members, and when the inevitable conflicts arose, the remaining members were unable to develop effective modes of cooperation.

When these problems were brought to the attention of the field staff of the Department of Cooperatives, they concluded that the situation was headed for disaster. They appealed for more personnel, fewer loans, and a slowing of the pace of registering new societies.[44] Their expressions of concern were met with an overwhelmingly negative response from the national political leadership. Kaunda's vision of rural Zambia anticipated no problems with cooperative development, and he interpreted their complaints as typical manifestations of bureaucratic fear of innovation. UNIP politicians with rural constituencies were delighted with the massive giveaway program because it offered them a new form of patronage. Most of the cooperatives were formed by local UNIP branches, and securing government funds for these societies was a good way

*In a study of thirteen Eastern Province farming cooperatives conducted by this author, over 80 percent of cooperative leavers found employment in other occupations, with fewer than 20 percent returning to subsistence farming.

for local and national politicians to strengthen their political positions. Because the political elite were more interested in distributing patronage than creating viable local societies, they dismissed the departmental requests for more staff as irrelevant. As a result, the new cooperatives continued to develop with little supervision or assistance in solving their problems.

The situation was highly unstable, however, because it depended on the continued availability of government funds and an absence of supervision of the cooperatives. Both of these variables changed radically in 1967. In that year the French agronomist Rene Dumont presented a report on cooperatives which was extremely critical of them and focused public attention on their problems.[45] In 1967 there was also a financial crisis in Zambia precipitated by transportation problems which limited the export of copper. Government revenue declined while expenditures continued to rise, and it became clear that Zambia would soon be running a budget deficit instead of the customary surplus. The deficit would be due largely to heavy government investments in infrastructure and education and a recent massive increase in civil service salaries.[46] The salary increase was deemed necessary to keep civil service pay in line with that of the multinational mining sector, whose workers had shortly before won a major wage increase. The infrastructure and education expenditures were also largely the result of pressure from the private sector, and thus it seems reasonable to argue that the budget crisis was an effect of the regime's encouragement of capitalism in the industrial sector. Despite this, the response to the impending deficit was an even greater encouragement of capitalism.

Many of the government's spending programs had strong support from powerful groups or classes in the society. Infrastructure investment was supported by private firms and multinational investors, urban social services by the labor aristocracy, government wage and salary increases by state employees, military spending by the increasingly powerful armed forces, and state subsidies of industrial production by the parastatal sector of the state elite. Given these constellations of interest and the general absence of effective mechanisms for central planning, the government was both unwilling and unable to carry out a thorough reexamination of its development strategy. Such a reexamination would have required scrutiny of all programs to evaluate their contribution to the achievement of national goals, and would almost certainly have necessitated some difficult political choices. Instead the government launched a "productivity drive" designed to improve performance in all areas of

state activity, rather than be forced to choose between different areas.[47]

This "productivity drive" required each ministry and department to justify its budget in terms of tangible benefits produced. In the service-related agencies, "tangible benefits" was rather loosely defined, but in the production-oriented agencies it quickly became clear that it meant short-term increases in economic output. In the agricultural sector, for example, departments were asked to demonstrate how their activities were contributing to the total volume of marketed agricultural produce. In a sense, production-oriented agencies were being evaluated in terms of profitability—i.e., the ratio between revenue (defined as contribution to output) and expenditure. It should come as no surprise that a major group pressing for the productivity drive was the parastatal managers—men who were convinced they could justify their existence in terms of profitability. One of the most important results of this campaign was a series of economic reforms which transferred many of the government's directly productive activities to the parastatals.[48] The productivity drive avoided a direct confrontation between different programs and different social goals by quietly adopting the capitalist values of productivity and profitability as evaluative criteria for state programs.

Productivity and profitability are the principal evaluative criteria of capitalist economic organization, and while they are by no means irrelevant to economic calculation under socialism, they are not the only standards by which socialist economic activity is judged. In Zambia, the lack of a planning system which could take other standards into account, and the unwillingness of the elite to make difficult political choices, meant that productivity and profitability became the sole evaluative criteria, which was disastrous for the cooperative movement.

The productivity drive was launched shortly after the Dumont report had drawn attention to the problems of the farming cooperatives, which meant that cooperatives were singled out as a special target for criticism. Many national politicians who had formerly endorsed cooperatives sensed a shift in mood and began to criticize them for wastefulness and inefficiency.[49] Further investigation of the movement by international agencies was sought, and their rather negative reports added to the chorus of criticism.[50] Within the bureaucracy, comparisons were made between cooperatives and other forms of agricultural production which indicated the superior economic performance of settlements and individual family farming.

The most interesting feature of the new criticism of cooperatives was that it was couched entirely in terms of economic efficiency. No attention was paid to the noneconomic aspects of cooperative production, even though these had figured prominently in Kaunda's original vision of the movement. No allowance was made for the fact that communal production was difficult and involved time-consuming social conflicts, and no attempt was made to inquire whether cooperatives were making progress in political and social change.

At this point, we should examine Kaunda's role in the productivity drive. Since it was he who initiated the cooperative movement and set noneconomic as well as economic goals for it, certainly he must have had something to say about the evaluation of cooperatives entirely in terms of economic productivity. The President was curiously silent on this question, however. The basis of this silence was apparently his discouragement over the facts brought out in the Dumont report. He thought that government policy had created cooperative members who were "just another class of exploiters," living off the government or off the labor of others.[51] Such a realization might have stimulated a close analysis of Zambian rural society, a reevaluation of basic ideological premises about "traditional" village socialism, and a detailed investigation of bureaucratic policymaking, but instead the President abandoned the cooperative movement in the face of the harsh public criticism and turned his attention to an alternative approach to rural development. Thus, like many utopian thinkers whose visions are confronted with practical obstacles, Kaunda chose to shift his attention to a new visionary project instead of dealing with the problems in the existing program. His new project was the creation of village productivity committees—organizations very similar to cooperatives, except that they would be independent of government finance.[52] Kaunda's shift meant that the cooperative movement was deprived of its main political support at a time when public criticism was becoming particularly intense.

The new criticism put the Department of Cooperatives in a difficult position. They confronted a myriad of mini-cooperatives located in isolated parts of the country, deeply divided by internal conflicts, and heavily indebted to the government. Given this situation, the department had two possible alternatives: it could try to improve the economic decision-making of the local societies, or it could try to centralize decision-making and run the movement from Lusaka. The first alternative would have required a large field

staff to educate members in conflict-solving and cooperation as well as government financing to restructure the incentive system to encourage productive behavior. Unfortunately, neither manpower nor financing was available to the department.

The productivity drive drew attention to the waste of government loans by cooperatives and by individual farmers, resulting in a decision to turn agricultural financing over to a parastatal organization which would (presumably) manage it in a more "businesslike" way. The new agency—the Agricultural Finance Company (AFC)—turned a deaf ear to departmental requests for more funds for cooperatives.[53] The agency insisted that until cooperatives had paid off their old loans in full they would be ineligible for new credit, which ensured the demise of those cooperatives which had wasted their old loans rather than improving their productive capacity. The productivity drive was followed by a massive reorganization of the bureaucracy and the creation of a giant Ministry of Rural Development which controlled all of the country's agricultural development resources. The new minister was unwilling to grant the Department of Cooperatives more field staff because he felt that the other, more productive rural development schemes had more justified claims on the limited personnel resources.*

Short of staff and short of funds, the department had no choice but to take over the movement. It consolidated small societies into larger ones by administrative fiat, creating new entities eligible to receive AFC loans. It hired farm managers to run the larger societies, and gave local cooperative officers operational authority over the smaller ones. These moves compromised the participatory character of local societies, and led to substantial resentment by members of their bureaucratic superiors. Membership in the cooperative movement plummeted, and by 1972 the movement which was supposed to have transformed not only Zambian agriculture but Zambian society as a whole consisted of a small handful of bureaucratically run societies which resembled settlement schemes more than cooperatives.[54]

The demise of cooperatives signalled the end of socialist experimentation in agriculture in Zambia. After 1972 government programs focused entirely on the extension of private farming

---

*The Minister of Rural Development went so far as to initiate a study about the possibility of abolishing the Department of Cooperatives as a separate department. (See "Letter from the Permanent Secretary, Ministry of Development and Finance, to the Permanent Secretary, Ministry of Rural Development, 2 December 1969" [Department of Cooperatives, Lusaka Files, File 2/392]).

coordinated through the market. The Ministry of Rural Development devoted its attention to improving the network of agricultural assistants, restructuring commodity prices to induce the types of output deemed necessary, developing new marketing agencies in rural areas, and assisting "progressive farmers" with their plans to innovate and expand.[55] The AFC focused its credit operations on the more successful African commercial farmers, and a new rural development parastatal began supplying advanced farming machinery to them. The principles of free enterprise, profit, individual ownership, and wealth accumulation which had guided economic activity in the urban sector since independence were now extended to the rural sector. So complete was the government's adoption of the "business-like" approach to agriculture that it seriously considered a scheme to import large-scale farming techniques from South Africa to set up a number of private agrobusiness concerns. The difficulties involved in such a move proved its undoing, but the proposal indicates clearly the extent to which capitalist values and principles were being applied to the development of rural areas.

IMPLICATIONS OF THE ZAMBIAN EXPERIENCE

What is the significance of the Zambian experience with rural socialism? It is clear that the cooperative program was badly conceived, half-heartedly implemented, and quickly abandoned when problems developed, but histories such as this abound in the literature on development. What makes the Zambian case important is that the failure of the socialist experiment in agriculture was the result of the country's inability to effect changes in other sectors of the society. Zambia tried an incremental approach to the creation of socialism, and the collapse of the experiment lends support to the hypothesis that a "socialism in one sector" approach will not work. Let us review briefly the ways in which failure to develop socialist practices in other sectors undermined the cooperative movement in agriculture.

In the industrial sector, a decision was made to encourage private ownership of the means of production by domestic entrepreneurs and multinational firms, perpetuating the existence of a class with its own special priorities for development spending and a distinct antagonism to socialist experimentation. The appeals by this class to maintain a "favorable investment climate" led to a heavy concentration of government spending in the education and infrastructure areas. It took years for expenditures in these

105

areas to produce tangible benefits, which helped to precipitate the budget crisis of 1967. When that crisis arose, the entrepreneurial class defended the specific programs it favored and actively criticized the "wastefulness" of the cooperative movement. More significantly, the capitalist class pressed for an acceptance of productivity and profitability as the sole criteria by which social and economic policies should be justified. This was particularly true of the banking sector, which was entirely foreign-owned and which continually criticized the COZ for its "unbusinesslike" approach to loan granting.[56] The acceptance by the elite of the evaluative criteria proposed by the capitalist class proved disastrous for the cooperative movement.

The continued existence of multinational corporate control over copper mining deprived the cooperative movement of a potential ally by encouraging the development of a labor aristocracy. The mining companies were willing to pay relatively high wages in return for labor peace, and were willing to Africanize certain areas of their management hierarchy. Their manipulation of material incentives focused the attention of the mineworkers on getting more pay and promotions and retarded the development of any links of identification or sympathy between the workers and the rural masses. When the "productivity drive" directed attention to the problems of the cooperative movement, the mineworkers were quick to join in the chorus of criticism: they were familiar with productivity agreements in the mines, and saw no reason why cooperatives should not be judged by similar criteria.* The failure to develop a sense of identification between the urban working class and the peasant masses hastened the demise of the cooperative movement.

In addition to pressing for evaluative criteria which shaped the elite consciousness in ways detrimental to socialism, the multinational mining companies argued directly for a capitalist approach to agricultural development. The Anglo-American Corporation, which owned several Zambian copper mines, offered to develop a number of private farms to be run by South African managers using the most modern machinery to produce huge yields of maize— Zambia's basic food crop. The regime's acceptance of this offer

---

*This does not mean that the mineworkers were enthusiastic in their acceptance of productivity agreements; in fact they resisted numerous attempts to use these agreements to limit the rate of increase in their salaries (see Robert Bates, *Unions, Parties and Political Development* [New Haven: Yale University Press, 1971], pp. 56-64).

shows clearly the influence of the multinationals on government policy, and suggests that corporate criticism was a major factor behind the "get tough" policy toward the cooperative movement after 1967. We have no *direct* evidence that corporate pressure was exerted in this direction, but it would be naive to think that the corporations were indifferent to the prospect of collectivized agriculture.

The existence of a private industrial sector further undermined agricultural cooperatives by imposing a drain on personnel from both the Department of Cooperatives and the cooperative movement in general. The higher salaries offered by private industry drew talented staff away from the Department of Cooperatives, as did the more attractive wages and working conditions in the parastatal sector. The existence of profitable employment opportunities in industry and retail trade also imposed a drain on the more industrious members of the cooperative movement. A regime less tolerant of private enterprise would have been able to control this flight of talented manpower more effectively.

In the realm of coordination, Zambia's decision to rely principally upon the market instead of central planning meant that the cooperative movement was forced to justify its existence in terms of market criteria. Noneconomic, social criteria were the basis of an important part of the contribution the movement could make to national development, but in the absence of effective planning, social criteria for evaluation could not be properly developed. It was not even possible to make an effective distinction between short-run and long-run measures of economic productivity.* This meant that the cooperative movement was called upon to justify its existence in terms of short-run economic profitability, and by this criterion it clearly failed. The inability to develop effective mechanisms for operationalizing social goals rendered any attempt at building socialism extremely difficult.

In the area of international linkages, the Zambian government continued to be dependent on foreign assistance from capitalist governments, and the parastatals became progressively closer associated with international capitalist firms. The advisors imported by Zambia from Britain, the United States, Germany, the Netherlands, Denmark, and Sweden were generally unsympathetic to the

---

*The Department of Cooperatives argued that cooperatives required set-up time to clear land and make capital improvements which would pay off in increased production in the long run, but these arguments were never even seriously discussed by the top echelon policymakers.

cooperative experiment in agriculture,[57] and their advice, along with that of several international economic missions, helped to persuade the government to pursue several different types of agricultural development at the same time. The decision not to adopt collectivization as the sole policy for development led to problems of bureaucratic competition which hindered the implementation of cooperative policy, and meant that alternative employment opportunities were available for those advisors frustrated by cooperatives. When the budget crisis developed, the critical views of these advisors provided ammunition for the political and bureaucratic enemies of cooperatives within the Zambian elite.

The parastatal sector was established shortly after independence to provide a means for government linkages with international firms. Parastatals were authorized to establish industries by themselves, but the usual pattern was for government agencies to participate in co-ventures with international firms. Parastatal managers were thrown into close association with the managements of multinational corporations—relationships in which the corporation managers had the advantage in education, expertise, consumption style, and economic power. The result of such associations was a gradual acceptance by the parastatal elite of the attitudes and values of the international managerial class. The emerging ideology of the parastatal elite stressed business criteria for evaluating government programs, the legitimacy of inequality in the distribution of social rewards, and the utility of market incentives for stimulating economic activity. This ideology naturally came into conflict with Humanism, but rather than engage in a direct assault on the Humanist worldview, the managerial class took the roundabout course of criticizing specific programs which originated in Humanism. Chief among these was the cooperative movement, of which the parastatal sector was one of the most persistent critics. Its opposition is most clearly apparent in the attitude of the parastatal Agricultural Finance Company toward granting loans to cooperatives, but it also appeared in the initial formulation of rural development policy, when the parastatal elite endorsed a multi-program approach to rural development. As noted, this approach led to serious problems for the cooperative movement and reduced elite support for collectivization.

While these developments in the areas of industry, coordination, and international linkages were important factors in the collapse of the cooperative movement, the basic cause of the collapse was the failure to transform the political sector in a way compatible with

socialist development. In the realm of ideology, Humanism failed to provide an accurate analysis of Zambian society; as a consequence, there was a failure to anticipate the problems to which cooperative-based rural development might lead. The counterproductive loan program was based largely on the false assumption that the rural population was ready for cooperatives; this same assumption provoked the President's subsequent resistance to departmental requests for more supervisory staff and a slower rate of registration of new societies. Kaunda failed to achieve the acceptance and internalization of Humanist values by the elite. In a sense, the whole tenor of the "productivity drive" was determined by the lack of strongly articulated support of noneconomic evaluative criteria. This support was lacking because of Kaunda's disillusionment with cooperatives and his rapid shift to the promotion of village productivity committees. This volatility is common to utopian thinking, but provides a very poor ideological basis for socialist development.

In the area of organization, the political superstructure was almost wholly unprepared to support a socialist rural development program. The party was allowed to disintegrate following independence, and in the rural areas it became largely a mechanism for the distribution of patronage instead of an effective instrument of mass mobilization. The party's unwillingness to initiate a campaign for cooperative development forced Kaunda to turn to the Department of Cooperatives for supervision of the movement. I have argued elsewhere that bureaucratic organizations are ineffective for bringing about the kind of popular mobilization which socialist rural development requires;[58] Kaunda's use of such an agency led to a host of problems in implementation. Since the cooperatives were the responsibility of a bureaucratic agency and not the party, it was easier for criticism of the movement to be voiced, and even party politicians could attack the movement without embarrassment. Because of the patronage orientation of the party in the rural areas, there was strong pressure on the department to give out loan funds without adequate supervision. This bolstered the prestige of the UNIP politicians, who claimed responsibility for securing the money, but exacerbated the problems of the movement.

A lack of measures to control elitism was another major weakness in the political structure. Not only were attempts to impose a leadership code effectively resisted, but national politicians became heavily involved in the ownership of private businesses and farms. In fact, a series of economic measures were passed which increased the ability of the political elite to gain access to property ownership.[59]

It is hardly surprising that the political elite showed little interest in saving the cooperative movement, since a wholesale organization of cooperatives in agriculture would have deprived many of them of their private farms. They were *at best* willing to tolerate a very limited program of cooperatives in agriculture, and were clearly unsympathetic to spending large amounts of government money in an attempt to make such an approach effective. The adoption of a market-oriented strategy for agricultural development would clearly benefit the property-owning section of the political elite, and this doubtless played a part in the final decision to move in that direction.

SOCIALISM IN ONE SECTOR?

This analysis has demonstrated how an incremental approach to the creation of socialism in Zambia quickly collapsed under pressure from the non-socialist sectors of the society. "Socialism in one sector" would thus seem to be an unworkable approach, despite its appeal as a "pragmatic" alternative for resource-poor third world countries. If "socialism in one sector" is unworkable, the apparent implication is that poor countries which are interested in socialism must be prepared to undertake a massive assault on all five major sectors of society *simultaneously*. Only this broad, frontal approach seems to stand a chance of success, but the complexity, expense, and difficulty of such an approach makes it highly unlikely that many poor countries will be willing and/or able to make this kind of effort.

While a conclusion of this sort seems to emerge inevitably from the preceding analysis, there are two problems associated with generalizing from a single case which make it difficult to accept this conclusion wholeheartedly. The first is the problem of reasoning from a negative to a positive: the incremental approach *did not* work in Zambia; therefore a comprehensive, integrated approach *will* work if attempted elsewhere. There is nothing in the preceding analysis which would suggest that an integrated campaign for building socialism would necessarily be successful if attempted in another African or third world country. It may well be the case that the obstacles to the creation of socialism in Africa are so great that even a comprehensive attempt would stall, become corrupted, or generate such resistance that the regime attempting it would be overthrown. Tanzania has attempted a far more comprehensive approach to building socialism than did Zambia, but the recent wave of critical literature on the Tanzanian experiment suggests that the fate of socialism there is very much in doubt.[60] Before we can discuss intelligently what it might

take to build socialism in Africa, we will need some information about successes as well as failures. The manner of the collapse of the Zambian experiment suggests some hypotheses about what might be required for the creation of socialism, but these will remain only abstract theoretical possibilities until we have some evidence that they have been productive of positive results in other contexts.

The second problem with the single-case generalization is that we lack sufficient data to establish that the creation of socialism requires simultaneous efforts in *all* major sectors. We have shown that confining the socialist experiment to the agriculture sector was an approach which failed, but this leaves unanswered the question of whether failure was the consequence of limitation to a *single* sector or of the choice of *agriculture*. It may be that agriculture is the worst place to begin a socialist experiment, and that the experimental, single-sector approach might work if initiated in a more important sector. (At the moment we have no way of knowing for certain if some sectors are more important than others to the process of building socialism.) Thus it may be possible for African countries to move toward socialism by concentrating on one of the nonagricultural sectors, or by concentrating on more than one sector—but not all five. I suspect that the sectors of politics and international linkages are more crucial than the others, and that a country which could move in a socialist direction in these two sectors might stand a fairly good chance of making a success of socialist development. Until we have more detailed information about African and third world attempts to create socialism, however, this must remain a hunch only.

Both of these problems point to the need for further research on the socialist development model and on other experiments with "socialism" in Africa. Of particular interest in this respect are the new governments of Angola, Mozambique, and Guinea-Bissau. These regimes have come to power after prolonged guerrilla struggles which helped to shape militant party/army apparatuses. Elites in these countries have become quite familiar with Marxism, and have established close ties with the socialist world. As a result these three regimes are likely to approach the task of building socialism more systematically than have past "African Socialist" governments. It is possible, therefore, that we may soon have some examples of more comprehensive and integrated approaches to the creation of socialism to set alongside our rather negative evaluation of the "socialism in one sector" approach.

111

THE DIFFICULTIES OF IMPLEMENTING SOCIALIST STRATEGIES OF DEVELOPMENT IN AFRICA: THE "FIRST WAVE"

Thomas M. Callaghy

WEAK STATES AND MUDDLED IDEOLOGIES

Socialist transformation requires massive state-directed policies of socioeconomic change. The role of the state is central and predominant. As a ruling, dominating organization competing for power with other political, economic, and social organizations both internally and externally, the state searches for sovereignty and compliance. The type of state that exists greatly affects the success of socialist efforts at transformation. Such a transformation is an extremely complex and difficult task requiring major structural and value changes. Generally there is little consensus concerning what the task is, how it is to be accomplished, or who is to benefit from it. Bringing about a socialist transformation is a highly conflictual process that directly affects the ideal and material interests of a wide variety of groups. If society is to be basically restructured, some groups are bound to lose a great deal in the process. Resistance, both active and passive, will be significant; as a result, high levels of state power are required.

There are essentially two sets of factors that affect the outcome of a socialist transformation: organizational and environmental. The organizational factors relate primarily to the structure and leadership of the state and the type of ideology used to guide the transformation. The environmental factors refer to the relationship of the state to the society it attempts to transform and to the world system within which it must operate. Many discussions of the difficulties of implementing socialist policies in Africa focus on environmental factors—particularly problems of dependence. The emphasis here will be on organizational factors in the belief that environmental problems are usually severe under preindustrial conditions, and thus socialist transformation becomes a question of the ability of organizational factors to cope with or compensate for environmental factors.

Environmental problems, both internal and external, were severe in the Soviet Union (as even a cursory reading of Merle Fainsod's fine book *Smolensk Under Soviet Rule*[1] indicates), but the Bolsheviks created a powerful organization of control which was able to mitigate and eventually overcome most of these difficulties. The state as an *organization of domination* is necessary for socialist transformation. Soviet theoreticians have long stressed the importance of the nature of state power in the transformation process. Consider this statement by I. Pronichev, a leading Soviet theoretician on "non-capitalist development": "In the political sphere, non-capitalist development manifests itself in two aspects: internal and external. The former involves, *first and foremost*, the nature of state power, for the problem of ways of development is *ultimately* always a problem of state power."[2] The state must be able to simultaneously maintain internal order *and* formulate and effectively implement coherent policies of transformation. There are three basic types of compliance: *voluntary normative* compliance, usually based on a consensus on values; *utilitarian* compliance, which benefits the individual usually as a result of some form of inducement; and *coercive* compliance, based on compulsion by force, violence, or terror.[3] All states rely on a mixture of the three kinds of compliance, but states attempting socialist transformation must rely on coercive compliance more heavily than other types. Most African states are weak in all three categories, but particularly in coercive compliance.

Above all, socialist transformation elites need considerable coercive capacity to ensure widespread compliance with their policies, to create enough room to maneuver to allow them to cope with environmental problems, and to allow them to make mistakes without threatening the survival of the regimes. This is because the short-term costs of such a transformation strategy are severe. The state must be able to cope simultaneously with resistance and sabotage by a wide range of groups, the tasks of cadre motivation and training, the formulation of coherent and systemic economic plans, and the accumulation of sufficient capital to implement such plans. The state must be able to reallocate cadre and resources easily as changing conditions dictate. All of these activities require considerable coercive capacity. Socialist transformation regimes use ideological appeals to achieve voluntary normative compliance, and bargaining and incentives for utilitarian compliance when they do not result in unwanted commitments or unintended consequences, but relying primarily on utilitarian compliance requires extensive resources to be used in bargaining and distribution, and voluntary compliance through persua-

sion and mobilization is not sufficient to bring about successful socialist transformation in preindustrial societies.

There are essentially two types of tasks for which state power can be used by ruling coalitions. The first task is basically nationalist and reformist in nature in that the regime is primarily concerned with the survival of the state, the maintenance of order, the pursuit of the ruling group's interests, and modest reforms affecting the standard of living of the masses. I have labeled this tendency in African states "neomercantilism." The second task is revolutionary in nature, and entails basic restructuring and redefinition of society—usually along socialist lines.

These different tasks and approaches reflect different value and normative commitments on the part of the ruling elites, and require different strategies of rule and different degrees of state power. The neomercantilist approach requires only a survival and order capability, a limited regulative and extractive capability, and some policy formulation and implementation capability. A modified form of the colonial conquest state is sufficient for this approach: administration is less direct, intensive, and continuous than is necessary in a state attempting socialist transformation. Such regimes rely heavily on bargaining and compromise in dealing with social groups, and thereby develop commitments to such groups which restrict freedom of movement. Political order is usually maintained, but traditional authority structures often coexist with those of the state, maintaining a sizable degree of formal or informal autonomy. A reformist, muddling-through strategy will not succeed in building a socialist state under preindustrial conditions.

A successful revolutionary strategy of socialist transformation requires what Kenneth Jowitt calls "breaking through"—i.e., "the decisive alteration or destruction of values, structures, and behaviors which are perceived by a revolutionary elite as comprising or contributing to the actual or potential existence of alternative centers of political power."[4] Society is to be restructured and redefined around new value premises. A breakthrough strategy implies an antagonistic orientation toward existing social structures and alternative centers of political and economic power. The object is to abolish or severely limit the influence of both these elements.

To be capable of implementing a socialist strategy, a state needs intensive, direct, continuous, and relatively efficient administration and control. Above all, intermediary authorities and competing groups and organizations have to be abolished or at least severely emasculated. A direct state-subject relationship must be established.

114

Tanzanian efforts at rural socialism provide a vivid illustration of the need for tight control of the population, including a viable coercive potential. Local groups frequently demand that Ujamaa structures coexist with existing socioeconomic structures. Because compliance is heavily voluntary, implementation is often weak even where a population is apparently predisposed to Ujamaa changes. Thus in Mnenia, which had long been an area of major party support, Frances Hill found that "the people . . . were not prepared for complete socialist transformation. Citizens and leaders alike were experimenting with a new way of life. At the very least the experiment could serve as a *defensive compliance with government policy that would protect the existing way of life from government sanctions.*"[5] It is clear that opposition was widespread, and cut across emerging class lines:

> No one except the Ujamaa village chairman supported collectivization. All demanded instead that they clear new land, although no one had any idea where such could be found. *They successfully insisted that Ujamaa coexist with socioeconomic patterns the Rangi now regard as normal, neither encroaching upon nor disturbing them.* Those with little land were as insistent as those with more to lose. TANU leaders and Ujamaa village members opposed collectivization as strongly as ordinary citizens not in Ujamaa villages. . . . The people . . . agreed to draft a letter to the area commissioner *stating categorical opposition to changing either their way of life or Ujamaa as it currently existed.* The letter was signed "People of Mnenia." . . . Irangi gradually became calm but not socialist. The district government had spent over $200,000 to produce this impasse.[6]

Despite his stated aversion to the use of coercion, President Nyerere finally permitted its use for the villagization portion of Ujamaa, but he has steadfastly refused to let it be used for collectivization. However, the effective collectivization of agriculture will probably require extensive use of coercion.

The revolutionary strategy emphasizes limiting commitments to both internal and external groups. Coercion is used to keep the commitments of the state at a minimum and to break them after they have served their short-term purpose. Coercion is also used to eliminate the authority of all non-state groups. A socialist elite needs an organizational weapon to carry out its tasks and implement its policies. It builds this weapon around an institutional core of dedicated cadre that comes to constitute a specifically change-oriented administrative subculture. Thus the state uses coercion to avoid spiraling

commitments, prevent or suppress open or covert opposition, obtain compliance when it is not voluntary or forthcoming as a result of incentives or non-coercive sanctions, control the staff of the state, and maintain room for maneuver for itself.

After a period of about twenty years of independence, the realities of the modal African state have become relatively clear. In general, African states are authoritarian, highly personalistic structures that have territorially extensive but relatively limited penetrative, administrative, and coercive capabilities. The colonial conquest state has been adapted to new conditions, but it has not been basically restructured. Prolonged and intense conflict with the colonial power might have forged distinctive and coherent revolutionary politico-military organizations capable of successfully undertaking socialist transformation, but the nature of the independence settlement was usually such that little actual struggle took place. After independence there was a general move among African states to turn independence movements into one-party states that could be used to ensure the survival of the new regimes and to mobilize the population for socioeconomic transformation. These single-party structures turned out to be very weak organizational weapons, however. Indeed they manifested more the characteristics of loose movements of representation and reconciliation and of political machines relying on exchange, bargaining, and the establishment of commitments and shifting alliances to maintain political order.[7] What started out as a mobilization strategy ended up as a muddling-through strategy in which the elites were unable to limit alliances and prevent spiraling commitments and demands.[8] Administratively these states still resembled the colonial conquest states, in which a loosely and superficially centralized domination was maintained via extensive and indirect (rather than intensive and direct) administration. Direct state-subject relations were not achieved because traditional intermediary authorities continued to exercise considerable authority. In addition, new urban groups were able to effectively pressure the new governments on key issues. Thus the structural orientation remained one of political control and extraction rather than of systemic transformation.

These new regimes also had relatively low coercive capabilities. Such capabilities were limited primarily to the maintenance of general political order and could not be widely used to enforce compliance with transformation policies. As initial resources were depleted and the demands and resistance of both internal and external groups increased, ruling elites rapidly lost their initial post-independence power reserves and moved more toward force as a way of maintaining

116

basic order and minimal support among social groups.[9]   Coercive slack (i.e., room for maneuver provided by a coercive capability) became increasingly scarce, and the margin for political error became narrower and narrower. Coercive slack can be partially supplied through external assistance, but no large-scale assistance from major world socialist powers was forthcoming for the several new African socialist regimes. Substantially different patterns of assistance have emerged for African states in the "second wave," but the type, level, and duration of such assistance remain undetermined. Will this assistance greatly increase the long-run control and penetrative capabilities of these regimes?

The military and police forces of the new states were rapidly Africanized, but remained basically colonial in structure and in patterns of training and supply. Often there were no close personal and ideological ties between the new military leaders and the new heads of state, and the military and police forces proved to be very difficult to control. The civilian elites moved to extend state coercive control over society in the face of mounting internal political and economic difficulties and increasing problems in implementing socialist policies. In doing so they ran up against Weber's "paradox of sultanism"—i.e., the more a ruling group seeks to expand its domain of discretion and lessen dependence on societal groups, the more it must rely on military force, and thus the more dependent it becomes on the military.[10]   The eventual result was the rash of military coups that swept Africa beginning in 1965.[11] The military regimes usually proved to be no more nor no less successful at governing than their civilian predecessors.   Until the recent advent of the "second wave," there have been no serious military attempts at socialist transformation in Africa; however, there have been several attempts by military elites to use socialist notions as the core of a "forensic ideology."[12]

In addition to regime commitments to societal groups, there is another kind of commitment involved in a revolutionary socialist strategy. It is commitment to and propagation of a revolutionary ideology which elucidates the revolutionary goals, redefines authority relationships, analyzes the faults of the existing structure, points out enemies of the revolution who are still active, and charts the course for the successful achievement of the revolutionary goals. The ideology gives the institutional core its mission, purpose, and coherence and—ideally—changes the values of the subject population, thereby encouraging voluntary compliance with socialist policies. The ideology should be coherent rather than diffuse, confrontational

rather than cooperative, and all groups lacking revolutionary commitment should be identified and excluded from the movement.

There are many variants of African socialism, but most of them share several specific weaknesses.[13] The first weakness is the tendency to portray traditional African culture, especially its egalitarian and communal aspects, as a traditional form of "socialism." As such it is seen as the foundation for contemporary efforts. The establishment of socialism then simply becomes a matter of modifying and updating traditional patterns and practices.*[14] This analysis (which is clearly incorrect) leads to a second weakness—i.e., the contention that socialism can be achieved without widespread conflict or struggle, class-based or otherwise, because there are no major social impediments to its establishment. The result is that there is no confrontational stance toward the old society or identification of internal enemies of the revolution. A third weakness is closely related. If socialism can be achieved without significant societal conflict, there is no need to use widespread coercion. Only political education, example, and non-coercive forms of mobilization are required. (Nyerere in particular is adamant on this point.)[15] A fourth weakness is that the ideology often lacks systemic focus—i.e., the linkages between agricultural and industrial development are not clearly established.[16] These weaknesses appear to be less prevalent in the socialist ideologies of the "second wave," but only time will tell if this will make a significant difference.

In sum, massive state power, a coherent revolutionary ideology, and effective leadership are the crucial organization elements that foster the success of attempts at socialist transformation. These organizational factors may make it possible to surmount severe environmental difficulties. A successful attempt at socialist transformation must meet stiff tests. Many such revolutionary attempts fail. Some elites have partial success; others fail outright. The most common cause of failure is premature reconciliation with internal and external groups due to insufficient control capabilities and/or ideological fuzziness.

TWO ATTEMPTS

The "first wave" of socialism in Africa has had only very limited success. Let us briefly analyze two African attempts at socialist

---

*Peasants in Tanzania become confused when asked to collectivize their holdings in Ujamaa villages. They have been told many times that traditional African patterns are socialist; why then must they change them?

transformation which failed—Ghana under Kwame Nkrumah and Mali under Modibo Keita. The eventual success of the "first wave" efforts at socialism in Tanzania and Guinea, which are examined in other chapters in this volume, also remains very much in doubt.

 Ghana under Nkrumah. In Ghana, Nkrumah attempted a socialist transformation during the period from 1959 to early 1966.[17] Formally it was a systemic, Leninist approach that concentrated on both the agricultural and industrial sectors. After independence Nkrumah "muddled through" to a radical socialist position that called for ending the dependence on agricultural export commodities and for state-directed industrialization. This attempt failed decisively, indicating the difficulty of forging transformation instruments *after* taking power by adapting preexisting state and party structures. These instruments are necessary to cope with the severe short-term political and economic costs of such a strategy.

There were many reasons for the failure in Ghana. The transformation ideology was vague and shifting, with the ideological focus wavering back and forth between nationalism, socialism, and Pan-Africanism. The changes in goal priorities resulted in very erratic policies complicated by short-term political considerations which made rational planning and resource allocation extremely difficult. The state-directed strategy was severely hampered by the lack of commitment of the state administrative staff and the grossly inadequate performance of the state enterprises which were to form the core of the industrial transformation. External dependency problems also aggravated the situation, especially a drastic fall in cocoa prices and a diminishing ability to generate external capital on favorable or even endurable terms. Internally, the Convention People's Party (CPP) was unable to limit spiraling commitments to social groups or to obtain widespread compliance with state policies. Externally, fraternal support by socialist states was minimal. The last—and probably most crucial—factor was a lack of adequate coercive capabilities. Coercive capacity to control alternative centers of power while maintaining basic order, to keep commitments to societal groups at a minimum, to accumulate sizable amounts of capital internally, and to force the implementation of major transformation policies simply did not exist. Regime control of the coercive apparatus was weak, and its capabilities were distinctly limited. Increased capabilities might have given the regime enough breathing space (or "slack") to begin coping with some of its multiple problems. Such a coercive capacity would not have guaranteed success, but it would have allowed the re-

gime to keep trying to solve its problems.

Nkrumah was unable to adapt or transform the inherited structures of the colonial conquest state or of his own CPP in order to use them to control internal groups. The party-state as a ruling organization did not dominate widely or intensely. Colonial rule left behind a fair degree of economic and social differentiation in Ghana which was reflected in the existence of numerous groups with the organizational capacity and resources enabling them to react effectively when their ideal and material interests were threatened. The CPP had to focus primary attention on survival and the maintenance of political order; transformation goals had to come second. It is necessary to be able to focus on both simultaneously. The demands and expectations of internal groups generated by the regime's ideological statements raised the problem of the "welfare paradox," which pits social and economic equity against the needs of economic growth and transformation. Demands from many groups for services in exchange for crucial political support collided with the need to accumulate the capital necessary for transformation projects. Because the CPP was a political machine rather than a disciplined revolutionary party, its ability to restrict demands and spiraling commitments was limited.

For example, two of the strongest societal groups were the Trades Union Congress (TUC) and the United Ghana Farmers Council (UGFC). Although both of these organizations were formally absorbed into the CPP under Nkrumah's inclusionary slogan "The CPP is Ghana, Ghana is the CPP," both of them retained strong autonomy and organizational viability which allowed them to oppose the party-state when its policies directly affected their interests. The two organizations were to be used by the party to carry out certain state projects. They had strong and ambitious leaders and large constituencies which demanded more and more of the action and resources in return for their support. The TUC espoused socialist ideas but was in constant conflict with the government over wage and welfare demands for the workers. The party, however, wanted to use the TUC to maintain order and to limit and channel worker demands in order to permit increased capital accumulation. The CPP managed to coopt the TUC leadership during certain periods, but the workers were still able to assert their power. In 1961, for example, workers in Sekondi-Takoradi opposed a CPP plan for compulsory savings for capital accumulation by an attempted general strike that was effective locally, and the government was forced to give up the plan. The coercive capacity to compel savings was not available, and voluntary saving was clearly not popular.[18]

The UGFC was to organize and maintain cocoa farmer support for the CPP. Eventually it also took on such tasks as the monopoly buying of cocoa and the administration of cooperatives and mechanization schemes. Its administration of these projects was abysmal, and victimization and corruption were rampant. The UGFC was often not able to control its members and ensure support for state policies. For example, a land rent act was passed which set reasonable annual limits which severely undercut existing exorbitant land rent rates. This act unleashed immense rural conflict led by the opposition of powerful owner-farmers who rented land to land-poor farmers. By 1963 the government had stopped trying to enforce the law, and after the military coup it was quickly repealed.[19] These examples indicate the party-state's inability, in the face of effective opposition and a low coercive capability, to enforce implementation of its policies of transformation.

Because of the colonial nature of Ghana's economy, Nkrumah decided to start with a mixed economic pattern before moving on to full socialism. As financial reserves were depleted by the expansion of the state apparatus, misallocation of resources, administrative inefficiency, corruption, and lack of motivation, it became necessary to rely heavily on foreign capital. At the same time, severe constraints and uncertainty came from other sectors as cocoa prices began to drop drastically and import prices began to rise. Nkrumah did not have a party-state organization powerful enough to accumulate capital internally as export earnings diminished, import prices rose, and the state overextended and overinvested in the industrial sector. Inflation, inefficiency, corruption, and political dissent rampaged, and dependence on external creditors increased.

These cross-pressures led to attempts to rely more on force and internal austerity. This approach most adversely affected the very groups socialist transformation was designed to aid—the peasants and the workers—at the same time that the ideology was leading them to believe that things were going to get much better. The situation was aggravated by continued conspicuous consumption by large sections of the party-state administration. Stratification gaps widened, power fragmented, and opposition increased everywhere. Through an increased reliance on force, Nkrumah was barely able to maintain basic order, but he was very unsure of the reliability of the military and the police. In an attempt to control his inherited compliance structures, Nkrumah emasculated the army and created a completely loyal alternative force, which alienated the military and the police. In February 1966 these groups staged a *coup d'état* toppling the Nkru-

mah regime and ending its attempt at socialist transformation in a clear manifestation of Weber's "paradox of sultanism." The socialist transformation attempt came to an abrupt end precisely when Nkrumah attempted to expand his coercive capacity by creating a completely loyal military/police force. The heavy short-term costs of the strategy proved too much for the limited and unreliable coercive apparatus at Nkrumah's disposal. Slack did not exist, and mistakes became increasingly costly.

Mali under Keita. Under the leadership of Modibo Keita, Mali attempted a socialist transformation during the period 1960 to 1968.[20] In many ways this effort was remarkably similar to the Ghanaian pattern under Nkrumah, but in a much poorer, less developed, more dependent, and isolated state. As in Ghana, it was formally a systemic, Leninist approach in which "scientific socialism" was to be adapted to Malian conditions in both the agricultural and industrial sectors. Using his strong pre-independence mass support as a base, Keita also "muddled through" to a radical socialist position that sought to lessen dependence by fighting neo-colonialism, to use an ideologically committed single party and a planned economy to greatly increase agricultural production, and to begin state-directed industrialization via a greatly expanded public sector. Mali's socialist leadership desired—and felt it could achieve—simultaneous structural transformation and rapid economic growth *in the short run*. Despite the obviously severe socioeconomic and political constraints and their stated belief that the socialist option was a real gamble in Mali, the leadership was initially very optimistic. For example, the first five-year plan projected major structural change in the agricultural and industrial sectors and set an annual growth rate of 11.2 percent (later scaled down to 8.9 percent). And this was to be accomplished without a major coercive capacity! There was no appreciation of the severe short-term difficulties of such a strategy. However, the outcome was the same as in Ghana—i.e., the results were minimal, and the experiment was brought to an end by a military coup. As in Ghana, the reasons for failure were multiple, and the inability to control what little coercive capability existed brought the experiment to an abrupt end.

The ideological orientation of the regime was basically Marxist, but it was not systematic in any way. The ideology was called "scientific socialism," but it was in fact an eclectic, often utopian, blend of Marx, Lenin, Rousseau, general tenets of African socialism, and Malian history and political culture—particularly the legacy of the

ancient empires and the powerful influence of Islam. This confusing, often contradictory, mélange of ideas was incapable of generating coherent and well-integrated policy proposals, much less intense commitment by a dedicated cadre. Keita sought to adapt "scientific socialism" to Mali's needs, culture, and history. He strongly believed that Mali's traditional culture was basically socialist and could easily be modified to accommodate the effort at socialist transformation. The resultant ideology was clearly not confrontational in nature.

Like Nkrumah, Keita believed in the primacy of the political. This emphasis on the political kingdom meant that the guiding principles of party organization were unity, discipline, democratic centralism, and collective leadership. Keita, like Nkrumah, attempted to transform a successful, mass-based independence movement into a disciplined party capable of coping with the severe short-term political and economic costs of socialist change. The Union Soudanaise was to become a vanguard party that was inclusionary rather than exclusionary. The elaborate control structure of a Marxist-Leninist party was to be extended over all organized groups, institutions, and regions of the country down to the smallest village. Discipline was to be maintained by party control committees, an inspectorate, *brigades de vigilance*, and eventually the popular militia, while ideological commitment was to be reinforced by party schools and methods of mass mobilization. As in Ghana, however, the structure proved to be a house of cards; the Marxist-Leninist veneer was thin. The transformation from a diffuse mass base to tight hierarchical control is extremely difficult to accomplish—especially *after* coming to power. Intra-party factionalism over ideology, policy, personnel, and particularistic, regional, and group claims was rampant. The party lacked ideological and political unity and policy coherence. Ethnic and regional criteria were often more important than ideological rectitude or class origin in the politics of party leadership. Keita was pushed and pulled from both the left and the right—first by "socialist radicals" and then by "moderates" who wanted economic stabilization and closer ties with France. By trying to placate both groups, Keita merely increased a pervasive policy incoherence underlying an intensifying public revolutionary fervor. He could not enforce his will inside or outside the Union Soudanaise. The party lacked a sufficient number of loyal, disciplined, ideologically knowledgeable, and committed cadre to implement policy programs, especially with regard to the establishment of rural cooperatives. It was not able to persuade *or* force peasants to farm collectively. An administrative subculture of dedicated socialist cadre did not exist, nor did the co-

ercive capability that might have compensated for it.

The socialist option in Mali stressed the need for "socialist planning founded on African realities,"[21] and the party created a mystique around "planned socialism" as a vehicle for simultaneous structural change and rapid growth. In fact, the plan was not at all based on the socioeconomic and political realities of Mali. It was wildly unrealistic as to levels of expected foreign assistance and state expenditure, the amount of borrowing required, the ability of the regime to impose austerity or accumulate capital internally, and the capabilities and efficiency of the state sector. The five-year plan for 1961-1966 was an overall failure. For the plan period, GDP increased at less than 2 percent per year, and when population growth is taken into account, the average citizen was poorer after than before the plan period.

In particular, socialism in the rural sector did not fare well. The village-based cooperative program was badly organized, poorly run, and generated few successful cooperatives. Most cooperatives barely functioned, and many existed only on paper. The regime expected enthusiastic voluntary participation by the peasants; in fact there was almost none. Powerful local groups manipulated the program to protect their corporate or individual interests, but government mismanagement and disorganization also played an important part in the program's failure. After 1965 some peasants began to withdraw from commercial agriculture, and by 1967 clear and substantial peasant opposition to the regime was apparent, particularly with regard to official marketing procedures and the artificially low prices set for crops. Production and marketing levels fell in the agricultural sector as a whole. The coercive capability needed to sustain these policies in the hope of overcoming short-term dislocations and obtaining long-term gains was lacking. Basic structural change requires control and slack, and neither was present in this case.

But the peasants were not the only ones who chafed under Malian "planned socialism." The interests of traders, small businessmen, the small "working class," and the large number of state employees were all threatened. As economic and financial problems accumulated, these groups became increasingly restive. Rather than coercively suppressing their demands, the regime had to buy them off in order to ensure its survival. These unwanted commitments seriously affected the ability of the regime to enforce its austerity measures, and the regime lacked the coercive capacity needed to avoid such commitments.

As a result of its heavy dependence on the international econo-

my, poverty, isolation, low level of development, and poorly conceived and implemented socialist plan, Mali experienced a series of
increasingly serious economic and financial crises. The country suffered from large government deficits, extensive borrowing, a huge
debt (by 1967 it was five times the national budget), rampant inflation, balance-of-payments problems, reduced foreign exchange
earnings, import and other austerity restrictions, commodity shortages, smuggling, widespread black market activity, a decline in commercial agricultural production, and a loss of major Western—particularly French—assistance without a compensating increase in socialist
aid. As a result of the lack of large-scale external assistance and weak
coercive capabilities, the regime was finally forced into a *rapprochement* with France, with all the attendant commitments that entails.

The *rapprochement* with France proved to be very humiliating
for the radical socialists in the Malian regime. As in Ghana, this led
to an increase rather than a decrease in "revolutionary" rhetoric and
activity. Keita unleashed the students and youth in what has been
termed the "active revolution," patterned somewhat after the Chinese cultural revolution. The youth of the *milice populaire* set out
in a cloud of Marxist-Leninist verbiage to increase ideological unity
and commitment and to root out all dissent and corruption. The
normative and coercive mobilizational effects of this "cultural revolution" continued, without much success, until the military reacted
against them. These efforts were accompanied by weak attempts
at increased administrative centralization, tighter party control
through various structural changes, and a greater use of coercion and
other repressive measures via the militia. Keita attempted to move
from power to force, as Nkrumah had done before him, and with the
same results—a military *coup d'état* staged by young army officers on
November 19, 1968. The Malian regime was severely shaken by
Nkrumah's downfall in early 1966 and took measures to assure the
loyalty of the army. However, Keita did not learn from Nkrumah's
mistakes, and like Nkrumah he failed to control the army while
threatening and insulting it. Above all, he allowed the roughly 3,000
armed and undisciplined youth of the popular militia to become a
threat to the 3,500-man army. The military saw its position directly
challenged, and it acted to protect its interests. The popular militia
was clearly not a viable alternative to a large, loyal, and efficient mi-
litary/police force, and without such a coercive apparatus, there was
almost no chance for the success of an ambitious socialist experiment.

The coup did not generate a popular reaction against it. As in

Ghana, the socialist experiment in Mali ended abruptly but quietly. The core problem in Mali was that the regime did not possess sufficient state power (normative, utilitarian, and, above all, coercive) to overcome the inherent constraints of poverty, isolation, and dependence *as well as* the severe short-term socioeconomic and political costs of a socialist transformation strategy.

THE POLITICAL ECONOMY OF AFRICAN NEOMERCANTILISM

Socialism has had very limited success in Africa. If socialist states have not taken shape, what has? Rather than comparing African countries with contemporary revolutionary socialist regimes, it may be more useful to compare them with the mercantilist states of early modern Europe.[22] Two major processes in African sociopolitical life today are state formation and the emergence and consolidation of an African ruling class. Both are central to African neomercantilism. Neomercantilism, not African socialism, captures the essence of the dominant political economy in contemporary Africa.

Mercantilism, both historically and now within African states, has been closely associated with state formation and a search for sovereignty—not with revolutionary change or welfare goals. Mercantilist policies are specifically designed to aid in the formation of stronger states, to help achieve unity, to centralize and concentrate power, and to struggle against internal particularism and external dependence. Mercantilism is not primarily an economic phenomenon: it is an attempt to force economic policy into the service of power as an end in itself.[23]

Like their early modern European predecessors,[24] most African states today are centralizing, but distinctly limited authoritarian patrimonial-bureaucratic states. They have low levels of development and penetration and limited coercive and implementation capabilities. Politics is highly personalized, and a ruling class is emerging, with the gap between the rulers and the ruled increasing. Mercantilist states are not welfare states: state power and the interests of the ruling elite—not mass welfare or basic societal change—constitute the central focus of state policy. In many African countries, welfare-oriented development policies are talked about a great deal, but development policies that augment state and elite power are the primary focus of implementation efforts.* These states have predomi-

---

*A particularly striking example is provided by Zaire. Walter Davis has discovered five basic goals of the Mobutu government during 1965-71: "(1) the resto-

nantly agricultural economies characterized by low levels of development and technology, a central role for trade, and enclaves of capitalist commerce, manufacturing, and extraction.

In the basic mercantilist equation of African state formation, the key element in the search for sovereignty and unification is power, the basis of power is wealth, and the foundations of wealth are foreign exchange and economic development. The crucial link between foreign exchange and economic development is external trade. Trade is pivotal to the mercantilist political economy because, in a period of relatively limited internal markets and low levels of economic development, it is the major source of foreign exchange. Thus, because it constitutes the foundation of state power and the ability to raise the level of economic development, African neomercantilist states seek to augment their supply of foreign exchange by attempting to increase the volume, terms, and types of trade. Development projects, in addition to fostering the well-being of the ruling elite, are designed primarily to expand the control capabilities of the state, increase exports, minimize imports, and promote economic autarky.

African neomercantilist states attempt to maintain a partially open, partially closed approach to penetration by external economic groups. The ruling elite can increase state power and further their own interests (and the two reinforce each other) by encouraging regulated investment and development of new enterprises by external groups. Mercantilism is opposed to laissez-faire or autonomous capitalism, but not to political capitalism.[25] As in early modern

ration of the authority and prestige of the state, (2) sound finances and monetary stability, (3) economic independence, (4) economic growth and infrastructure improvement, and (5) improvement in individual well-being." The data in Davis's thesis clearly show that this listing indicates the priority of the state for each item. Item (5) is the lowest priority of the state: "Social justice as defined in this [Davis's] study consists of three components: (1) the satisfaction of minimum needs in income, employment, education, health, nutrition, and housing; (2) the reduction of disparities in these six variables; and (3) popular participation and leadership accountability. . . . In every variable except education, minimum needs have not been met. However, since 1965 modest progress has been achieved in some aspects of income, health, and nutrition. On the other hand, disparities in all six variables have increased during the 1965-71 period, and popular participation and leadership accountability have decreased. This has resulted in passivity on the part of the masses and the pursuit of private interest on the part of the elite" (Walter Thomas Davis, Jr., "An Ethical Evaluation of the Development Goals and Achievements of the Government of the Republic of Zaire from 1965 through 1971" [Ph.D. dissertation, Boston University, 1974, esp. pp. v-vi]).

Europe, neomercantilism provides a favorable framework for the early development of politically regulated and controlled capitalism in Africa.[26]

The African neomercantilist state has an important role in the economy. Neomercantilist policies result in a mixed condition of state-regulated and coordinated capitalism and some state enterprise in the parastatal sector. The goal is not, however, the extensive state ownership and operation of the economy characteristic of socialism. The role of the state emphasizes direction and regulation with some direct investment in state enterprises. The state encourages trade, regulates imports and exports, grants subsidies, monopolies, and incentives for manufacturing and extractive industries, searches for new mineral deposits, improves the transportation and communications infrastructure, promotes inward technology transfer, establishes some state enterprises and participates in others, and seeks to create a unified internal economy.

Such is the *intent* or *thrust* of African neomercantilist policies; successful implementation, however, is another matter. Like their European predecessors, African neomercantilist states do not engage in effective, large-scale economic planning. Although there is much talk about and promulgation of economic "plans," they are seldom implemented in a serious way. Planning is indicative at best. Again, like early modern European mercantilist states, African neomercantilist states often seem to be in serious financial difficulty—even on the brink of bankruptcy. Regular sources of revenue are not adequate or are poorly organized; extensive borrowing and debt are common; corruption is rampant; scarce resources are squandered by ruling groups. A key characteristic of the limited patrimonial-bureaucratic states of early modern European mercantilism was the enunciation of elaborate and ambitious policies which were scarcely implemented. This is also characteristic of African neomercantilist states. They are not fully developed modern bureaucratic states, which is vividly attested by the general failure of their implementation efforts. Heckscher's assessment of early modern European mercantilism might well apply to contemporary Africa: "The ability of mercantilist statesmen to achieve what was required by their programs was very limited. . . . Generally it may be said that mercantilism is of greater interest for what it attempted than for what it achieved. It certainly paved the way for its successors."[27]

CONCLUDING REMARKS: THE FUTURE

The short-run future of most African states will probably be as weaker or stronger versions of neomercantilist states achieving, at best, moderate rates of growth and development. Successful socialist transformation attempts may well be out of the question under current African conditions. It might be possible in the future for some African states to "muddle through" to a radical socialist position resembling what I would call "client socialism," but considerable outside assistance would be necessary to give ideological direction, assist in capital accumulation, provide technical expertise, strengthen coercive capabilities, and ensure regime survival. (Cuba is an example of such a "client socialist" state.)

Most African states will continue to have internal groups that espouse various forms of socialism. In the short run, however, the best these groups can hope for is to pressure ruling coalitions in neomercantilist states toward policies that emphasize equity and distributive justice. It is also highly unlikely that military elites taking power can succeed in instituting viable socialist regimes under current conditions.

The best long-term hope for socialism in Africa probably lies in the appearance of "second revolutions," in which truly revolutionary movements overthrow the neomercantilist states and transform them into socialist states, but at present there is no clear trend in that direction.

Perhaps one of the beneficial outcomes of the "first wave" attempts at socialist transformation is that they have made the realities of African sociopolitical life and the obstacles to change so clearly evident that political thinking and action may take account of them. The belief in easy or quick solutions is gone, and that in itself is an important accomplishment. Although African socialism has not lived up to expectations under current conditions, socialist hopes for the future of Africa remain.

SOCIALIST IDEOLOGY

IN AFRICAN POLITICS

SCIENTIFIC SOCIALIST REGIMES IN AFRICA: POLITICAL DIFFERENTIATION, AVOIDANCE, AND UNAWARENESS

Kenneth Jowitt

INTRODUCTION

> "We have not been preoccupied with labels or categories, for these are particularly misleading in the African context."
>
> Secretary of State Cyrus R. Vance[1]

Currently there are a number of self-designated "scientific socialist" and "Marxist-Leninist" regimes in Africa.* Their most striking feature is the absence of ideological commitments, developmental strategies, and institutional developments consistent with their formal identity.

In Mozambique, according to Conor Cruise O'Brien, "a favorite Frelimo word is, or was, *dinamizar*. It was a principal duty of a *responsavel* to 'dynamize' the masses. In Maputo at least the *responsavels* seem to have been singularly unsuccessful in this aspect of their task. It would be hard to imagine any group of people less *dinamizado* in their demeanor than the population of Maputo on that afternoon when they were supposed to be choosing their municipal leaders."[2]

In Guinea, R. W. Johnson notes that "since 1964 the disjuncture between what Touré says and what actually happens . . . has grown increasingly radical and severe—indeed one has the impression that Touré has long ago run up against the outside limits of all that organization and exhortation to mass mobilisation can achieve."[3] And in Congo-Brazzaville, Africa's first people's repub-

---

*Guinea, Congo-Brazzaville, Benin, Mozambique, Angola, Somalia, and Ethiopia.

lic, Samuel Decalo reports that "rhetoric and the new structural trappings of a Communist state aside . . . N'Gouabi's regime has been remarkably nonrevolutionary and devoid of striking socialist policies or changes."[4]

Several possible explanations exist for this striking juxtaposition of rhetoric and reality. Their value rests as much in the questions they raise as in the answers they offer. There is first the argument that African "scientific socialist" or "Marxist-Leninist" regimes are non-dogmatic, indigenous instances of national communism. Viewed in this light, their failure to resemble the Soviet (or Chinese) models should not be equated with failure to build a Leninist regime.[5] This argument poses a vital question for the analyst and the leaders of Leninist regimes: What is general or common at the levels of ideology, strategy, and institutions to all Leninist regimes? In the absence of an authoritative political and ideological center, leader, and organizational means of enforcement such as the Soviet Union, Stalin, and the Comintern, the ability of academic analysts, on the one hand, and Leninist leaders, on the other, to agree on an answer has not been impressive. But (for both groups) the question remains.

A second argument is that the designation of an African regime as Leninist or "scientific socialist" is a purely instrumental act—an effort by its leaders to secure military and/or economic aid from Communist countries. The problem here is that self-designated Leninist regimes, such as Benin, are not favored recipients of aid from Communist countries.[6] In fact, certain non-Communist countries like Nigeria and India receive a great deal more attention from the Soviet Union (as does Zaire from China). Still the designations remain.

A third argument is that the gap between aspiration and achievement in these regimes is explained by the overwhelming environmental resource difficulties they face: low levels of commercialization and industrialization, shortages of trained manpower, lack of natural resources, low levels of effective state power (as reflected in the incidence of smuggling), small national markets, and ethnic-tribal fragmentation. In this view the gap between political aspiration and achievement can be overcome as social and economic development proceeds.[7] There is even an argument that the significance of "Marxist-Leninist" or "scientific socialist" rhetoric rests in the elaboration of a symbolic framework which can provide the meaning for and shape the quality of socioeconomic development as it occurs.[8] The problem with this argument is that it takes the ideological commitments of these regimes at face value. The

implicit assumption is that socioeconomic development not ideological commitment is problematic—or that it is primarily the low level of socioeconomic development that makes the ideological designation inoperable. *These assumptions are questionable.*

A fourth possible argument is that the leaders of these regimes are simply "left-wing" versions of the personal dictators that abound in Africa, and that the choice of ideological format reflects the personal idiosyncracies of the leader more than anything else. Viewed in this light, the self-styled "Emperor" Bokassa of the Central African Empire has his "left" counterpart in Sékou Touré, the "Responsable Supreme" of Guinea. Without denying the element of personal arbitrariness or even rage that may at times accompany the ideological references and designations of certain African elites and individual leaders, it is incumbent to ascertain what—if any— situational and ideological constraints shape the choice of political references and ideological designations. Certainly the pattern of references and designations among former French colonies suggests the operation of general as well as idiosyncratic factors.

Finally, rather than viewing these regimes as poor copies of Leninist organization, or as "scientific socialist" symbolic containers to be "developmentally" filled in over time, one might approach them as identifiable instances of *non-Leninist* regime types. In this vein Gregor has argued that "African socialism shares . . . more compelling affinities with paradigmatic Fascism, the Fascism of Mussolini, than with any form of socialism."[9] Of course, it is possible that the perceived resemblance between African socialism and fascism is as superficial as African socialism's resemblance to "any form of socialism," something Arnold Hughes and Martin Kolinsky have recently and convincingly argued.[10] However, while the reference to fascism misleads more than clarifies, this should not prevent consideration of the general point that African "scientific socialist" regimes might best be considered as organizations with identifiably non-Leninist characters who for particular reasons have formally adopted Leninist facades.

In fact, there is very little in the way of case studies or interview material (let alone survey data) that the comparativist can use to make sense of the actions taken by elites in these regimes. My purpose in this article is to suggest a set of directions that research might take—some hypotheses and concepts that students of African affairs might find useful in their empirical studies of these regimes. I clearly intend this article as a supplement to and not a substitute for such studies—a supplement whose empirical limits are hopefully

compensated for to some degree by the hypotheses and concepts it introduces.

My analysis of African "scientific socialist" regimes is not meant to deny the *possibility* that certain self-designated "scientific socialist" or "Marxist-Leninist" elites are indeed Leninist in intent and prevented largely by resource obstacles from acting on their ideological commitments. However, I want to go beyond this argument and suggest other, equally important reasons for the striking gap between the ideological rhetoric of these elites and their political practice. Nor am I unaware of the significant diversity within the African group of regimes self-designated as either "scientific socialist" or "Marxist-Leninist," but in this article I want to specify the common or general features of elites and regimes that have adopted these designations.

The analysis that follows rests on three notions—political differentiation, political avoidance, and political unawareness—and their relationship to the material *and* ideal interests of particular African elites and *the types of choice—not simply resource—environments** that they confront and to varying degrees favor.

I. POLITICAL DIFFERENTIATION

THE INTERNATIONAL DIMENSION

In many instances African elites have designated themselves "scientific socialist" or "Marxist-Leninist" in an attempt at political differentiation. These cases may be seen as special instances of the more general phenomenon of African elites adopting a socialist designation, which prompted Kopytoff to point out that "at the present historical juncture, the adoption of the term 'socialism' . . . enhances the symbolism of the separation of Africa from the colonial ('capitalist') powers.[11] This observation needs to be developed: (a) political acts of differentiation may have *domestic as well as international dimensions*; (b) at times they may be efforts at *relation as well as separation.*

Resource environments refer to the social and material resources an elite has available for its developmental efforts. *Choice environments* are bounded but not strictly determined by resource environments. Choice environments refer to an elite's ability or inability to avoid or remain unaware of the practical (i. e., strategic and institutional) implications of its formal political identity. This ability or inability varies with how "hard" or "easy" its choice environments are. These concepts and distinctions are developed in the final section of this article.

136

As attempts at political differentiation in the international realm, the adoption of Leninist or "scientific socialist" designations may be motivated by survival, autonomy, and/or status concerns. With respect to survival concerns, a weak country must often find an ally able and willing to counter the direct military and political threat posed by an occupying power or neighboring country. Success in this effort depends in good measure on the weak country's being politically *visible and intelligible* to its potential ally. Visibility and intelligibility are at least superficially achieved by adopting the political idiom and format of the potential ally. Instances of this phenomenon are frequent throughout history, including contemporary history. Outer Mongolia's adoption of Leninist rhetoric and organization in the 1920's was directly related to the threat posed by China to Mongolia's national independence and cultural autonomy.[12] Albania's identification first with the Soviet and then the Chinese variant of Marxism-Leninism was directly related to its fear of Yugoslavia. Romania's adoption of a Western liberal facade in the nineteenth century and through the interwar period was an effort at visibility and intelligibility vis-à-vis the West: an effort at separation from first Russia and then the Soviet Union through the claim of identification with the West. The recent adoption of Marxist-Leninist facades by Ethiopia, Angola, and Mozambique may be partially interpreted as survival efforts by regimes faced with the threat of political extinction from powerful opponents.

Closely related to the immediate concern with survival as an independent regime is the concern with autonomy. Here the typical situation is that of a weak country bordering a more powerful one. While concern about the military expansion of the more powerful country may be less than immediate, there is a general apprehension about being overshadowed by a more economically viable, politically visible, and militarily developed (at least in terms of size) neighbor. One can approach the cases of Benin, Congo-Brazzaville, and Tanzania from this perspective. These regimes have acted to differentiate themselves from the more powerful neighboring countries of Nigeria, Zaire, and Kenya. These attempts at differentiation have consisted in good measure of self-designations strikingly different from the political and ideological formats of the "threatening" neighbor.

Just as survival and autonomy concerns may be hard to distinguish in particular cases, so the concern for autonomy and status may overlap as motives for attempted differentiation. In examining status concerns as a motive for an elite to designate itself "scientific socialist" or "Marxist-Leninist," one is struck by the fact that such

KENNETH JOWITT
</cite>

designations occur more often among former French than among former British colonies. The existence of a powerful French Communist party and the absence of a powerful British Communist party has a great deal to do with this. For the elites of Benin and Congo-Brazzaville, presiding over countries with disproportionately large urban-intellectual strata aware and resentful of the downgrading of their regimes in France's attention, and of their countries' personnel in Francophone Africa's affairs, formal identification with Marxism-Leninism may be an attempt to upgrade their status by simultaneously *relating* to a prestigious and powerful component of French national life (i. e., the French Communist party) and *separating* themselves from exclusive identification as former colonies and "national supplicants."* Finding themselves effectively excluded by the French political center from recognition proportionate to their expectations, the elites of these countries have attempted an "end run" similar to that of many Italian voters in Rhode Island when they discovered the Democratic Party was unavailable to them: they have identified with the "minority" party.†[13]

Lacking such an alternative referent in Britain and given its leader's philosophical orientation, Tanzania has attempted to differentiate itself—in the sense of upgrading its status—by in some ways identifying with the socialist-egalitarian orientations of Scandinavian countries (and China). Such identification is designed to provide material and ideal support for its efforts at political and economic autonomy as well as regional and continental status.

Diverse as the motives for differentiation may be and diverse as the expressions of attempted differentiation are, there is a common feature to such attempts. In all instances those African elites claiming the designation "scientific socialist" or "Marxist-Leninist" want to simultaneously relate and separate themselves from two referents: their formal ideological and political reference—i. e.,

*Note Decalo's characterization of the Beninois situation as one where "the extreme dependence of the government on French largesse and the semi-annual hat-in-hand pilgrimage of Dahomean officials to Paris and other world capitals has fostered deep resentments among the more militant and proud intellectuals and students" (Decalo, *Coups and Army Rule in Africa*, p. 43).

†In Rhode Island the minority party was the Republican. Presumably the French Communist Party and Rhode Island Republican Party saw in these "excluded" constituencies new sources of political support; thus the "benefits" of the relationship are to some extent seen as reciprocal. The analogy holds further inasmuch as not all Italians in Rhode Island vote for the Republican Party, just as not all small former French colonies attempt to align themselves with the PCF.

138
</cite>

the "socialist camp"—and their effective economic and cultural references—i. e., the former colonial powers of Western Europe. In this respect the adoption of "scientific socialism" by a number of African elites reminds one of nothing more than the adoption of Arianism by the Germanic tribes in the fourth and fifth centuries.

As they came into regular contact with the Roman Empire, the Germanic tribes simultaneously attempted to *relate to* and *separate themselves from* what they perceived to be a prestigious, authoritative, powerful, and useful set of institutional and what we would today term ideological references. Too close an identification would threaten their claims to and desire for an identity of their own; too little relation would separate them from sources and symbols of power and status. To differentiate themselves (rather than to be isolated from or identified with Rome) "they unanimously adopted Arianism rather than Catholic Orthodoxy and thereby assured their *separate* religious identity *within the common universe* of Christianity."[14] In a remarkably similar fashion a number of African elites have adopted a particular variant of "scientific socialism" and a particular manner of relating to the "socialist camp." While self-designation as "scientific socialists" or "Marxist-Leninists" ideally offers them access to prestigious symbols associated with powerful and/or high status regimes such as China, the Soviet Union, and Vietnam, selective rejection of critical tenets such as dictatorship of the proletariat, class war, and/or bloc alignments marks them as heretics from the Leninist point of view. As such, African "scientific socialist" regimes maintain respect for *and* distance from the powerful and prestigious regimes they in some measure identify with.* The value of the Arian analogy is that it emphasizes the

---

*The effort to relate yet maintain distance is illustrated by the practice of requesting political and economic advisors from either smaller Communist countries or from Communist parties out of power. In some cases this has a technical rationale, as when Congo-Brazzaville recruits Marxist instructors from France (see Decalo, p. 166). Language considerations go a long way (but not the whole way) in explaining the choice. In other cases this practice reminds one of the historical tendency of newly converted pagan states to choose religious instructors from either weaker Christian areas, so that conversion wouldn't threaten their autonomy, or from a more powerful but distant center (i. e., Rome) that could balance the attempts by more powerful neighboring, regional Christian states to convert and control them. While there is evidence in Africa of the first practice, as of yet there is none of the second. Should a country like Ethiopia become a viable regional Leninist regime, one should see evidence of the second practice as well.

The tendency of newly converted Christian states to choose instructors from

dual—i. e., relating and separating—quality of "scientific socialist" designations in Africa. On the one hand, adoption of the idiom and institutional facades of Leninism ideally means access to the material and symbolic resources of powerful international and national actors. On the other hand, from the point of view of a regime like the Soviet, the rejection of certain Leninist tenets and practices by African "scientific socialist" elites makes them at worst impostors, at best heretics—a status these elites may well consider desirable for its Arian-like shielding quality.

THE DOMESTIC DIMENSION

As suggested earlier, the adoption of "scientific socialist" labels may serve as a basis for domestic as well as international differentiation. Decalo's observation that "the new radical pronouncements emanating from Cotonou (Benin) attest . . . to the coming-of-age of a new political class more attuned to the militancy in other parts of the Third World"[15] can be extended geographically and analytically. What one sees in many African countries is *the emergence of an unestablished elite*: one lacking the authoritative credentials of high social and political status in their societies, as well as the long-standing social, cultural, educational, and political ties that transform a functional into an established elite. Members of an established elite supplement their power roles with shared experiences and personal ties that contribute to their political confidence, interpersonal ease, and organizational coherence.[16] In the absence of such experiences and ties, a premium exists for new elites (such as those in many African regimes) to adopt formal symbols, idioms, and facades that differentiate them from their more established predecessors. *The adoption of a new political and ideological designation formally provides an unestablished elite with internal bonds and external boundaries*—with an enhanced capacity to offset its regional, tribal, religious, generational, and educational diversity, a common dimension along which to relate to one another,

less threatening areas is outlined by Marc Bloch in *Feudal Society* I (Chicago: University of Chicago Press, 1970)—e. g., the Hungarian recruitment from Czech rather than German bishoprics and the desire of Scandinavian princes to have a direct relationship with distant Rome in favor of subordination to the more proximate and powerful Bremen bishopric (see pp. 14 and 34). This practice of "leapfrogging" has parallels in relations among Communist states. Perhaps the earliest instance was Albania's identification with the distant Soviet Union and dissociation from neighboring and more powerful Yugoslavia.

and the corporate capacity to distinguish or separate themselves from others. One might even hypothesize that, other things being equal, the less established an elite the greater the propensity to adopt political and ideological designations that sharply distinguish them from their more culturally and socially secure political rivals and the latter's international supporters.

Adoption of "scientific socialism" can provide an elite that is relatively unfamiliar with one another, and very unfamiliar with the domestic and international tasks confronting it, with *a formal set of ideological, strategic, and regime references*. These can increase such an unestablished elite's sense of security and confidence by providing an ideological idiom that allows it to at least formally identify and map its problems, a set of policies and strategies that appear to address these problems, and perhaps material resources to implement those policies and strategies.*

Self-designation as "scientific socialist" or "Marxist-Leninist" also offers a new elite the rationale for and image of a new political format that presumably favors its authority and power. Adoption of a new political idiom and organization ideally allows an unestablished elite to change the criteria of political competence and status. While older, more established elites have an advantage in manipulating existing political arrangements, adoption of a new idiom and institutional facade *presumably* undercuts this advantage and shifts it to that group with ties to the sources of the new format, with less to *un*learn in operating it, and with the initial advantage of being its author. In short, unestablished elites comprised of individuals coming from previously subordinate tribal groups, neglected regions, or generational strata that have been excluded from the highest power positions (and/or who lack educational-status achievements) will tend to adopt designations that compensate for their low status, lack of experience, and need for internal bonding and external boundaries. In many cases "scientific socialism" and "Marxism-Leninism" are appropriated to serve just those purposes. Examples are to be found in Congo-Brazzaville, where the "rise of Fort Rousset-born N'Gouabi ended the neglect of Congo [Brazzaville]'s undeveloped central and northern regions and the political and administrative superiority and dominance of the Bakongo";[17] in Ethiopia, where can be seen the emergence of the Galla and the consequent challenge to Amharic leadership, and the antagonism between the previously subordinate social elements that now comprise

*Here again the case of Outer Mongolia is very relevant (see note 12).

the support and membership of the Dirgue and the opposition Ethiopian People's Revolutionary Party (EPRP)—a largely student-youth group that draws support from the families of the urban "established" intelligentsia;[18] in Guinea, where the rise of the Parti Democratique du Guinée meant both the displacement of traditional notables and the educated elite in favor of the less educated and members of the *petit fonctionnaire* and union groups;[19] and in Benin, where the success of the Kerekou group in 1972 meant the displacement of the established political notables who had dominated political life up till then and the senior army stratum predominantly staffed by members of the traditionally powerful Fon tribe.[20]

However, to establish a plausible relationship between the emergence of an unestablished elite and its need for a new political idiom and format to bolster its coherence, effectiveness, and self-esteem doesn't explain why the particular formal designation in a number of contemporary African cases tends to be "scientific socialist" or "Marxist-Leninist." Some reasons have already been mentioned. Regime survival, as in the Ethiopian-Soviet connection, is an obvious one. Status is another—particularly for the elites of countries that, unlike those in the Ivory Coast and Kenya, are not inheritors of relatively successful economies or led by men with long-standing contacts with the former metropole or favored by the former colonial power. Adoption of "scientific socialism" is a way of identifying with a powerful "alternative" sector of the world, compensating for the absence of material development, *and offering a new—symbolic—criterion of development and achievement.* In this last respect, African "scientific socialist" regimes do closely follow Communist precedent. It was Stalin (in his *Dialectical and Historical Materialism*) who noted that "Belgium lags a whole historical epoch behind [the USSR], for in Belgium the capitalist system prevails, whereas the USSR has already done away with capitalism and has set up a socialist system."[21] More recently Enver Hoxha has asserted that Albania "positively influences the course of events in the world, not by the size of her territory or by the number of her population or atomic weapons, but by the inspiring force of the Marxist-Leninist ideas, which she applies, defends, and spreads throughout the whole world. From this viewpoint Albania's force is unmeasurable."[22]

In cases where the neglected African country has the possibility of linkage with a significant Communist party in the former metropole, the incentive to designate itself "scientific socialist" or "Marx-

ist-Leninist" is even clearer. To reiterate and expand on this point: In such cases the neglected African elite can attempt simultaneously to find a *new* point of entry into the former metropole's political system *and* into the camp of the Western metropole's international rival—the "socialist camp." Partial relation to that camp and to its "ally" in the metropole's political system (e. g., the PCF) ensures separation from as well as relation to the ambivalently viewed metropole.

A third reason may be the formal congruence betweeen certain tenets and features of "scientific socialism" or "Marxism-Leninism," on the one hand, and the cultural orientations, social organization, and colonial experiences of African countries, on the other. In explaining the adoption of the Arian variant of Christianity by Germanic tribes, Bury suggested that it was "simpler for their intelligence than the difficult doctrine of Nicaea."[23] If instead of intelligence one focuses on cultural orientations and social organization, then Bury's point can be fruitful—not just controversial. I would suggest that at one level the doctrine of Nicaea and the doctrines of liberal or social democracy share an important feature—as do Arianism and "scientific socialism." The former contain more abstract features, while the latter stress more the personal and concrete. In short, Arianism not only related and separated (i. e., differentiated) the new Germanic elites vis-à-vis the Catholic Roman Empire, *but it also demanded less of an internal identity shift insofar as the tenets of Arianism could (at least formally) be related more readily than Catholicism to existing German-tribal notions of authority and organization.*[24] Similarly, "scientific socialism" or "Marxism-Leninism," with its emphases on the heroic role of cadres, the significance of the party leader, its paternalistic concern with welfare, and substantive rather than procedural orientations, fits more readily with African traditional and colonial experiences than do the procedural and individualistic emphases of liberal or social democratic political and economic tenets.

A fourth reason may be the belief among certain African elites that Leninist regimes have specific techniques, experiences, and resources relevant to their problems.

Finally, the particular designation "scientific socialist" or "Marxist-Leninist" may appeal to certain African elites precisely because an authoritative center no longer exists within the Leninist group of regimes. As I have emphasized, differentiation in the case of African "scientific socialist" or "Marxist-Leninist" regimes refers

to the dual effort to separate from and relate to conflicting political referents. The absence of an authoritative center of Leninism comparable to the Communist Party of the Soviet Union under Stalin allows self-designated "scientific socialist" African elites *to avoid the hard identity choice of bloc alignment internationally and exclusive political choices domestically.*

THE GENERAL PURPOSE OF "SCIENTIFIC SOCIALIST" DESIGNATIONS

For an unestablished African elite, the "adoption" of "scientific socialism" appears to have the same general domestic and international purpose—to achieve *limited political differentiation.*

At the international level, "scientific socialism" provides a formally distinct identity selectively separating as well as relating African elites to their formally positive references—communist regimes—and relating as well as separating them from their formally negative references: Western regimes. *Nonalignment* is the central political and ideological tenet in this dual and differently weighted act of international differentiation. Nonalignment serves to separate formally designated African "scientific socialist" regimes from the "socialist camp" and to relate them to non-Communist regimes (e. g., in the West). Nonalignment is designed to secure a relationship with the liberal and Leninist worlds that enhances the status and material well-being of African elites while avoiding hard-choice situations that would directly affect their international autonomy and domestic political character.

Domestically, self-designation as "scientific socialist" operates in the same fashion. On the one hand, it identifies new constituencies from which an unestablished elite can try to secure support. Appropriation of the symbols and facades of "scientific socialism" directs unestablished elites to social groups (e. g., students and workers) that can ideally serve as political constituencies. Reciprocally, appropriation of these symbols might serve to focus the interest and commitment of unattended-to social groups on the new regime. In these senses self-designation as "scientific socialist" performs a *relational* function to what *presumably* are available and valuable social bases of support. Being uncommitted these bases can contribute to and enhance the domestic political autonomy of a new elite concerned with establishing and stabilizing its political identity. Relation to these presumably unattended-to and available urban (and rural) constituencies is simultaneously an act of separation from existing and constraining elite-constituency patterns with their built-in resource distribution and status-ranking commitments.

However, as is the case internationally, the identification of new domestic political references means limited rejection of old references and limited reliance on new ones. How limited that reliance is comes out quite clearly in the contrast between regime preference for "scientific social*ism*" and antipathy toward "scientific social-*ists*." In Somalia President Siyaad Barre has purged socialist ideologues, in Ethiopia the Mengistu-led Dirgue has imprisoned a variety of "left-wing" groups, while in Guinea Sékou Touré purged the left-wing Mamou section of the Parti Democratique de Guinée and its leader Pleah Koniba.[25] It should be noted that African regimes with formal claims to "scientific socialist" status are not the first to combine divergent ideological facades and political practices. The paradigmatic case is that of Ataturk in Turkey. Throughout the initial period of the Ataturk regime, the Soviet Union was an important source of support. The limits of this support were dramatically demonstrated when along with their first diplomatic mission the Soviets sent a group of Turkish Communists: "The Kemalist authorities had them drowned."[26] More recently Nasser jailed Egyptian Communists and the Iraqi regime hanged a number of Iraqi Communists.[27]

If on the one hand self-designation as "scientific socialist" favors identification of but limited reliance on or relation to new constituencies, on the other hand it means limited rejection of or separation from old or established elites. Members of established elites are displaced from power and authority, and presumably placed at a disadvantage with respect to their access to and familiarity with the new "scientific socialist" or "Leninist" organizational facades and rhetoric. However, the particular meaning African elites give to "scientific socialism"—an ideal as well as practical commitment to religion,[28] hostility not only to political interference from Communist countries but also to domestic Communists, rejection of systematic recruitment and training of Communist cadres and of the Leninist tenets of class war and the dictatorship of the proletariat—favors only limited, not decisive, political separation from established elites. African regimes formally committed to "scientific socialism" resemble what Iliya Harik in his perceptive analysis of Egypt terms a "collaboration regime"—one in which a "nationally dominant leader enters into an 'alliance' with regionally and locally influential persons; the party organization [serving] as a kind of 'formal contract' between them."[29]

The character of collaboration will vary significantly from country to country. However, the emphasis placed by African

"scientific socialist" elites on displacing the established *political* class, designating a new *political* format, and *politically* organizing existing but presumably unattended-to constituencies suggests that the new elites' separation from established sociopolitical practices will be limited. For these new unestablished "scientific socialist" elites, formal political organization rather than substantial social mobilization seems to be the basis of political differentiation.

Self-designation as "scientific socialist" or "Marxist-Leninist" may be seen as an act of limited political differentiation, as an attempt by certain African elites to simultaneously balance the imperatives of political relation and separation in three arenas: (1) domestically, (2) in connection with former colonial powers, and (3) in connection with the "socialist camp." The defining feature of self-designation by an African elite as either "scientific socialist" or "Marxist-Leninist" appears to be its effort to establish an intermediate domestic and international political position—*to avoid hard (i. e., mutually exclusive) choices of international alignment and domestic political organization.*

II. POLITICAL AVOIDANCE

OVERWHELMING CONSTRAINTS AND DESPERATE RESPONSES

The limited extent to which African elites have acted on their formal ideological and political commitments is undoubtedly related to resource constraints. These elites face overwhelming resource obstacles that make the translation of "scientific socialist" facade, language, and symbol into strategy and policy extremely difficult. Lenin himself noted that "without a certain level of capitalist development, we would get nowhere."[30] However, the relationship between resource constraints and the particular way in which African elites have appropriated "scientific socialism" is not a simple one. Many of the outstanding characteristics of these regimes can be viewed as desperate responses to overwhelming constraints. I begin this line of argument with the following hypothesis: *situations of great constraint generate a climate of elite desperation with a consequent tendency to adopt quasi-magical solutions to overwhelming problems.*

Commenting on the fervor with which socialism has been at least symbolically appropriated by many African leaders, Aristide Zolberg observed that "for those who are faced with the overwhelming burdens of government in Africa, socialism is more than a sci-

entific method. It is a modern gnosis which promises to unveil to its initiates the secrets of economic development."[31] Similarly, Andreski explains what he considers to be the unwillingness of African politicians to "face reality" on economic questions, to "fall into word magic when talking about economic problems," by the hopelessness of their economic situation. He goes on to note that the relationship between hopelessness (or desperation) and magic is consistent with Malinowski's "theory of magic," the main point of which is that "people . . . think rationally about processes which they can control, but fall into an autistic mode of thinking when dealing with completely unmanageable and unpredictable phenomena."[32]

The same relationship may hold in the sphere of political organization. In regimes where the elite is *unestablished*, where factionalism is ever present and sustained by familial, tribal, and regional divisions in the country, and where nationalism promises disunity not unity, Leninism with its emphasis on centralization may well appear to be organizational magic.* It may be seen as a way of skipping the nationalist as well as the capitalist stage, of moving directly from a decolonization phase (not to be confused with a nationalist phase)[33] to a "socialist" phase.

The frequently noted tendency in self-designated "scientific socialist" or "Marxist-Leninist" regimes to develop what P. Erny in his comments on Congo-Brazzaville youth terms a "culture of the word" may have similar bases.[34] The attention to and emotional investment in Leninist language very likely reflects the serious resource obstacles to action facing these elites and the consequent premium they place on formal mastery over one of the few realms subject to their control, as well as the importance given to speech in a traditional culture and the importance an unestablished elite places on gaining control over its own status-idiom.

The symbolic adoption of "scientific socialism" by certain African elites may also reflect the impotence-rage, cynical-utopian dualities Henry Roberts found in his study of small Balkan states. Roberts suggests that the highly constraining and vulnerable environments these states operate in alternately produces postures of political impotence and rage.[35] For a country like Benin, faced

---

*Lenin once commented that "The effort to prove the necessity for centralism to the Bolsheviks, who are centralists by conviction, by their programme and by the entire tactic of their Party, is really like forcing an open door" (V. I. Lenin, "Can the Bolsheviks Retain State Power?," in *Collected Works*, 26 [Moscow: Progress Publishers, 1964], p. 116).

with overwhelming economic difficulties, dependent on France for economic largesse, and resentful of France's refusal to accord Benin and its elite groups the regional status they desire, adoption of "Marxism-Leninism" may well be an instance of political rage produced by political impotence.

For unestablished African elites dependent on foreign economic largesse, lacking traditional domestic status and having no material base for international status, and resting on a fragile political base, appropriation of a free good like Marxism-Leninism may in a fundamental respect have quasi-magical meanings—e. g., it may to some extent be seen as a "guarantee" of development and as a "political amulet" capable of offsetting the neo-colonial threat to a recently acquired and fragile political autonomy.

POLITICAL AVOIDANCE AND IDEAL INTERESTS

The limited extent and quasi-magical fashion in which African "scientific socialist" elites act on their formal ideological and political commitments can be seen not only as desperate responses to resource obstacles, but also as more or less deliberate attempts to avoid the practical (i. e., strategic and policy) implications of their "scientific socialist" designations. Viewed in this light the particular way in which African elites have appropriated "scientific socialism" can be said to reflect their ideal interests as well as the resource obstacles they face. An examination of the role *elite ideal interests* play in shaping the political character of these regimes should in no way exclude an appreciation of the role played by elite material interests, or of the impact of resource constraints on elite policy choices and political psychology. However, it does add an important and neglected dimension to our understanding of the gap between rhetoric and practice in African "scientific socialist" regimes.

"Not ideas, but material and ideal interests directly govern men's conduct." According to Reinhard Bendix, Weber never developed this "cryptic remark."[36] Perhaps not in a definitional fashion, but the distinctiveness of Weber's analytic approach can be said to rest with his notion of ideal interests. In any case my analysis of African "scientific socialist" elites calls for a clear conceptualization of what Weber refers to as ideal interests.

Elites may be said to have material interests, values, and ideal interests. Whether a given elite has all three and how they are weighted is an empirical matter. *Material interests* refer to an elite's concern with power and economic well-being, and its efforts to

148

organize bases of support in order to pursue them. *Values* refer to organizationally relevant personal qualities (e. g., honesty, obedience, loyalty, initiative) an elite sees as essential and valuable, and to socialization efforts (i. e., education and indoctrination) favoring their development.

Ideal interests refer to an elite's concern with identity and self-esteem; its designation of a particular social group as embodying and guaranteeing those virtues, skills, and dispositions on which its own and the organization's integrity are seen as depending; and its efforts to ensure that social (reference) group a privileged position. In contrast to values, ideal interests have a specific sociological component: it is through the designation of a particular social group (e. g., class, tribe, religious sect) as the appropriate, not simply expedient, base of a regime that an elite attempts to stabilize and integrate its material interests and value commitments.

While an elite can try to foster particular values through education and indoctrination, and pursue its material interests by building *expedient* support coalitions, its ideal interests lead to and are signalled by the identification of a particular social group that in the elite's view offers the most *appropriate* setting for the generation and stabilization of valued dispositions and qualities on the one hand and power and economic resources on the other. *An elite's ideal interests refer to its efforts to locate, develop, and favor the social group it sees as indispensable for the effective integration and realization of its ideological and material goals.* Thus West European elites in the nineteenth century looked to the middle class not simply out of expediency or because of their social origin (Lenin after all looked to the workers while himself of middle class origin), but because for these elites the middle class was believed to be best suited to ensure the *proper* development of their countries—not simply the adequate generation of power and economic resources. Similarly, in the Soviet case industrialization meant not only material gains in the form of industrial plant, defense capacity, and technical skills, but also gains in the development of the proletariat—the group believed to possess the virtues and dispositions essential to a particular type not simply level of development and consequently to the long-term maintenance and integrity of regime identity not simply capacity. Elites and regimes can be compared along the dimension of ideal interests. One can ask: What, if any, social group is designated by a particular elite as the *ideal* or *appropriate* base of its rule? To what extent does such a base exist? To what extent must an elite find *expedient* bases of support in the absence (numerically or

organizationally) of an *appropriate* social base? What political consequences are there for an elite that must rely on expedient bases of
support? Should the hoped-for social base exist, to what extent are
its cultural qualities and material resources consistent with elite
expectations, and to what extent and in what manner are they
available to the elite?

Our task here is to identify the character of elite ideal interests
in African "scientific socialist" regimes. Recently, a Soviet student
of these regimes—P. I. Manchkha—observed that "some revolutionary democrats treat socialism not as a historically inevitable social
and economic formation but only as the most effective method of
eliminating age-old backwardness and bondage to the imperialist
metropolitan countries. . . . [They] frequently underestimate the
role of the working class in the socialist transformation of society. . . ."[37] Almost without exception, statements like Manchkha's
about "the role of the working class" are dismissed by scholars as
a ritualized Soviet reference and/or as inappropriate for countries
that don't have much of a working class either in size or in the
sense of a social group whose style of life and institutional patterns
are differentiated from other groups (e. g., tribal, peasant). Needless
to say, there is a great deal to these objections; however, they don't
exhaust the significance of Manchkha's statements, which speaks
directly to the divergence in African "scientific socialist" regimes
between elite ideal interests and organizational-ideological forms.
Manchkha's checklist of Leninist features *absent* from these regimes—an oppositional attitude toward religion as a social institution
(not simply toward religious elites), centrality of the working class as
appropriate support base and/or ideal referent, development of a
party based on a "correct line," and greater appreciation of the
general features of socialist revolution regardless of setting[38]—
provides useful clues about the ideal interests and political identity
of these elites. That identity appears to be more populist than
Leninist.

To develop this argument one must first gauge the extent to
which the substantial as opposed to rhetorical definitions of these
regimes approximate the central political and ideological features
of populism or Leninism. To do this requires a clear statement of
the contrasting features of populism and Leninism. Second, one
must ascertain whether the national and international environments of African "scientific socialist" elites call for hard choices or
easy choices. *Hard choices* are those demanding an either-or response to the practical (i. e., strategic and policy) implications of

their formal ideological commitments; *easy choices* are those that allow an elite to avoid understanding and acting on the practical implications of their formal ideological commitments—i. e., having to make either-or choices. In the absence of environments demanding hard choices, there is uncertainty about the political character of these regimes both for the analyst and to some extent for the regime elites themselves. In the remainder of this section, I shall contrast populism and Leninism, and in the final section examine the types of environments African "scientific socialist" elites currently face.

Populism. It is by no means easy to isolate the populist features of elites who in good measure employ a non-populist (i. e., Leninist) terminology. Trying to specify their ideological character would be easier if one could find regimes that do not employ a Leninist idiom, but whose organization and practical behavior approximate those of African elites designating themselves "scientific socialist" or "Marxist-Leninist." Two such African regimes exist—the one founded by Cabral in Guinea-Bissau, the other led by Nyerere in Tanzania. Furthermore, both Cabral and Nyerere have been quite explicit in characterizing their political beliefs. From their statements and actions one can draw a composite profile of African populism which can be used as a benchmark for examining the ideological statements and political actions of self-designated "scientific socialist" elites.

In Cabral's and Nyerere's statements one can readily discern six characteristic features:

(1) The *national leader* is identified as the key element determining the revolution's continued success. To be sure, designation of the leader as the most important political element doesn't preclude the need for a vanguard party,[39] but that party's character derives more from the qualities of its leader than from its program. Cabral was most explicit on this point that continuation of the revolution depended on the development of revolutionary consciousness: "This dependence necessarily calls our attention to the capacity of the leader of the national liberation struggle to remain faithful to the principles and to the fundamental cause of this struggle."[40]

(2) Populists place primary stress on the *ethical dimension* of leadership and development. In the statement cited above, Cabral goes on to observe that "if national liberation is essentially a political problem, the conditions for its development give it certain characteristics which belong to the sphere of morals."[41] Nyerere's

emphasis on the ethical dimension is even greater than Cabral's, and his language reminds one more of Thomas Aquinas than of Marx or Lenin. Related to this concern with the ethical, populists stress personal attitudes as being the critical determinant of social change. For Nyerere the first step in changing Tanzania "must be to reeducate ourselves, to regain our former attitude of mind."[42] This primary emphasis on the ethical and attitudinal does not preclude organizational and sociological orientations: Cabral's analysis of Guinean social structure is impressive, and Nyerere's at least formal appreciation of organizational development is on record.[43]

(3) Typically, populists attempt to achieve national homogeneity through political mobilization rather than social mobilization. Political mobilization consists of elite efforts to activate people, to direct their actions and affect (negative or positive) at particular targets—without, however, *directly* challenging the social identity or institutional commitments of those activated. Reliance on political mobilization as the basic means of social change results in the superimposition of new social elites on largely unreconstructed social institutions, and new political loyalties on existing ones. Social mobilization consists of elite efforts to undermine existing institutional frameworks and social identities (e. g., religious and kin) and create alternative ones. The populists' avoidance of social mobilization stems as much from self-imposed ideological and political restraints as from limits on their organizational capacity. (In fact, the ideological constraints directly affect organizational capacity.) Populists have an approach-avoidance relationship to mass social mobilization. Social mobilization threatens the asserted unity of the people. However, as social, economic, and political inequalities increase and the political elite fails to uphold strict moral standards, the leader of a populist regime *approaches* the option of social and political mobilization. (Nyerere's stance on collectivization is pertinent here.) Then, as the social, cultural, and political implications of acting on a mobilization policy become clearer, the leader usually *avoids* them by limiting himself to personnel changes, emotional-rhetorical efforts, and campaigns against corruption.[44] Thus approach-avoidance tends to be a continuing political pattern in these regimes.

(4) Populists are levellers: their symbolic referent is *the people*. While recognizing social differences, they assert the *political* unity of the people and deny the existence of fundamental social divisions. Nyerere's "nation of socialist villages" and Cabral's nation in which the "vestiges of tribalism have been eliminated" are representative

images of a homogeneous *political* nation. The elevation of *the people* as the central ideological referent clearly expresses the ideal interests of a populist elite *and* its practical difficulty in locating specific social strata that conform to the elite's ideological and political expectations—social strata in a position to offer the elite appropriate cultural, economic, and political support. One major difference between nineteenth-century West European romantic nationalism and contemporary African populist nationalism is that in the former case there existed significant middle class or bourgeois groups possessing appropriate cultural, economic, and political resources—i. e., *resources consistent with the political aspirations and ideological self-conceptions of their countries' political elites.* For most African regimes such a group does not exist. Such regimes often find the practical or substantial implications of Leninism unacceptable, a social base for an effective nationalist policy unavailable, and reliance on social (e. g., tribal) groups with neither resources nor orientations consistent with a policy of *national* identification and development unavoidable.

(5) For [African] populists the *colonial experience* is defining. According to Cabral: "Even more than the class struggle in the capitalist countries and the antagonism between these countries and the socialist world, the liberation struggles of the colonial peoples is the essential characteristic, and we would say the prime motive force, of the advance of history in our times. . . ."[45] Linked to this appreciation is the idea that the colonial state, not the class struggle, was the defining experience for African countries, and that the impact of this state was primarily cultural, with its major feature the denial of an indigenous history and racism.[46]

(6) Finally, populist leaders typically emphasize the *particular* and not the *general* features of their developmental efforts. Nothing characterizes populists more than this. Cabral is explicit on the point. While arguing that a clear ideology is an essential element in any effort to secure genuine sovereignty, he goes on at great length (in a commentary on the Cuban experience) to point out that "we have certain reservations about the systematisation of phenomena. . . . We are not completely certain that, in fact, the [Cuban] scheme is absolutely adaptable to our conditions."[47] To be sure, Cabral was right that the Guevarist approach was not "absolutely adaptable" to Guinea-Bissau, but he was questioning more than the applicability of Guevarism. He was questioning the "systematisation of phenomena." One might question this distinction between populists and Leninists by pointing out that Leninists argue that general

principles must be adjusted to national differences, and that regimes like the Yugoslav and Romanian argue vociferously in defense of "many roads to socialism" and against Soviet attacks on the possibility of various kinds of socialism.[48] From the populist side, one could cite Nyerere's remark that "socialism is [not] a vague concept which can have as many different meanings and variations as there are people who advocate it."[49] However, for populists like Cabral and Nyerere, the general features of political and social development have *a symbolic—not a standard institutional and strategic—dimension.* For populists it is the particular or national, not the "systematised" or international, dimension of a country's development that is central. And while Nyerere asserts that socialism is not a vague concept, when he identifies its general features as the "well-being of the people" and "acceptance of human equality," he illustrates what he denies.[50]

Leninism. The basic differences between Leninism and populism become more interesting when one pursues their similarities. In his discussion of Marxism and modernization, Robert Tucker asks why Marxism has "exerted such influence upon intelligentsia minds in underdeveloped societies." His answer is that "Marxism portrays a totally polarized pre-revolutionary society, a society divided into two hostile class camps." He goes on to point out that while the fact that in third world countries the two classes are not those Marx spoke of "creates problems for Marxism as sociological theory, it does not deprive it of great force as political ideology. It does not prevent elements of the radical intelligentsia from seeing their bifurcated society through Marxist eyes, from assimilating the realities around them to Marx's vision of class polarization." Tucker observes that Lenin ("who had acquired from experience and from foregoing generations of Populist revolutionaries the consciousness that there existed two Russias"—an omnipotent officialdom and the peasant mass) successfully superimposed "the class war doctrine of Marx upon the bifurcated society of semi-modern Russia and other societies like it."[51] There is a great deal of merit in what Tucker says. However, if Leninism primarily means the adoption or assimilation of Marxist terms to a populist reality, how does one explain the fact that in Russia, China, and elsewhere Leninists broke through the basic social institutions of their countries instead of ideologically and politically limiting themselves to attacks on the urban, rural, and educated elites?[52] Why didn't Lenin, Stalin, and Mao speak like Marxists and act like national populists? If Tucker is right, then

Lenin did to Marxism what Marx saw the German literati doing to French revolutionary ideas. According to Marx, "the work of the German literati consisted solely in bringing the new French ideas into harmony with their ancient philosophical conscience, or rather, in annexing the French ideas without deserting their own philosophic point of view. . . . They wrote their philosophical nonsense beneath the French original."[53] But in the light of the institutional and strategic actions taken by Lenin (and Leninists), it is clear that Lenin did more than subvert Marxist "originality" with populist "nonsense" or superimpose the class war doctrine of Marx "upon the bifurcated society of semi-modern Russia and other societies like it."

The differences between Leninism and populism are not absolute, but they are, as I shall point out, defining.

(1) In contrast to populist movements, the integrity of a Leninist party is seen to rest primarily on a *charismatically impersonal* "correct line"*—not an ethical leader. While leaders in Leninist regimes have often been the effective loci of authority, power, and policy, ideally this has always been a usurpation. The practical significance of an ideal commitment to a "correct line" extends from providing a political challenger a legitimate base in the Party's charter to oppose a "cult of personality," to increasing a Communist regime's stability by reducing its ideological dependence on a single leader.

(2) Related to the "impersonality" of the Leninist party, ethical considerations are subordinate to sociological ones. While Leninists stress the importance of socialist culture, party education, revolutionary morality, and ideological consciousness, they consider fundamental changes in social-institutional patterns as the necessary and prior condition for substantial changes in attitudes and ethics. Ideologically this orientation is captured by the contrast Leninists make between "scientific" and "utopian" socialism; politically it is

---

*For a discussion of the Leninist "party of a new type" as an instance of what I term *charismatic impersonalism*, and of the central place of the "correct line" as an ideal element in its organizational definition, see Jowitt, *The Leninist Response to National Dependency*. It is worth noting here that Stalin at the height of his personal power felt it incumbent to point out at the Eighteenth Party Congress in 1939 that only "after a correct political line has been worked out and tested in practice, the Party cadres become the decisive force in the leadership. . . . *A correct line is of course the primary and most important thing*" (J. V. Stalin, "Report to the Eighteenth Congress of the CPSU [Bolshevik] on the Work of the Central Committee," in *The Essential Stalin*, ed. Bruce Franklin [Garden City, N.Y.: Doubleday, 1972], pp. 373-74).

captured by the Leninist commitment to collectivization. As much as any Leninist, Mao Tse-tung emphasized culture, consciousness, and revolutionary morality, but he did so in the context of a regime that had collectivized the largest and one of the oldest rural societies in the world.

(3) This sociological emphasis expresses itself politically as sustained efforts at *mass* social mobilization. The emphasis on mass social mobilization—or better, the use of political organization as a means of institutional transformation, of generating new types and mass bases of political power—is what Benjamin Schwartz points to in Mao's case. Referring to the Chinese Communist Party's founding, Schwartz notes that

> Mao Tse-tung was probably one of the few among these early party members equipped by experience to appreciate Leninism as an organizational technique rather than as simply another doctrine. . . . it was his experiences in organizational activities in Hunan which made him realize that only *mass political power secured through mass action* could guarantee the realization of dynamic reforms.[54]

Unfortunately, Schwartz's language is somewhat confusing. Perhaps because he wishes to emphasize the organizational novelty rather than the ideological features of Leninism, he emphasizes organizational *technique*. The tendency to identify Leninism's distinctiveness with its disciplined organization has some merit. However, it often leads to the conclusion among practitioners and academics that the organizational form is the political substance.[55] Though his language suggests this, Schwartz's argument and quotation from Mao suggest something else—i. e., that the Leninist is more a "political sociologist" than "political scientist." For Leninists the party is more the means of breaking through existing social and cultural institutions, uprooting old and creating new mass sociopolitical constituencies, than a vehicle for superimposing new social elites on largely unreconstructed social institutions, and new political loyalties on existing ones.

(4) Populists like Leninists are interested in finding appropriate, not simply expedient, social constituencies. They differ with respect to the social groups they deem appropriate and the means employed to develop and upgrade them. It is here that the Leninist emphasis on *class* and the populist emphasis on *the people* have political, not merely symbolic, import. A populist regime with a solidary conception of the people as its ideal referent is largely

limited on the one hand to political organization and on the other to political violence directed against individuals and elites as means of rule and development. In contrast, the Leninist recourse to mass social mobilization involves the deliberate use of political violence against social-institutional features of the "solidary" nation, provides political resources to strata seen by populists as lacking the appropriate virtues, skills, and orientations for national development, and favors the creation of political formats that challenge the ideological emphasis populists place on the leader.

Harik's analysis of Egypt under Nasser speaks directly to these points. Nasser's populist leadership favored the emergence of a particular social constituency —farmers and professionals—who were to replace the upper urban class and large rural landlords (the previously *established* elite). The political upgrading of this new social elite meant significant but limited attempts to transform Egyptian social and cultural institutions—e. g., land reform, but not collectivization. The limits of social change in Egypt were as much due to self-imposed political and ideological constraints as to resource constraints. These limits created a recurrent situation in which Nasser was confronted with socially based political opposition that he thought he had done away with, and with new social groups that effectively withheld resources necessary for the implementation of his developmental policies. In 1965 he responded by beginning to act on his radical socialist commitments. The result over a two-year period was the limited but visible strengthening of the "party"—the Arab Socialist Union—at the expense of local social elites. ASU activists "took over political responsibility from locally established leaders; this resulted in conflicts with those whose power and interests were adversely affected by the new party organization." Nasser's upgrading of the ASU under Ali Sabry's leadership meant that "peasants and workers soon proved to be a competing elite."[56] Some two years after Nasser initiated this process he called it to a halt *because of its success, not its failure.* As Harik points out, the radical strategy of 1965-67 threatened the type of regime Nasser had created. However, the threat wasn't simply a material one. With his personal charisma and control of the army, it is likely that Nasser could have controlled the development of a "scientific socialist" regime as well as Castro has.* The threat was also to the ideal interests of Nasser and sectors of the Egyptian elite.

*It is unlikely that this capacity was equally distributed at other levels of the Nasser regime. Consequently, concern with material interests would be an inhibiting factor at some levels and for some individuals.

The Egyptian developments of 1965-67 are instructive in at least two respects: (1) as a clear instance of the approach-avoidance pattern of populist leadership to social and political change, and (2) as a vivid illustration of the political significance of an elite's designation of *the people* (rather than a class) as its ideal referent. Faced with the implications of acting on his radical socialist claims—i. e., with a hard choice—Nasser made his preference and the regime's political identity clear. Sadat's redesignation of the Egyptian regime along explicitly non-"scientific socialist" lines is rooted in the hard choice made by Nasser in 1967.

The Leninist commitment to a *class* view of society (even when the party's identification of favored social groups is clearly based more on ideological designation than sociological analysis) favors a quite different policy and organizational syndrome. At crucial developmental points, the ideal commitment to the "international proletariat" contributes to a Leninist elite's capacity to politically and expressively detach itself from and attack indigenous social and cultural institutions *as well as* displace established political elites. And its positive appreciation of the West's scientific and industrial abilities—not just products—along with the designation of the proletariat as its ideal social referent (i. e., appropriate social base) favors an industrial program with cultural and social as well as economic targets. The Leninist negative evaluation of dominant rural peasant institutions works in the same direction.*

(5) Leninists, like [African] populists, identify colonialism as a negative historical phenomenon. However, they tend to diverge from the populist evaluation of colonialism in three respects. First, they contend that colonialism had a number of positive consequences insofar as it included the "backward" parts of the world in the capitalist, industrial, and secular developments of "historically progressive" Western Europe. Second, for them European colonialism is not the defining feature of historical and political development in Africa. Finally, they do not feel that colonialism's major features are racial and cultural.

(6) In some ways the most telling difference between Leninism and populism is the stress placed by Leninists on the *general* features of social change. Here, as in many other instances, the difference is relative but defining. Lenin and Leninists have always stressed the need to interpret general principles in light of particular or national

*If one distinguishes between peasant institutions and selected peasant traditions and "virtues," this statement applies to Mao as much as any other Leninist.

conditions. In the post-Stalin period a central theme for regimes from North Korea to Yugoslavia has been the need to appreciate the many roads to socialism. Without ignoring the significance of ideological and political statements in Leninism about the importance of particular conditions, it is important to point out that historically Leninism has stressed the *general institutional and strategic* features of revolutionary socialist change. Writing in 1920, Lenin began his famous *"Left-Wing" Communism: An Infantile Disorder* with a section entitled "In What Sense We Can Speak of the International Significance of the Russian Revolution." In it he asserted that

> certain fundamental features of our revolution have a significance that is not local, or peculiarly national, or Russian alone, but international. I am not speaking here of international significance in the broad sense of the term: not merely several but all the primary features of our revolution, and many of its secondary features, are of international significance in the meaning of its effect on all countries. I am speaking of it in the narrowest sense of the word, taking international significance to mean the international validity or the historical inevitability of a repetition, on an international scale, of what has taken place in our country.[57]

Lenin went on to note that one shouldn't exaggerate this point beyond "certain fundamental features" of the Russian Revolution, but the thrust of the point is clear—the "fundamental features" are to be interpreted in "narrow" institutional-strategic terms, not "broad" symbolic terms. Leninism (like Roman Catholicism), while formally sensitive to the "particular," is biased in favor of the general—i. e., institutionally and strategically standard approaches to social change—while populism (like Protestantism) reverses the weightings.

The differential weighting of the general and particular features of social change that characterizes Leninist and populist elites is more than a matter of style. It directly affects the quality of populism and Leninism as modes of political organization and action, and raises for investigation the extent to which cross-national movements based on *standardized institutional and ideological formats* or those based on *a deliberate diversity of formats* are successful in bringing about social change.

The General and the Particular. There are periods in history when a standard institutional, ideological, and strategic format is authoritatively enforced across a number of diverse settings. More

often one finds periods of organizational diversity when no such authoritative format exists. There are some parallels in the realm of intellectual formulations. At times primary emphasis is placed on the need for and value of general theories, while at others there is a marked suspicion of such theories and a corresponding emphasis on analyzing the "trees" with little concern for conceptualizing the "forest."

Historically, the authoritative position and cross-national institutional standardization enforced by the Roman Catholic church, and more recently by Stalinist Russia, are striking instances of the dominant role of the "general," while the Protestant Reformation and the joint phenomenon of national communism and "populist socialism" are equally striking instances of the dominance of the "particular."*

For several reasons Western scholars are likely to prefer cross-national formats that are diverse in practice and principle. First, there is the association between diversity, pluralism, and democracy. Second, there is the historical association between the unique pattern of development in Western Europe and the oft-noted fact that from the fifth century on it lacked a long-standing, effective, and area-wide imperial structure. Weber, G. R. Elton, and most recently Wallerstein have argued convincingly that there is a direct and positive relationship between the historically innovative quality of social development in Western Europe and its diversified regional political structure.[58] Finally, there are experimental findings about leadership within small groups that indicate the relative absence of motivation and originality among the members of an authoritarian group.[59]

The association of authoritarian organization and social stagnation can be extended outside the social-psychological "laboratory." The consequences of a highly dogmatic, authoritarian institution failing to adequately consider the diversity of elite interests, resource bases, and cultural definitions in the varied environments in which it operates are clearly evident in the Catholic and Stalinist cases. The irrationalities (e. g., trying to literally replicate Soviet collectivization in Outer Mongolia)[60] and the obstacles to social, institutional, and policy innovation that organizations of this order created *at certain points in their development* are more than obvious.

*Currently political science is in a marked "particularization" phase—a pendulum-like reaction to the previous ahistorical-theoretical phase. These pendulum-like developments are not very fruitful: one baby and then the other suffers the same fate as the bath water.

However, for all their empirical and analytical value these observations are inadequate. Simply stated, one must ask *when* authoritatively enforced, standard institutional, strategic, and ideological formats favor innovation and when they don't. For example, how favorable a given format is to innovation will depend in part on what task elites see as critical to their development. Thus, in the social-psychological literature referred to above, "If the group is faced with a need for emergency action . . . authoritarian leadership is practically demanded under such circumstances."[61] Rather than categorically associate innovation with diversity of institutional and ideological formats, one should investigate to determine the occasions when an emphasis on the standard or general favors development as well as when it obstructs development (and when diversity obstructs development as well as when it favors it). For example, rather than simply seeing Protestantism (or national communism) as favoring a wide range of social innovations and Roman Catholicism (or Stalinism) as nothing but historical impediments to such innovations, two possibilities must be entertained.

First, there may well be a developmental relationship between the period of Roman Catholic (or Stalinist) standardization or generalization and the succeeding phase of Protestant (or national communist) diversification or particularization. It would be shortsighted not to consider the possibility (even likelihood) that many of the gains associated with the later developments would have been impossible without the earlier "standardized" developmental forms. This does not mean that developments from standardized to diversified formats are peaceful or automatic. *Quite the contrary*: the movement from one to the other format in both Christianity and Leninism has been a highly conflictual and even violent one. And the extent to which "later" developments toward diversification entail gains in certain values (e. g., personal liberty, national sovereignty) is dependent on a wide if bounded range of contingencies.

Second, one must consider the possibility that *at certain points in their history* elites that authoritatively impose standard or general institutional and ideological forms on a diversity of social and cultural settings are highly innovative. Here the questions should be: What innovative purposes does an organization emphasizing the cross-national quality of general definitions serve? When does it serve them and when not? To respond to the first question: For elites attempting to establish radically new forms of organization in hostile settings, there is a premium on *insulating* the new movements' fragile achievements by *concentrating* their scarce human and material

resources and *focusing* the loyalties and commitments of their memberships. In such situations a political and ideological orientation that emphasizes the general, cross-organizational, standard, and compulsory features of institutional and ideological life may indeed be innovative. One can make such an argument for both the Catholic church and Stalinist bloc at certain points in their development—when a non-local unit of mutual identification and support (i. e., Rome and Moscow) facilitated elite differentiation and social transformation in diverse local settings.

To respond to the second question: General institutional formats depend for their innovative quality on an unequal distribution of power within the movement. However, the potentially most powerful representative of the movement (i. e., a Rome or Moscow) must be limited in the extent to which it can equate cross-national commitment to standard institutional definitions with the uncritical acceptance by "associate" elites of its political interests as their own. Such a limitation depends on the *inability* of the potentially most powerful representative to fully realize that potential, and the related ability of "associate" elites to control to some extent a major uncertainty—ideological, military, economic, political—affecting the development of the potentially most powerful representative of their "bloc."

Should the potentially most powerful representative of the movement realize its potential and others lose their local bases of power, then the shared commitment to an ideology (or religion) that stresses the value and necessity of a cross-national standard institutional format and set of practices will lead to a situation where shared commitment to the general institutional features of development becomes shared subordination not only to the specific institutional features but also the specific political interests of the bloc's dominant representative. In all these respects the histories of *Roman* Catholicism and *Soviet* Leninism are pertinent.

From this discussion a number of conclusions can be drawn. *First*, at present in the intellectual and political worlds there is an indiscriminate emphasis on theoretical and political formats that emphasize the particular and diverse against the general and standard. *Second*, one should avoid categorically identifying movements like Leninism that stress the general features of development at the institutional—not simply symbolic—level with lack of innovative power, and movements like populism that stress the value of particular modes of development with such innovative power. *Third* (as has happened elsewhere, so in Africa), the creation of effective political

organizations integrated with social constituencies offering appropriate support for programs of social, cultural, and economic change may depend at a certain developmental point on the appearance of a regional hegemon(s) able to insulate, concentrate, and focus resources of various types, and overcome the diversities that in some respects work against regional and national development. *Hegemony, not self-reliance or regional federation, may be the major condition for development within a country and region at critical points.* Regarding *national* development, Karl Deutsch has emphasized the significance of "core" areas such as Paris in France, Prussia in Germany, and New England in the United States. "Cores" have a "surplus" of resources—e. g., administrative, military, economic, and cultural—that facilitate the emergence of a nation in a given area at a given time.[62] I want to extend this point by arguing that *supranational ideologies like Christianity, liberalism, and Leninism became internationally effective political forces because at critical points a single core power—Rome, Great Britain, and the Soviet Union— monopolized their strategic and institutional meanings.* To be sure, the means, bases, and extent of such control varied significantly in each case. But that shouldn't prevent one from appreciating what underlay the political success of Christianity, liberalism, and Leninism at critical points in their history—i. e., a monopoly over the institutional definition of the ideology by a hegemon with a "surplus" of power and prestige, and a "minimum" of effectively organized competition from ideologically related rivals. *Fourth,* the importance of a hegemonic core is only partially appreciated by African elites, as their reference to Pan-African symbols suggests. What they give with one hand they take back with the other when they insert the proviso that African unity in no way affect their national sovereignty. *Fifth,* while hegemony of a particular power (rather than regional confederation) may at a certain point be a condition for sustained and successful development in Africa, this does not mean that the appearance of a hegemon(s) is inevitable, *or* that should it appear it would be a Leninist hegemon. *Sixth,* it would seem that an ideology like populism that politically and ideologically emphasizes the particular, and limits general considerations to those of a symbolic order, works against the emergence of cross-national organizations with the inclination and capacity to play a hegemonic role, and may thus work against the radical transformation many African elites are formally committed to.

We now have one of the two elements necessary to get a better

"fix" on the political identity of self-designated "scientific socialist" regimes—an analytic contrast of populist and Leninist features. If one considers the case of Guinea (and its leader Sékou Touré)—a "scientific socialist" regime with a very elaborate set of ideological pronouncements and a long radical history—the utility of such a contrast becomes clear. For all of the rhetorical emphasis Touré places on class war, cultural revolution, dialectical materialism, and vanguard party, he and his regime appear to be radically populist—not Leninist or "scientific socialist." According to R. W. Johnson (whose analyses of the Guinean regime are consistently marked by detailed knowledge and sensitivity to context), "Touré's conception of socialism [has] remained essentially idealist." While Touré, unlike Cabral and Nyerere, has gradually adopted the position that class struggle is a central feature of domestic and international change, and at one point was even intent on discussing dialectical materialism, he has remained committed to the idea that "the socialist revolution is first and foremost a heightened consciousness, a willing determination to see the good of all." Touré's "Stalinist"-like purges and "Maoist"-like mobilization of students and extra-party organizations have taken place in the absence of sustained efforts to transform or break through major sociocultural institutions. Collectivization in Guinea, in both its 1960 and 1975 incarnations, has apparently failed. In part this is due to resource constraints: "[Touré's] regime is almost certainly too rickety and fragile for him to attempt such measures against the kulaks of the Fouta Djalon." However, the failures of measures like collectivization also appear to be linked to the "ideological limits [Touré] has set himself." These limits express themselves in several ways: in the use of ideology to "disadvantage members of certain social groups in their public and political activities . . . as an instrument of control over individuals rather than groups"; in the notion that development depends most on the "radicalisation of language and the development of psychological conditions"; in the greater antipathy toward educated elites than "hostile" social classes (an antipathy clearly revealed in the "Teachers' Plot"); and in the emphasis on Guinea's "particular" experience (which helps account for Johnson's observation that Touré's "often scathing clarity frequently deserts him when faced with the problem of conceptualising or analysing original or purely Guinean phenomena"). In short, Touré is a radical populist—not a Leninist revolutionary.[63]*

*Jean Suret-Canale examines the many factors leading to the attacks on

One can find related features in the Ethiopian, Somali, Congolese, and Beninois elites, strengthening the presumption that these elites also are populist not Leninist.* However, to refer back to the Egyptian case, while one could be more or less clear about the Nasser regime's political identity by noting the political and ideological tenets it emphasized and rejected, only in a crisis situation, such as existed in 1967, could the analyst—and in a real sense the elite itself—be certain. Having a clear concept of the political and ideological features of populist and Leninist elites is valuable insofar as it provides *initial clues* about an elite's political identity—i. e., how it is likely to respond to crises. But an adequate test of a regime's political identity also rests with a clear conceptualization and empirical investigation of the types of choice environments it faces.

III. POLITICAL UNAWARENESS AND CHOICE ENVIRONMENTS

In important respects all self-designated "scientific socialist" elites in Africa face easy-choice situations. Let me be clear as to what I mean by this. I do *not* mean that any of these elites face easy situations. All of them confront enormously difficult problems with inadequate resources. What I mean is that, difficult as these problems are, *at present* they do not require these elites to respond in an either-or fashion to the practical implications of their formal ideological designations.

In their international environments, contemporary African (or Middle Eastern) elites who designate themselves as revolutionary or "scientific socialist" do not confront an either-or political choice between East and West. The post-World War II emergence of "third world" and North-South dimensions makes it possible for them to avoid hard political identity choices. The current groupings in international politics provide African "scientific socialist" elites with an international reference group—the third world—that, at a minimum, symbolically supports their avoidance of an exclusive or even primary *organizational* identification with the "socialist camp" even as they reject identifying with the West.

and political demise of the chieftaincy in Guinea. The hostility shown by Touré and the PDG toward this traditional political elite stratum is consistent with our interpretation of the Touré regime as radical populist (see "The End of Chieftancy in Guinea," *Journal of African History* 7, 3 [1966] : 459-93).

*Even more so than in Guinea, where (as in Angola and Mozambique) the elite has had occasion over a long period of time to familiarize itself more with Communist organizations and ideology.

In addition to a *multi-dimensional* international order (in which North-South identifications complement East-West ones) that favors easy over hard identity choices, there are developments in the realm of ideology that work in the same direction. No longer must an aspiring revolutionary of the left rely solely on Marx, Lenin, and Mao. In recent years, Fanon, Cabral, and in an important respect Fidel Castro*—with their stress on the uniqueness of each national situation, the centrality of culture and colonialism, and the primary significance of the third world—have been afforded at least equal status.

Ironically, developments in the Communist world also contribute to the existence of an easy-choice international environment. The absence of a single authoritative Leninist state capable of setting and enforcing an internationally "correct line" means that self-designation as a Leninist or "scientific socialist" regime has no real political consequences. For various reasons the Soviet Union is unwilling and/or unable to enforce (or even loudly assert) its "papal" convictions, while the United States finds it more difficult to immediately intervene wherever an elite designates itself "scientific socialist" or Leninist. There is no longer an obligatory Leninist model—or automatic American threat. If one adds to this the desire of Leninist regimes such as the Chinese, Romanian, Yugoslav, and North Korean to retain their political and ideological sovereignty— a desire that leads them to argue vociferously against the reappearance of a powerful center and obligatory model[64] —the "contribution" of the Communist world to an easy-choice international environment for African "scientific socialists" is substantial.

Finally, one must take into account the Soviet Union's current stage of *national* development. At one point the Soviet elite identified the success of its own institutional and ideological development with the enforced replication of Soviet features in parties and regimes identified as Leninist. This appears to have changed in part because the Soviet Union is politically and militarily unable in most cases to demand conformity with Soviet practice from self-designated "scientific socialist" elites, and also because the Soviets now see their material and ideal interests best served if these elites adopt gradualist programs of political change *and* link themselves directly with the Soviet (and East European) economies.[65]

When one looks at the domestic environments of African "scientific socialist" elites, the idea that these are easy-choice en-

*As I shall point out below, references to Fidel Castro's position are likely to diminish in frequency and be limited to his pre-1969 statements.

vironments seems at best ignorant, at worse perverse. However, if one maintains the distinction between an easy situation and easy-choice situation, it is neither. While these regimes face serious economic, technical, social, and cultural obstacles, *the very obstacles that make certain types of development impossible make other types of development unnecessary*. For example, the near complete absence of industrially based socioeconomic strata possessing politically relevant resources, occupying distinct institutional bases, and making demands that don't readily allow for symbolic or cooptive individual responses means that African "scientific socialist" elites lack the environmental incentive and opportunity to fully understand or act—positively or negatively—on the organizational and strategic implications of their formal revolutionary designations.

In short, African "scientific socialist" elites do not confront hard-choice situations internationally or domestically. Rather than forcing them to come to grips with the incompatible features and strategic implications of their political and ideological orientations, their environments favor continued unawareness of such and continued ability to avoid making hard (political identity) choices. By contrast, an examination of the choice environments that Mao Tse-tung confronted in the interwar period may highlight the type of situation that favors increasingly conscious, exclusive, substantial, and high-risk identity choices. Initially, Mao (and Ho Chi Minh) were as unclear about the practical implications of Leninism as many contemporary African "scientific socialists." No Leninist emerges fully formed from reading *What Is to Be Done?*—a point that should emphasize the situationally contingent quality of Leninist political and ideological developments.

To understand Mao's (and Ho's) political development, one must look to the environments they operated in—environments that forced hard choices. *The starting point must be the differences between the post-World War I and post-World War II periods*. It is difficult today to appreciate the impact the October Revolution had on radical Chinese and Vietnamese nationalists like Mao and Ho.[66] In the aftermath of World War I, they viewed the Bolshevik victory in Russia as an heroic challenge to the colonial system. The Soviet Union was not a global superpower; rather it was seen as the most dramatic national challenge to the international system of colonialism. There was no "third world" or "third world" international organizations that could act as alternative political and ideological frames of reference for radical nationalists, nor were there any

alternative Leninist models.* Internationally, the choices of radical alignment and identification were much more limited than in the 1950's and 1960's. Domestic developments also worked in favor of hard political choices. By the late 1920's, Chiang's policies within the Koumintang and China confronted Mao with exclusive choices, while the impact of foreign invasion, commercialization in rural areas, and some industrial development created new mass constituencies potentially available to a Leninist party.

Finally, one must be sensitive to the stage of Soviet national development during the 1930's and 1940's. This was precisely the period when under Stalin the Soviet regime placed a marked, even absolute, stress on the transnational adoption of common institutional and ideological features. It is not enough to point to the "particular" or unique qualities of the Chinese (or Vietnamese) revolutions. In their development one must be equally sensitive to what at certain points and in major respects was seen by Chinese and Vietnamese leaders as their authoritative referent—the Soviet model. Unlike contemporary African "scientific socialist" elites, the Chinese and Vietnamese had a less diverse set of "left" ideological formulations to choose from. They had a single and authoritative international political referent demanding conformity, and domestic incentives as well as occasion to act practically on their ideological tenets.[67]†

In light of the heterogeneous and often conflicting ideological orientations of African "scientific socialist" elites (e. g., Fanonist-populist, Leninist, and religious), the absence of any state referent able to authoritatively establish institutional and strategic if not policy standards, and the lack of social and material resources to

---

*While this was true of the immediate post-World War I period, by the 1930's fascism began to offer itself to some as an attractive radical alternative to Leninism. In fact during the 1930's some adherents of fascism saw Stalin, Hitler, and Mussolini in much the same terms. For a relevant case see Lloyd E. Eastman's discussion of the Blue Shirts in *The Abortive Revolution: China under Nationalist Rule 1927-1937* (Cambridge, Mass.: Harvard University Press, 1974), pp. 31-85.

†Again one must note the variation that exists in the experience of African "scientific socialist" elites. The difference between Mozambique and Benin is profound with respect both to elite familiarity and connection with European Communist organizations and to guerrilla experience and consequent opportunity to "operationalize" and clarify ideological tenets. However, one should still be prudent about any conclusions regarding the political identity of the elite in Mozambique. One would have to know a great deal more about the scope and intensity of social and political mobilization in Mozambique, and the heterogeneity-homogeneity of political preferences within the elite.

act on their formal political and ideological commitments, one has every reason to doubt that the "scientific socialist" or "Leninist" language employed by African elites *is politically substantial in any revolutionary sense*. I have already suggested that the appropriation of Leninist terminology serves several elite purposes ranging from attempted increases in status, to being more politically visible and intelligible to Communist powers, to helping differentiate and *perhaps* bond an unestablished elite attempting to provide itself with a minimally coherent and common identity. However, none of these purposes is revolutionary. Still, one finds arguments that "scientific socialist" *language* serves revolutionary purposes in Africa. Recently Conor Cruise O'Brien suggested that "Marxist rhetoric can buttress the legitimacy acquired by transition, by bonding the new ruling class—including inter-tribal bonding, providing it with a dialect of rule, with the means of inculcating its legitimacy and the dialect which upholds it into those whose education it controls . . . it permits group flexibility in practice, together with an impressive style and vocabulary for the denunciation of those who criticize any course of action the rulers may decide on."[68] Where O'Brien speaks of the (possible) intra-elite bonding function or the value of a new language as a political weapon against elite opponents, there is little to disagree with. However, where he suggests that political language per se can provide inter-tribal bonding and inculcate elite legitimacy through education, one finds a measure of intellectual idealism that parallels the political idealism of many African "scientific socialist" elites.

One finds a similar argument in David Laitin's article on Somalia in this volume. He also suggests the value of "scientific socialist" language may be more semiotic than programmatic.[69] The same criticism applies to both authors—i. e., without institutional transformations that relegate traditional cultural meanings and social practices to the private and out of the public sphere, and without ideological tenets such as class war that provide the political incentive and strategic disposition to do so, the effective meanings and consequences of "scientific socialist" language in these societies will diverge fundamentally from their supposed meanings and consequences. "Scientific socialist" or Leninist rhetoric *may* indicate the developmental mission these African elites have chosen. However, as Selznick observes, "the mission of an organization cannot be adequately defined without also determining (a) its basic methods, the main tools or ways of acting with which it should be identified, and (b) its place among organizations that carry on related activities. . . . An institutional role

cannot be won by merely wishing for it or by verbalizing it clear-ly."[70]* As it happens, African "scientific socialist" elites have neither verbalized their political mission very clearly nor adopted strategies consistent with their formal ideological and political designations.

The logical question to ask is: What types of developments would lead to greater elite awareness of the incompatibilities in their current definitions of ideological mission and political role, and lessen their ability to avoid the practical or strategic implications of their political self-designation? Or more succinctly: What sort of developments might favor hard political choices by African "scientific socialist" elites?

One such development would be a more tightly organized Communist world. Two recent events are significant in this regard. The first is the hard political choice made by Fidel Castro in the aftermath of the Czechoslovak invasion. From that point on Castro began to align himself more strictly with the Soviet Union.[71] The second is Vietnam's decision in 1978 to join the Soviet-sponsored Comecon. These two actions are important because Cuba and Vietnam are the Leninist regimes with the greatest symbolic and political significance to most African "scientific socialist" regimes. Presumably, in the international environment at least, Cuba and Vietnam's closer identification with the Soviet Union has reduced the easy-choice quality of African "scientific socialist" elite political identification. However, while significant, the "hardening" impact of Cuba and Vietnam's moves should be lessened by (among other things) the continuation, proliferation, and exacerbation of political and military conflicts within the "socialist camp."

A second recent development that should favor hard over easy choices is the "new colonialism" in Africa. Cuban, French, and Soviet actions can quite plausibly be seen as favoring more categoric political responses from African elites. However, the qualification in this instance refers to the content of these hard choices. Should they be made, the likelihood is that they will be more racially or ethnically populist than Leninist.

There are also potential domestic developments that bear on the likelihood of hard choices having to be made. Failure to achieve

*Selznick's contention that "an institutional role cannot be won by merely wishing for it" is almost a restatement of Lenin's comment that "socialism is not a figment of the imagination" in "'Left-Wing' Childishness and the Petty-Bourgeois Mentality," in *Collected Works*, 27 (Moscow: Progress Publishers, 1965), p. 350.

international status, secure aid, bring about economic development, and/or enhance a country's regional position may favor consideration of harder political and ideological choices, but *developmental failures—while threatening particular incumbent elites—do not provide the social or economic base for substantial political alternatives, or lessen the tendency to adopt quasi-magical political and ideological facades.* On the other hand, should (or as) some of these countries develop socially and economically, then hard choices are likely to become the order of the day. At that point those elites formally designated as "scientific socialist" are likely to face socioeconomic constituencies and developmental issues *calling for more exclusive and allowing for more substantial strategic choices.* It is in anticipation of this situation that the Soviet Union currently limits its criticisms of "heretical" radical regimes in Africa. At the point when African elites must and can make more exclusive and substantial sociopolitical choices, the Soviets want to influence some of those elites and some of those choices. At the point when political choices become substantial—not simply rhetorical—the Soviet concern is that Africa become more East European than Latin American.

Another potentially major impetus for making hard political identity choices would be the appearance of an indigenous and powerful regional hegemon in Africa, a state with a surplus of some valuable resource—organizational, economic, or military. Such a state's appearance would create a crisis for many elites. Should a Leninist regional hegemon appear in Africa, this would force neighboring and weaker elites to either sharply *dissociate* themselves from "scientific socialism" in an attempt to avoid de facto political subordination, or *substantiate* their formally radical commitments by drawing on the greater resources of the hegemon and/or more distant Leninist powers.*

IV. CONCLUSION

The gap between the rhetoric and practice of African "scientific socialist" elites is due only in part to resource constraints. *It*

---

*In this context, recent developments in Ethiopia are significant—not because Ethiopia will inevitably become a stable Leninist regional hegemon. There is no inevitability that it will become any of these things. In fact on the basis of what is known about Mengistu, it appears he would favor the role of Chiang Kai-shek more than Mao Tse-tung. Ethiopian developments are significant because whatever their outcome they will be a shaping influence on the political choice environments of many African elites.

also reflects the reciprocal influence of populist ideology and easy-choice environments. While all self-designated "scientific socialist" elites confront extremely difficult problems, none is faced with hard-choice environments. Should they develop, these elites will be faced with political choices of a more exclusive order. The cases of Sultan-Galiev in the Soviet Union and Fidel Castro in Cuba are excellent illustrations of two likely directions initial responses to a change in choice environments may take.

Sultan-Galiev was a Tatar Communist who became Stalin's protegé in the Commissariat of Nationalities. He became "the most important Moslem in the entire Soviet hierarchy and had acquired a unique position from which to influence the Eastern policies of the Communist regime."[72] Galiev argued that Communist efforts should be focused on the East, not on Europe, and should be more accommodating to the religious convictions of the Moslem population. By the early 1920's he was arguing that "the war against the imperialism of industrialized societies, not the war against the bourgeoisie . . . was the real conflict for universal liberation." Not the dictatorship of the proletariat over the bourgeoisie but rather "the establishment of the dictatorship of the colonies and semi-colonies over the metropolitan areas" was the goal.[73] Galiev moved on to political demands "by advocating the creation of a Colonial International which would unite all the victims of colonial exploitation and would counterbalance the Third International, dominated by Western elements. He also desired the establishment of a Soviet Moslem (or Turkic) republic and the revival of the Moslem Communist Party." In Pipes's words: "At this point the heavy hand of party discipline fell on his shoulder."[74]

The easy-choice environment that at first "supported" Sultan-Galiev's unawareness or avoidance of the incompatibilities in his political and ideological commitments was superseded in the early 1920's by the emergence of a hard-choice Soviet political environment—one that forced him to become more ideologically aware and to make more exclusive political commitments. He did both and became more and more of a radical national (Moslem) populist.

Like Sultan-Galiev, Fidel Castro also enjoyed an easy-choice situation during the first decade of his rule. Self-designation as a Leninist did not critically affect the latitude he enjoyed in defining the institutional and strategic features of Cuban policy—definitions with a markedly idealist, populist, and "particular" thrust. For Castro the critical year was 1968. Cuban economic developments, the direction of the Vietnamese war, and defeats in Latin America

coagulated around the Soviet invasion of Czechoslovakia. The result was apparent in Castro's speech at the Algiers Conference in 1973 when he denounced the "circumstantial unalignment" of the "third world" and the identification of the Soviet Union as an aggressive superpower, argued for closer identification of the unaligned with the Soviet Union, and stressed the historic significance of the October Revolution.[75] After 1968 Castro was faced with a set of choice environments that demanded greater political awareness of the practical implications of his ideological self-designation, and in that situation the weight of his responses was more Leninist than populist.

Should hard-choice environments emerge, *initial* developments in African "scientific socialist" regimes are likely to range from Galiev- to Castro-like in character. The particular pattern of choices will vary according to whether or not regional hegemons appear, their political character, the pattern of international alignments, the political and ideological makeup of national coalitions, and the level and quality of socioeconomic development in a given country. My purpose in this article has been to offer some general analytic leverage to those better equipped than I to deal with those particular outcomes.

SOMALIA'S MILITARY GOVERNMENT AND SCIENTIFIC SOCIALISM

David D. Laitin

On October 20, 1970—one year after his successful *coup d'etat* in Somalia—President Maxamed Siyaad Barre announced:

> In our Revolution we believe that we have broken the chain of a consumer economy based on imports, and we are free to decide our destiny. And in order to realise the interests of the Somali people; their achievement of a better life, the full development of their potentialities and the fulfillment of their aspirations, we solemnly declare Somalia to be a Socialist State.[1]

Siyaad then made a frenetic trip throughout his country explaining to the people, as best he could, what "scientific socialism" meant for them. He articulated its goals and attempted to show how socialism was consistent with military rule, with Somali traditional values, and with the state religion of Islam. Economic enterprises were nationalized, foreign policy was altered to be more eastward looking, large numbers of Russian and Chinese military and civilian technicians were invited to help with Somali development, and Somalis began to call each other "comrade" (*jaalle—lit.*, playmate or team-member).

On June 27, 1976—after nearly seven years of rule by a Supreme Military Council—Siyaad announced the creation of a socialist party in which he would serve as First Secretary. As Somalia begins to chart a new course in its socialist development, it will be useful to evaluate its socialist experience thus far, in which certain trends can be clearly identified. In this article I will discuss those trends and will suggest that scientific socialism—understood as a *programmatic* ideal for economic and political development—has had little impact on political choice in Somalia. The failure to achieve the

---

This is a revised version of a paper delivered at the annual meeting of the American Political Science Association, Chicago, 1976. It was written before hostilities began in the Ogaden desert, and before the Russian military advisors were expelled from the Somali Republic.

major transformation required by socialist ideology has been so overdetermined by Somali bureaucratic, organizational, and cultural constraints that no further explanation (e.g., "the ideology was ill-formulated") is needed.

I will therefore propose that analysts of the socialist experience in Somalia look at socialism not as program but rather as *semiotic*. If socialism is analyzed as program, the analyst examines the extent to which policies fulfill their goals. If socialism is analyzed as semiotic, the analyst examines the extent to which, through the creation of symbols, new goals begin to be shared among the people. When programmatic failure has been overdetermined, the study of the creation of utopias through symbolic manipulation can be of value.

I. SCIENTIFIC SOCIALISM AS PROGRAM

The civilian regime which attained independence in Somalia in 1960 operated in a tumultuous environment. The nation was linguistically, religiously, and ethnically homogeneous, but the Somali people had a long tradition of resisting authority—both foreign and indigenous. The Somalis had an equally long tradition of democratic participation, however, and adapted easily to the institutional democracy "granted" them—a bastard child of English and Italian institutions. In this very lively political environment, parties proliferated, propaganda pamphlets were disseminated with only minimal censorship, parliamentary debate was vociferous, and parliamentary seats were usually available to the highest bidder. That almost nothing ever got done—that, for example, foreign aid grants were used to line the pockets of ministers, government-procured medicines were sold at local pharmacies, and civil servants were rarely at their desks—seemed to bother only Somalis. Most Western observers saw in Somalia a model of democratic performance, with its changes in government based on electoral returns and healthy internal debate.

The military intervened in 1969 only after the civilian institutions collapsed under the weight of their own talk. In October 1969 President Cabdurashiid Cali Sharma'arke was assassinated, and Prime Minister Maxamad Ibraahiim Cigaal, then on a state visit to the United States, quickly returned home. The Parliament, after hours of debate, was unable to set up a new government which could have any real claim to legitimacy, and the military, long disgusted with civilian performance, staged a *coup d'etat*.

The first year of military rule was dominated by a campaign

against corruption, and each former minister was scrutinized carefully concerning his use of public funds. This campaign, referred to as "accounting without shame," uncovered a wide range of offenses against a people who were among the poorest in the world. But no regime can survive for long on uncovering the sins of its predecessors; eventually, after the sins of the past have been exposed, the regime must be judged on its own merits. With this thought in mind, Siyaad announced the commitment to socialism on the first anniversary of the "revolution."

Because the term "socialism" has so many different meanings, it is difficult to assess a socialist program. Since Siyaad's "scientific socialism" has elements of Soviet influence based on present alliances, of Fabian influence based on intellectual currents throughout Africa from the colonial period, and of "national socialist" influence based on Mussolini's vision of "La Grande Somalia" and Siyaad's early contacts with the Italians, an assessment is even more difficult. In addition, the notion of "class," which is so central to socialist analysis, is virtually irrelevant to Somalia. As President Siyaad has noted: "Our [Somalia's] enemies are hunger, disease, ignorance, colonialism, and a few Somalis who, although they have no capital, yet believe in the capitalist ideology. They are as poor as the rest of us but their ideology is wrong."[2] Ideas about how to develop an economy, not relationships of production, are the key to understanding political action in Somalia.

Despite the difficulties in defining socialism, there are some general criteria for judging socialist development. First, it is to be expected that a socialist country will attempt through government ownership of the means of production (and hence popular control and government planning) to avoid economic development which is beneficial to a single person or small group at the expense of the masses. Popular sovereignty over the market, with a keen distrust of Adam Smith's "invisible hand," is the first benchmark of socialism. Second, it is to be expected that a socialist state will actively pursue egalitarian policies. Socialists have always been very concerned about social equality: their distrust of the "invisible hand" is based on the conclusion that the free market makes the rich richer and the poor poorer. Third, based largely on the Soviet socialist experience, it is to be expected that any socialist experiment (and especially those in the third world) will emphasize rapid economic growth. As Nyerere has frequently observed, equality in poverty cannot be a goal of socialism.[3] Fourth, it is to be expected that any socialist state will begin to disengage from the world capi-

176

talist economy, which by virtue of its reliance on the free market could wreak havoc on any program to establish a socialist society. Fifth, and finally, it is to be expected that under "scientific socialism" there will be continual ideological analysis and refinement. It is assumed that only through "scientific" ideological methodology can any socialist leadership group know when the time is ripe for the various steps associated with socialist development.

In summary, then, popular control of the means of production, egalitarianism, rapid economic growth, disengagement from world capitalism, and ideological refinement are the essential parts of a program of scientific socialism. The performance of any self-proclaimed scientific socialist state can be evaluated on the basis of the degree to which it fulfills this program. It is to the evaluation of the Somali socialist experience that we now turn.

A. POPULAR CONTROL OVER THE MEANS OF PRODUCTION

Socialist economic theory generally interrelates three components—public ownership of the means of production, worker participation in industrial management, and centralized control of the marketplace. We will discuss each of these components separately.

In Somalia, government ownership of various economic sectors has been effected through nationalization. Thus banks, insurance companies, petroleum distribution firms, schools, and the sugar-refining plant have been nationalized, and national agencies have been created for construction materials and foodstuffs.

On the other hand, small shopowners are frequently reassured that socialism does not mean the end of small private enterprise, and that their investments will be protected. Similarly, camel owners have been told that the government will not interfere in their sector either: they are considered to be workers rather than capitalists (even though camels are still the chief indicator of wealth in Somalia). In addition, Siyaad has stated—primarily for Western consumption—that the banana plantations can remain in private hands "in so far as they continue to contribute to our national development."[4] The two major export items, then—bananas and livestock—are still under private ownership.

In this matter, Siyaad's regime is conforming to the pattern set by most mixed economies in today's world. A year after he declared Somalia a socialist state, Siyaad made this statement at Muqdisho's annual trade fair:

Because the first year of the Revolution brought a period of change to the country's affairs, there was perhaps some justification for suspicion among [the businessmen]. But since that time the Revolution has made it clear that "clean business" had nothing to fear. In fact, we have made several appeals to businessmen to invest their money in this country.[5]

More than mere appeals have been made. As reported in *Africa*:

The present investment code restricts the right of transfer home of profits in any one year to 15 per cent of the capital initially invested in the business, while in case the profits do not reach that level the difference can be added to the remittance over a period of three years.[6]

Revolutionary socialist rhetoric aside, then, the Somali government's position on local capitalist enterprise and foreign direct investment seems to be "reformist capitalist" with a few symbolic nationalizations. Furthermore, these nationalizations occur at points of high visibility or in connection with discoveries of unethical practices—not as part of a planned development program.

Nationalization can mean "state capitalism" rather than "socialism" if the workers in the nationalized enterprises are not active participants in the managerial process. It is not enough that government bureaucrats rather than private entrepreneurs run an enterprise if the effects for the workers in that enterprise are to be more than minimal. Therefore the Siyaad regime has attempted to adorn its governmental apparatus with all the accoutrements of modern revolutionary socialism. National guidance or "orientation" centers have been established throughout the country to disseminate socialist ideas; young Somalis are recruited into a revolutionary task force known as the "Victory Pioneers," who are vigilantes in the city, arbitrators in disputes among neighbors, and initiators of self-help schemes; a fascist-built military camp now called "Halane" has been turned into a reorientation center where government officials and would-be officials go through paramilitary and ideological training to make them better socialists. The orientation centers, Victory Pioneers, and Halane are meant to bring the government closer to the people, so that the administration of programs and nationalized industry will reflect the workers' views. But as in all participation schemes under an authoritarian regime, participation is used more to control the masses than to respond to its initiatives.

More significant than the participation in orientation and re-

orientation centers are the numerous self-help schemes. From a socialist point of view, the most interesting of these is the sand-dune stabilization project. The coastal sand dunes had been moving inexorably inland, had begun to encroach upon some of the better farmland in Somalia, and were threatening the major road connection from the capital (Muqdisho) to the south. The government "recruited" a permanent work force for this project (as for others of a similar nature), and temporary workers were requested to help out on Fridays, the Islamic day of rest. The project caught the imagination of the white-collar workers in Muqdisho, and soon many other Somalis—from the President to the bureaucrat to the nomad—could be seen, tool in hand, shoveling sand. A truly classless society was together doing battle with nature. One Somali observed that "here is the true fusion of socialist theory and practice." But not all self-help schemes have enhanced the socialist ideology. Since local administrators derive status from having self-help schemes in their districts, many went to the clan councils in the bush to collect camels—a traditional mode of taxation (*nabadon*). They then used the money derived from this tax to get projects constructed. While the nomads saw themselves as exploited by the regime, the administrators advertised these projects as nomadic self-help.[7] The central government has dirty hands in this business as well; as was noted in a recent British private security report: "Jail terms await those who fail to volunteer."[8]

Another major inducement to obtain worker participation is related to language reform. Although it is a linguistically homogeneous state, Somalia could not—for political, religious, and technical reasons—agree upon an orthography for its language. In government administration, therefore, it was necessary to rely on the languages of foreign contact—English, Italian, and Arabic—which few Somalis spoke and in which nearly all were illiterate. The administration of the state in languages not indigenous to the state was a barrier against citizen participation. On the second anniversary of the Revolution, the Supreme Revolutionary Council stipulated a script for the Somali language, and Somali soon became the official language of the republic. This decision opened the possibility of popular control of citizens and workers over the state bureaucracy.[9] A major literacy campaign was undertaken, which involved closing the secondary schools for a year so that the students could teach the new script to the nomads. This was an invitation for worker participation, but both this campaign and the sand-dune stabilization project are examples of widening the scope of government control

179

rather than examples of extending popular control over the means of production.

A central component of socialist economics is government planning. As most critics of laissez-faire capitalism are quick to point out, the free market operates not rationally but randomly, and often rewards individuals at the expense of the society. One example of the irrationality of free market forces in pre-revolutionary Somalia involves a milk factory built with Russian aid. The factory, which homogenized cow's milk, would have been profitable if most Somali herders had brought their milk to it for processing. But they did not, with the result that the factory had a very low scale of operation and could not afford to pay a decent price for raw milk.* The factory almost ceased to function, and the urban populations were obliged to pay more for unhomogenized milk in the milk markets than they would have paid for homogenized milk in the factory outlets if all the herders had brought their milk to the factory. In addition, the herders would have received more for their milk if all had sold directly to the factory. None could break the irrational cycle in the marketplace, however, because any herder would suffer if he acted first. The revolutionary government acted to make the government-owned enterprise profitable by forcing all herders to sell to the factory and by closing the open milk market.

A second example of the irrationality of the "free market" suggests that if it were allowed to operate in Somalia without constraint, the nomadic population would have destroyed itself. It was rational for nomadic groups to dig wells and line them with concrete in order to have semi-permanent water supplies. Unfortunately, too many of these wells were dug, depleting the water table and severely reducing the grazing opportunities for livestock. (While it was rational for *some* nomadic groups to build wells, it was irrational for *all* of them to do so.) This problem, along with the serious drought of the early 1970's, led the government to attempt to induce the nomads to become peasants. Resettling a nomadic population, proud of its calling, into agricultural areas and an activity most nomads scorn is no easy task, but the severity of the drought (and the legitimacy of his revolutionary regime) has

---

*Somali nomads believed that use of the factory-distributed milk containers would kill the cows, and Somali urbanites maintained that factory-processed milk had no flavor. Both arguments are spurious. While the milk loses the charcoal flavor which comes from the lining inside the traditional containers, I can attest that it approaches ambrosia. If the Somalis want true ambrosia, camel's milk—which does not have to be homogenized—is available in the bush.

given Siyaad considerable resources to effect this change. Stopping activity which is individually beneficial but socially destructive is the essence of socialist action.

While the Somali government has become involved in the development of national economic plans, its intervention in the free market is more in keeping with the demands of the early socialists. But such intervention is now characteristic of government in all mixed economies, and need not have scientific socialism as its ideological basis. The Somali government has become more active in economic activity, and Somali workers are supposedly participating more in production decisions, but the relationship of workers to the productive process in Somalia has changed little since the declaration of socialism.

B. SOCIAL EQUALITY

For Somali males, the traditional Somali social structure was quintessentially egalitarian. Any Somali man had the right to participate in governing councils, and wit and poetic skill rather than designated authority roles were the key to political influence. The lack of deference by Somalis to governmental authorities has attracted the attention of many foreign observers, and the leading English-speaking ethnographer of the Somalis—I. M. Lewis—considers egalitarianism to be a core element in understanding Somali society.[10]

Modern institutional forms have been in part responsible for the emergence of social stratifications in Somalia. Two sources of stratification have been especially distressing to Somalis: (1) the differences between the life chances of urban dwellers and those of bush dwellers and (2) the difference between job opportunities for residents in the former British protectorate of Somaliland (the northern region) and those for residents in the former Italian colony and then trusteeship territory of Somalia (the southern region). Important steps have been taken by the revolutionary regime to eliminate both these differences. To the extent that socialism entails a commitment to inhibit social stratification, the military regime's definition of its objectives is consistent with socialist ideology.[11]

While 86 percent of the Somali people are engaged in either nomadic or agricultural life, and only about 14 percent are urban residents, most of the benefits obtained under the civilian regime went to the cities. The nomads were virtually ignored: they received no economic aid, and the government invested few resources in

attempting to exert its authority in the bush or to put an end to clan warfare. By contrast, the socialist government has emphasized equality, as a comparison of the development (capital) budgets in the pre- and post-revolutionary governments clearly indicates. In Table 1, the non-recurrent expenditures of the two governments on development programs in agriculture, fisheries, forestry, animal husbandry, and irrigation are distinguished from those in industry (which have primarily an urban impact). The post-revolutionary regime has reversed the priorities. In the 1963-68 period, there was approximately 33 percent more investment in industry than in agriculture, etc., while in the 1971-73 period of Siyaad's tenure, two-and-a-half times more development money went into the rural programs than into industry. Similar changes were made in the design of a new electrical power grid. The original design would have augmented capacity in the three major cities, but the socialist government began to decentralize the grid "in line with our socialist principles that the benefit of electricity facilities be spread to cover the maximum number possible in an effort to reduce the gap between urban and rural areas."[12]

When the program of the Somali Revolutionary Socialist Party was announced (August 1976), matters of industry, trade, and capital were discussed, but they were given low priority. The first specific program task was "to spare no efforts in improving the living conditions of the nomads and their livestock, which are the

Table 1

NON-RECURRENT EXPENDITURES OF SOMALI GOVERNMENTS
IN DEVELOPING PROGRAMS

(*In million Somali shillings*)

Area of Investment	Years	
	1963-68	1971-73
Industry	214	87.3
Agriculture, fisheries, forestry, animal husbandry, irrigation	142	220.3

Source: Economic Commission for Africa, *Summaries of Economic Data, Somalia*, compiled January 175, M75-168, 6th year/no. 9.

182

backbone of the national economy; to improve the pasture areas, veterinary and husbandry services and to plan the introduction of higher and more productive breeds of livestock. . . ."[13] Related to the high priority given economic development for the nomad is a commitment by the regime to political penetration of the bush. Conversations with a number of Somalis have led me to believe that internal warfare among Somalis in the bush has been virtually stopped by the government; in addition, the government seems intent on cancelling the special benefits gained by urban residents during the post-independence period.

Because of the differences in the colonial administration of British Somaliland and Italian Somalia, problems of "reintegration" were bound to occur when the two colonies combined to form the Somali Republic.[14] These problems were exacerbated by the lack of a common administrative language for the two regions. As time went on, English began to dominate in Somali administration over Italian and Arabic, which gave an advantage to Somalis who were educated in the north (Somaliland). Since the central government is the major employer in the modern sector of Somalia, and since language ability is crucial for most modern sector jobs, those Somalis who were literate only in Italian found their skills to be of diminishing value. By the late 1960's, although there was no clan basis for it, a "southern identity" was beginning to form—especially as more and more northerners were migrating south and getting the best jobs. By then a unified school curriculum with instruction and exams in English had reached the secondary level, which put students in the south, whose education in English was often given by teachers who did not speak English themselves, at a disadvantage. The problem faced by the southerners is clearly indicated in the results of the first centralized Standard Eight leaving exam, which are shown in Table 2. While there are twice as many people in the south as in the north, the number of southerners who took the exam was only 50 percent greater than the number of northerners. More northerners passed the exam than did southerners, which meant that northerners would get the majority of available jobs. As a consequence of a recent decision by the Supreme Revolutionary Council to change to a Somali-language curriculum, northerners will begin to lose their advantage in the competition for jobs.

The decision to make Somali the official language has had a significant impact on emerging social stratification. A problem most African states faced at independence was that either there was no single indigenous language which most of the citizens spoke or

Table 2

REGIONAL RESULTS OF THE STANDARD EIGHT
CENTRALIZED EXAMINATION IN SOMALIA: 1971

Region	Total Standard Eight Enrollment	Number of Passes	Percent Passed
Northern region (former British colony)	1178	1038	88%
Southern region (former Italian colony)	1695	907	54

Source: Somali Democratic Republic, Ministry of Education, *Annual Report* (Muqdisho, 1971), p. 32.

(as in Somalia's case) there was no acceptable orthography for the common language. Therefore, most of the newly independent African states continued to administer their affairs and educate their youth in a foreign language. Obviously, literacy in a foreign language takes longer to achieve and is more difficult to maintain than literacy in one's mother tongue. If a state demands literacy in a foreign language of its administrators, then that state must ensure that they have a secondary-level education in the foreign language. What then happens to the primary school leavers? They are not sufficiently literate in the foreign language to maintain their literacy in it, and they soon begin to lose the benefits of their primary school education. The long-term result of such a language policy is to create a core of literate administrators who govern an essentially illiterate mass. The uneducated or ill-educated can penetrate the bureaucracy only minimally, and the educated, administrative elite, by guiding their children up through the educational pyramid, becomes self-perpetuating.

Since nearly all citizens in Somalia speak Somali, once Somali became the official language of the state, mass literacy became a feasible goal. The regime worked first toward urban literacy, especially among the civil servants (who were already literate in Arabic, English, or Italian); then in March 1974 it launched a literacy campaign in the rural areas. The intermediate and secondary schools in the urban areas were closed for a year while the students and

other cadres went into the bush to teach the nomads how to read Somali. Previous rural literacy campaigns had failed because of nomad resistance, the lack of a script for the indigenous language, and the necessity to teach a foreign language as well; even in this campaign the police played a fundamental role as "group gatherers."[15] Vast strides were made in the development of rural literacy (the Ministry of Information and National Guidance estimated a countrywide literacy rate of 55 percent in 1975),[16] a fundamental requisite for a balanced urban-rural development.

Especially in a homogeneous society, the use of an indigenous language as the official language fosters egalitarian educational policies. Primary education provided in an indigenous language is generally self-maintaining, and makes it possible to recruit literate primary school leavers into the bureaucracy. In addition, since fewer expatriates are needed to teach in the primary schools, the egalitarian goal of a universal primary education is much more likely to be achieved. Table 3 shows a rapid expansion in school enrollment at the primary level during the post-revolutionary period, which further demonstrates how language policy can help promote social equality.

Because one of its functions is to create a technical elite, any educational policy will foster new types of social stratification. In Africa the bureaucratic elites, certified by their diplomas and retaining many of the perquisites of their colonial predecessors, are clearly a new social stratum. Such stratification is inevitable in any attempt to establish a modern state in a traditional society. Siyaad has attempted to reduce the inequalities to the greatest extent possible. He has turned his "accounting without shame" review board from an anti-corruption focus to a focus on bureaucratic salaries and benefits. The board studies every ministry and resets salaries and reduces perquisites where they are considered too high. Civil servants still live well, but under Siyaad's stewardship the gap between their life style and that of others has been reduced. In his public addresses to civil servants, Siyaad has spoken of the mutterings of civil servants concerning their salary cuts and their "orientation courses" at military camps, which suggests that they have begun to lose some of their advantages.[17]

Perhaps even more important in Siyaad's mind than salary reductions is the elimination of the "cosmopolitanism" of the civil service. When Somali became the official language of the civil service, those Somalis who had studied abroad and viewed themselves as a special elite by virtue of having been to London, Paris, Rome, or

Table 3

INCREASES IN SCHOOL ENROLLMENT IN SOMALIA:
1966-1974

Level	School Year							
	1966-67	1967-68	1968-69	1969-70	1970-71	1971-72	1972-73	1973-74
	Pre-Revolution				*Post-Revolution*			
Primary	21,050	23,121	24,697	23,842	25,939	31,364	53,465	69,493
Intermediate	7,532	10,056	10,609	14,129	14,761	16,027	24,668	24,410
Secondary	1,836	2,066	3,133	4,185	5,244	5,810	9,457	10,500
TOTAL	30,408	35,243	38,439	42,156	45,944	53,201	87,590	107,403

Sources: 1966-71: *Current Statistical Trends in Somali Education*; 1971-72: *Statistics of Education in Somalia, 1971-72,* Dept. of Planning (III), May 1972, and Ministry of Education, *Annual Report, 1973*; 1973-74: *UN Statistical Yearbook,* 1976. When the years overlap in these different sources, different figures are given for the same years; the figures should therefore be considered estimates only.

Washington lost their elite status. Only these Western-educated Somalis, Siyaad observed, would obey the commands "of those who were their inferiors in terms of education or intelligence . . . because they were members of the colonizing regime in our country."[18] An indigenously educated civil service would be less estranged from the people they are serving, which also promotes equality. A modern state must give some perquisites to its technical elites, but to be effective they need not have all the advantages. Here Siyaad was being consistent with Somali tradition and socialist ideology.

The one form of social stratification supported by traditional Somali society is that based on sexual differences. The post-revolutionary regime has made some efforts to change this, but it is proceeding cautiously. Thus while some practices relating to inequalities in divorce and to bride-price have been challenged, while the penalty for murdering a woman is now equal to that for murdering a man, and while liberal maternity leaves and equal pay for women are now part of the Somali labor code, the government has remained fairly quiet about the continued practice of female infibulation. At least in Muqdisho the social restrictions on women seem to have lessened since the revolution, but as the Ministry of Information and National Guidance points out, norms on these issues change slowly because most Somalis do not "put theory into practice lest their daughters remain unwedded."[19]

It is in education that opportunities to increase social mobility for women are greatest. As Table 4 shows, since the last school year of the pre-revolutionary period, the increase in the percentage of girls in the total school enrollment at the primary level has been 72.7 percent. On the intermediate and secondary levels, however, the progress for females has not been any greater than under the non-socialist civilian regime. (At the university level, before the revolution only eleven women were enrolled in the "University Institute"; in 1974, 181 were enrolled.)[20]

In terms of employment in the modern sector, the situation of women is not clearly defined. The Somali government reports that 65 percent of those who passed the first civil service literacy test in Somali were women, which attests both to their ability and to their presence in significant numbers in the civil service. However, no one lost his (or her) job for failing the test, nor was promoted for passing it, so the test did not serve to increase the social mobility of women. Progress for women in terms of employment can perhaps be assessed more accurately in the Ministry of Education, which publishes the sex ratios of its teaching employees. As Table 5 shows, the per-

Table 4

PERCENTAGE OF FEMALES IN TOTAL SCHOOL ENROLLMENT IN SOMALIA:
1966-1974

Level	School Year							
	1966-67	1967-68	1968-69	1969-70	1970-71	1971-72	1972-73	1973-74
	Pre-Revolution			Post-Revolution				
Primary	23.4%	22.9%	23.2%	21.8%	22.7%	24.3%	27.0%	30.0%
Intermediate	19.9	24.5	20.7	20.0	21.4	21.6	22.9	23.9
Secondary	9.7	10.2	11.4	14.1	15.6	14.7	15.4	16.9

Sources: Somali Democratic Republic, *Current Statistical Trends in Somali Education* (Muqdisho, 1971), and Ministry of Education, *Annual Report, 1973.*

Table 5

PERCENTAGE OF WOMEN TEACHERS IN SOMALIA:
SELECTED YEARS, 1966-1974

	School Year			
	1966-67	1971-72	1972-73	1973-74
Educational Level				
	Pre-Revolution	Post-Revolution		
Primary	10.0%	14.6%	13.1%	13.1%
Intermediate	25.2[a]	5.3	6.7	4.9
Secondary	9.8	16.3	12.5	11.9

Sources: Same as Table 4.

[a]This figure reflects the presence of the American Peace Corps. The statistical office usually factors out expatriate teachers, but did not do so in this case.

centage of women teachers in Somalia declined between 1971 and 1974, with only a small overall improvement since 1966-67—a representative pre-revolutionary year. Of course, it is difficult to increase the proportion of women teachers until the percentage of girls passing through the school system has been increased; thus the figures in Table 5 do not necessarily reflect a declining interest in sexual equality. However, despite the rhetoric of the revolution—

The Blessed 21st October Revolution under the leadership of SRC President, Jaalle Maxamed Siyaad Barre, has assumed the task of emancipating women from the exploitation of reaction and has given its attention to their mobilization toward production and development. . . . The basic answer to benefitting from this vast untapped labour source has been found to be education[21]—

women have made only limited gains, and suffered at least one setback, under the socialist regime.

The information presented here concerning social equality, though limited, indicates a basic trend. Under the institutional forms of democracy in the early years of independence in Somalia, there was an increase in social stratification. Under the authoritarian

189

regime, whether for reasons of "socialism" or a desire to return to traditional Somali values—and despite the fact that a new military stratum has achieved considerable status and control of resources— action has been taken to restore social equality to the Somali polity. (The socialist element must have played some role, because only that can explain the movement toward sexual equality.)

C. ECONOMIC GROWTH

With no reliable figures for GDP, any discussion of socialist progress in economic growth in Somalia becomes highly conjectural. The regime's claim that Somalia is approaching "take-off" is, of course, far-fetched, but for those people who have seen Somalia both before and after the revolution, the economic progress since the revolution has been astounding. Many new roads, new factories, and new buildings have appeared, and even the development projects finally seem to be underway. Many more people appear to be working, and the results are beginning to be evident. Even a well-trained observer is likely to be amazed at the "progress."[22]

But this apparent progress is not reflected in the available statistics. It is almost as if the "revolutionary progress" were occurring in a different time-space continuum than the society represented in the data provided by the Statistical Office. In the revolutionary pamphlet "Agriculture in the Service of the Nation," published by the Ministry of Information, it is stated that "agriculture was a thriving occupation for the Somali people even in the ancient times. . . . It was lamentable, however, that Somali agriculture should suffer a severe setback during the era of foreign domination."[23] The pamphlet is replete with accounts of successful cooperative schemes, irrigation schemes, land development projects, underground water utilization projects, grain storage projects, etc., and visitors have confirmed the enthusiasm and apparent efficiency of the Ministry of Agriculture in developing these schemes. But when the statistical data are examined, a different picture emerges.

In the production of bananas, for example—the country's second biggest export (livestock is first)—the Ministry of Agriculture claims that the takeover of their marketing in May 1970 by the National Banana Board was "a great leap forward for the Somali banana!" Furthermore, "considerable improvements" have been made "in the yield per hectare due to the adoption of better irrigation application and drainage practices, fertilizer application and intensive spraying methods," and new markets for Somali bananas

have been developed in the Middle East and the German Democratic Republic, reducing the constricting effect of Italian monopsony.[24] In addition, the ministry reports, new roads for bringing the bananas to the ports have been built, as well as a new banana packaging plant to ensure better marketing with less waste. "The export of bananas has," the report concludes, "shown a tremendous rise from 1970 onward,"[25] but the complete figures (not the selected ones provided by the ministry) show otherwise. While the ministry propagandists claim that 1973 was a bad year for bananas because of weather problems, the figures for banana exports have fluctuated since the revolution, with no clear secular trend evident since the overthrow of the civilian regime (see Table 6).

The situation with respect to grains is similar. A governmental "crash program" in agriculture had as its primary goal "to increase national food production toward the attainment of sustained self-sufficiency with emphasis on import substituting crops." It was claimed that new hectares had been brought into production, that new schemes for making nomads into peasants had been developed,

Table 6

SELECTED EXPORT AND IMPORT FIGURES FOR SOMALIA:
1967-1973

(*In million Somali shillings*)

	Year						
Product	1967	1968	1969	1970	1971	1972	1973
	Pre-Revolution			*Post-Revolution*			
Banana exports	68.4	59.7	55.7	62.4	64.3	78.2	67.4
Imports of rice and other cereals	35.3	35.2	48.8	50.5	104.8	56.4	57.5
Meat and preparations exports	2.4	3.0	3.0	6.7	21.4	22.6	16.0

Source: Economic Commission for Africa, *Summaries of Economic Data, Somalia*, compiled January 1975.

and that production levels had been raised. But a look at imports of rice and other cereals (see Table 6) reveals a different situation. Even with the drought year of 1971 omitted, the level of imports of basic foodstuffs has been consistently rising.

There is no doubt that the drought, which lasted for several years and threatened the very existence of the Somali nation, was at the heart of Somalia's agricultural problems. The figures suggest that agricultural progress in Somalia, which has been central to Siyaad's concerns, will continue to be erratic. In Siyaad's espousal of socialist ideology he has demonstrated the importance of changing the basis of the Somali economy from nomadic herding to settled agriculture. He has not only overcome nomadic resistance to settled life, but has even generated enthusiasm among the civil servants and the new farmers. The drought may have helped him recruit nomads for farming, but it has also made reasonable yields more difficult to attain. While the ideology can mobilize nomads, it cannot create rain.

In at least one area—the production of tinned meats—the statistics provided in Table 6 confirm the reports of visitors and the revolutionary rhetoric. Prior to the revolution, Somali tinned meats could not penetrate the international market. While tinned meats are still but a small percentage of total Somali exports (7.57 percent in 1972, 5.44 percent in 1973), revolutionary ardor and organization has in this case produced modest but positive results.

Economic growth requires an educated citizenry. In terms of total enrollment, the figures for education in Somalia are encouraging. In the years 1972-73 and 1973-74, there were substantial increases in school enrollment, especially at the primary level. While I have no data concerning what is happening in all the classrooms, it seems likely that a high percentage of Somalis will both be literate and have the basic skills needed for them to be mobilized for productive activity. It is not clear whether such productive activity can be found in the Somali environment, but it is clear that through its educational policy Somalia is making a major effort to prepare its citizenry for "take-off."

In summary: In the post-revolutionary period, economic growth in Somalia has been more apparent than real. Where available, the statistics have shown only limited gains and some losses in various economic sectors. In terms of economic output, there has been little overall difference between Somalia under the socialist regime and under the previous civilian regime.

D. FOREIGN POLICY

Since the socialist declaration, the Somalis have consistently sought to reduce ties with the Western capitalist world and to increase ties with the socialist states. The Somali military leaders were trained by the Soviets, which helps to explain their initial openness to socialism. Under civilian rule, the republic had attempted to modernize its armed forces with the aid of the United States, but the U.S., which was already supporting both Ethiopia and Kenya— the two countries against which Somalia has had border claims[26]— did not want to risk its friendships with those countries by arming Somalia. The U.S. offered to help the Somali police force, but refused to give military aid. The Somalis therefore turned to the Soviets, who agreed to provide military assistance. Close ties developed between the Soviets and the Somali military, and when the army seized power in the period of anarchy following the assassination of President Sharma'arke, the Soviets were in a position to exert great influence. The national commitment to socialism and Siyaad's Marxist-Leninist rhetoric follow from this marriage of convenience.

The remaining ties with the U.S. soon began to erode. The American Peace Corps was expelled some three months after the revolution, and shortly afterward, when Somalia permitted its flagships to transport goods to North Vietnam, the U.S. cut off other aid. Relations between the U.S. and Somalia became icy when a countercoup was attempted by the leaders of the police force, who were suspected of being spurred on by the U.S. Central Intelligence Agency.

Somalia thereafter became actively and vociferously identified with the "third world." Its first Revolutionary Charter included the following foreign policy guidelines:

1. To support international solidarity and national liberation movements;
2. To oppose and fight against all forms of colonialism and neo-colonialism. . . .[27]

Indeed Somalia joined the vanguard of third world radicalism in giving ideological support to the committee for the liberation of southern Africa in the Organization of African Unity, to Guinea's stand against Portuguese aggression, and to the Arab stand against Zionism. Siyaad even issued a joint communique with Enrico Berlinguer* at

*Since 1972 the Secretary of the Italian Communist Party.

the 1976 Soviet Party Congress declaring their "mutual support."[28] Finally, Somalia permitted the Soviets to construct a major military facility at Berbera on its northern coast—a facility the Russians feel will be useful in their attempt to achieve naval hegemony in the Indian Ocean.[29]

In exchange for the use of the port of Berbera, Somalia received enormous amounts of military aid from the Soviets, as well as support for its radio facilities, its schools, its port facilities, and its canning factories. The Chinese, meanwhile, are financing and building a major north-south road which will provide a permanent connection between the former colonies of British Somaliland and Italian Somalia for the first time. Wells will be built every few kilometers, which will be helpful in encouraging nomads to engage in agriculture. Somali officials were pleased with the effects of "socialist aid."

But there are problems associated with this ideological shift in foreign policy. For one thing, Somalia's external public debt to the Soviet Union stood at 275.8 million shillings in 1971, accounting for 52.5 percent of its total external debt.[30] A socialist foreign policy requires that a country seek economic autarky, but Somalia became very much dependent on the Soviets. (The public debt to the Soviets has always been high, however—even under the civilian regime.) The Soviets supplied the Somalis with sufficient arms to make a reasonable attempt at "reuniting the dismembered Somali people and . . . restoring the integrity of her territory" (in the words of former Foreign Minister Cumar Arteh Ghalib),[31] but by retaining control of Somali supplies of petroleum, oil, and lubrication, they had a decisive voice in Somalia's most important foreign policy arena, perpetuating dependency rather than autonomy.

A second problem results from the fact that most Somalis see the Russians as Europeans and therefore to be despised. Stories of sabotage against Russian projects circulate throughout the republic. A third (and perhaps the most serious) problem is a result of Somalia's joining the Arab League in a desire to procure oil at an affordable price and to support anti-Zionism. Aid from Saudi Arabia and Kuwait was forthcoming, but the Saudis and Kuwaitis are far more afraid of the Soviets than of the Israelis, and both countries have attempted to reduce Soviet influence in particular (and socialist influence in general) in Moslem Somalia. Prime Minister Qaddafi of Libya has promised aid, and has suggested the creation of a "Libyan-Somali-Arab Bank" to assist in development projects, but Qaddafi's influence in Arab politics has been so reduced that Somalia has had to defer to Saudi Arabia and Kuwait in order to obtain cheap

oil and to be accepted in the Arab League. The Saudis have made diplomatic attempts to wrestle Somalia from the "Soviet camp," and the recycling of petrodollars by OPEC states in the form of aid to friendly countries has been of only marginal benefit to the Somalis. Thus, while Somalia maintains a strong socialist foreign policy "rhetorically," it is under considerable pressure from non-socialist Arab states to modify it.

To return to the issue of dependency: Siyaad has advised his people that political autonomy is the key to success in building socialism. But as the figures on Somalia's importation of rice and its external debt to the Soviet Union indicate, economic autonomy is not being achieved. This is made even clearer in Table 7, which shows the steady increase in Somalia's external debt, the fluctuations in foreign contributions to its recurrent budget (with a sharp rise in 1974), and its increasing trade deficit (except for a decline in 1970) since the revolution. It is ironic that, unlike most of the

Table 7

INDEXES OF SOMALIA'S DEPENDENCY: 1966-1974

(*In million Somali shillings*)

Index	Year								
	1966	1967	1968	1969	1970	1971	1972	1973	1974
	Pre-Revolution				*Post-Revolution*				
External debt	281.7	313.9	355.7	394.0	498.6	525.2			
Foreign contributions to recurrent budget		26.5	22.0	15.5	18.0	13.7	13.7	13.0	27.0
Trade deficit		87.9	127.8	137.9	98.3	201.2	225.5	342.2	

Source: Economic Commission for Africa, *Summaries of Economic Data, Somalia*, compiled January 1975.

socialist third world countries, which are trying to eliminate cash crops as the core of their economy because cash crops are subject to the vicissitudes of the capitalist marketplace, Somalia considers it part of its socialist purpose to "return" Somalia to cash cropping.[32] Despite a constant striving for socialist autonomy, then, Somalia is getting further in debt, further enmeshed in international economies (both socialist and capitalist), and closer to severing its treaty of friendship with the Soviet Union.*

E. IDEOLOGICAL REFINEMENT

If the adjective in "scientific socialism" is to mean anything, it must mean that scientific methods can be used to determine how best to tackle various problems in socialist development. Scientific research as the fundamental basis for policymaking is the hallmark of scientific socialism. In the original counsels held by President Siyaad, a number of socialist ideologues had important roles, but many of these people have since been excluded. For example, Cabdulaziz Nur Hersi, founder of the Hawl iyo Hantiwadaag [Work and Socialism] party in the pre-revolutionary period, was first ignored by Siyaad, then consulted, and then sent to jail. Arrested with Hersi was Dr. Maxamed Adan, a former secretary of higher education. In addition, two other Marxist intellectuals— Maxamed Wairax, former secretary of finance, and Axmad Hashi, a lawyer educated at the University of Moscow—were jailed, and Yusuf Cusman Samatar, a leader of the left prior to the revolution, has been in and out of jail since the revolution. Some Somalis argue that these men were jailed because they were too Peking-oriented or too closely identified with Eurocommunism, but most with whom I have talked believe that Siyaad saw in their ideological expertise a power which could become a threat to his freedom of action.†

*In the summer of 1977 the Soviets began to support the Ethiopians in their war against the Somalis. Soviet advisors were expelled from Somalia in November of that year.

†Maxamed Adan is now chairman of the editorial board of *Halgan* [The Struggle], a monthly publication of the Central Committee of the Somali Revolutionary Socialist Party. This journal, published in Somali, Arabic, and English, attempts to relate Marxist theory to Somali realities. Other scholars are attempting to reassess Somali history from a Marxist perspective. I do not mean to suggest that there is no critical examination of society from a socialist perspective in Somalia, but only that little of this criticism seems to penetrate the military command.

Not surprisingly, Siyaad's socialist thinking is confused. On the one hand he says that there is no such thing as "African socialism"—that there is only "scientific socialism"—but on the other hand he says that "a Soviet socialist cannot tell me about Somalian problems, which must be put in an African context."[33] And rather than finding class enemies of socialism ("The Somali people as a whole are workers"),[34] he finds the enemies of socialism to be former parliamentarians, pseudo-religious men, and pseudo-intellectuals.[35] This is "shoot from the hip" ideology, and shows a "school of hard knocks" sensibility; by no means does it show policy directions born of scientific analyses of economic problems from a socialist perspective.

F. SUMMARY

While the data are inconclusive, and while seven years is a short time to complete a social transformation, it is clear that in terms of socialist economics the Somali regime is doing little that is not being done in other liberal, not avowedly socialist third world states. While there have been determined efforts at the development of worker control of production, the overall thrust of initiative is still coming from the political center. Government activity has gotten the market moving, but this is more a reflection of military energy than of socialist ideology.

As for social equality, there is little doubt that the Siyaad regime has deterred emerging stratifications not essential in a modern society. The distinctions between rural and urban residents, northerners and southerners, and civil servants and private citizens have begun to diminish due to government policy. That some movement has been made to enhance opportunities for women and to promote sexual equality (in opposition to Somali tradition) suggests that the commitment to social equality derives in part from socialist ideology.

Rapid economic growth in a desert country with almost no exploitable resources is not to be expected with even the best of ideologies and governments. Promises of rapid growth and the reality of economic stagnation have created tensions within Somali society which reflect poorly on its socialist experiment.

Somali foreign policy has become "socialist"—in diplomatic terms. During the past few years Siyaad and Cumar Arteh have become leading spokesmen for "progressive" causes in the world, and close ties developed between Somalia and the Soviet Union, South Yemen, North Korea, China, and the Sudan. There also has

been a clear thrust at integrating Somalia's economy with the socialist world. In military terms, Somalia has lost some degree of autonomy, and the Soviets' control over Somali petroleum, oil, and lubricants will enable them to veto any attempt by Somalia to engage in independent foreign policy adventures with regard to its neighbors.

In terms of theory, "scientific socialism" in Somalia is rather a mishmash. Some of the leading socialist ideologues have been purged since the revolution, and "socialism" as a guide for action becomes more meaningless with every Siyaad speech. Decisions on economic policy do not seem to be based on the scientific application of socialist theory.

The record suggests that a non-socialist but vigorous, development-conscious military in control of the Somali government would have acted in much the same way as the present socialist regime. While the Siyaad regime has made commendable progress along certain lines associated with socialist ideology, no radical transformations or uniquely socialist programs have been essayed. But this achievement can be considered relatively successful in comparison with other socialist experiments in the third world.[36] The possibilities for economic development are too limited for poor countries to effect radical transformations, but many have opted for "socialism" nonetheless. Perhaps a different tack—treating socialism not as a program but as a symbol—will lead to more insights concerning the meaning of socialism in Somalia.

II. SOCIALISM AS SEMIOTIC

An important concept in the Marxist tradition is "universalism." Marx argued that expressions of cultural differentiation by various nationalities were a threat to the international unity of the working class. Lenin was appalled by the support given to each European nation by its proletariat: he expected members of the working class to see beyond their loyalties to particular nations. A second key concept in Marxism is "materialism." In their attacks on related traditions, Marx and Engels disputed Hegelian "idealism" and "utopian" socialism because of their emphasis on the role of ideas as forces in history. For the true Marxist, relations of production—not ideas—determine history.

Based on their concern for "universalism" and "materialism," Marxist critics, even if they were to ignore its programmatic failures, might well make two major criticisms of Siyaad's "scientific social-

ism." First, they might say that the regime's emphasis on the use and development of the national language represents "Somali chauvinism" rather than "socialist universalism." Of course it is commendable to use the national language (Stalin himself resurrected a number of national languages to counter what he called "Great Russian chauvinism"), but to view the use and development of the national language as an integral part of the socialist revolution is, from a Marxist standpoint, to misdefine the country's priorities. (The Bolsheviks supported the development of national languages as a concession to the nationalities, but not as an integral part of the socialist program.)

A second criticism they might make would relate to the continued support of the Islamic faith by the socialist regime. Stalin was willing to tolerate expressions of national consciousness in the Soviet Union, especially when directed against the Great Russians, but he was horrified by the implications of a national policy which would sanctify the power of the reactionary Mullahs.[37] Religious principles have always been considered by Marxists to be antirevolutionary. The language policy threatens the Marxist ideal of universalism; the religious policy threatens the Marxist ideal of materialism.

To put the matter a different way: If Marxism is *epochal* in the sense that it envisions a future unencumbered by the oppressions of the past, then Somali policy, in supporting the national language and religion, is *essential* in that it seeks to support those values which inhere in the Somali tradition.[38] A tension between epochalism and essentialism is clearly seen in Siyaad's speech announcing the new script for the Somali language: "As dedicated revolutionaries we must now ensure that what has been handed down to us over the centuries is no longer lost."[39] How can Marxist epochalism be reconciled with Somali essentialism?

I shall begin with the tension between socialist universalism and the national language policy. Before 1789, according to E.J. Hobsbawm and Raymond Williams, words such as "middle class," "socialism," "liberal," and "capitalism" had not yet been invented in Europe or had meanings very different from their modern ones.[40] A similar situation existed in Somalia of the 1960's. The development of any new social theory—especially one with the ideal of changing a society into something very different from what it has been for centuries—requires the development of a new vocabulary. If the new theory is articulated in a foreign language, one which few of the indigenous people speak, theoretical discussion becomes

very limited. It is one thing, for example, for people to be told about the evils of "surplus capital" when each word is rich in connotative meaning; it is quite another thing for them to be told about such evils when the words have no independent significance. When the new social theory is translated into the indigenous language, with new terms invented where needed, any citizen can speculate about the theory; the social theory comes, as it were, alive.

The language of "scientific socialism" in Somali translation indeed came alive. The very choice of the name of the ideology—*hantiwadaag*, which means "livestock sharing" in Somali—stirred criticism. Some Somalis argued that livestock sharing is what Somalis have always done when their brethren were in trouble, while others argued that *hantiwadaag* suggests that the have-nots would get livestock but the haves would lose theirs. This set off a debate, in which Siyaad was forced to engage, concerning whether *hantiwadaag* implied that nomads were "capitalists" or "workers," and whether nomads' property would be owned by the state.

Other semantic battles spilled over into substantive ones. The initial translation of "scientific" was literally "which sits on knowledge." Many Somalis thought that this phrase assigned too passive a role to theory. With the hope that theory would be more prominent in policy formulation, the translation was changed to "which is built on knowledge" in later government statements. At first the revolution was called *afgembis* (*lit.*, "turning over of the mouth")—a term used to refer to people tripping over themselves. This was seen as too frivolous a term to refer to a socialist revolution. The regime soon began to employ the Arabic-derived *towradda*, but this word was foreign to Somalis and had significance only insofar as it connected Somali politics to revolutionary politics in the Middle East. This was unacceptable to those Somalis convinced that they were engaged in a unique social movement. Finally, *kacaan*, which connotes "standing up" or "growing up," became the accepted term.* This connotation is commensurate with the regime's ideals of leading Somalia to greater autonomy and greater responsibility for its own future.

The message of the revolution is often spread through popular poetry and song. The choice of words for propagandizing a new political line in the indigenous language is of considerable import. Consider the first two lines of perhaps the most popular song of the revolution, which is sung by schoolchildren before classes, by

*In Muqdisho, *kac*—the root of *kacaan*—can mean "go to hell." The connection between this street-meaning and the term for revolution is unclear to me.

workers before their shift begins, and by all groups of Somalis as they are transported, for whatever reason, through the country:

Guul wadoo Siyaad, aabahii garashada gayiga yagoo
Hantiwadaga wa habka barwaaqo no horsedayee

You the winner Siyaad, the father of understanding to all of us; Socialism will lead us to prosperity.

Of several points which can be made about this couplet, two are particularly noteworthy. First, in the attempt to create a charismatic aura around Siyaad, traditional imagery of understanding (*garashada*) rather than ideological purity or correct vision of Somalia's future is used. Siyaad is therefore portrayed not as someone who is committed to rapid socioeconomic change, but rather as someone who will judge fairly. The conciliator rather than the pathbreaker is the ideal of the charismatic "winner," and socialism is thereby metaphorically tied to traditional values concerning leadership. The second point is that the word used for prosperity—*barwaaqo*—is also the name of the richest grazing grass in the country. No higher praise is possible for someone in Somalia than to be known as one who brings *barwaaqo*. Ironically, then, even though the revolution led by Siyaad is committed politically to the gradual elimination of the nomadic way of life, the imagery used to describe the revolution relates it to the *summum bonum* of nomadic existence: milk-laden camels. These images are understood at a very deep level by the Somali population, and the regime cannot in the future easily escape, as it were, its own rhetoric.

The use of Somali as the official language of state, then, has forced the government ideologues and induced the population at large to engage in popular debate concerning what socialism "means" in both its semantic and pragmatic senses. The semantic debate, by forcing articulation of socialist theory in the Somali context, is more than anything developing revolutionary consciousness. The national language policy is not, then, a concession to Somali essentialism, but rather it acts to encourage epochal thinking.

Karl Mannheim, in an important revision within the Marxist tradition, has brought into question Marx's insistence on a universalist socialism. Whereas Marx argued, for example, that Judaism must be abolished before socialism can be attained, because only then could all men achieve "species consciousness,"[41] Mannheim has suggested that the visions of counter-reality which foster revolutionary consciousness and will are nurtured in specific cultural milieux.[42] Revolutionary program and consciousness will not emerge

from a universalist society, Mannheim suggests, but only from the various sects, religions, and cultures that use special symbolic forms to postulate alternate universes (i.e., utopias).

The Somali language community, like Mannheim's anabaptists and chiliasts, has through the use of its own symbolic forms nurtured revolutionary consciousness and will. The Somali proverb *Af somaaliga waa mergi*—"The Somali language is sinuous, like the larynx"—suggests that the language can be changed to suit different purposes. The use of this sinuous language in national politics has provided Somalis with an opportunity to rethink socialism, and through the creation of new symbols to make socialism so much theirs that they might have the motivation, as Mannheim's argument suggests, to help realize socialist goals.

But one caveat is necessary here. That the ideological debate in the Somali language has induced popular participation and has engaged many intellectuals in the polity is clear. That more and more Somalis from all walks of life are petitioning the government on a variety of issues is also clear.[43] But the current rate of emigration by young educated Somalis to Kenya, Saudi Arabia, England, France, and the United States is far higher than before the revolution. This is in part because while Siyaad in his language policy has fulfilled one of the necessary conditions for popular participation, he has systematically stifled free expression through his authoritarian practices. Most Somalis are afraid to speak out politically—perhaps the ultimate irony in Siyaad's socialism. Through his statements concerning scientific socialism, he has provided the grist to entice his people to speculate about politics, but he has refused to allow them to mill it. Like Tantalus, the Somali people have a vision of a better life, but Siyaad denies them the right to reach for it. Scientific socialism seen as a symbolic system can only "work" if the people are permitted speech—for only through speech can revolutionary consciousness and will develop.

The relationship between socialism and religion in Somalia is far more complex than that between socialism and language. While Siyaad makes continual use of the symbols of Islam, he has been ruthless in his dealings with reactionary Islamic leaders. He has threatened that he would confiscate their land if they did not modernize their schools, or if they objected to the use of a non-Arabic script for the Somali language. When a number of them protested the egalitarian sexual policies he had developed, Siyaad used that occasion to put ten of them to death. When elements in the religious community have tried to denigrate socialism by sug-

gesting that it is contrary to the principles of Islam, Siyaad has excoriated them in public, calling them *wadaad honka* (pseudo-religious men). At one point in the heat of the socialism campaign, Siyaad observed that

> As far as socialism is concerned, it is not a heavenly message like Islam but a mere system for regulating the relations between man and his utilization of the means of production in this world. . . . The reactionaries want to create a rift between socialism and Islam because socialism is not to their interest; therefore, they have not even reverenced misinterpreting the words of God.[44]

Siyaad has made clear that for him "there is no conflict between Islam and socialism, as they both enshrine the principles of human dignity, mutual respect, cooperation, progress, justice and well-being for all."[45] And in a speech commemorating the end of the annual Islamic fast in 1970, he attempted to articulate a more progressive Islamic ideology:

> Our Islamic faith teaches us that its inherent values are perennial and continually evolving as people progress. These basic tenets of our religion cannot be interpreted in a static sense, but rather as a dynamic force, as a source of inspiration for continuous advancement. . . . Hence the need for our religious leaders to probe within the social reality of our people, and wrest from our religion its practical teachings, thus making available its ideas and actions in the interest of general progress. Among our people, religious leaders must play a galvanizing role to activate a society advancing towards the high values of Islam, which have always been the foundation of our social and political organization. The Somali Democratic Republic will spare no effort to follow the path to prosperity. . . . This path is clearly laid out by Islam. . . .[46]

Marxists abhor religion because of its anti-materialism. Less critical of religion's role in socialism are many sociologists who have cogently argued that while there is nothing essential in Islam which is a constraint on capitalism, neither is there anything in Islam which especially promotes or opposes socialism.[47] Siyaad has gone even further: he has decided to use Islam and its symbols to further his socialist revolution. In its propaganda the regime provides examples of the congruence of socialism and Islam which go back to Caliph Umar, who "established a well-defined basis of socialism" by assigning the lands of Azzabad to public ownership.[48]

By bringing religion and its symbols into the heart of the revolution, Siyaad is countering the materialist thrust of socialism. For if language is sinuous, religion is like a moral anchor—a constant reminder of the eternal principles which impel men to act morally and humanely. And if language acts through its cultural particularism to counter socialist universalism, then religion acts through its humanistic idealism to counter socialist materialism. To an increasing degree, furthermore, the religious and socialist doctrines amplify each other in the Somali context. In the same way as Siyaad repeats ad nauseam in many of his speeches, "There is only one socialism and that is scientific socialism"—a clearly materialist message—he is compelled to redefine Islam and recommit himself to its teachings in almost every speech. The more tension he creates on a philosophical level between state ideology and state religion, the more he is forced to articulate the symbols of the religion. Support of the religion even gets prominent space in the Program of the Somali Revolutionary Socialist Party.

Without a programmatic ideology such as socialism to relate them, the sinuous language and the anchoring religion would lead Somali politics to bounce endlessly between novelty and tradition. Socialism provides a bridge between the Somali language and the Somali religion—and the language and religion provide dialectical antitheses to socialist universalism and materialism. On a symbolic level, then, scientific socialism in conjunction with the Somali language and Islamic religion create the synthesis of epochalism and essentialism so necessary if people in the third world are to have symbolic maps telling them where they have been, where they might go, and why they should expend their energy (with the concomitant risks of failure) to support radical change.[49]

III. CONCLUSION

Immanuel Wallerstein, in a distinguished contribution to social theory, has argued that "*states* as such are neither progressive nor reactionary, and thus there are no socialist states within a capitalist world economy. At best, semi-peripheral states can attempt a mercantilist retreat from the world economy, as was the case of England vis-à-vis the Netherlands . . . France vis-à-vis England . . . Germany vis-à-vis Britain . . . the Soviet Union vis-à-vis the U.S."[50] This general conclusion based on a Marxist analysis of the world system helps to make sense of much of the socialist experience in Africa when treated as program.

In an earlier work on Africa, Wallerstein (as he emphasizes in the preface to his most recent book)[51] tried valiantly to find differences in colonial experience, ideology, and other factors which might explain differences in programmatic outcomes of different African states. Since most African states followed similar developmental patterns no matter what their colonial background or professed ideology, the comparative approach to African development came under some criticism.[52]

Rather than finding causes based on the existence of international capitalism, students of African socialism were developing state-oriented explanations of the failure of socialist programs in various African states. Socialist ideologies were criticized because they were intellectually flawed. Socialist experiments were criticized because African bureaucracies were not considered sufficiently developed to carry out the complex and centrally planned programs associated with socialist ideals. The lack of vanguard parties and committed cadres was also mentioned as a cause of the failure of socialism in Africa. But why scrutinize state structures when, with the world system as the unit of analysis, it is possible to show conclusively that, within a capitalist world economy, progressive and reactionary programs (while perhaps "the daily bread and butter of local politics")[53] are of only limited significance for political and economic outcomes?

Without denying the cogency of Wallerstein's argument, I nonetheless think that to lump together rightist and leftist retreats from the international economy as essentially the same (mercantilist) is to miss too much in the understanding of political life, and to be insufficiently sensitive to important distributive decisions. The evidence in this paper suggests that while the socialist program in Somalia has not transformed the Somali economy, it has led the country down a path where general participation in economic life and relative social and economic equality are more likely than under the previous regime. Furthermore, the evidence suggests that it may be useful to ask whether socialism in Somalia, when seen in a symbolic perspective, can influence future utopianizing in Somali political life.

The answer provided here is that scientific socialism as an ideology can be a useful bridge for Somali social and political development. The Somali language is sinuous, spontaneous, and suggestive. It induces neologizing, and in the Somali-language community utopians utopianize for the sake of the pun. In political terms, what it lacks is a formal structure of ideas to serve as a foundation for creative thinking.

The Somali religion, in contrast, is steeped in tradition, and any small change is regarded as a threat to the totality. In Somali society Islam provides an anchor. As the nomad roams the bush, he is certain at least of the humane morality of the five pillars of Islam, and what he must do to remain moral. This anchor is invaluable in times of flux, when the problem of meaning becomes salient, for then the individual is able to return to the religion for reassurance before he goes too far in exploring new social and political arrangements. But while Islam provides the anchor, it does not provide the political program in which the anchored man, secure in his position, can venture to improve his condition.

Between sinews and anchors (if my mixed metaphor is not hopelessly confusing), there needs to be an intermediate ideology for any regime intent on bringing about social change—an ideology which will provide structure for the sinuous language but allow the ship of state to roam a little in the search for a better mooring than the religion has provided. Of course, intermediate social and economic policies to induce some equality and public control of economic enterprises must complement the ideological symbols. The symbols which in Somalia revolve around scientific socialism, through their inducements to national economic independence, social, regional, and sexual equality, and economic growth through state control—all mediated by language and religion—could help transform Somalia's political culture by inducing Somalis to internalize new norms, to envision new goals, and to see their own culture as a dynamic entity which could adjust to a vastly different social and economic system when and if resources allow.

IDEOLOGY AND LEADERSHIP IN
POST-NKRUMAH GHANA

James A. McCain

Ten years after the exile of Kwame Nkrumah from Ghana, Ghanaians are experiencing a renaissance of "Nkrumahism." During the ten-year interval, Ghana has had military regimes and an intervening civilian regime. Currently there is an effort underway to construct a "Union Government" allowing for greater political participation by including more civilian groups in the decisional process. There are few indications that Nkrumah's notions of "scientific socialism" have been incorporated in recent regimes, but Nkrumah himself is revered as a hero in Ghanaian culture.

For the ten years following Ghana's independence in 1957, Nkrumah lectured throughout the country about "scientific socialism," "consciencism," and "Pan-Africanism." The meanings assigned to these concepts by Nkrumah and his followers remain ambiguous, however. These ambiguities are not surprising given the fact that Nkrumah's writings on socialism lack the rigor that scholars tend to associate with discussions of formal socialist ideology. On the one hand, Nkrumah argues that there is no such thing as African socialism: there is only scientific socialism,* which is valid the world over, and is the basis of Ghanaian efforts to build a socialist society.[1] On the other hand, he argues that socialism in Ghana needs to be pragmatically adapted to the specific requirements of African society. In addition, socialist development must be independent of ideological pressures from both East and West: non-alignment is essential to its success.

---

*As derived from Engels, "scientific socialism" asserts that there are laws of history which dictate that the proletariat will challenge the bourgeois order and instigate revolution, and that the forces of production and distribution will ultimately be controlled by the state, which will order the economy in such a way that the profits of industrial enterprise are reinvested in state enterprises and do not accrue to individuals.

It seems probable that Nkrumah was more interested in political mobilization and constructive mythmaking than ideological clarity. The applicability of scientific socialism to any particular situation was not as important as the belief by Ghanaians that their society was (for example) egalitarian, anti-colonial, income-distributing, non-exploitative, and incorrupt. The maintenance of the cultural order was more dependent on the persistence of these implicit, latent ideological beliefs than on the existence of state farms and nationalized breweries. Therefore, Nkrumah's regime attempted to ensure the transmission of the culture's norms and myths throughout the process of socialization. To Nkrumah, ideology was a tool to be used both to socialize Ghanaians with the values of the modern state and to exercise political control.*

My purposes here are (1) to survey the extent to which the ideology of African socialism remains salient for Ghanaians in the post-Nkrumah era, (2) to analyze differences of opinion between mass and elite audiences with respect to socialism in Ghana, and (3) to indicate areas of consensus or agreement between such audiences.

The orthodoxy of African socialism in the Ghanaian context is not a matter of concern here. It is assumed that people operate on the basis of their beliefs, and whatever African socialism means to Ghanaians is best evaluated from *their* point of view (whatever that happens to be) at any given point in time. This perspective is important to an understanding of how well socialized Ghanaians have become to the ideology of Nkrumah's African socialism.

African socialism in the Ghanaian context has been variously defined as (1) a vague expression of solidarity with the anti-imperialist world, (2) a nonaligned version of "second world" socialism, (3) a social synthesis for the reconciliation of modern technology and human values,[2] (4) the defense of communalism in a modern setting,[3] and (5) the nation-state viewed as an extended family system.[4]

People assign meaning to ideological expressions on the basis of their own experiences, beliefs, and values, and they often project their own values into ideological statements and treat them as matters of fact rather than opinion. We are seeking to determine the

*Nkrumah believed that the socialist revolution could not fulfill itself without "a strong and well-organized political party . . . and decisive leadership . . . to guide and lead it." The function of an ideologically elite party was to serve as an educative and disciplinary vanguard for government policy. Nkrumah's training program at the Winneba Ideological Institute and the creation of the Young Pioneers are well known. (See *Some Essential Features of Nkrumaism* [New York: International Publishers, 1964], pp. 50, 128.)

degree of adherence to such ideological statements as they may reflect the cognitive maps of mass and elite audiences. This inquiry is consistent with Zolberg's observation that political scientists need to acquire a greater understanding of normative concepts and the cognitive apparatus concerning politics "in order eventually to be able to answer the question, how do Africans perceive the political world?"[5] To acquire this understanding, not only must the explicit ideology of the leaders be studied, but also the "latent" ideology of non-leaders.

METHODOLOGY

In this study, conventional scaling techniques were employed to measure the degree of agreement or disagreement with socialistic statements made by African leaders and writers. The statements to which respondents were asked to indicate their agreement, disagreement, or uncertainty were carefully selected to ensure results of maximum reliability and validity. In a previous study conducted in 1973, the author employed intensive, experimental techniques to determine *how* Africans and Africanists view the ideology of African socialism.[6] Utilizing Q technique, subjects were asked to arrange seventy-five statements made by African leaders pertaining to African socialism along an opinion-continuum. Responses were intercorrelated and factor analyzed to produce three principal axis factors, or patterns of perception—"mind-sets"—toward African socialism: "pragmatic," "scientific," and "internationalist."

Once the *qualitative* question "In what ways do Africans perceive the ideology of African socialism?" had been answered, answers could be sought to the *quantitative* question "With what frequency are the various mind-sets to be found in a specific African population?" Those statements which had proved most salient in differentiating the three types of socialist mind-sets in the 1973 study were included in the new scale, along with several statements which were regarded as "consensual" among all three of the types.*

*In most survey work focusing on socialization patterns or attitudes (toward the civic culture, for example), the investigator *assumes* that agreement or disagreement with certain statements necessarily indicates the existence of a certain mind-set (e. g., an authoritarian personality). In this case, no such attributions were made with regard to the respondents until after they had arranged the statements under experimental circumstances. Thus the statements used during the course of this study were selected not at random, but because there was empirical evidence to suggest that they were responsible for the respondents' consensus or cleavage on important issues related to their views of African so-

Data gathering took place in Ghana in 1974-75. Of a total of 316 people interviewed, 187 were second- and third-year political science students at the University of Ghana. They represent the elite audience of the survey by virtue of their educational status. In Karl Deutsch's terms, they constitute "a politically relevant strata of the population,"[7] or what James Coleman would term "an elite subsociety."[8] Hanna is more specific:

> As university students are recipients of the most advanced Western education available, they understandably consider themselves, and are regarded as, actual or prospective members of this elite. They are conscious of their exclusiveness and their preeminence, and are often deferred to and imitated by the masses.[9]

Not only are the students educated in the ideas of African socialism reflected in the survey statements,* but many of them can expect to occupy positions in the Ghanian government in which they will have some responsibility for implementing policies emanating from such socialist principles.

The remaining 129 respondents, who comprise the "mass" audience, were selected randomly from the greater Accra area. An effort was made to exclude individuals who by other socioeconomic-status indicators might be considered "elite" (e.g., corporate executives, middle-level bureaucrats). The resultant group is composed of sales clerks, cooks, secretaries, factory workers, market women, laborers, grocers, and people of similar occupational status. The rationale for selecting people living in or near the capital was (1) they were likely to be more sensitized to governmental activities then those living in remote regions, and (2) they were wage-earners operating in a cash economy. The latter was considered important

cialism. The effect of this procedure of experimental pretesting to determine the salience of statements to the respondents in the survey was to increase our level of confidence in the results. The Ghanaian respondents in this study were initially asked to respond to the specially selected statements by indicating whether they "strongly agreed," "agreed," were "uncertain," "disagreed," or "strongly disagreed" with them. (After a preliminary inspection of the results, the categories were collapsed to agree, uncertain, and disagree, which simplified their interpretation.) Upon completion of the questionnaire, each respondent was interviewed to determine the specific grounds for his/her indicated agreement or disagreement with or uncertainty about the various statements.

*The statements were presented to the student respondents in English rather than their native languages, but the students had no difficulty with them. The newspapers, which are the principal vehicles for regime rhetoric, are printed in English, and all lectures are given in English. Therefore, in terms of comprehension, the salient properties of the statements were not "lost in translation."

because, unlike those who barter for goods, wage-earners are engaged in the type of commercial activity a modernizing country seeks to foster. None of the respondents in the "mass audience" were farmers, and in this sense the "mass sample" is an urban mass sample only, which tends to limit the generalizability of the findings. (At the time the survey was made, it was believed that urban residents were a more politically mobilized group and would have a stronger basis for making informed judgments about the material contained in the statements. This belief was considerably shaken by subsequent research conducted in rural areas which confirmed Fred Hayward's reassessment of the conventional wisdom about rural mass audiences.[10] My own experience has convinced me that rural dwellers are much better informed about political life than is generally assumed. However, constraints of time, access, and resources precluded the selection of a larger "national" sample for the study.)*

*For the mass audience, the questionnaires were administered verbally by two interviewers from the African Languages Centre of the University of Ghana (Legon) who had training in survey techniques. The statements were initially translated into the local language and were subsequently retranslated into English by a third language specialist to ensure that the proper meanings had been conveyed during the inverview process. [For these services I would like to thank the staff of the African Languages Centre and Mr. Kofi Safo-Kantanka of Legon.] A breakdown of the respondents by ethnic identity and sex is provided below.

SURVEY RESPONDENTS BY ETHNIC IDENTITY AND SEX

	Masses		Elites	
	Percent	Number	Percent	Number
Ethnic Group[a]				
Akan	47%	(61)	49%	(92)
Ga-Adangbe	29	(37)	9	(17)
Ewe	17	(22)	25	(47)
Mole-Dagbani	7	(9)	3	(5)
Other[b]	0	(0)	14	(26)
Total	100	(129)	100	(187)
Sex				
Male	70	(90)	92	(172)
Female	30	(39)	8	(15)

[a]The source for the ethnic divisions is the *1960 Population Census of Ghana*, Special Report "E," *Tribes in Ghana* (Accra: Census Office, 1964), pp. 1-5. All percentages have been rounded.

[b]Includes Hausa, Yoruba, Mossi, and those who gave no response.

SURVEY DATA ANALYSIS: TYPES OF SOCIALIST MIND-SETS

PRAGMATIC MIND-SET. Of the three socialist mind-sets revealed in the 1973 experimental study—pragmatic, scientific, and internationalist—the pragmatists were differentiated from the other two by (1) a predisposition toward economic flexibility in development policies, with a preference for a mixed, planned economy; (2) cultural assertiveness with respect to indigenous African values and institutions, and (3) skepticism about African politicians and a preference for decentralized political institutions with effective checks on those who rule. The first four statements which the respondents were asked to assess reflect these concerns of the pragmatists.

STATEMENT 1. *We have no intention of applying a rigid, doctrinal authoritarian socialism. Our socialism will be empirical. As required by circumstances, we will adapt. Our country's development must be planned in this way.*[11]

Response	Masses		Elites	
	Percent	Number	Percent	Number
Agree	67%	(86)	74%	(136)
Uncertain	19	(24)	17	(31)
Disagree	14	(18)	9	(17)
Total	100	(128)	100	(184)

$X^2 = 2.2$ P = .333   N = 312

Comment. Most Ghanaians—both masses and elites—express a willingness to adapt socialist economic development programs to circumstances.

STATEMENT 2. *Rather than the utilization of the most efficient techniques, socialism is a sense of community, a return to Africanism. It involves a merciless struggle against social dishonesty.*[12]

Response	Masses		Elites	
	Percent	Number	Percent	Number
Agree	45%	(57)	65%	(120)
Uncertain	39	(50)	16	(30)
Disagree	16	(20)	18	(34)
Total	100	(127)	100	(184)

X^2 = 21.3   P = <.001   N = 311

Comment. The elites are more inclined than the masses to believe that socialism is a sense of community and a return to Africanism, involving a struggle against social dishonesty. In the follow-up interview, it became evident that some of the elites believe that socialism presents a unique opportunity to assert an African identity within a framework which is egalitarian and just—a notion the masses generally regard as dubious. The masses have seen a "socialism" in which a few people receive excessively high salaries, embezzle public funds, or engage in illicit trading or bribery. While these things may be regarded as tolerable by the elites, the masses regard them as intolerable and as neither the foundation for a sense of community nor a return to pastoral Africanism. From their point of view, both socialists and non-socialists have been too willing to tolerate dishonest practices.

STATEMENT 3. *What we desire is the creation of freemen—physically, intellectually, and spiritually integrated. Our first goal, therefore, must be a fully developed socialist economy. Without this economic base, we cannot advance our freedom.*[13]

Response	Masses		Elites	
	Percent	Number	Percent	Number
Agree	74%	(95)	65%	(120)
Uncertain	14	(18)	15	(28)
Disagree	12	(15)	20	(36)
Total	100	(128)	100	(184)

X^2 = 3.79   P = .147   N = 312

Comment. Both the mass and elite audiences share a desire for personal freedom, but the masses appear to feel a stronger need for a solid economic base.

STATEMENT 4. *Scandals are numerous: ministers grow rich, their wives doll themselves up, the members of parliament feather their nests, and there is hardly a soul who does not join in the reprehensible procession of corruption. These problems must be overcome before we can attain the socialism for which we yearn.*[14]

Response	Masses		Elites	
	Percent	Number	Percent	Number
Agree	86%	(111)	82%	(153)
Uncertain	7	(9)	8	(14)
Disagree	7	(9)	10	(19)
Total	100	(129)	100	(186)

$X^2 = 1.06$ $\qquad$ P = .594 $\qquad$ N = 315

Comment. Both the mass and elite audiences have a profound distrust of politicians and perceive their leaders as corrupt. (It would be an understatement to say that most politicians and civil servants in Africa do not enjoy honorable reputations. Public service in the Ghanaian context is often viewed primarily as an invitation to partake of the spoils which public office may offer. The *Final Report of the Commission of Enquiry on Bribery and Corruption,* released in 1975, concluded that corruption is endemic to the body politic of Ghana and, if not controlled, "will seriously undermine the effectiveness of the present or any future government of Ghana."[15] Within such a context, government is likely to be tyrannical and unresponsive, and the distribution of scarce goods, services, and resources is likely to be capricious. These dangers are readily apparent to both the elites and the masses.)

SCIENTIFIC MIND-SET. In the 1973 experimental study the "scientific" socialists were characterized by dogmatic adherence to the principles of orthodox Marxism-Leninism, including the belief that class distinctions will perpetuate divisions within society which will ultimately lead to class warfare and a more perfect form of so-

cialism. The scientific socialist mind-set is reflected in positive responses to statements 5, 6, and 7.

STATEMENT 5. *We seek to promote the economic development of the people through the common ownership of the essential means of production and distribution and, ultimately, through the abolition of power to live by rent, interest, and profit.*[16]

Response	Masses		Elites	
	Percent	Number	Percent	Number
Agree	52%	(67)	70%	(130)
Uncertain	17	(22)	12	(22)
Disagree	31	(40)	18	(33)
Total	100	(129)	100	(186)

$X^2 = 11.18$ $P = < .005$ $N = 314$

Comment. While the elites may honestly believe that they seek to promote development through common ownership of the means of production, etc., the masses are less likely to believe that this is the goal of the present government—or of the elites in general. During the interview process, representatives of the masses frequently commented that they desired to "live better"—to acquire more wealth, land, and luxury goods; in short, they aspired to the material position of the elites, who possess those items from which the masses are generally excluded. Ironically, a reordering of the economic system might foreclose the possibility of the masses improving their lot in a society they already perceive to be rigged against them.

For their part, the elites—in response to a follow-up statement—generally agreed (69 percent [127] so indicated) that "African scientific socialism, specific to the needs of Africans, is the only answer for our people; the presuppositions and purposes of capitalism would be a betrayal of our personality and conscience."[17] (Seventeen percent [32] of the elite respondents expressed uncertainty about the statement, while 14 percent [26] disagreed with it.) Such agreement may represent a temporary point of view of students and other types of elites (e. g., civil servants, businessmen) who are engaged in capitalistic enterprise but retain an emotional attachment to the notion of scientific socialism. On the basis of a

215

number of general comments made by the elite/student respondents, this pro-socialist sentiment is likely to fade over time as the students assume other elite roles for which they are being groomed.

STATEMENT 6. *Classes do exist in Africa in terms of social and economic groups occupying different positions in the political system. This can only lead us to revolution and eventual socialism.*[18]

Response	Masses		Elites	
	Percent	Number	Percent	Number
Agree	53%	(68)	48%	(90)
Uncertain	20	(26)	17	(31)
Disagree	27	(35)	35	(66)
Total	100	(129)	100	(187)

$X^2 = 2.45$ $P = .293$ $N = 316$

Comment. In the follow-up interview it was found that while a majority of the mass audience and a plurality of the elite audience agree that class differences exist in African society, they are less inclined to believe that these differences will lead to revolution or socialism. They insist that classes have always existed in their society. As Nkrumah puts it:

> The phrase "African socialism" seems to espouse the view that the traditional African society was a classless society imbued with the spirit of humanism and to express a nostalgia for that spirit. Such a conception of socialism makes a fetish of the communal African society. But an idyllic, African classless society (in which there were no rich and no poor) enjoying a drugged serenity is certainly a facile simplification; there is no historical or even anthropological evidence for any such society. I am afraid the realities of African society were somewhat more sordid.[19]

Ghanaians—especially those at the lower end of the socioeconomic spectrum—are not unaware of these "sordid realities" but their knowledge of them does not give rise to expectations of a unified proletariat turning the society on its head through violent revolution. Rather, since violence is not regarded by most Ghanaians as an effective means of social transformation (and given their pre-

disposition for discussion), social change is likely to be peaceful and evolutionary.

STATEMENT 7. *If our economic and industrial policy is to succeed, then those responsible for running our affairs must acquire a Marxist perspective and a socialist drive keyed to socialist needs and demands.*[20]

Response	Masses		Elites	
	Percent	Number	Percent	Number
Agree	48%	(62)	64%	(118)
Uncertain	19	(25)	8	(14)
Disagree	33	(42)	28	(52)
Total	100	(129)	100	(184)

$X^2 = 12.30$ $P = < .005$ $N = 313$

Comment. There is substantial agreement between the mass and elite audiences concerning the perspective they believe should be adopted by their political leadership. The interviews indicate that the elites see a need for more rigorous organizational and management techniques to be applied to a faltering economic policy; as a result they tend to favor leadership—even Marxist leadership—which might better coordinate industrial activities within the state. The mass audience is somewhat more cynical about leadership in general. They seem to think that it makes little difference what ideological perspective their leadership has with regard to economic policy: there will be little discernible improvement in *their* living conditions. They recall that Nkrumah, an avowed "socialist," had limited success in guiding the economic policies of the state. Finally, they perceive themselves as being politically impotent.

INTERNATIONAL MIND-SET. In the 1973 experimental study the "internationalist" socialists were characterized by their perception of the world as economically interdependent; from their viewpoint, national characteristics and policies should be subordinated to a more global political and economic integration. This orientation was distinguished by (1) a belief that future African economic development will require assistance from non-African sources, (2) a

perception that, in terms of socialist development, Africa is essentially a proletarian continent, and (3) a rejection of the political mythology and folklore supportive of indigenous African culture.

STATEMENT 8. *Economically, Africa cannot do without the other
continents, except at the price of increasing our relative backwardness.* [21]

Response	Masses		Elites	
	Percent	Number	Percent	Number
Agree	79%	(101)	61%	(112)
Uncertain	10	(13)	8	(14)
Disagree	11	(14)	32	(58)
Total	100	(128)	100	(184)

X^2 = 18.02   P = <.001   N = 312

Comment. Although there is a general sense of global inter-
dependence, interviews reveal that many elite respondents deny that
Ghana is "relatively backward" in comparison to other countries.
Moreover, many of them do not regard the presence of foreign,
multinational corporations in Ghana as a positive influence; they
tend to see these firms as a form of neocolonialism since they extract
profits from Ghana, but do not adequately reinvest in indigenous
enterprises. The mass respondents tend to regard foreign economic
enterprises favorably—not only because they provide increased employment opportunities, but also because they are a source of scarce
luxury items which would otherwise be completely denied to the
masses if they had to rely on domestic firms alone.

The elites amplified their views of Africa's international status
in response to a follow-up statement. Fifty-eight percent (106) of
the respondents disagreed with the statement "The image we have of
our continent is that of a proletarian continent. Socialism has created
a bond of poverty between us and has contributed to Pan-African
sentiments at large."[22] Twenty-four percent (44) of the respondents
expressed uncertainty, and only 18 percent (33) agreed with the
statement. They do not believe themselves to be part of an international, revolutionary proletarian fellowship—nor do they define
poverty in material conditions alone. Thus they do not conform to

the ideal internationalist mind-set delineated in the experimental study.

STATEMENT 9. *"They talk 'til they agree." This is the very essence of African democracy. It is a clumsy way of conducting affairs in a world impatient for results, but discussion is essential to any democracy, and the African is expert at it.*[23]

Response	Masses		Elites	
	Percent	Number	Percent	Number
Agree	66%	(85)	63%	(116)
Uncertain	18	(23)	15	(28)
Disagree	16	(20)	22	(40)
Total	100	(128)	100	(184)

$X^2 = 1.94$ $\qquad$ P = .62 $\qquad$ N = 312

Comment. The general nonconformity of Ghanaians to the internationalist orientation is found in the mass and elite reponses to statements about indigenous African traditions, mythology, and folklore. Both the masses and the elites seem to prefer discussion to direct confrontation as a means of social change. Perhaps neither group has access to structures which would allow for their participation in policymaking; their preference for "talking things out" is probably a carryover from the pastoral tradition in which chiefs, linguists, and elders sat under a shady tree exchanging views until a consensus emerged concerning an appropriate course of action for a given situation. Thus the democratic-centralist notion of arriving at a group decision or "party line" through discussion is legitimated in the Ghanaian context.

STATEMENT 10. *Our African personality contains elements of simplicity and wisdom that are to be found more easily in the common man than in those who have tried to learn the complicated new language of the modern world—and this is why we must not lose touch with the common man whose sense of individual mission guides our democratic socialism.*[24]

Response	Masses		Elites	
	Percent	Number	Percent	Number
Agree	78%	(100)	80%	(148)
Uncertain	11	(14)	11	(20)
Disagree	12	(15)	9	(17)
Total	100	(129)	100	(185)

$X^2 = .502$ P = .78   N = 314

Comment. African peasant-based wisdom is regarded as effective by both the masses and the elites, and the notion of the "African personality" forms part of the mythology of the political culture of Ghana. To a follow-up statement 70 percent (129) of the students disagreed that "the African personality can only remain a glorious myth. At best it is a focus, a coming into consciousness. It is no use pretending that it means anything to any given individual."[25] These respondents believe that the myth of the African personality is useful in the construction of the modern culture of Ghana and the resurrection of a favorable image of the pre-colonial culture.

STATEMENT 11. *We in Africa have no more need of being converted to socialism than we have of being taught democracy. Both are rooted in the traditional society which produced us, and will foster our security in the modern world.*[26]

Response	Masses		Elites	
	Percent	Number	Percent	Number
Agree	59%	(76)	51%	(94)
Uncertain	19	(24)	21	(39)
Disagree	22	(29)	28	(52)
Total	100	(129)	100	(185)

$X^2 = 2.08$ P = .35   N = 314

Comment. Masses and elites believe that the pre-colonial culture in Africa was both socialistic and democratic. To the extent that socialism and democracy are seen as part of an interrupted ancestral

heritage in Ghana, they are nourished in the belief that they will contribute to the future welfare and culture of the country.

ELITE/MASS CLEAVAGES. Several statements which elicited consensus responses among the three socialist mind-sets in the 1973 study tended to indicate cleavages between masses and elites in the Ghanaian context. These cleavages are reflected in differing degrees of agreement with the statements rather than in "agree-disagree" splits. Statements 12 through 15 reflect some of this cleavage.

STATEMENT 12. *In our African society we are individuals of various status within a community. We take care of the community's needs, and the community takes care of ours. That is socialism.*[27]

Response	Masses		Elites	
	Percent	Number	Percent	Number
Agree	76%	(97)	47%	(87)
Uncertain	10	(13)	19	(36)
Disagree	14	(18)	34	(62)
Total	100	(128)	100	(185)

$X^2 = 26.02$ $P = < .001$ $N = 313$

Comment. The follow-up interview revealed that many students believe that *they* (as elites) are not "individuals of various status" in their society. In contrast, the masses appear to perceive clearly that there are persons of differing status within the community. They see that their status is lower than that of the elites, but they are inclined to believe that through their labor they are making greater contributions to the development process: they can see the physical results of their manual labor, but know little of the work of government planners. While the masses tend to have faith that society in general, and the elites in particular, will take care of their needs, the elites are less convinced of their obligation to provide for such needs.

The faith in society expressed by the masses reflects more a traditional community arrangement than a modern, urban one, and is consonant with Nyerere's linking of traditional social arrangements with his definition of socialism:

Both the "rich" and the "poor" individual were completely secure in [traditional] African society. Natural catastrophe brought famine, but it brought famine to everbody—"poor" or "rich." Nobody starved, either of food or of human dignity, because he lacked personal wealth; he could depend on the wealth possessed by the community of which he was a member. *That was socialism. That is socialism.* [28]

STATEMENT 13. *The best and most ethical way to achieve lasting economic progress is to assure equality of sacrifice in all walks of life—i. e., to give each according to his needs, and take from each according to his abilities.* [29]

Response	Masses		Elites	
	Percent	Number	Percent	Number
Agree	77%	(99)	69%	(127)
Uncertain	13	(16)	9	(17)
Disagree	10	(13)	22	(40)
Total	100	(128)	100	(184)

$X^2 = 7.44$ $\qquad$ P = <.05 $\qquad$ N = 312

Comment. The masses appear to believe more strongly than the elites that economic progress requires sacrifices by all who make up a community. The follow-up interviews indicate, however, that while such conditions may obtain under ideal circumstances, the masses believe that "real" sacrifices need to be made now by those who are more wealthy, better educated, and have a higher standard of living if their society is to make progress in escaping from its present situation—i. e., a situation in which they perceive the quality of life of a majority of individuals continuing to deteriorate uncontrollably.

STATEMENT 14. *We have to face up to an act of conditioning our people psychologically so that we can destroy in them the various complexes created by the colonial system—ignorance, inability, insecurity, desire for the easy life.* [30]

Response	Masses		Elites	
	Percent	Number	Percent	Number
Agree	72%	(92)	92%	(171)
Uncertain	9	(12)	3	(6)
Disagree	19	(24)	4	(8)
Total	100	(128)	100	(185)

$X^2 = 24.15$ $P = <.001$ $N = 313$

Comment. While the masses sometimes blame the elites for deteriorating conditions in Ghana, the elites blame the colonial system of twenty years ago for creating a predisposition toward an easy life. There is a tendency on the part of the elite respondents (many of whom were not alive during the colonial period, but were raised in the Nkrumah years) to blame all social ills on colonialism twenty years after independence, and deny any responsibility for present conditions. The "complexes" and "desire for the easy life" do exist among the people, and one way of coping with them is to blame them on a colonial history over which they had no control.

LEADERSHIP, ISSUES, PRIORITIES. One defense mechanism a society can employ to cope with a lack of tangible progress and development is to emphasize those unique, mythological, and intangible aspects of culture which satisfy an inner faith that, despite material shortcomings, a sense of purpose and mission can be achieved by the resurrection of a usable past. Such intangibles often include a reliance on political folklore, the veneration of dead national heroes, and a rather chauvinistic belief that one's countrymen share a common code of behavior demonstrating rectitude and therefore deserving of international respect.

STATEMENT 15. *If the white man shuts his eyes to the good that is in my culture, he is the poorer for it, and I am one up on him.*[31]

Response	Masses		Elites	
	Percent	Number	Percent	Number
Agree	84%	(108)	75%	(137)
Uncertain	5	(6)	11	(20)
Disagree	12	(15)	14	(26)
Total	100	(129)	100	(183)

$X^2 = 4.71$ $\qquad\qquad$ P = .09 $\qquad\qquad$ N = 312

The creation of a usable past, a recalling of former times of national greatness, a belief in the African personality to endure hardship, and the perpetuation of political mythology is important to the maintenance of the cultural order in Ghana. Nkrumah was part of that process, and he helped to manipulate it constructively. Mythology cannot end famine, however. A resurrected national history which masses and elites alike can regard with a sense of pride is laudable, but it is no substitute for pipe-borne water, access to health clinics, a reliable food supply, and a stable economy. Ultimately leaders are responsible for giving their populations a sense of vision and purpose in contemporary terms. Nkrumah's notion of "scientific socialism" may have been a useful basis for national norms at the time, but in the modern period it is no substitute for the tangible improvement in the quality of life for the citizens of Ghana.

The current military regime in Ghana is perceived as incapable of providing the necessary leadership required to accomplish pragmatic policy goals. A large number of Ghanaians desire a prompt return to complete civilian rule. The apparent concession by the military regime of strengthening the civilian component of the civil service, and allowing for greater input into the decision-making process by civilians, is regarded as too little too late. When asked to name an "ideal leader," the mass audience tended to mention the names of local or regional leaders more often than did their elite counterparts, but majorities of both groups agreed that there is no ideal leader in Ghana (see Table 3).

When asked what they expected of their government, the masses specified—in order—guaranteed employment and a reduction in the cost of living, housing, better roads, free education, more and better food, and more health clinics (see Table 4).

Table 3

Whom Do You Consider an Ideal Leader?

	Masses			Elites	
Leader	Percent	Number	Leader	Percent	Number
No one	49.6%	(64)	Nyerere	55.1%	(103)
Nkrumah	27.1	(35)	No one	28.3	(53)
Nyerere [Tanzania]	7.8	(10)	Nkrumah	10.2	(19)
Acheampong [Ghana]	5.4	(7)	Kaunda [Zambia]	1.6	(3)
Amin [Uganda]	3.9	(5)	Busia [Ghana]	1.1	(2)
Bernasko [Ghana]	1.6	(2)	Touré	1.1	(2)
Touré [Guinea]	1.6	(2)	Machel [Mozambique]	1.1	(2)
Others[a]	3.1	(4)	Others[b]	1.6	(3)
TOTAL	100.0	(129)	TOTAL	100.0	(187)

[a]Ya Na, Nii Olenu, Aggery, and Backo were each mentioned once.
[b]Neto, Nasser, and Acheampong were each mentioned once.

Table 4

What Do You Expect the Government to Do for You?

Activity	Percent	Number
1. Guarantee employment and reduce the cost of living	23.7%	(27)
2. Provide housing	17.5	(20)
3. Provide better roads	14.0	(16)
4. Provide free education	12.3	(14)
5. Provide more and better food	6.1	(7)
6. Provide more health clinics	5.3	(6)
7. Guarantee political freedoms	4.4	(5)
8. Better communications system	4.4	(5)
9. Provide piped water	2.6	(3)
10. Other[a]	9.6	(11)
TOTAL	100.0	(114)

[a]Personal expectations (e. g., "Increase my salary").

When asked what issues the Ghanaian government should deal with quickly, the mass audience mentioned economic matters most frequently. Next in order of importance were issues of housing, transportation, and aid to the rural areas (see Table 5).

CONCLUSION

The elite and mass respondents in this survey tend to come closest to sharing the "pragmatic" orientation defined in the 1973 experimental study. Also there is an affinity, especially among the elites, for the rhetoric of "scientific socialism." There is little preference among either group for the "internationalist" position. There is no evidence of support for a violent proletarian revolution, an authoritarian government, or an embracing of non-African, socialistic political and economic models. Both groups acknowledge the role of political mythology in their national culture; in fact they tend to believe that democracy and socialism are rooted in their traditional

Table 5

What Issues Should the Government Deal with Quickly?

Issue	Percent	Number
1. Guarantee employment and reduce the cost of living	24.6%	(28)
2. Housing	14.9	(17)
3. Transportation	14.0	(16)
4. Aid to rural areas	14.0	(16)
5. End bribery & corruption	13.2	(15)
6. Guarantee political freedoms	7.9	(9)
7. Food supply	7.0	(8)
8. Health care	4.4	(5)
TOTAL	100.0	(114)

society and that such concepts as the African personality are instrumental for defining the norms of their polity.

Few citizens of any country desire corrupt leaders, unresponsive political institutions, or an abundance of economic problems. Ghanaians are no different in this respect. Increased employment opportunities, reduced inflation, an improved physical infrastructure, and honest leaders are more important to them than Marxist principles. When the leadership cadre is seen as corrupt, it is difficult to inspire modernizing activities and to mobilize the masses for participation in social programs. Ghanaians are aware of the hard work and deferred gratification that is required to modernize their country, but they do not want to be the victims of a class struggle in which their sacrifices produce no discernible improvement in their living conditions, but instead contribute to a situation where a small influential group monopolizes a disproportionate amount of wealth and power.

The data presented in this study tend to suggest that Nkrumah filled the role of a political folk hero. He lent a degree of constructive mythmaking to Ghanaian culture. His importance as a weaver of dreams was recognized beyond Ghana, beyond Africa, and extended to all foreign capitals of the modern world. More importantly, Ghanaians were aware of this. Nkrumah's political style and

charisma make his attraction as a leader understandable. He represented something vital in African life; his charismatic character pervaded African culture and helped to maintain a sense of order in the African setting; he was a shrewd politician and demonstrated bold, if not always wise, leadership on major issues. He became a symbol of the modern African culture.

The routinization of the new order involves the transmission of the myths of the culture over time. This mythology gives a unique dimension to Ghanaian culture which distinguishes it from the cultures of other countries in the minds of native Africans. All this suggests that Nkrumah served as a condensation symbol for Ghanaian society.[32]

Since his death, Nkrumah has been replaced by Nyerere as the leading African spokesman in the minds of the elites (and by no one in the minds of the masses). He has not been replaced by any other Ghanaian, and his recent veneration is not surprising in a culture which wishes to salvage something useful from the post-independence, "modern" past. Ghanaians like Nkrumah because he made Ghana important in the eyes of the rest of the world. His notions of "scientific socialism" were not particularly contagious, and are probably not his most important legacy.

Ghanaians feel a need to resurrect a "modern usable history" not only because their country has lost its preeminence on the ideological front, but also because it is dwarfed geographically by Ivory Coast and Nigeria in West Africa, and lacks a sense of purpose in resolving its current domestic difficulties. The present regime has proved incapable of meeting either the material or the psychological needs of its people.

Given their plight and their cynicism about politicians and political schemes it is remarkable that Ghanaians have persisted in attempts to carry on a political dialogue. The Acheampong government has signalled its willingngess to abdicate in favor of a "Union Government"—a parliamentary government based on consensus, where the army, police, and civilians would share power in a "no-party" state. All nongovernmental political organizations have been prevented from speaking against the Union Government proposal, leaving no one to campaign against it legally. Some form of the Union Government proposal will emerge by default, but the military regime would be naive to believe that it will represent a lasting solution to Ghana's political problems. The predictable embrace of Union Government by both the elites and the masses will derive

less from the assumed durability of the proposed scheme than from the shared belief that anything is preferable to the status quo.

The elites are critical of the Union Government proposal because it does not provide a mechanism for the formation of political parties, which the elites view as essential for the organization of government in a modern state. Moreover, the proposal does not appear to allow any protection for the expression of divergent ideological viewpoints. The proponents of Union Government cry for consensus, but there will be no consensus—at least not in a parliamentary model—without structures for opposing views to be aired.

The elites believe that in the proposed government parliamentary caucuses will form based on the ideological preferences of the individual participants. This will give rise to partisanship on major issues, and political parties will then emerge. The elites feel that it would be preferable to allow political parties to organize and campaign on the Union Government proposal from the outset.

The masses also will support the proposal for Union Government. When the military lashes out at the lazy, corrupt intellectuals in society, the masses applaud. When they speak in favor of returning rule to the civilians, the masses applaud even louder. If previous history is any index, the loudest applause from the masses will be reserved for the denunciation of the military regime by its civilian successor. The behavior of the Ghanaian masses is not difficult to explain: they will support any form of government which will respond effectively to the pressing economic problems of triple-digit inflation, food shortages, inadequate distribution of medical supplies, and the like. Change is now needed because it is clear that the military regime is no more capable of solving these problems than any other post-independence Ghanaian government has been. (Many respondents in this study would argue that the problems are due primarily to the post-independence trade structures that favor Europeans.) The masses seem prepared to support any form of government so long as it is more effective than its predecessor. The ideology of the regime is less important than the solutions it provides to the problems which affect the masses directly.

An important ingredient in the success of any future proposal is the definition of the role to be played by traditional leaders and chiefs. Over the course of the past twenty years no Ghanaian government has survived which has ignored the legitimacy and credibility of the traditional leaders. They are critical to the success of any government's operation in Ghana—especially in the rural areas. Here

the fundamental themes of African identity, beliefs, and practices are integrated with the goals of the state. The proponents of Union Government argue that parliamentary representation should be based on this traditional composite of chiefs, ethnicity, regions, and villages. They claim that these structures have more relevance to Ghanaians than the corrupt party structures.

It does not seem reasonable to attribute all previous disunity, violence, and corruption to party competition alone, especially since the military has proved no less corrupt and equally prone to tailoring its operations to the various ethnic divisions within the country. In the absence of parties, however, the influence of chiefs is likely to grow, and traditional leaders are likely to support Union Government because of their increased strength in a no-party system.

The crises faced by Ghanaians today are profound: crises of inept leadership, ideological rhetoric without government action, economic retrogression, parliamentary proposals and European-dominated trade structures will not be solved by a Union Government alone or by socialism in the abstract. The situation presents opportunities for a renewed experimentation with the socialist alternative as it may be applied to concrete problems. The fact that Ghanaians have remained actively interested in their own political processes is encouraging.

IDEOLOGICAL RHETORIC AND SCIENTIFIC SOCIALISM
IN BENIN AND CONGO/BRAZZAVILLE

Samuel Decalo

Superficially there may appear to be few significant similarities between the two former French colonies of Benin (ex-Dahomey) and Congo/Brazzaville. In terms of their historical evolution and socio-economic infrastructures, the two countries are quite different, and even in their conversion to the status of "People's Republics" (with the adoption of Marxism-Leninism as the official state ideology)— seemingly their only contemporary common denominator—the two have followed quite distinct paths: Congo declared for the socialist option in 1963 (becoming Africa's first People's Republic in 1968) and Benin over a decade later.

All this notwithstanding, the basic systemic similarities of the two geographically distant countries is quite remarkable. Both present strikingly similar patterns of praetorian instability, socioeconomic turmoil, urban radicalization, rural stagnation, and political maladministration. And in the spheres of ideology and socioeconomic development, both Congo and Benin manifest—much more than any other African states—immense cleavages between rhetoric and reality, between a stridently vocal concern (especially in Congo) with ideological militancy, vigor, purity, and autocriticism ("Socialist rectitude") and a near-total failure of all leadership strata to direct or control socioeconomic development (in *any* manner, let alone along socialist lines) or to arrest corruption and mismanagement in their own ranks. Indeed, the immense gap between, on the one hand, ideological and ideologically derived policy-goals, incessantly hammered at with an insistence and ferocity reminiscent of the ideological clashes of early Stalinist Russia (and accompanied by similar purges), and on the other, the pragmatism and continued dependency-relations with former colonial powers not only tolerated but encouraged by the ruling elites tempt the critical observer to discount African radical ideology as but "opium for the masses."

Yet while socialist rhetoric and radical ideology are used quite opportunistically by contemporary elites to balance, "correct," or buttress their legitimacy or ethnic credentials, or to fend off other factions aspiring to power, it cannot be disputed that increasingly larger proportions of the urban masses have become radicalized and open to class appeals. Moreover, the failure of the contemporary elites to achieve a rapid, radical socioeconomic transformation of their societies (beyond the selective expropriation of expatriate capital) should be viewed within the context of the enormity of the task being undertaken. Even were the leaderships concerned united, sincere, and selfless (which in the cases of Congo and Benin they unequivocally are *not* on all three counts), the socioeconomic realities, existing neocolonial relationships, and other international limitations may preclude more than very modest advances toward the goal of a better society they so ardently espouse. However this may be, a proper assessment of the role Scientific Socialism plays in both Benin and Congo, and the manner in which radical ideology has been utilized there, requires a basic understanding of the nature of power in these two countries and the origins, motivations, and concerns of the current decision-making elites. Any analysis of socialism in these two countries cannot help but be in part the study of the highly complex struggle for political control and power in them.

BACKGROUND TO THE BENIN REVOLUTION

Nothing in the personal backgrounds of the members of the young military junta that now (1978) rules Benin in the name of the "Revolutionary farmers and workers" could have forewarned observers of the impending transformation of the country that followed the 1972 *coup d'etat*. Indeed, in most circles the coup through which the junta came to power was viewed as merely another in a succession of meaningless and debilitating "power-grabs" by a faction of the highly politicized and praetorian army. The coup—the sixth in Benin in twelve years of independence—brought to power a young group of middle- and low-ranking officers who were, for all practical purposes, political unknowns even in their own country. A few had appeared in the national limelight previously (during previous coups), but their role had always been subservient to the main actors—the senior officer hierarchy. If as a group they were distinguished by anything besides youth and junior rank, it was by their being by and large politically uncommitted to anyone or anything. Though one or two were known to be favorably disposed to one or another of the domi-

nant political leaders of the past, and a few had acquired reputations as "conservatives" or "radicals," there was little to indicate that the 1972 coup was different from the other power-grabs—i.e., nonideological, personalist—and that Dahomey had reached a crossroads, with radical rhetoric to become the staple of the state.

At the time of the coup, Benin had just completed the first peaceful change of political leadership in its turbulent history as President Hubert Maga passed the rotating chairmanship of Benin's unique Presidential Council to Justin Ahomadegbé.* Though the council had proved unsatisfactory and costly in several respects, it had restrained the ambitions of the country's three ethnic leaders—Maga, Ahomadegbé, and Apithy [Vice-President of Dahomey 1960-63, President 1963-65]—and kept intra-elite strife within manageable limits. In all previous instances one or two of the three had eliminated the other(s), and political succession had been consequent upon a military intervention.[1] Divided sharply along ethnic-regional lines into remarkably cohesive and stable political camps,†[2] Dahomean politics during the period 1945-72 is essentially the history of a three-cornered tug-of-war, of occasional alliances and frequent intrigues, purges, and forced exiles, punctuated by increasingly praetorian military intervention and periods of military rule. Almost every possible combination of these three had had its day in the sun and failed to provide either stability or development, but the Dahomean electorate, loyal to its traditional ethnic leaders, has refused to support any alternate contenders for the political throne.

This Dahomean version of musical chairs inevitably eroded political legitimacy and destroyed the corporate integrity of the armed forces. Long before the 1972 coup catapulted to power the

*Maga had been President of Dahomey between 1960 and 1963, when he was overthrown in a coup due in part to mismanagement of official finances. Briefly imprisoned and then self-exiled in Paris, Maga returned to Cotonou to compete in the 1970 elections, emerging as the first chairman of the Presidential Council (see Decalo, *Historical Dictionary of Dahomey*). Ahomadegbé, who was imprisoned by Maga during Maga's first tenure as President, became Vice-President (and Head of Government) of Dahomey after the 1963 coup, sharing power with Sorou-Migan Apithy, who was President. Constant bickering between the two led to a 1965 coup and an interlude of military rule under General Christopher Soglo. Like Maga, Ahomadegbé became a self-exile in Paris until 1970, when he returned to Dahomey and was elected to the Presidential Council.

†The Fon in the southwest have been solidly organized behind the candidacy of Ahomadegbé (of the Agonglo branch of the pre-colonial Fon Danhomé kingdom); the Yoruba and Goun of the southwest (and especially the Porto Novo area) have long been the fiefdom of Apithy; and Maga has controlled the northern Bariba and other groups through a series of ethnic lieutenants.

latest clique of military power-seekers, the armed forces had become a patchwork of competing personalist/ethnic allegiance-pyramids centered around popular officers of all ranks in which superior rank or authority was only grudgingly acknowledged.[3] Moreover, not only had the armed forces become the vehicle for political aspirations of specific officers, but they had also acquired the appearance of being the fount (or repository) of ultimate political legitimacy. In justifying his 1972 coup, Major Mathieu Kerekou stated—in terms almost identical to those used by Colonel Maurice Kouandété when he had assumed power three years earlier—that he had not "seized" power but had "collected" it back: "The ousted civilian regime held its power from the Army. The Army has taken back what it gave."[4]

In the economic sphere Benin has continuously been on the brink of bankruptcy, with large budgetary deficits and overwhelmingly negative balances of trade—all covered by French subventions.[*5] Producing mostly agricultural products within the context of a stagnating agrarian sector, while voraciously consuming Western commodities at a level befitting its colonial reputation as the "Latin Quarter of Africa"[6] and supporting a bloated bureaucracy[†] and extensive social services (especially education for an upwardly mobile southern population), Benin seemed destined to remain in a dependency relationship with France for a long time.[7] Half-hearted attempts by several leaders at fiscal restraint and budgetary austerity (hiring freezes, cuts in personal allowances, heavy "solidarity" levies and taxes) have foundered against the demands of militant trade unions, increasingly radicalized and ever ready to defend their prerogatives. Indeed, paralyzing general strikes (linked with student upheavals) against austerity policies preceded two of the coups in Benin.

Within this context of intense intra-elite strife and periodic clashes between the government and various interest groups over the distribution of benefits in a societal framework of acute scarcity, ideology had rarely played a significant role. Each party or faction, each interest group, and each military faction had been primarily interested in preserving its status, enhancing its position, or gaining ascendance over all others, as the case may be. All efforts to inject radical or socialist ideology into Benin politics had failed dismally. Even in the turbulent 1950's, an era of intense jockeying, a miniscule

*For the period 1960-75, exports have ranged between a high of 59% (1960) and a low of 15.9% (1975 provisional estimates) of imports, with a median of 41.3%.

†The bureaucracy consumes upwards of 65% of the national budget.

Parti de la Revolution Socialiste du Benin collapsed due to the lack of interest in it in the "proletarianized" urban centers of the south. The more moderate Mouvement de Liberation Nationale also collapsed when it compromised its basic platform and merged with the traditional hierarchy, while the inter-territorial Mouvement Socialiste Africain had barely fifty members in all the south.[8] Of the ethnic parties and leaders, only during Ahomadegbé's 1963-65 tenure as Vice-President was there even a semblance of ideology.[9] While radical rhetoric was reflected in the progressively radicalized schools and unions (especially in the late 1960's and early 1970's), it seemed curiously artificial and out of keeping with the generally conservative social ethos.

In like manner all attempts to set up non-ethnic political parties have come to naught. The various *partis unique* set up have been forced mergers of ethnically incompatible clientelist formations. Following each coup the parties have collapsed into their individual components, under new names, providing a complex representation of a basically simple tripartite cleavage.[10] The best example of Dahomey's classic ethnic division—of electoral loyalties that take precedence over any ideological or non-ethnic appeals—was provided by the four-cornered Presidential elections of 1970. Emile Derlin Zinsou, the veteran politician who as President during 1969-70 had given Dahomey its most astute leadership since independence, stood as the modern non-ethnic alternative to the established ethnic triumvirate; he received barely 3 percent of the vote. The stability of ethnic-regional politics in Dahomey is attested by the fact that virtually the same percentage of the vote went to the country's ethnic leaders in 1970 as in the 1960 elections.[11]

Even the military—for several years prior to the 1972 upheaval a dominant political force—was totally lacking in interest in either ideology or "African Socialism." A few junior officers were suspected of being "radical," and amorphous factions were slowly forming around popular officers such as Captains Kerekou, Michel Aikpé, and Janvier Assogba, but ultimate power revolved around four senior officers: Major Benoit Sinzogan, Head of Gendarmerie; Lt. Colonel Alphonse Alley, Chief of Staff; Lt. Colonel Philippe Aho, former Deputy Chief of Staff; and Major Kouandété, Deputy Chief of Staff. Sinzogan, despite a power-gambit in 1970 that surprised observers, was a timid and drab officer with little proclivity for intrigue and less for ideology; Alley, immensely popular, had few intellectual pretensions or political ambitions, and was widely known as the "wine, women, and song" officer; Aho was singlemindedly preoccupied with

promoting his own and Fon military interests (he was soon retired); and Kouandété—although his intense drive to be Head of State contributed to much polarization and politicization of the armed forces—not only was not committed to any ideology or platform of action, but in 1971 could not cite a single major reform to be initiated under his aegis should he assume (by coup) the Presidency.*[12] Those who have often been referred to as Dahomey's "intellectual officers" were by and large devoid of any interests beyond their country's boundaries or their own private and military preserves, and the country that had spawned so many of Francophone Africa's progressive, cosmopolitan, and intellectual elements was ruled at home by narrow, isolationist, and ethnic elites who were uninvolved in any movements, structures, and ideologies transcending the immediate present.

The picture began to change subtly in the 1970's. Two years of the Presidential Council—though for the first time providing a power arrangement that satisfied all three ethnic leaders—had exposed the population once again to the *immobilisme* and sterile bickerings of the past. The spectacle of the old triumvirate back on the political throne despite being discredited during previous terms of office deeply rankled the more militant coastal elements.[†] The inability of any elite—civilian or political, northern or southern—to suggest alternative solutions to the country's perennial economic problems alienated the students and intellectuals always at the forefront of the more strident and ideological elements. Biannual "hat in hand" pilgrimages to Paris and French pressures or local expatriates' patronizing attitudes further offended long-suffering Dahomean pride. To many the gap between the glories of the not-too-distant (highly romanticized) past and the semi-pauper status of the present was intolerable, as were the revelations of corruption at the highest levels of the government.** While the coup that finally erupted in

*From interviews in Cotonou, July 1972. All four officers, and several of those who rose to prominence shortly later as avowed Marxists, were uninterested in socialism of any variety or form when interviewed in 1972.

†Despite this, the coastal vote in 1970 split more or less along traditional ethnic lines because Zinsou, the only non-ethnic candidate, had threatened too many southern vested interests during his Presidency.

**One allegation of corruption—the "Kovacs Affair," which related to improprieties by the holder of a monopoly on stationery supplies to the government—was levelled against Kerekou and was to pursue him through 1978. Both a 1975 attempted putsch by Captain Assogba and the disenchantment (and subsequent murder) of Captain Aikpé are related to this allegation—never fully detailed or laid to rest.

1972 had specific *military* reasons,[13] all the factors cited above played a role in widening the gap between rulers and ruled and in discrediting all aspects of the *ancien regime*—political, economic, and military. The 1972 upheaval swept out of power (probably for the last time) the entire array of civil and military leaders that for so long had dominated the Dahomean center stage. A completely new elite—unknown, untried, and to a considerable degree unsure of itself—percolated to power. In part from conviction and in part from an absence of viable options, but at least to an equal degree to seek legitimacy from the radicalized coastal populations uneasy with the "northern" leadership of the coup, Dahomey was wrenched onto a path of Scientific Socialism.

SOCIALISM IS OUR CHOSEN PATH; MARXISM-LENINISM IS OUR GUIDE*

As an ideology, a prescription for action, a framework of policies, Dahomean Socialism (as it was originally referred to) or Beninois Scientific Socialism (its more recent appellation) neither stems from previously held convictions in the officer corps nor constitutes a truly cohesive set of premises. The "doctrine" is essentially composed of ad hoc nationalistic decrees, edicts, and prescriptions only much later superficially tied to the "legitimacy" of a comprehensive radical ideology (Marxism-Leninism), whose dialectic the Beninois leadership still does not appear to have mastered. The tortuously slow radicalization of the jargon emanating from Cotonou—evident in any comparison of early with later proclamations or discourses—is a clear manifestation of the self-taught, ex post facto nature of the Benin Revolution. Beginning with a rejection of all "external" guidelines from socialism, communism, or capitalism,[14] and progressing through a period of rationalization that "Marxism is *not* the Devil,"[15] the revolutionary regime finally opted *over two years after the coup* for Marxism-Leninism, which was now regarded as an "authentic" Dahomean doctrine.[16] As one Beninois close to the regime only half-humorously observed: "They only started reading their Marx after the coup had succeeded."[17]

Because of the highly ad hoc and changing nature of the doctrine, as well as the disagreements within the officer corps concerning its provisions and even its necessity, there is no single document that can serve as the "bible" of Beninois Socialism. Benin's "intellectual officers" have been so devoid of literary proclivities that nothing along the lines of the "collected works" of Julius Nyerere,

*Motto of Benin.

Kwame Nkrumah, Moussa Traore, Kenneth Kaunda, or Marien Ngouabi exists in Benin. However, the basic policy imperatives of Beninois Socialism—as expounded by Kerekou*—are quite clear, and were formally spelled out in detail in a speech celebrating the second anniversary of the 1972 Revolution.[18] Stripped of jargon the central tenets include (1) independence from external economic control (i.e., "capitalism") through the centralization of most means of production in the hands of the state and narrowly circumscribing the limits within which private capital will be tolerated, (2) the transformation of society through various reforms and structures into a model socialist alliance of farmers and workers, and (3) a realignment of Benin's foreign policy toward the "progressive bloc." To these should be added a fourth tenet, enunciated clearly much later—i.e., democratic centralism, defined as total loyalty to the head of the newly established revolutionary party (Kerekou) and the subordination of the "minority to the majority."[†] These tenets are, *mutatis mutandis*, an integral part of Benin's fundamental law as published in August 1977.[19]

In some of his earliest speeches, Kerekou inveighed against the evil of the control of Dahomey's economy by foreigners (the "main cause" of the country's problems), sparking the flight of some French capital.[20] (French investors were already uneasy over the prominence given to the announcement of the nationalization of the French-owned water and electricity monopolies—nationalization that had been planned for years.) Pent-up anti-French feeling burst out in an orgy of riots and looting on February 28, 1973, when a demonstration against France's alleged support for a counter-coup by Colonel Alley got out of control. Kerekou had added insult to injury by charging the expatriate community with "exploitative" characteristics that had triggered the resentment, but the reaction in Paris was so negative that he offered a retraction,[21] and few further policy ventures were attempted for the duration of the "revolutionary regime's" first year in office. Indeed a conscious effort was made to play down previous statements implying a disengagement from

---

*As noted, there are significant disagreements within the officer corps regarding most matters of doctrine. Most of the sharp ideological divergences within the elite are underreported, however, and a few *very* divergent ideological postures (those of Captains Aikpé and Bodjogoumé, for example) have never been printed.

†The principles of the new party, as enunciated by Kerekou, include submission of the individual to the organization, but the party as a whole is subordinate to its Central Committee (see *West Africa*, December 22-29, 1975).

France's "apron strings,"[22] but diplomatic relations began to be established with the East,* and there was talk of a break with both the Organisation Commune Africaine et Malgache (OCAM) and the Council of the Entente.

It was not until November 30, 1974—fully two years after the revolution—that the first two nationalizations were announced, on the heels of Kerekou's anniversary speech and ten-point delineation of Dahomey's new Marxist-Leninist commitment. The latter sent shock waves through Cotonou's expatriate community, but the first announced takeovers—of the oil distribution network and private education—were not taken very seriously. The oil network was of such minor dimensions that its nationalization appeared merely a symbolic gesture, while the "takeover" of private schools (50 percent of all schools and mostly Catholic) was viewed as meaningless because all instructors were asked to remain in their posts. These two nationalizations were but the tip of the iceberg, however. Soon after, the insurance industry, transport, and two banks were brought under government control, and in mid-1975 other banks, the brewery, the popular Hotel de la Plage, all Protestant and Moslem schools, and other sectors of the economy came under state monopoly.[23]

The expansion of the public sector resulted in the establishment of a wide array of state trading, marketing, and purchasing organizations that by 1976 (on paper at least) placed most aspects of commercial activity in Benin under state control.[24] The proliferation of state activity in the economic sector—and the concomitant appointment of military personnel to supervisory posts in the economy—strained the capabilities of Benin's small (80-odd) officer corps, while the usual problems attending such a reorganization and centralization of commercial life led to a decline in productivity and inefficiency and—inevitably—created opportunities for corruption.[25] The deterioration in Benin's economy and its balance-of-trade[26] is to some extent linked to the dislocations and repercussions attending the generally poorly planned extension of state control over the economy. In most instances arrangements were made for the payment of compensation for private companies or for shares expropriated. All indications are that the Kerekou regime had not really anticipated such expenditures, however, but was forced into paying them when it realized that forthcoming French state subventions,

*A large, interest-free loan was obtained concomitant with the opening of relations with China, and the following year the construction of a major sports complex was pledged.

subsidies, loans, and grants—frozen pending a resolution of the compensation issue—greatly exceeded the sum total of all the nationalized enterprise. Indeed, despite all the patriotic fanfare and the emphasis in official rhetoric, bringing the major sectors of the economy under state control involved the expropriation of assets valued at a mere 2,000 million CFAF (barely $8 million!). French aid blocked in 1974 exceeded this sum, and French aid between 1970 and 1974—40 percent of all aid granted to Benin—amounted to over 10,200 million CFAF.[27] The influence of French expatriate capital on economic activity in Benin has been heightened by the weakness of the country's economy and its small modern sector, which has also limited the prospects for rapid and radical socioeconomic development.

Hand in hand with the extension of state control over the economy, the Kerekou regime undertook a "reorganization" of Benin's administrative structure. During a week of high-level deliberations in November 1973 involving prefects, subprefects, formerly self-exiled radical ideologues, and a number of military officers, a formula was arrived at for the "decentralization" of the administration that would allow "the organized masses to recover control of the state apparatus."[28] Strongly criticizing the old system in which "a minority of petits bourgeois numbering 30,000 had placed the state in the service of an imperialist and neo-colonial system of exploitation,"[29] the planners renamed Dahomey's regions and administrative officials and called for the establishment of Revolutionary Councils and the appointment of Political Commissars at each level of the administration—i.e., regional, district, etc.* Villages, townships, and urban communities were to have Revolutionary Committees, and at a later stage all quarters and places of work were to organize Committees for the Defense of the Revolution charged with the function of detecting and denouncing enemies of the Revolution. Regional centers for rural development were established in each province in 1975 for managing developmental projects and organizing and helping the rural population in general,[30] and as a further effort at revamping the structures of government there was a reorganization of ministries and creation of several superministries. According to Interior Minister Aikpé, one of the more militant leaders at the time, these reorganizations "responded to the needs of the oppressed masses."[31]

*Major Michel Alladayé, Captains Aikpé and André Achadé, Lieutenants Albert Koyami and Martin Azonhiho, and Sublieutenant Philippe Akpo were appointed political commissars on December 2, 1974; they were responsible for the "organization, instruction, and mobilization of the people."

The failure of the masses to respond with alacrity to the opportunities allegedly offered them by these new structures was explained by the continued presence of "impenitent enemies of the Revolution," including "short-term idealists, opportunists, fishers in troubled waters, and reactionaries of all trends."[32]

By 1975 much of the new apparatus had officially been operational for two years, and, according to the regime, there were 1500 Committees for the Defense of the Revolution dotting the countryside.[33] However, most were only "paper structures,"[34] while those that were genuinely operational were either practically moribund or merely control mechanisms for the central government (or power bases for its top competitors for power) rather than agencies for grass-roots participation in the building of a new socialist order.[35]

The regime's penchant for the *trappings* of a Marxist-Leninist state were manifest in the great attention given to the superficial and tangential: the promulgation of an edict concerning the proper "revolutionary" way of ending letters,* a drive against "neo-colonialism" in clothing, continuing diatribes about the lack of "Socialist morality" in attendance at nightspots (whose hours were curtailed because they were seen as a "hotbed of reactionary forces")[36] and in weddings lasting until midnight, the change in Dahomey's name and flag in November 1975, etc. Though a number of quasi-political structures had been set up shortly after the 1972 coup,† there was no attempt either to bring civilians into top decision-making organs (which remained solidly military) or to institutionalize a revolutionary party. The idea of setting up a legitimizing proletarian party had been suggested to Kerekou as early as January 1973 by the militant union elements that had formed the United Democratic Front (which had been behind the anti-French demonstrations), but the suggestion was rejected by Kerekou as impractical because it would encompass only "a fraction of Dahomey."[37] By 1975, however, with the military regime's prestige at its nadir and sources of opposition against it proliferating both internally and externally, the legitimizing facade seemed more desirable (though little had occurred to make Marxism more widespread), and the Benin People's

---

*"Kindly accept the assurance of my revolutionary commitments."

†These included a Military Council for the Revolution watchdog body over the activities of the government (see *West Africa*, January 1, 1973), a National Council for the Revolution composed of sixty-nine individuals from three corporate "fronts"—workers, youth, women—and a thirteen-man mixed civilian-military Political Bureau. All three (but especially the National Council) were by 1974 riddled with "counter-revolutionaries" and allowed to ossify.

Revolutionary Party (BPRP) was born under tight military control in May 1976. It is too early to tell whether or not the BPRP will turn out to be another largely hollow structure, but certainly the indications to date are that the party is *not* truly operative. Since the murder of Aikpé (see below), the alienation of labor, students, civil service, and the south in general has been so complete that it is hard to point to any source of support for Kerekou outside the army itself.

Youth—increasingly vocal, strident, and radical in the 1970's in Benin's coastal cities—spearheaded the opposition to the regime when its radical idols Captains Nestor Beheton and Hilaire Bodjogoumé were returned to the barracks in August 1973 after only eight months in the cabinet. Though Kerekou had lifted the ban on the Union Général des Elèves et Etudiants du Dahomey (UGEED)* and appealed at the outset for the support of youth, the intransigence of the Union, its call for a "true revolution," its barbed attacks on the army's petit-bourgeois mentality, and continuing friction between the regime and students in general brought the regime the same confrontations with youth that every regime had faced in the past—and the same consequences.† Moreover, though pretending to be radical, youth in general has been unwilling to forgo the fleshpots of the city and accept the twelve months of civic duty in the countryside promulgated late in 1975.[38]

Kerekou has also been unable to retain control over the officer corps, which has been divided from pre-revolutionary days into a multitude of personalist and ethnic loyalty-pyramids. Early in 1975 the internal schisms within the officer corps resulted in a challenge to Kerekou's faction by Assogba,** whose attempted coup was grounded in claims that Kerekou had accepted a 35 million CFAF bribe[39]—part of the Kovacs Affair fiasco extending back to 1972 and the era of the civilian Presidential Council.[40] Within six months, Aikpé—the strong man of the regime and architect of the 1972 coup—was murdered. Aikpé, who for some time had been rumored to be plotting Kerekou's demise both because of his disillusionment

---

*The highly politicized and ultra-left UGEED in December 1971 had called for the transformation of Dahomey into a "vast battleground."

†Particularly annoying to the regime was a January 1974 strike in Abomey and Porto Novo. Kerekou lashed out viciously against the students on this occasion, claiming that they were influenced by petit-bourgeois intellectuals who are mostly cut off from the "working masses" and whose "verbalism and infantile Left-wingism . . . benefit reaction" (*Africa Research Bulletin*, Economic Series, April 1974; see also *West Africa*, May 6, 1974).

**At the time the Minister of Civil Service and Labor.

with the latter's socialist commitments and his acceptance of Assogba's charges as true,[41] allegedly was killed during an assignation with Kerekou's estranged wife.* Aikpé's death triggered a massive wave of revulsion in Benin, where coups and previous periods of military rule had been largely bloodless and assassinations practically unknown. In the subsequent union strikes (grossly underestimated abroad) in which placards calling for Kerekou's arrest for murder were prominent, only the readiness of the regime to use brute force (again highly "un-Dahomean") prevented it from being overthrown.[42] The cost in terms of popularity and legitimacy has been immense however; by the time the riots of 1975 were subdued, practically every stratum of Beninois society had been totally alienated.

The unionists, brutally dispersed in 1975, have for all practical purposes deserted the Revolution; indeed many have physically deserted the country itself. Despite their periodic militancy and slow radicalization over the years, labor has usually judged all regimes in Cotonou according to their ethnic base. The northern leadership of the Revolution and the brutal eclipse of its southern component (Assogba, Aikpé, and others), combined with the packing of the civil service and top levels of administration with northerners,[43] assured that despite Kerekou's protestations of socialist commitment† few in the civil service would regard him in any other light than as a *northern* (and *military*) usurper of political power.

So great was the exodus from Benin of southern civil servants in the aftermath of the 1975 tumult that in July the government clamped down on the granting of exit permits[44] and later, after a warning, confiscated the property of all civil servants who had not returned from self-exile in Togo. Indeed, friction with Togo developed, in part, over the embarrassingly large—and potentially threatening—presence in Lomé and Anécho of large numbers of Beninois exiles. Many of these joined in the groundswell of support for an opposition party set up in Bruxelles (and undercover in Porto Novo) after the resignation of fifty-three members of Benin's diplomatic staff (including senior ambassadors) who refused to continue to represent the regime internationally. The proliferation of opposition to the regime from all quarters, dedicated to topple from power what they termed "one of the most inhuman and implacable fascist dictatorships in Africa" and "a caricature of Marxism, . . . a blind

*Most analysts assume he was cold-bloodedly murdered.

†These protestations ring false to many dedicated militants while threatening conservatives.

and sinister dictatorship installed by a band of criminals who call themselves Marxists,"[45] sparked a witchhunt in Benin led by Lieutenant Martin Dohou Azonhiho—Kerekou's only wholly trusted ally.* A "gigantic Zinsouist plot" was discovered that made possible a systematic purge of the residual sources of opposition to Kerekou.[46] (It is paradoxical how Zinsou—whose weak traditional support had threatened no one in the 1970 elections—had in 1975 become the most implacable and feared foe of the military junta and Benin's public enemy number one.)

In assessing the course of the Benin Revolution and the nature of Benin Socialism, several observations are inescapable. First, protestations to the contrary notwithstanding, most of the leaders of Marxism-Leninism in Benin today are either moderates or apoliticals. Kerekou himself—whether viewed primarily as a sincere and dedicated leader attempting to lift Benin from its economic morass or as an opportunistic and ambitious northern power-seeker (the two are not mutually exclusive)—is acknowledged by most to be a political moderate straining to juggle the various factions in his command. Brought into the plot that led to the 1972 coup at a late date (due largely to his prestige in the armed forces),[47] he has shunted aside the true radicals—officers such as Beheton, Bodjogoumé, and Aikpé—while alienating both the domestic and exiled radical civilian elements that initially rallied to the Revolution.† The slow tempo of radicalization in Benin is in part a function of the conservative nature of its leadership. The ideological rhetoric emanating from Cotonou is hardly comparable to that from Brazzaville. The Benin regime at first had to maintain the pace of radicalization and militancy in order to appeal to elements among the unions, students, intellectuals, and selected strata of the urban masses, who could provide a measure of legitimacy, as well as to its own small leftist wing. Until 1975 these groups were its supporters. After Aikpé's murder, however, Kerekou's regime became isolated from most of the progressive elements and hence the more earnest efforts to institutionalize power in Benin. In short, despite Benin's need for reforms and possibly even radical solutions for its perennial political and economic instability, much of the rhetoric in Cotonou is merely the current socially

*Despite his low rank, Azonhiho is a key figure in the gendarmerie and in the military junta; he has been Kerekou's right-hand man since the 1972 coup and one of the principal ideologues and directors of the Revolution.

†Such as radical ideologue and Sékou Touré-protege Louis Behanzin, who returned to his native Benin after the Revolution only to return to Guinea in disgust in 1975 (see Decalo, *Historical Dictionary of Dahomey*, pp. 25-26).

accepted *lingua franca* of a legitimacy-seeking extra-constitutional ruling clique increasingly perceived in purely ethnic terms in the advanced coastal areas.

These facts explain at least in part the vast gap between socialist rhetoric and reality in Benin. Since the leadership is not really dedicated to revolutionary change despite the continual clamor for it, little more than moderate change can be expected. Whether or not the editors of *West Africa* are correct in concluding that 99 percent of Cotonou socialist rhetoric is irrelevant because it merely "expresses generational rivalries in more flattering ideological terms,"[48] Kerekou's regime has been extremely reluctant to antagonize French interests in Benin—or France in general. Indeed, apart from the outburst of anti-French sentiment early in 1973, the regime has been ultra-sensitive in its efforts to assuage French investors and expatriates. These efforts have at times verged on the ridiculous, as when after the nationalizations accompanying the declaration for Marxism Kerekou noted that he "did not have particularly revolutionary motives,"[49] and that Benin's opting for Marxism "should not spread fear among private investors."[50]

Since Benin is dependent for much of its foreign aid upon French subventions, with no other donors willing to subsidize the perennially deficit-ridden economy, the implementation of the regime's commitment to total control over means of production would be, in very short order, suicidal. Moreover, there is actually very little in Benin to nationalize. There are hardly any private extractive or industrial concerns: most expatriate capital was in the areas of import/export, commerce, and services. With the nationalization bout of 1974-75 Kerekou for all practical purposes reached the limits of nationalization in Benin. The burden of compensation (to keep French public capital flowing) has been heavy, the benefits of the new public sector have been few, and the international fiscal response has been mostly negative. Little Eastern aid has been committed to develop the "new" ideological ally, even less Arab petro-dollar funds, and almost no new French private capital.[51]

The nationalizations have been the easiest part of the Revolution. The transformation of society along more equitable and socialist lines, the fulfillment of the pledge of a new morality and greater public accountability, and the spread of Leninist-Marxist ideas and structures have been very much more difficult to achieve (especially in light of the regime's transparent lack of sincerity in this domain). As noted, most of the "reforms," structural "reorganizations," terminological innovations, and involvement of the "revolutionary

masses" in the building of a "Marxist-Leninist society" have not much affected the *reality* of political and economic power in Benin—even where they left the drawing board and were implemented. The preoccupation of the Benin Revolution with *structural* "reorganizations" may be a function of the difficulty of achieving real reforms. The "great emphasis on structures, minutely detailed but powerless, meaningless"[52] that so many observers have commented upon seems to indicate that the leaders of the Benin Revolution have confused or substituted "paper change" and "epistemological change" for real socioeconomic change. Their ventures into the countryside to "explain" to farmers the meaning of Scientific Socialism and the sacrifices it entails clash oddly with the style of their own arrival[53] and their general deportment in the cities. The inability of the small officer corps—vanguard of the Revolution—either to provide leadership or to control, guide, or supervise the various state industries and enterprises under their charge (even though in comparison to other African states Benin is small, compact, and easy of access) has only added to the inconsistencies between rhetoric and reality.

A final observation about Benin Socialism: It is striking how ideological dialectics have become for many the socially approved jargon of the day and a weapon to ward off personalist, ethnic, and factional challenges to the leadership of the Revolution. Almost all opposition to Kerekou's rule—whether personalist, ethnic, or ideological—has been defined exclusively in terms of ideological deviation and classified according to its position on a Left-Right continuum. The regime is to some extent a captive of its own jargon, and especially since mid-1975 has fabricated "ideologically motivated" plots in order to weed out real or imagined enemies.* It is due largely to the well-known artificiality of much of the "class struggles" that Kerekou periodically announces (though the country has had more than its share of plots and opposition) that Benin's claim of an "imperialist" assault on Cotonou airport early in 1977 was widely dismissed abroad—at least initially.[54] The airborne mercenary assault resulted in few casualties and little damage, while reports about its casual execution raised serious doubts abroad that it had ever occurred. The usually astute *West Africa* doubted the report of the bizarre attack: "Benin has nothing Imperialism could conceivably want. . . . Benin would come very low on an aggressor's list."[55] The truth about the January 1977 attack is still shrouded in mystery (though Gabon, Morocco, and France appear to be implicated in a

*This phenomenon will be discussed in detail in the section on Brazzaville.

Zinsou-sponsored plot), but in its glorification of that date (of Benin's "victory" over imperialism), Benin shows remarkable parallels with Congo/Brazzaville, to which we now turn.

BACKGROUND TO THE CONGOLESE REVOLUTION

What Brazzaville somewhat imprecisely calls the "Congolese Revolution" refers to the overthrow of the venal, autocratic, and reactionary regime of the defrocked priest Fulbert Youlou, following three days ("Les Trois Glorieuses") of popular demonstrations.[56] The upheaval was in many ways the culmination of a process of urbanization, radicalization, and ethnic strife that had made Congolese politics tumultuous, with periodic bloody confrontations, even prior to independence.

The Benin case-study illustrated the largely artificial nature of the Revolution in Cotonou and of Benin's Marxism-Leninism. It also underscored the way in which socialist rhetoric has been utilized in Benin to buttress support for a military clique perceived in the developed coastal areas mostly as a "northern" leadership and challenged from both Left and Right by opposing factions. By comparison, Congolese socialism is more sophisticated (though similarly riddled with inconsistencies) and its ideological dialectic is on a much higher plane. In addition, the Congolese military regime (also "northern" and governing a country where southerners dominate most sectors of society) has had to control a militant civilian elite, a large politicized conservative bureaucracy, and a powerful ultra-left challenge, which give Congolese politics several dimensions lacking in Benin. Congo's internal contradictions have resulted in bitter factional clashes for supremacy that have been more frequent, extensive, and bloody than those in Benin, and have involved a much greater use of socialist ideology as a weapon, requiring a greater awareness of the political context within which the "ideological" clashes have taken place.

However, as one observer has succinctly observed: "Socialism has made little difference to either the vast mass of the people, living on subsistence agriculture in the country and largely unaware of the political leaders in the towns; or to the country's economy, which remains largely under the control of French interests."[57] Even in the cities, despite violent exhortations, purges, and counterpurges, few have been sufficiently dedicated to the official state ideology to renounce bourgeois tastes or privileges. This is true of both the "vanguard" Marxist-Leninist party, which has twice been

truncated by near-total purges of its membership, including the Central Committee and Politburo, and the People's Army, which has also been a leader in the tendency toward embourgeoisement to the detriment of the state sector over which it has been given supervisory control.

Despite Congo's considerable natural resources and economic potential, the country remains (much as Benin) in a classic dependency relationship vis-à-vis France. Until recently, investment conditions in Africa's first People's Republic have been much more liberal than in non-socialist states such as Ivory Coast.[58] Unwilling to risk a break with the former metropole, all Congolese leaders since the Revolution have strained to assure France and French investors that neither Marxist rhetoric nor revolutionary postures emanating from Brazzaville were prejudicial to private capital. Having declared for the Marxist option as early as 1963, Congo has been saddled ever since with the task of assuring potential investors that *in reality* nothing has changed. The frequency with which ministerial delegations have been dispatched to Paris and other Western capitals, and the laments to Brazzaville at the drying up of sources of private capital, testify to the difficulties inherent in such dualistic postures.

At the same time, Congolese leaders have attempted to rationalize the dissonance between the socialist doctrine of the various "stages" in Scientific Socialism and the maintenance of the status quo. In this they have satisfied neither the ultra-left (especially youth and intellectuals) nor the residual Youlouist right. Since 1963, politics in Congo has involved the hazardous juggling of various ambitious civil and military factions and personalities, purges of both radicals and conservatives, and adherence to the largely immobilist center while projecting the image of being the true guardian of the Left. Thus, Congolese Marxism has been suffused with symbolic decrees and preoccupied with dialectics and the creation of "revolutionary structures" bereft of significant content that might be defined as either socialist or Marxist. Hence, while it has radically realigned the country's foreign policy, diversified the sources of foreign aid, and slowly expanded the perennially deficit-ridden, mismanaged, and corrupt public sector ("organized bungling"),[59] Congolese socialism has not extended to the acquisition by the state of the most profitable segments of the economy. Until recently, a policy of nationalization has been applied only to ailing or unprofitable industries whose French principals have been on the verge of withdrawal. The lucrative Hollé phosphate mines, for example, which were originally handed over to private French capital under condi-

tions more favorable than those granted in much of Francophone Africa, were nationalized (in 1978) only after the mines were disastrously flooded[60] and were about to be abandoned.

Much of the rhetoric emanating from Brazzaville, including lengthy discourses on ideological purity and socialist rectitude, very soon became the institutionalized vehicle for factional strife (intramilitary and civil/military) and a cloak for the promotion of sectional, particularistic, ethnic, and personal interests. Since the 1963 Revolution, factional strife in Brazzaville—the "politics of permanent plots"—has become the most distinctive aspect of Congolese political life. There have been repeated assaults on the center of political power by segments of the armed forces, the civilian elites, youth, and opposition elements outside the country. Some have been pure power-gambits by ambitious elements; others have been ethnically inspired, while others have aimed at radicalizing or reversing the course of socialism in the country. As in Benin, however, the leadership of the socialist revolution has been solidly in the hands of moderates (Alphonse Massemba-Debat, Marien Ngouabi) or conservatives (Joachim Yhombi-Opango). Revolving around the power apex has been a composite of radicals and conservatives whose common denominator has been personal allegiance to the leader of the moment.

All this is not to suggest that there is little dedication in Congolese circles to the cause of a radical restructuring of the society in the direction of socialism—even though many who profess socialism do so only opportunistically. Rather, it underscores the difficulties inherent in breaking old patterns of social interaction, the intensity of residual ethnic animosities that now emerge in ideological guises, the tumult of praetorian politics that works against meaningful social development, and the havoc created where radical rhetoric is not matched by radical action.*

Following an unusually brutal and inept colonial administration and economic exploitation,[61] Congo emerged at independence with sharp ethnic animosities (between the advanced southern Bakongo and the northern Mbochi), a potentially rich (though mostly extractive) economy dominated by expatriate concessionary interests, and

---

*It is ironic that during the period of the U. S.—Congo diplomatic break (1965-77), which was a result of continuing harassment of the U. S. Embassy and its personnel by revolutionary youth gangs, the only American visitors granted easy access to Brazzaville were what were defined as "international capitalists and financiers."

one of Africa's most urbanized and youthful populations.* Major demographic dislocations subsequent to the construction of the Congo-Ocean railway that links Brazzaville with Pointe Noire on the Atlantic (in which almost 25 percent of the population had been engaged), along with the country's advanced educational system,[†] had created conditions leading to large pools of unemployed youth in the cities of the south. Urban unemployment had already been exacerbated by the dissolution of the colonial federation of French Equatorial Africa.[62] Overnight Brazzaville was transformed from a small federal headquarters into an oversized national capital—with a grossly bloated civil service—of a small country. Indeed, part of the economic strife in Congo (including during the Revolutionary era) can be traced to a relatively sophisticated civil service jealously guarding its prerogatives** under intense pressure from large pools of unemployed urban youth—appearing in ever-increasing numbers— and a continuation of the rural-urban drift, bringing more antago- nistic northerners to the southern towns.[63] Frustration at the inability of the potentially rich economy to provide adequate jobs for Congo's upwardly mobile youth has been a basic element in much of the strife in the country,[††] aggravated by perceived prefer- ential treatment for one or another of the country's ethnic groups. The sensitivity of this issue is possibly attested by the banning in Brazzaville of all copies of an edition of *Le Monde* that suggested that Congolese politics be reconceptualized as intense competition for jobs rather than for ideological rectitude.[64]

Youth has been a constituency that all politicians in Brazzaville have had to mollify and keep attuned to. Derided and scorned by Youlou, they played a major role in the collapse of his regime. Organized into small quasi-anarchic bands "to defend the Revolu- tion" in the aftermath of Youlou's collapse, later used as stepping- stones to power by ambitious leaders, and still later organized into ancillary paramilitary units, youth has to a considerable extent

*According to a 1974 census, 33% of the 1.3 million population lived in towns and cities and roughly 60% of the population was below the age of 16 (*West Africa*, August 12, 1974).

[†]Congo has a 70% school attendance rate (1971) and leads Africa in a num- ber of educational indices (see the education tables in Donald G. Morrison et al., *Black Africa: A Comparative Handbook* [New York: The Free Press, 1972]).

**Despite an official freeze on recruitment to the civil service by all regimes to date, Congo's bureaucracy grew by 636% between 1960 and 1972—from 3,300 to 21,000 (see *West Africa*, April 19, 1976).

[††]According to Ngouabi, unemployment could reach 450,000 in 1985— mostly youth (*West Africa*, January 8, 1972).

dictated the pace of radicalization of all regimes to date.[65] Yet even while official rhetoric has been radicalized to meet this challenge from the Left, all regimes have acted to subordinate and control these youthful elements.

Ethnicity has also played a major role in Congolese politics—both prior to and after the 1963 upheaval. All governments in Brazzaville (which has dense, solidly northern quarters), civil as well as military, have been judged essentially in terms of their ethnic composition and leadership. The rise of the southern socialist regime of Massemba-Debat following Youlou's demise did not please northerners smarting from their neglect under Youlou, and the subsequent more militant administration of Ngouabi was perceived in the south as nothing more than a vehicle for northern ascendance. As one self-exiled southern politician noted: "*Who* the leader of the Congolese Revolution is matters as much as *what* his specific policies are. Socialism under a petit-nordist is simply not socialism to us."[66]

In economic terms, Congo is in a completely different category from Benin.[67] It produces a large array of commodities and is one of Africa's more industrialized countries, with large reserves of exploitable minerals and ores. Yet growth and development have been stunted by a host of factors—including the economic stranglehold and exploitative policies of expatriate concessionary interests that have depleted resources without contributing to long-term development,* and the more recent virtual looting of state sector industries by civilians and military alike. The declaration of Marxism in 1963 and of a People's Republic in 1968 dried up the flow of international risk capital (despite French government guarantees against expropriation) and strengthened the tendency of existing enterprises to seek to maximize immediate profits and to minimize further investments out of fear of eventual nationalization.

Congo has had negative trade balances since 1963. Its shrinking agrarian sector is unable to feed both itself and the burgeoning urban population, and the local and expatriate elites consume directly up to 40 percent of the country's imports. In the years 1963-72 exports have ranged between 50 percent and 73.1 percent of exports, with a mean of 60.9 percent.[68] Though hidden exports have raised these percentages, the Congolese economy has been dependent on France for budget-balancing subventions—as well as for investment capital and other grants. By 1969 Congo's accumulated debt to the French Treasury was 4,511,764,000 CFAF; the retirement of this debt, if

*In particular those in the timber sector—Congo's prime foreign currency earner until the early 1970's.

demanded, would have required the immediate dismissal of 75 percent of the Congolese civil service.[69] The inability and/or unwillingness of all governments to date to disengage the Congolese economy from the apron strings of the metropole, as opposed to the desire of many to forge in the direction of a new Marxist society, is another element in the backdrop against which the evolution of Congolese socialism must constantly be assessed.

In terms of building a Marxist state in Congo, there are few differences between Massemba-Debat's efforts and those of Ngouabi. There are major differences between the civilian era (1963-68) and the military period (1968-) of the Revolution, and the three leaders who have controlled the Revolution (including Yhombi-Opango since 1977) differ significantly in their commitment to it. Massemba-Debat was a schoolteacher who became moderate socialist Speaker of the National Assemby; purged by Youlou, he was catapulted to power in 1963 by virtue of his sober, unpretentious character. Ngouabi was a popular northern (Kouyou) Chief of Staff whose conservative outlook as early as 1964 brought him into conflict with Massemba-Debat; transformed into a Marxist he intervened in the political arena in 1968 essentially to preserve the army's corporate autonomy and—especially—his primacy within the army.

Though Ngouabi rapidly learned to use the jargon of the Revolution, his rhetoric always sounded hollow in comparison to the fiery dialectic of other Brazzaville leaders. Yet whether or not Massemba-Debat's commitment to socialism was genuine and Ngouabi's commitment only a learned response to the ideological exigencies of power in Brazzaville,* both leaders—and Yhombi-Opango today—faced quite similar tasks when they assumed leadership of the Revolution, and they reacted in a similar manner. Put succinctly, these tasks included *primarily* charting a zigzag course between the competing political, ethnic, personalist, and ideological factions in Brazzaville and *secondarily* expanding state control over the economy without frightening nervous French private and public investors. The first task demanded an opportunistic policy subordinating rhetoric to the pragmatic dictates of remaining in power and assuring that no powerful antagonistic combination of interests coalesced; only the second involved efforts to construct a socialist society. Because of the near-continuous challenge to the stability of the regime since 1963, the elite in power has spent much less time on economic

*"To survive at such a time you had to know the revolutionary jargon, at the very least" (see "Brazzaville: Ten Years of Revolution," *West Africa*, August 20, 1973).

planning than on political maneuvering, making protestations of socialist commitment sound less than sincere. As *Le Monde* commented fully fourteen months after Ngouabi's rise to power: "[He is] less concerned with ideological options than with remaining in control of the State."[70] Such a judgment has been made, *mutatis mutandis*, of all leaders in Brazzaville and of most socialist "militants" in Congolese politics.*

"SOCIALISM UNDER THE SIGN OF THE GUN, INSTRUMENT OF PROGRESS AND OF POLITICAL CONSCIENCE OF THE CONGOLESE PEOPLE"[71]

Though Massemba-Debat formally achieved in months what had always eluded Youlou—a one-party system and unified ancillary organizations—he was never fully in control of the forces unleashed by the upheaval of the Revolution, and the "centralizations" he achieved were largely meaningless. The Catholic unionists—at the forefront of the anti-Youlou revolt—resisted their forced merger within the unified trade union movement. Many of their leaders and parliamentary deputies were silenced, arrested, or forced into exile. The nationalization of the private schools (i.e., Catholic) and youth movements increased discontent and added to the growing base of resistance to the Revolution. In the countryside the Lari (the most important subgroup of the Bakongo), many of whom as Matsouanists[72] had been Youlou's electoral backbone,† rejected Massemba-Debat's Lari ethnic ties and retreated from the political arena. Later, hounded and brutalized by roving youth vigilante gangs, they were to lend support to periodic plots against the regime—especially those originating from the Bakongo "diaspora" in Zaire and Angola. In the 1964 elections fully 48 percent of the eligible voters shunned the polls—a significantly higher percentage than in other electoral contests. Tract warfare and clandestine plotting by purged elements added to the tumult in Brazzaville.

The extreme caution with which Massemba-Debat moved vis-à-vis French expatriate interests polarized the militant left into increasingly ideological factions that forced the administration to

Le Monde (March 24, 1970) observed with reference to the many ideologically justified plots and coup attempts: "It is all a matter of rivalry between factions in Brazzaville," and *Africa Contemporary Record, 1973-74*, referring to a major 1972 challenge to Ngouabi from the "Left," said: "There appear to be no clear-cut ideological differences between the sides" (p. B584).

†Youlou rose to power by gaining the support of the Matsouanists—a sect of supporters of André Matsoua that played an extremely important anti-French role during the decade prior to independence.

radicalize its socialist commitment without, however, instituting corresponding radical policies. Although the youth was eventually "organized" as the Jeunesse du Mouvement National de la Revolution (the youth wing of the new MNR party), it at all times acted independently, appropriating to itself various "revolutionary" functions in the cities and the countryside. It mounted security checkpoints, kidnappings, and assassinations, and plotted revenge against self-exiled enemies of the Revolution. Whether or not the JMNR is viewed as a distinct age-group,[73] many of its activities and preoccupations confirmed Erny's observation that Congolese youth ";had developed a culture of the word, in which spoken words seemed all powerful . . . [and] the management of words . . . was regarded as the key to the social drama in which they were all involved."[74] That the "management of words" was to become the key to political power in Brazzaville as well may be an extension of Erny's insight.

However that may be, the JMNR rapidly acquired independent sources of materiel and funds from friendly Eastern embassies. Falling under the control of ambitious political aspirants (such as André Hombessa, who became Minister of Interior in 1964 by skillfully manipulating his power base),[75] recruiting unemployed youth and swelling into an inchoate body of 35,000 youth, the JMNR in many ways became the major threat to the stability of the regime and sparked both a 1966 mutiny* and Ngouabi's 1968 *coup d'etat.*

Throughout his five years in office, Massemba-Debat tried to juggle the various political and personalist factions that buffeted his regime from Left and Right. He was faced with incessant intrigue and a series of plots to unseat him. The militant and ambitious Politburo tried to shackle his administration to its control—even forcing him to accept a more doctrinaire Marxist (Amroise Noumazalay) as Prime Minister in 1966. Confrontations and endless "dialogues" with the unruly JMNR and unrest in the increasingly politicized armed forces showed the political instability of revolutionary Congo. Yet despite a strong commitment to Marxism-Leninism, the prime goal of the Left—i.e., nationalization of all the means of production, seen as the solution to all Congo's ills—was not

---

*In 1966 Ngouabi refused to accept the political indoctrination of the army, and was detached from his Brazzaville command, demoted, and reassigned outside the capital. In a subsequent mutiny his loyal paracommando troops arrested senior officers, ransacked the MNR offices, and chased the party Politburo and cabinet to the municipal sports stadium before cooler tempers prevailed. Ngouabi was promptly reinstated in his old command.

attempted and was firmly rejected as an option. Massemba-Debat once exclaimed in exasperation at the pressures for nationalization: "There is nothing to nationalize in the country!"[76]

Under Massemba-Debat diplomatic relations with the East proliferated (Youlou had been paranoically anti-Communist), and Congolese foreign policy and UN postures acquired a distinct Marxist hue. The state sector slowly expanded as fiscal commitments were secured from Eastern donors. But for the development of the country's most lucrative extractive sectors, French private capital was assiduously sought by Marxist ministers. Only marginal enterprises were nationalized, and few barriers were placed in the way of existing private capital in Brazzaville.

The gap between socialist rhetoric and pragmatic reality that developed in the Congo stemmed from a very deliberate policy decision at the outset of Massemba-Debat's rule. In a very non-doctrinaire manner, what was feasible and infeasible, desirable and undesirable with respect to the undeveloped Congolese economy was defined. A policy emerged that aimed at (a) establishing state control over international commerce, trade, and transport (easily centralizable), (b) the creation of a public industrial sector with Eastern funds (the future "motor" of the Revolution), and (c) protecting existing royalty-generating expatriate companies and courting new private capital for similar areas of enterprise while allowing radical elements to express themselves (since they could not be muzzled).[77] With minor variations and only slightly different ideological rationalizations, this economic policy was retained by the Ngouabi successor regime at least until 1973-74, and perhaps has been renewed by the essentially conservative Yhombi-Opango since Ngouabi's assassination in 1977.

The factors that brought about Massemba-Debat's collapse and the emergence of the army at the center of the political arena are both simple and complex, and in any case have been outlined elsewhere.[78] They were complex in that they involved both purely military factors and civil-military tensions (cloaked as a struggle for socialist rectitude)* set loose by (or inherent in) the 1963 upheaval and the formation of a politicized People's Army; they were simple in that Massemba-Debat's juggling role in the midst of Congo's swirling cauldron of factions, ideologies, and personal ambitions had for a long time been regarded as highly untenable. However, an assessment of the course of Congolese socialism under Ngouabi requires an

---

*Ngouabi's main *overt* criticism of Massemba-Debat when he moved against him was that he had paid only "lip service" to the Revolution.

awareness that Ngouabi's coup was motivated by non-ideological factors, that his personal outlook had always been moderate, and that his regime was essentially perceived as a vehicle for Mbochi ascendance in the country to the detriment of Bakongo interests.*

Though under Ngouabi the structural underpinnings of Congolese Marxism-Leninism were firmly set and socialist rhetoric was heightened and became more militant, the *economic* reality changed very little. Under Ngouabi's aegis, two new constitutions were promulgated (in 1969 and 1972), a new vanguard party was established, several far-reaching structural reorganizations were decreed, and a new (red) flag adopted along with Congo's designation as a People's Republic. Ngouabi developed into a more and more outspoken ideologue (compared to the somewhat drab, schoolmasterly Massemba-Debat), projecting the image of a "revolutionary intellectual, in a state of constant debate with his party militants, always ready to deliver long harangues to rally the faithful."[79] His collected speeches (minus his earlier dialectically naive discourses), including the oft-cited "Pour un programme du Parti Congolais du Travail" (1972) and "Reflexions et directives du President du P.C.T. au Comité Central" (1973), were published in France[80] and distributed free of charge to the party faithful in Brazzaville. A more dashing and charismatic figure than his predecessor, at times donning camouflage fatigues (along with loaded grenades and pistols) to lecture on the prevalence of enemies of the state, but equally at ease in diplomatic attire, Ngouabi's zigzag leadership of Congolese socialism was in most respects no different from Massemba-Debat's—nor were his travails in office any less or different. As *West Africa* commented on the occasion of his assassination: "Once in power President Ngouabi established the appearance of a socialist order, led by the P.C.T.,[†] but left the running of the economy to French expatriate capital and proprietors."[81]

One of Ngouabi's first actions was to shackle the leftist JMNR and its paramilitary units to the army. A bloody confrontation between his paracommando troops and the youthful defenders of the Revolution left over one hundred youths dead in their self-dubbed "Camp Biafra." Most of the units were brutally disbanded, others were left under the firm control of loyal Ngouabi appointees, while the most militant ones were integrated into the armed forces under

*Ngouabi's first actions in office were attempts to placate Youlou, to purge the Left in the army and bureaucracy, and to pack the civil service with northerners.

†Parti Congolais du Travail—the new vanguard party.

Lt. Ange Diawara, the ambitious Political Commissar of the army. (Diawara was to try to rise to power in 1972 with the help of segments of the armed forces and his young protegés, along with the blessing and ideological assistance of several French Marxist teachers in the country who had been specially recruited by France at Congo's request.)

Ngouabi, like Massemba-Debat, faced a multitude of challenges to his rule from both inside and outside the country. In almost all instances, segments of the armed forces (and especially the gendarmerie and the police) either actively participated, knew of the plots but did not report them, or straddled the fence when they erupted. The plots, whether officially defined as leftist or rightist,[82] were generally linked with ethnic grievances against the ascendance of the north (through the army and Ngouabi's efforts to promote northerners in the administration)[83] and were spearheaded by politically ambitious elements or individuals who had been purged. Ngouabi's main allies in the intensive struggle for primacy in Congo were his loyal ethnic (Mbochi-Kouyou) paracommando units, and especially the southern (though Fort Rousset-born) Major Yhombi-Opango* and Cabinda-born (i.e., southern) Captain Alfred Raoul. The former had been attacked on several occasions by militant elements for his bourgeois tastes,† while the bon vivant Raoul had never made any attempt to conceal his quite overt pro-French sympathies, capitalist aspirations, and irreverent attitude toward Marxism. (The paradox of a "Marxist" leader from the north being sustained in power by arch-conservative southern subordinates is resolved if one bears in mind that, rhetoric aside, personal allegiances are of greater importance in Congo than ideological affinities.)

Ngouabi's experience with his "new" revolutionary vanguard party likewise underscores the futility of using claims of socialist allegiance as a basis for analyzing politics in Brazzaville. The carefully pre-screened and hand-picked PCT membership was riddled from the outset by a multiplicity of conflicting allegiances to differing ideologies, ethnic camps, and personalities—both radical and conservative. In the aftermath of Diawara's attempted putsch, it—

---

*Yhombi-Opango saved the regime in 1972 at the time of Diawara's attempted putsch and was consequently promoted to the rank of colonel—then the highest rank in Congo.

†Among the charges levelled at him were that he "lives like a capitalist in his luxurious villa" and that he had "a false revolutionary attitude" (see *Jeune Afrique*, March 11, 1972, and *Africa Research Bulletin*, Political Series, December 1971).

along with the gendarmerie and police—was for all practical purposes dismantled (including its Central Committee and Politburo) by a massive purge. In the process of weeding out "state enemies" of all hues (e.g., the "deviationist gang" of Diawara, the "incorrigible anti-Marxists," and "tribal reactionaries")[84] during what was seen as an ideological clash reminiscent of those of early Stalinist Russia,* the PCT all but disappeared except in name and on paper. Hundreds of the party's elite were purged for "ideological insufficiency," the Central Committee and Politburo were reduced to only five and three members respectively, and most party branches closed due to lack of leaders or members; total membership of the PCT declined to barely 160.[85] The scheduled 1974 Party Congress was hurriedly convened soon after in order to infuse new blood into the party, but virtually the same criticisms were levelled against the new party membership less than four years later. A subsequent "systematic purge" again virtually decimated the party and its leadership. The four pillars of Congolese socialism and the vanguard party were defined as (1) revolutionary theory, (2) iron discipline, (3) close liaison with the people, and (4) autocriticism.[86] Neither the PCT nor Ngouabi paid much attention to any of them; yet the Congolese experiment with socialism was repeatedly praised as a major contribution to the history of socialism.

Throughout these tumultuous power-clashes in Brazzaville— usually described as a battle between international capitalism and Congolese socialism or as a fight against "deviationists" (i.e., ultra-left), "infantile Leftism" (the JMNR and youth in general), "fetishism" (i.e., countryside resistance), or "unrepentant anti-Marxists" (usually applied to Bakongo in the bureaucracy)—the economics of Congolese socialism remained virtually the same. The 1970 assessment of Ngouabi's first fourteen months in office† was no less applicable eight years later. Congolese Socialism was frequently extolled as an "experiment which will be set down in the history of political parties of the world"[87] but even as Ngouabi was extolling the Congolese experiment (in this case in 1972), the Marxist-Leninist

---

*"Who would have thought that Lin Piao would disappear from circulation? Or that Trotsky would betray Lenin's ideas? The Socialist path is long, tortuous and full of pitfalls" (see *Africa Contemporary Record, 1972-73*, p. B534).

†"For all its revolutionary language and outward forms, the ruling group set its face against taking over control of the means of production, or of ending the country's financial dependence on France" (*Africa Contemporary Record, 1969-70*, p. B419).

state hardly had a state sector worthy of note* and was continuing Massemba-Debat's policy of offering the economic plums to private French capital.

Though negotiations had commenced under the previous regime, Congo's valuable phosphate mines[†] were handed over in 1969 for exploitation by a French combine in exchange for a state share (15 percent) "much less than in similar enterprises in African states with no revolutionary pretenses."[88] While Ngouabi continued to assert the inevitability of "socialization of the means of production," he rationalized the fact that there had hardly been any nationalizations since the Revolution on the grounds that any such action would merely strengthen the internal class enemies (specifically, the "reactionary bourgeoisie") that would have to be placed in control of such enterprises. As with the phosphate industry, so with forestry—the country's major export industry until the mid-1970's. Despite a long history of blatant exploitation by expatriate combines, this sector remained largely in private hands. (In this case the state's lack of competence in technical forestry skills may have played an important role.)[89] From the ideological point of view, nationalization was rejected as inappropriate for Congo's stage in the evolutionary process of the Revolution. Thus, though the "the ultimate goal of the Party is socialism, then communism, . . . Congo is not yet socialist. . . . There cannot yet be a Socialist Revolution. . . . Our actual stage is a National Democratic and Popular Revolution,"[90] which necessitates accommodation with world capitalism.[91]

The few expropriations that were decreed by Brazzaville during the first decade of the Socialist Revolution occurred not as a logical consequence of the socialist course of Congolese politics but in spite of it. The classic example is the disastrous 1970 labor-management confrontation in the SIAN-SOSUNIARI plants.** The French management's decision to halt production[††] forced the hard-pressed

---

*The state sector included essentially only the cement works, textile factory, and a match factory, plus control over the purchase and sale of certain commodities (see *Africa Contemporary Record, 1970-71*).

[†]The richest in the world, they collapsed and were closed down in 1977 for technical reasons.

**SIAN (Société Industrielle et Agricole du Nairi) and SOSUNIARI (Société du Sucre du Niari), Congo's largest and third-largest enterprises, owned sugar works, refineries, and plantations, mostly in the fertile Niari valley, and were very much symbols of Congolese neo-colonialism.

[††]The companies argued that low world prices for sugar together with wage increases and other benefits demanded would make production of sugar in the

Ngouabi regime to declare the nationalization of the industrial complexes. Unable to operate profitably with the wage increases the government decreed to the "revolutionary workers," and mismanaged and corruption-ridden under a series of political appointees and quasi-commissars, the nationalized sugar industry (now SIA Congo) had continuous fiscal deficits even after world sugar prices stabilized. According to expert cost-accounting, SIA Congo should have produced clear profits in the mid-1970's on the order of 2,000 million CFAF annually instead of deficits of 1,000 million CFAF each year.[92]

In 1973-74, the economic picture changed dramatically, if only briefly. The phosphate industry's development (despite major technical problems) combined with increased production from offshore oil deposits (boosted by sharply rising oil prices following the Middle East War)* all at once started pumping huge royalties into the Congolese treasury. The extent of the windfall comes into sharp perspective when one notes that *anticipated* oil revenues in 1973 were on the order of 3,500 million CFAF while *actual* royalties paid by ELF-Congo totalled 21,400 million CFAF—a sixfold increase that equalled 75 percent of Congo's budget. The windfall allowed the regime to buttress the sagging fiscal infrastructure of the state industries,[†] increase minimum wages across the board (including a 70 percent boost in 1975),[93] initiate a new series of takeovers (including the petroleum distribution network, private insurance, and some banking)** and retire some of Congo's huge external debt.[††] The government also announced a new Three Year Plan (1975-77),[94] the first since the 1964-68 Plan that had achieved only 63 percent of its scaled-down targets, and declared that henceforth private investment would not be allowed in the country unless linked with state participation. Despite the greater confidence with which the regime now spoke, however, private capital was again reassured that "Congo

country uneconomical; they then halted production until the government "imposed order" on the workers (*Marchés Tropicaux et Méditerranéens*, October 3, 1970).

*Congo received 20 percent of the profits from this production (see *West Africa*, February 4, 1972).

†These required subsidies of 4,000 million CFAF annually (*ibid*; see also *West Africa*, February 11, 1974).

**West Africa*, October 4, 1976. In September 1976 it was announced that the phosphate industry was to be centralized under a new state company—SONAMINES.

††This would otherwise have required major international loans.

was wide open to foreign trade and investment, especially from France" and that the state's more insistent socialist policies would not threaten private interests.[95]

The euphoria of 1974 was soon dispelled, however. Falling levels of oil extraction, continued difficulties with the phosphate mines (which were soon to close down), and "heavy-handed contempt for expertise" in the recently centralized forestry sector[96] created major strains and financial shortfalls that sparked frustrated accusations of economic sabotage of the Revolution.[97] Fully committed state revenues fell sharply, throwing the barely commenced Development Plan into a shambles and straining the state's overextended resources now obligated also to compensations for the recent round of nationalizations.* Possibly it is because this sharp economic downswing and vicious fiscal squeeze coincided with a marked surge of materialism in Brazzaville that the regime lashed out with a new, extensive round of purges and autocriticism. No stratum in society was immune from what became, in official state jargon, the "systematic purge" of 1975-76. The armed forces—already referred to as "a sink of corruption"[98] and purged for their "embourgeoisement" tendencies, mercantilist proclivities,[99] and anti-Marxist views—again fell under sharp attack by Ngouabi. With the gendarmerie and police disbanded and their functions assumed by other structures, Ngouabi began to rely more and more on his paracommando units, which had several times been "reorganized" to purge them of class enemies. The appointment of paracommando officers to supervisory roles in the public industries in order to arrest rampant corruption[100] did not achieve its aim, however; it merely proliferated the number of sinecure-holders and sources of corruption. Perhaps the ultimate paradox occurred in the state sector early in 1978 when it granted one month's pay bonuses to all workers at a time when every industry was deficit-ridden; seven directors in the sector were promptly jailed for one month for this action.[101]

The civil service and, in particular, the PCT came under sharpest attack in the new bout of autocriticism. As official socialist structures in Congo, their failure was much more serious and their penalties were greater. Among the charges levelled at them in marathon lectures and harangues were "weakness of party leadership," "lack

---

*No new projects under the Plan were commenced. Of a budget of 52 billion CFAF (lower than that for 1975), only 3 billion could be spared for developmental purposes (see *West Africa*, April 26, 1976). A later issue of *West Africa* (May 19, 1976) noted that the current cost of Congo's 1,700 agricultural extension officers was equal to what the whole rural sector earned in 1972.

of dedication to the Revolution"; they were criticized for their "complacency and lethargy," self-enrichment ("frantic race for material advantages"), "false revolutionary attitudes," and "incompetence and irresponsibility."[102] The "connivance of the bureaucratic bourgeoisie and foreign capitalists" was attacked as well as "the natural tendency among our Party and State cadres to become bourgeois," "the morbid nature of the vanguard party," the "use of Marxist phraseology only out of political opportunism," and "possession of many cars and the holding of champagne parties."[103] These were only *some* of the myriad charges against what for all practical purposes had been the leadership of Socialism in Congo and its most visible agents. Only seventeen of the original ideologically pure, hand-screened fifty-member Central Committee were regarded by Ngouabi as "while not perfect, at least capable of carrying on the Revolution."*[104] So massive were the purges and so small the pool of eligible "socialist" cadres who could replace them in the government, party, and civil service that an Extraordinary Party Congress was called in order "to allow formerly disgraced party men to regain their old positions" and to set up "new structures capable of leading the Revolution onwards."[105] Indeed, so acute was the need for immediate staffing of positions left empty by the recently purged cadres that many previously purged leaders (in the 1973 bout) were allowed to reassume their old posts in advance of the Congress; who among them would percolate to the top was left to depend "upon the perceived sincerity of their self-criticism before the Party leadership."[106]

Simultaneously with the purge, fiscal orthodoxy was imposed on the state sector, and several punitively high taxes were levied on the private sector—especially the oil companies, which were seen as the main culprits in the developing fiscal squeeze in Congo.[107] These measures were, for all practical purposes, the final straw for many of the larger companies, and a major disengagement of private capital from Congo commenced. As *West Africa* summed up this process: "High taxes, the incompetence of those drafted to run State economic organizations and the world recession have all played their part in persuading many foreign companies, including the oil companies, to abandon participation in projects in Congo."[108] As the process intensified, so did Ngouabi's pique. He attacked France for its attempt to bring about the "suffocation" of socialism in Congo[109] by encouraging the exodus; the fall in domestic oil output was categorized by him as "deliberate," while the technical problems

*The rest were termed "misfits."

of the Hollé phosphate industry were "sabotage."[110] All this helped to plunge Franco-Congolese relations to one of their periodic nadirs, and ultimately forced Congo to draw upon the International Monetary Fund reserves—for the very first time. It was during the slow normalization and readjustment of the Congolese economy that Ngouabi was assassinated.*

It is much too early to evaluate Colonel Yhombi-Opango's socialist credentials, but it should be noted that there is little doubt of his conservative and essentially pro-Western outlook.[111] Indeed, shortly after he came to power he normalized relations with the U. S. and mended the break with France. He has gone out of his way to assure private capital that "it cannot at any time remain uninvolved in the development of this country which certain foreigners regard as their second homeland."[112] The ideological tenor of his speeches has been quite restrained compared to those of Ngouabi, while his criticisms of the state of the economy—especially of the perennially problematic state sector—have to date been remarkably free of Marxist dialectic.[113]

* * * *

There is little doubt from the analysis of these studies of Benin and Congo that there exists considerable pressure among at least some strata of the urban elites for a readjustment of their countries' economies in the direction of greater state control over resources and economic processes. In both instances, because of the relative sophistication of the urban elites, this discontent with the existing neo-colonial economic reality has been expressed in the vehement language of a radical socialist ideology. That the complexity and dialectics of the ideology are poorly grasped and selectively adopted is a function of the elites' claim that Scientific Socialism allows for national variations in the achievement of a socialist society. The extremely liberal interpretations in Cotonou and Brazzaville of the variations tolerated by Marxism-Leninism mean that—rhetoric aside—neither the parastatal sectors of Congo or Benin nor their

*Ngouabi had been the target of several attempts in the past, and his assassination resulted in a spate of executions (including that of Massemba-Debat, allegedly behind the plot) and revenge-killings (including the Cardinal of Brazzaville) by Ngouabi's kin. The unusual haste with which the investigations into the murder and the executions were carried out, and the fact that Ngouabi's latest purges (and rumors of more to come) had hurt leading figures in the armed forces, suggest that the principals behind the assassination (not yet identified) may be close to the top of the current political leadership of Congo.

economies in general are radically different from those of several states that reject Marxist doctrine and links with the East. That the bulk of the masses have been uninvolved in the process of radicalization (of thought and language, at least) is obvious in the untouched countryside, which has been largely immune to the turmoil in the urban areas. Perhaps most striking in the evolution of Marxism in both Benin and Congo are (a) the preoccupation with the largely insignificant outward trappings of a new Marxist order and (b) the intensity of the struggle for leadership.

The preoccupation with externals is a basic characteristic of the elites in Cotonou and Brazzaville. Psychologically it may well be an anticipatory preparation for the Marxist "take-off" stage, but it may be as much a function of the inability of elites to attain any meaningful economic change outside the realm of rhetoric and "structural reorganizations" of society and the economy. Reorganizations, even if followed through—and as has been noted, they seldom are—do not change reality; they change only the *structures* that interact with reality—something often misunderstood in both Cotonou and Brazzaville. Neo-colonial realities and dependency relationships cannot easily be changed, and underdeveloped and fiscally weak economies cannot easily be transformed—and certainly not by mere words, will, and "reorganizations." Symbolic change, strident rhetoric, ideological defiance, and militancy—all poor substitutes for meaningful restructuring of reality—may nevertheless be psychologically satisfying immediate options (possibly the only ones) for elites facing continued dependence on outside economic forces for the foreseeable future.

The intensity of the power struggles in Benin and Congo is possibly best seen as but a continuation of the pre-revolutionary free-for-all tug-of-war that even then was a striking aspect of their political systems. It is for this reason that the two countries' basic sociopolitical infrastructure has been so emphasized throughout. The political tug-of-war is today played under somewhat different rules and in different (ideological) garb, but the forces interacting in it are the same: ethnicity, regionalism, civil-military competitions and tensions, personal power ambitions, and incipient class considerations. If political life is a function of the myriad components that make up the polity, politics in Congo and Benin—both before and after their revolutions—remains inevitably captive to these forces.

A "SECOND WAVE"

OF SOCIALIST REGIMES

THE STRUGGLE FOR SOCIALISM IN MOZAMBIQUE, 1960-1972

Edward A. Alpers

This article is an attempt to explore the history of the development of a socialist commitment within FRELIMO—the Mozambique Liberation Front—with particular attention to the dialectic between theory and practice and the contradictions between various political lines in the Mozambican national liberation movement. Without minimizing the importance of the leadership of FRELIMO, it will seek to turn the discussion about the political direction of FRELIMO away from one centered on personalities toward a proper appreciation of the emergence of a coherent, collectively determined revolutionary socialist ideology.

ORIGINS AND EARLY DEVELOPMENT, 1960-1962

FRELIMO was formed at Dar es Salaam in June 1962 by the merging of three preexisting and competing exile nationalist organizations—UDENAMO (União Democratica Nacional de Moçambique), MANU (Mozambique African National Union), and UNAMI (União Africana de Moçambique Independente)—and the incorporation of a number of independent Mozambican nationalists. There was at this time no clear political line within FRELIMO, and each of its constituent organizations was perhaps as much an ethnic as a nationalist union. MANU, for example, had been formed in 1960 by several Mozambican exile groups (including the Makonde African Union) in what was then pre-independence Tanganyika.[1] In its tenth anniversary evaluation of the significance of the 25th of June—the date "celebrated by us as a symbol of our unity"—FRELIMO took a characteristically hard look at its past:

It is true that the unity which was established in 1962 was extremely fragile. The existing, externally based organisations which joined hands to form FRELIMO at that time did so reluctantly, and largely at the urging of younger, unattached militants with more direct and recent experience of the harsh realities which

existed inside Mozambique itself. The causes which kept these organisations separate in the past—namely tribalism, regionalism, lack of a clear and detailed set of goals and of agreed and relevant strategies—continued to exist. The only thing which was common to them was their opposition to Portuguese colonialism. On all other particulars, including the actual aims of the struggle, the mode of military activity to be undertaken or the very definition of the enemy, there was no consensus.[2]

But if there was no consensus, there was also no clear awareness at the time within FRELIMO that these were even problems of fundamental importance. Interviewed a year after the formation of FRELIMO, Marcelino dos Santos, one of the original exile leaders and now the Vice-President of FRELIMO, was asked if "unification entailed difficult political problems?" To this his response was a firm "No." He explained that "the division of the Mozambican forces was not the result of irreconcilable political positions, nor of tribal differences, as frequently happened in other places," suggesting instead that its fragmentation was the result of Mozambique's encirclement by white-dominated Southern Africa—a situation which was changed by the gaining of independence in 1961 by Tanganyika.[3] Nevertheless, the differences were there, and in the following years, as the liberation struggle took concrete forms of action, they were to become increasingly defined.

How were these differences resolved at the time of FRELIMO's birth in 1962? According to dos Santos (in a 1973 interview), the young militants from inside Mozambique who provided the main impetus for the formation of a unified national liberation movement gained control of the movement from the very beginning: "Only four of those elected to the leadership came from the exile group. The rest were from inside. Thus a unity was created with the major part coming from activists in Mozambique." Thus, although the condition of being exiles from their country gradually created a sense of self-awareness as Mozambicans, "in some ways the level of political consciousness of those who were outside and who founded [the nationalist] organisations, was really comparatively lower than the activists inside, despite the fact that the latter never reached the point where they succeeded to launch a real national organisation."[4] In the context of this analysis, one can see the significance of the role played by the two most distinguished Mozambican exiles of the time—Eduardo Mondlane and dos Santos.

Neither of these two men was identified with the narrow interests of the three organizations which merged to form FRELIMO.

After completing a Ph.D. at Northwestern University, Mondlane had an opportunity to visit Mozambique unofficially in 1961, while working for the United Nations, so that he was well aware of conditions inside the country and saw clearly that the kind of neocolonial solution being worked out elsewhere in Africa by the British and French could not succeed there, as events in Angola were already demonstrating. He also recognized that unity was essential in the hard struggle ahead, explaining that

> All of the . . . Mozambique political organizations wrote to me asking me to join them individually, but I insisted that the only way I can join a political party for the independence of Mozambique is if they would promise to take immediate steps to unite with other Mozambique groups forming a united front. . . . I then came to Dar es Salaam and helped to organize the conference in which the Mozambique Liberation Front was formed.[5]

From the beginning, then, Mondlane was a leading proponent of a unified Mozambican liberation movement and a realistic analyst of what needed to be done to achieve independence.

No less significant was the role played by dos Santos. Like Mondlane, he had been forced by political persecution in Portugal to continue university studies elsewhere. He studied at the Sorbonne under Georges Balandier, and his political consciousness was raised and participation accelerated by the North African struggles against French colonialism—in particular by the liberation movement in Algeria, which as a settler colony bore striking resemblances to Mozambique. Dos Santos was instrumental in coordinating activities among the liberation movements in the other parts of Portugal's colonial empire, and was elected secretary-general of the Conferência das Organizacões Nacionais das Colónias Portuguesas formed in 1961 at Casablanca. From this organizational base dos Santos took a leading role in creating the conditions for the emergence of FRELIMO.

The FRELIMO that took shape at the First Congress in September 1962 bears striking evidence of the alliance between the insiders and the Mondlane-dos Santos forces. The constitution, program, and resolutions of that gathering stress unity of action above all else. They also contain the seeds of the radical, revolutionary ideology with which FRELIMO is today identified. Significantly, however, the radical thrust was not limited to this coalition; indeed a number of the leading progressive ideas contained in these documents have close antecedents in the political program of UDENAMO.

Two things are striking in a comparison of the UDENAMO and FRELIMO political documents.[6] First, the official programs are virtually identical, save for some differences in wording and organization. For the moment I want only to observe that while each commits itself "To unite and mobilize Mozambicans of all social classes, residing in Mocambique and outside, without discrimination of tribe religion, ideology, or sex" (FRELIMO program, item 2; UDENAMO program, item 1), it would appear that the word *ideology* was too charged politically to be included in the definition of either organization's constitution (Art. III in each). Second, the similarity of the first eighteen articles of each constitution strongly suggests that the UDENAMO constitution served as a model for the FRELIMO constitution. However, the language of the "aims and objectives" (Art. IV in each case) of the UDENAMO constitution is clearly more radical than that of the FRELIMO constitution, indicating that the need to create a united front among all Mozambican nationalists forced a compromise:

UDENAMO CONSTITUTION

The aims and objectives of the UDENAMO are:

To serve as a vanguard in the relentless struggle for freedom of the African people and the independence of Moçambique.

To foster the spirit of Pan-Africanism in order to rid Moçambique of imperialistic economic exploitation, social degradation, and all traces of colonialism and imperialism.

Total liquidation of Portuguese colonial domination in Moçambique.

To defend and realize claims made by all the people of Mocambique, coming from any social strata enduring oppressions and exploitation, particularly the claims made by peasant and worker masses.

FRELIMO CONSTITUTION

The aims and objectives of FRELIMO are:

A total liquidation of Portuguese colonial domination and of all vestiges of colonialism and imperialism.

The achievement of immediate and complete independence in Moçambique.

To defend and realize the aspirations of the Moçambican people, who have been exploited and oppressed by the Portuguese regime.

One contrast between the two documents is revealed in the UDENAMO commitment "To serve as a vanguard in the relentless struggle for freedom of the African people and the independence of Moçambique"—a statement which casts UDENAMO in a political role with internationalist dimensions—and the more limited FRELIMO aim to gain "The achievement of immediate and complete independence in Moçambique." Other differences between these declarations are the inclusion of references to "imperialistic economic exploitation," "social strata," and "peasant and worker masses" in the UDENAMO constitution which are lacking in the FRELIMO constitution.

How is one to interpret these differences? One possibility is to see the wording of FRELIMO's "aims and objectives" as a defeat for the progressives and a victory for the more conservative petit-bourgeois nationalists at the 1962 congress. Another is to see the situation as a defeat for the ultra-leftists by the progressives, who were sensitive to the necessity of maintaining a broadly based front during the initial phase of the struggle. Evidence that this may have been the case is the fact that some of the most important dissidents in FRELIMO were originally UDENAMO members, including the former president of UDENAMO—Hlomulo Chitofo (Adelino) Gwambe (later suspected of being a Portuguese agent).[7] In any case, it is clear that the FRELIMO constitution produced by the First Congress was the culmination of three months of intensive discussion, bargaining, compromise, and canvassing. To draft a constitution in September which would undermine the delicate unity created in June would have amounted to an abandonment of the revolution and a return to the kind of factionalism which today besets Zimbabwe. Thus the apparent concessions made in Article IV of the FRELIMO constitution were necessary in order to attain the higher objective of "unity," which was surely the essential first *palavra de ordem* ("word of command") of FRELIMO.

In Article V of the FRELIMO constitution, for example, it is stated that

In order to achieve these objectives [Art. IV], FRELIMO will: Proclaim the necessity for unity to all Moçambican people. Organize, mobilize, and unite all Moçambicans.

This wording reverses the order of the parallel article of the UDENAMO constitution and expands the call for unity from "all the patriots" and "all patriotic forces" of Mozambique to "all Moçambican people" and "all Moçambicans." When it came time to deter-

271

mine the structure of FRELIMO, everyone appears to have been convinced of the need to assure that unity would be maintained at all levels of decision-making. The appropriate provisions of the UDENAMO constitution were taken over with only slight alteration to emphasize this dominant theme, but in words which provide a framework for a decidedly more radical political structure than the more conservative nationalists can have recognized.

Article XVIII of:

UDENAMO CONSTITUTION	FRELIMO CONSTITUTION
The structure of the UDENAMO is strictly based on the principle of democratic centralism, and the method of work of its organs is based on the following principles:	The structure of FRELIMO is based on Democratic Centralism. Its organs shall work and be oriented on the following basis:
(a) Democratic spirit.	(a) Democratic spirit.
(b) Unity of action.	(b) Collective spirit.
(c) Sense of responsibility.	(c) Unity in action.
(d) Criticism and self-criticism.	(d) Criticism and self-criticism.
(e) Mutual assistance.	(e) Mutual help.

Thus a clearly defined concept of "democratic centralism" was established from the outset by FRELIMO—primarily (I would argue) on the basis of the preexisting constitution of one of its three constituent organizations, and therefore without recourse to external models of socialist political organization, which would almost certainly have alienated a considerable number of the eighty delegates and more than five hundred observers at the First Congress.[8] In the hard years ahead, this structure would provide the Central Committee with the framework for defining the nature of the contradictions within FRELIMO, and for determining what to do about them, while the other provisions of its organization—from the cells to the supreme organ of FRELIMO, the Congress—would enable it to act appropriately.

Looking back over the development of FRELIMO on the occasion of the tenth anniversary of the initiation of armed struggle on 25 September 1964, and only five days after the investiture of the transitional government between Portuguese rule and independence, President Samora Machel made the following assessment, which shows the critical importance of the achievement of unity and the form in which it was embedded in the FRELIMO constitution:

Since FRELIMO's First Congress, a battle has been waged between revolution and reaction, centering on the following essential questions: defining who is a member of FRELIMO and, consequently, defining the interests to be served by the Front; defining the targets of our struggle and hence, in the last analysis, FRELIMO's objectives.

The victory of the revolutionary line at the First Congress was concretized by the declared need for the unity of all Mozambicans, men and women, bound together by the same oppression, exploitation and humiliation, mobilized to build a new and popular social order.

The victory scored against the reactionary racist forces, against conservative forces clinging to outdated tribalist patterns, the fight against various forms of adventurism and opportunism, enabled FRELIMO to start the process of organizing and mobilizing the masses, and training vanguard cadres.

Thus, in 1964, the minimum conditions were created for going over to a higher form of struggle: the general armed insurrection of the Mozambican people against colonialism and imperialism, for the establishment of a popular social order free from exploitation.[9]

The point I wish to emphasize is that the victory of the revolutionary line involved not only "the declared need for unity," but also the precise structure it was given in the constitution.

At the beginning of this article I noted that an awareness of what was beginning to take shape within FRELIMO was not yet grasped by even its highest leadership, citing an early statement by dos Santos to support this interpretation. Asked in 1973 about the lack of an ideological line at the beginning of FRELIMO's history, dos Santos responded in terms which substantiate the general description of its early development which I have suggested:

It is true FRELIMO as such had no clear ideological line apart from primary nationalism. But the very fact that the leadership was heterogeneous meant that different types of ideologies were represented in it from the start. . . . But the tasks facing us in those early days demanded that we create a collective which would accommodate all those who were prepared to work together to get the basic struggle off the ground. So, the nature of the political, social and economic realities of the situation as it then was, demanded a pragmatist attitude. But the struggle grew and new situations emerged and in the process political consciousness

and political awareness were increasing and developing even though in some ways our approach still remains pragmatic.[10]

Similarly, in response to a question concerning the "secret" of FRELIMO's success over the years, Machel stated categorically in 1976 that it was "the priority of ideology." When pressed by his interviewer (Pietro Petruzzi) to the effect that not everyone accords priority to ideology and that "in the first phases of a liberation struggle the 'ideological question' can divide forces instead of uniting them," he qualified his assertion as follows:

Our experience is there to demonstrate the contrary. It is true, there is an initial phase, that of national unity, in the course of which it is necessary above all else to constitute a first platform which is the point of unity of a collection of forces. But once these forces are mobilized around the platform it is imperative to define their unity at the ideological level. To give them a clear and common perspective.[11]

I think it can be definitively established that a dialectic between revolutionary ideology and cautious pragmatism has been rooted in the development of a socialist commitment in FRELIMO from its very inception. It is not that these two concepts are unrelated or somehow contradictory to each other (as some commentators apparently believe) or that the acquisition of state power unexpectedly confronted the leadership of FRELIMO with a situation which forced them to adopt a pragmatic approach. Rather, the gaining of independence by Mozambique under the direction of FRELIMO undercut the propaganda of the Portuguese fascist regime, which was accepted so uncritically by most of the capitalist press, and forced the West to begin the slow process of trying to understand what had really been taking place in that country during the previous decade.[12] Even in the initial phase of its development, the history of FRELIMO demonstrates the validity of the basic Marxist-Leninist tenet that for revolutionary change to be achieved there must be a complementary unity between theory and practice.

THE INTENSIFICATION OF INTERNAL CONTRADICTIONS, 1963-1969

All accounts agree that it was the launching of armed struggle which heightened the contradictions within FRELIMO and eventually made apparent to all the existence of the two ideological lines which had existed at its core from the beginning. The conflict was

not, however, a problem of competing elites, as Walter Opello has suggested; instead, it was the working out of an emerging class struggle over the future shape of independent Mozambique.[13]

As early as January 1963, FRELIMO cadres were sent to Algeria for military training, and political organization inside Mozambique was in progress to pave the way for the beginning of armed struggle.[14] During the course of that year there was a great deal of confusion in some quarters about the aims of the struggle that was to take place, and numerous defections from FRELIMO by individuals who were unable to work within its framework. There was also a good deal of provocation by Portuguese secret agents who had infiltrated the loosely defined united front.[15] Political education during this trying period was aimed at preserving the fragile unity which was being so severely tested, mainly by focusing on the dangers of succumbing to the narrower loyalties of ethnicity and regionalism, but when the armed struggle began on 25 September 1964 and FRELIMO found itself gaining control of significant areas of both Cabo Delgado and Niassa provinces, the fundamental issue of what kind of society FRELIMO sought to build in the liberated zones had to be addressed.

Certain guidelines existed in the FRELIMO program hammered out at the First Congress, but these were still extremely general ideas which had not yet taken any material form. Article 8 of the program proclaimed FRELIMO's determination "To establish a democratic government based on total independence, in which all Moçambicans will be equal before the law and have the same rights and duties," while Article 9 promised "To form a government of the people, by the people, and for the people in which the sovereignty of the nation will reside in the will of the people." On the economic front, FRELIMO declared its commitment (in Articles 13 and 14) "To liquidate all traces of a colonialistic or imperialistic economy" and "To reconstruct the economy and develop production in order to transform Moçambique from a colonial and underdeveloped country to an independent, industrial, developed, modern, prosperous, and strong country." Finally, with respect to education and culture, the program declared both a commitment "To end colonialist and imperialist education and culture; to reform the educational system now in force; and to energetically and rapidly combat illiteracy" (Article 17) and "To develop education and culture in order to serve the free and peaceful progress of the Moçambican people" (Article 18). Thus, although the historical context of the liberated zones from 1965 on was distinctly different from that of the inde-

pendent Mozambique only hazily envisaged in 1962, there can be no doubt that FRELIMO's fundamental political line throughout was people-centered. It was not mere rhetoric, then, when dos Santos observed in May 1970 that FRELIMO "has always taken the correct position, basing its decisions on the genuine interests of the whole Mozambican people."[16]

The problem, of course, was determining exactly what were "the genuine interests of the whole Mozambican people." It is one thing to decide for a people what those interests are; it is quite another to listen to the people themselves and engage in a process of political dialogue with them. With the beginning of armed struggle, FRELIMO depended critically upon the support and sacrifices of the people of Mozambique. Failing a deeply rooted mutual respect between the rural peasantry and the guerilla army, successful prosecution of the war for independence would have been impossible. The same was true for the successful operation of the liberated zones: historical circumstances dictated that FRELIMO listen carefully to what the people under their protection had to say about the society they were trying to build together.

FRELIMO's dialogue with the Mozambican people began even before the outbreak of armed struggle in the process of preparing the ground for the war through political mobilization. FRELIMO understood full well that the war being forced on them by the intransigence of Portuguese colonialism was a political as well as a military struggle. Victory depended as much on political mobilization as on military preparation, so that when the first cadres were sent abroad for military training, FRELIMO organizers were starting to work within northern Mozambique. As Barbara Cornwall, an American journalist who travelled with FRELIMO in northern Mozambique in 1968, puts it:

> The question was not only that of arming and supplying a guerilla force, but equally important, how an ignorant and intimidated peasant mass, which had already learned the hopelessness of earlier rebellions, had been persuaded to support at whatever personal sacrifice, the embryonic revolt then being organized by FRELIMO.
>
> The answer was careful and prolonged mobilization of the peasants long before the first shot was fired in September, 1964, and long before the first arms or guerilla bands were filtered across the border into Northern Mozambique, where the new, peasant-based revolution was to begin.[17]

This was not a simple task. According to Ali Thomas Chidudu, an original FRELIMO mobilizer among the Makonde: "When I first began to organize, the people did not know about politics. They only knew that they had been miserable all of their lives."[18] Cornwall comments that "The peasants had neither the time nor the background for theoretical argument and abstract thought. They were complete pragmatists and illiterate as well." By listening to their grievances and addressing them in language that they could understand, FRELIMO was able to gain the support of the peasantry and to recruit its sons and daughters into its ranks both as combatants and as civilians.[19] An Anglican missionary in Niassa province at this time remarked: "Most of the Frelimo people who came to the Mission to see me were ordinary villagers with a gun, though there were some who had been to Algeria and elsewhere for training."[20] Thus, as Eduardo Mondlane emphasized: "The army is representative of the population at large, in that the vast majority of the guerillas are peasants initially uneducated, illiterate and often unable to speak any Portuguese." As the war progressed, the army became the focal point for economic and social progress within the liberated zones, "but more important . . . is the fact that the army is the people, and it is the people who form the army."[21]

Political mobilization became a permanent task for FRELIMO, but a question remained concerning its political content. FRELIMO first addressed this question publicly in an editorial in *A Voz da Revolucão*, the internal organ of the front, in April 1966, which reiterated the overriding importance of the political mobilization of the people to its own militants:

Political mobilization consists of explaining to the people WHY IT IS that we are fighting and FOR WHAT IT IS that we are fighting. The people must know well that we are fighting for the expulsion of the Portuguese colonialists and for the liberation of Mozambique, so that Progress, Liberty and Equality should return to our country. An end to misery, slavery and discrimination.

The editorial went on to explain that "every militant of FRELIMO thus has the duty to explain to comrades who do not know the reasons and the objectives of our Revolution. Teach them the principles and the program of FRELIMO." It advised that this should be done in common language, drawing specific examples from the experience of the people in the area, after which it could be related to the general condition of the Mozambican people as a whole. The

specific examples chosen for illustration were FRELIMO's commitment to an end to forced labor and to equal pay for equal work, both of which were revolutionary concepts in colonial Mozambique, but neither of which in any way indicated the development of a socialist commitment.[22]*

This should not come as a surprise. The task of political mobilization in the areas still under Portuguese domination posed very different problems from the task of economic, social, cultural, and political reconstruction that faced FRELIMO in the liberated zones. One involved explaining to people a way out of the predicament in which they found themselves by struggling against an oppressive system, while the other involved the more demanding challenge of creating a new society on the foundation of the unity and successes achieved in the armed struggle. This is what was now taking place in the liberated zones, where for the first time socialist practice was beginning to emerge in the heart of FRELIMO, thereby giving impetus to the development of a socialist ideology at its head.

Yet the process was never as simple as this. Even in the sphere of political mobilization among the peasantry and waging the war, there were many contradictions in FRELIMO's practice because the process of political education was uneven at every level within the movement. According to Machel:

> In 1965, because many of us still had not properly understood the principle that the people are the main force, we made mistakes. We gave priority to technical aspects, looking upon weapons as the main factor and neglecting work among the masses.
>
> As a consequence we suffered reverses. We lost weapons, we lost militants and fighters, and the enemy exploited our ignorance of the main force.[23]

The earliest signs that a socialist line was developing within FRELIMO are to be found in the political articles which began to appear in *A Voz da Revolucão* and *Mozambique Revolution*. As early as November 1965 a lengthy statement defining colonialism

*Interesting in this context is the experience of Mariano Matsinge, chief of political mobilization inside Mozambique during this period: "We . . . found that the length of time needed to mobilize a group of people differed according to the intensity of their colonial experience. For example, the people who had returned from forced labor contracts in the towns were the most receptive to us. Or those who had been used for bridge- or roadbuilding, or for work on plantations growing sugar, tea, rice, or coconut" (quoted in Barbara Cornwall, *The Bush Rebels* [New York, 1972], p. 35).

and neocolonialism was published which clearly was shaped by the ongoing struggle to create new forms of social organization in the liberated zones:

> Today we are fighting against Portuguese colonialism. At the same time, we are creating the conditions so that neo-colonialism cannot be established in our country. . . .
>
> Colonialism is the direct exploitation and domination of one country by another country (in our case: the domination and exploitation of Mozambique by Portugal). . . .
>
> Neo-colonialism is a modern form of colonialism. . . . The principal difference in relation to colonialism is that here there is no occupation of territory: there is only economic exploitation. The Portuguese would not need to have either troops or adminis- trators in Mozambique: it would be Mozambique's own puppet government which would open all the doors to the Portuguese, obliging Mozambicans to work for them. . . .
>
> We are fighting so that in Mozambique there should exist a government chosen by the people, which represents the will of the people and which works for the good of the Mozambican people.[24]

Less than six months later this definition of the enemy against which FRELIMO was fighting was augmented by a biting analysis of imperialism and the international capitalist system which argued that both colonialism and neocolonialism were the products of imperialism.[25]

That a definite trend was taking place within FRELIMO toward a more clearly defined socialist ideology is made explicit by a long editorial entitled "The African Lesson" which appeared in early 1966. It had already been made clear to the leadership that the Portuguese regime against which it was struggling was only able to carry on the war because of "the intensification of imperialist aid to Portuguese colonialism."[26] At the same time, the leadership was confronted with the problem of how to organize society in the liberated zones. In looking elsewhere in Africa for models, they were saddened by what they observed: "Imperialism insinuated itself in the daily life of the people, fomenting divisions, murdering leaders, substituting regimes, dictating the destiny of the African nations, in a crescendo of aggressiveness. . . . Today, many of the African countries have only a formal independence, an independence of anthem and flag."[27] This was not the kind of independence that FRELIMO wanted for Mozambique. The successful prosecution of

the war provided it with a "laboratory," however, in the liberated zones, and it seized upon this opportunity to construct an integrated revolutionary ideology and practice which would serve as a basis for the reconstruction of the nation as a whole.

In "The African Lesson" the blueprint for this task was laid out:

> It is necessary to create in each country a party with a clear and popular programme, able to arm the people with a revolutionary ideology. It is necessary also to put weapons in the hands of the people. . . . These two factors must co-exist. An ideology without weapons to defend it will be easily neutralised by any armed group. Weapons in the hands of people who are not conscious of their political responsibilities can launch the country into chaos and anarchy.
>
> And, fundamentally, it is necessary to encourage the people to participate in the political life of the country; further, it is necessary to reject a concept in which the Revolution (socialism) is built by an active nucleus of leaders who think, create and give everything, and who are followed by a passive mass, who limit themselves to receiving and executing. This concept is the result of weak political conscience, and expresses lack of confidence in the fighting and revolutionary capacity of the people.
>
> This is the lesson that recent events in Africa teach us. [28]

Any remaining doubts about the direction in which FRELIMO was moving were dispelled by the clarification of FRELIMO's political line by President Mondlane on the occasion of the second anniversary of the beginning of the armed struggle: "Our struggle . . . is not only for the liberation of a piece of earth called Mozambique, but it is also part of the universal struggle for the complete liquidation of the exploitation of man by man."[29]

But if the dominant political line within FRELIMO was now explicitly revolutionary and socialist, it was by no means embraced by everyone within the leadership. It was probably to the dissident elements that "The African Lesson" was particularly directed. There was still hope among the dominant revolutionary faction that common struggle within the framework of "democratic centralism" would persuade their comrades-in-arms to share this political line, but in the following two years the reactionaries demonstrated their unwillingness to submerge their personal ambitions to the cause of socialism.

The first sign that a political struggle was shaping up within the

leadership of FRELIMO between two opposing ideologies came with the report of the ordinary session of the Central Committee in October 1966. This meeting was especially noteworthy in that "besides the members of the Central Committee, several military and political leaders from Cabo Delgado, Niassa, Zambezia and Tete attended . . . at the invitation of the Central Committee."[30] The opening up of the deliberations of the Central Committee to militants from the "inside" was undoubtedly the work of the adherents of the revolutionary line within the leadership: it both continued the historic domination of the "insiders" in the movement and led to the institutionalization of this domination at the Second Congress of FRELIMO in 1968. At this important Central Committee meeting two problems that had plagued FRELIMO's progress from its inception were addressed—discrimination against women and tribalism:

> The Central Committee condemned the tendency which exists among many male members of FRELIMO to systematically exclude women from the discussion of problems related to the Revolution, and of limiting them to executing tasks. . . . The C.C. vehemently condemned the tribalistic tendencies shown by some comrades in their functions . . .; it stressed that the struggle against tribalism and regionalism in our midst is equally as important as the struggle against colonialism itself, and is fundamental to safeguard our national unity and freedom.[31]

Directives were issued concerning both these problems, but solutions were not found for either one.

In the following months, however, the tasks of extending the armed struggle and transforming the liberated zones appear to have diverted nearly everyone's attention from these internal conflicts. Considering the explosiveness of the situation, which culminated in the brutal assassination of President Mondlane in February 1969, it is remarkable that public statements by FRELIMO during this period concentrate exclusively on the positive achievements of the struggle and make no mention of the leadership problems simmering beneath the surface calm.[32] How was this possible?

The explanation given by the Central Committee at its meeting of April 1969, when the contradictions in the movement had clearly manifested themselves many times over, bears full citation because it demonstrates that the structures established by a political movement are valid only if the people are politically conscious enough to live up to them.

But something completely new happened at this meeting, distinguishing it as an historical landmark in the development of FRELIMO: like a fresh wind there appeared a completely new element of criticism and self-criticism, resulting in the elimination of erroneous conceptions enabling us to lead some misguided comrades back to the correct revolutionary line, and to re-establish a sense of reciprocal confidence among us.

This confidence had been prejudiced by differences among the leadership. We were not very clear about where the basis of these differences lay, but we perceived that, when important decisions had to be taken there was a clash of standpoints, revealing the existence of two lines, each represented by a certain number of comrades, defending different positions.

All of us were conscious of this division—but because we thought we would aggravate the situation if we brought the question into the open, because we were convinced that it was necessary and convenient to present at least an appearance of unity in the FRELIMO leadership, we never discussed the problem.

These divergencies were manifested in many important instances. For example, in the definition of who is the enemy, in the question of deciding on the strategic line to take (a protracted people's war), on the importance to be given to the armed struggle in relation to the other forms of struggle, etc. This situation had become more evident since 1966, when we started having liberated zones in our country. Certain events had taken place since March, 1968, which seriously affected our organisation. We all felt that the origin of this situation was the division existing within FRELIMO—but we were unable to locate the roots of the contradictions and consequently, we were even less able to solve them.[33]

This is a political statement of remarkable honesty. In a word, FRELIMO's leadership had engaged in a process of self-deception, mystifying the process of their own ideological development to the point where they were unable to act critically and collectively in response to a situation which they all knew to be upon them. What had been taking place during this period was an increasing divergence between the revolutionary leadership and the reactionary leadership, who were increasingly inclined to cooperate with the Portuguese in an attempt to subvert their opponents in the Central Committee. In these circumstances the possibilities for Portuguese *agents provocateurs* were legion, and they were quick to exploit FRELIMO's division.

Foremost among these provocateurs was a Catholic priest named Mateus Gwenjere, who represented an extreme pole of racist and elitist ideology in the history of the movement.[34] Gwenjere arrived in Dar es Salaam late in 1967 and because of FRELIMO's open membership policy was able to establish himself as an instructor at the Mozambique Institute. (As Barbara Cornwall has observed, at about this time "no one asked the new recruit whether he was right, left, or center, and no one cared particularly.")[35] Almost at once Gwenjere began to attack the revolutionary white members of the staff and administration of the Institute. By March 1968 his outrageous activities could no longer be tolerated, and after an acrimonious debate he was censured by the Central Committee. Gwenjere then formed an alliance with Mozambicans living in Dar es Salaam but not involved in FRELIMO. Early in May, two attacks were made by this group against FRELIMO headquarters in Dar es Salaam. During the second attack, two FRELIMO officers were seriously injured, one fatally. Disturbances by students at the Mozambique Institute during this period, and the insistence of the Tanzanian government that whites working with FRELIMO leave Tanzania, marked a low point in the fortunes of the movement.[36]

At about the same time, complaints began to reach the Central Committee from the people of Cabo Delgado that they were being exploited by Lazaro Nkavandame, a member of the Central Committee who was responsible for the commercial section in Cabo Delgado. Nkavandame had been a leading figure in the cooperative movement in Cabo Delgado before FRELIMO was formed. Not surprisingly, his efforts were opposed by the Portuguese, and he had channeled his energies into FRELIMO.[37] With the securing of the liberated zones in Cabo Delgado, Nkavandame was able to reinstitute his old producers' network and build upon it to his own advantage.

Surveying the achievements of national reconstruction in 1967, FRELIMO had observed:

In Cabo Delgado . . . we have established or revived the old agricultural producers' cooperatives which the Portuguese had deliberately discouraged or destroyed. The Portuguese had . . . forced the people of Cabo Delgado to produce only those cash crops which were of immediate value to Portuguese European industries, such as cotton and sisal. In doing so, the cultivation of subsistence crops had to be sacrificed, with the result that the people suffered frequent periods of famine. We have put an end

to this system: the people now plant those crops which are of direct use to them.[38]

Similar efforts were being made in the commercial sphere, as was pointed out by Calisto Mijigo, the military commander in Cabo Delgado:

Before FRELIMO began the war, the people always got the short end of the bargain in any barter with the Portuguese. All shops belonged to the colonials and when the revolution started they stationed troops inside the posts where the shops were. After the Africans fled, they began to exchange their crops across the Ruvuma river at barter points operated by the movement. They are better off now and can produce more for trade. . . .[39]

Given the history of economic exploitation in Cabo Delgado, it is not surprising that its people should have been extremely jealous of the gains they had won with FRELIMO's help and that FRELIMO should have been especially sensitive to any criticism of its practices by the people themselves. The people's accusations against Nkavandame clarified his behavior and his class position for the revolutionary faction in FRELIMO, and helped to refine their definition of revolutionary. As the Central Committee concluded in April 1969:

Nkavandame and his group . . . wanted . . . to substitute themselves for the Portuguese colonialists in exploiting our people . . . before the people were politically mature: because then they would oppose resolutely any form of exploitation. The development of the struggle, the existence of liberated areas had thus made appear a specific category of persons—the exploiters of the people.[40]

By the middle of 1968 a number of things were becoming clear to the revolutionaries in the Central Committee. First, when "differences of opinion" arose in the Central Committee, they always found the same people lined up against them. Second, the nature of the opposition had been brought into sharp focus by recent events. Third, the views of the opposition were supported by the Vice-President of FRELIMO, Uria Simango, who found himself dangerously suspended between two increasingly hostile factions.

Crystallization of the issues now centered on the time and location of the Second Congress of FRELIMO, originally scheduled for September 1968 to coincide with the twin anniversaries of the First Congress and the beginning of the armed struggle. The events of

early May, however, made an earlier gathering imperative, especially as they highlighted the widening gap between FRELIMO in Mozambique and FRELIMO in Dar es Salaam, between a revolutionary movement based on a socialist ideology nurtured in socialist practice and a counterrevolutionary movement based on a petit-bourgeois nationalist ideology which in practice looked little different from Portuguese colonialism. In a statement on May 26, President Mondlane announced the congress for July 31, but without indicating where it would be held. The issues to be resolved could not have been made clearer: "The Mozambican people have a right to know what has recently been happening in Tanzania. . . . It is in the Congress that this matter will be brought before our people." Furthermore, delegates to the congress would examine

the problems of the developing political-social structures which need general discussion among Mozambicans within our own country. Some of these problems are (1) the working relationship between the military and the civilian administration; (2) the ways to increase production through agriculture, cooperatives, commerce, cottage industries, etc.; (3) the establishment and improvement of schools, adult education, medical centres and other social services; (4) the rationale of our foreign policy, which tends to favour friendship and cooperation with progressive forces, and is antagonistic to imperialism.[41]

Thus the Second Congress was to be an arena for establishing the political direction of FRELIMO more clearly, for political education at all levels within the movement, and for making the external FRELIMO responsible to the internal FRELIMO.

Mondlane and the insiders wanted to hold the congress inside liberated Mozambique, while Nkavandame and the outsiders argued for a site in southern Tanzania.[42] Another issue for debate concerned the composition of delegations from the three provinces where fighting was taking place—Cabo Delgado, Niassa, and Tete. In the end, each province was to send seventeen delegates—nine military and eight political—a decision which signaled a defeat for Nkavandame's faction (as did the decision to hold the congress in Niassa province). Thus, sensing that a major political defeat was at hand and no longer capable of maintaining an appearance of unity where none existed, the political delegation from Cabo Delgado refused to attend when the congress convened in July and remained in Tanzania.

Momentous decisions were made at the Second Congress,

but they neither completed the process of revolutionary change within FRELIMO nor brought an end to counterrevolutionary tendencies within it. A new set of statutes was drawn up to replace the original constitution of 1962, a new program was detailed, and an extensive series of resolutions was adopted. No less important was the reelection of Eduardo Mondlane as President: he was clearly the key representative of the revolutionary forces within FRELIMO and the particular object of attack by their opponents both from within and without. The essential thrust of the deliberations was to make certain the priority of the armed struggle in the liberation of Mozambique, and to define more precisely than ever before both the enemy against whom the struggle was being waged and the kind of society which was to emerge from that struggle.

An examination of the new statutes reveals how much the situation had altered since the First Congress.[43] Some of the greatest changes are to be found in the section on membership, which in the original constitution included only three brief lines and entailed virtually nothing beyond general support for FRELIMO. Both duties and rights were now clearly spelled out, and members were required to be politically conscious, used to military discipline, and ready to defend what they believed in. Similarly, in place of the cryptic definition of "democratic centralism," there was now a straightforward section on "Methods of Work," bearing witness to years of struggle within the Central Committee and demands by the people to have the nature of FRELIMO defined in words they could understand. The ideas were no different, but the way in which they were expressed indicates a victory for the mass of Mozambicans and the fighting cadres over the elitist manipulation of language characteristic of many African nationalist movements.

Most significant, however, was the new apportionment of power, authority, and responsibility in the section on "Structure and Organization." Of fundamental importance was the enlargement of the Central Committee from twenty members to forty and the requirement that most of the new members were to be popularly elected from constituencies inside Mozambique. Under the old constitution, the Central Committee had been composed of only the heads of departments and their assistants; now its membership included provincial secretaries, representatives elected from the provinces and by the congress, and representatives of mass organizations. Mondlane noted soon after that "nearly all these new members were party leaders permanently resident in Mozambique."[44] A number of them were military leaders who had made their mark

among the peasants of the war zones, according to Iain Christie.[45] At the same time that it enlarged the Central Committee, the Second Congress decided to restrict its activities mainly to legislative functions—that is, "To formulate the political line of FRELIMO, within the principles defined by the Congress," which remained the supreme organ of the movement. It also was entrusted with the selection of successors to the offices of President and Vice-President in case of death—a provision which took on great significance after the assassination of President Mondlane a half year later.[46] The development of the movement was reflected in the establishment of a political-military committee charged with the prosecution of the war as both a military and political struggle, the creation of an executive committee to carry out the resolutions of the congress and the Central Committee, and the clarification of the offices of the President and Vice-President.

Critical to the restructuring of FRELIMO was the drafting of a new program "adapted to the new reality," reflecting the lessons of the armed struggle and national reconstruction in the liberated zones. "This program placed a stronger emphasis on the necessity of the unity of all the People, on national reconstruction and on the reinforcement of ties with all anti-colonialist and anti-imperialist forces."[47] Fundamental to all its provisions is the commitment to eradicate all forms of social and economic inequality in free Mozambique (e.g., the need to include women in every phase of the struggle and to ensure that their participation is that of equals to men is prominently discussed in both the program and the resolutions).[48] Finally, in a statement which set the seal on the ideological path along which FRELIMO was then moving, the congress resolved that "This struggle is part of the world's movement for the emancipation of the peoples, which aims at the total liquidation of colonialism and imperialism, and at the construction of a new society free from exploitation of man by man."[49] Summing up the work of the Second Congress, Machel wrote in 1974 that "It analyzed the struggle, reaffirmed and further developed revolutionary principles and introduced the structural changes demanded by the advance of the people's liberation war."[50]

If it was widely believed that the air had been cleared by the defeat of Nkavandame's faction, this illusion was brutally shattered by the assassination on December 22, 1968, of Paulo Samuel Kankhomba, deputy chief of the section of operations of the defense department, on the Tanzanian border. FRELIMO's leadership saw this action as an indication of Portugal's increasing desperation. "The

more meaningful is our military action against Portugal," Mondlane wrote at year's end, "the more trouble we should expect from her."[51] Nkavandame was charged with being responsible for Kankhomba's death, and on January 3, 1969, he was stripped of all responsibilities in the movement, though he was not detained.[52]

The Portuguese continued to believe that FRELIMO's strength derived from its leaders rather than from the Mozambican people, and finding several other potential allies among the remaining counterrevolutionaries in the FRELIMO leadership, they stepped up their activities. On February 3, 1969, President Mondlane was killed by a package bomb, and within the next four weeks similar devices were intercepted that were intended for dos Santos and Uria Simango, Vice-President of FRELIMO. The leading figures implicated in these attacks were Silverio Nungu, secretary for administration at the Dar es Salaam headquarters, and Nkavandame. Nungu was sent back to Mozambique, while Nkavandame fled across the border to escape the Tanzanian police and defected to the Portuguese.[53]

We have already remarked on the confusion that obstructed FRELIMO's ability to perceive what was happening in its own ranks during this difficult period (see pp. 281-82 above). Now confusion was aggravated by profound demoralization, but the assassination of the President provided a shock through which "the Mozambican Revolution transformed its sorrow into new strength."[54] As FRELIMO accounted in its annual assessment of the preceding year's struggle:

> This situation was fought by intense action of mobilisation on the part of our political commissars, who explained to the people and to the fighters the necessity to continue the struggle, to avenge the death of our President, so that his death would not be a useless sacrifice.
>
> The answer of our people and fighters was completely positive: transforming sadness into intense hatred, and stronger determination, they continued with the war and advanced, thus frustrating the plans of the enemy to stop the struggle by the physical elimination of its leaders.[55]

By the time of the critically important Central Committee meeting of April 1969, the stage was set for the identification of the essential ideological division that had always existed in the heart of FRELIMO. Once again this was primarily the result of steady pressure from the ranks below, of listening to the people whose ideas had been forged in struggle:

The fundamental objective was to seek means of furthering our national liberation struggle—not, as the foreign press speculated, to look for the successor to our late President. Our people warned us against this danger: in numerous messages received from the Provincial Representatives at all levels, the same concern was expressed: "We must not preoccupy ourselves with personalities, who will be the President of FRELIMO—we must study the means of intensifying the struggle". And this is what was done.[56]

Specifically, the Central Committee posed the question "Might not this crime [the assassination] be related to the differences existing among us?" In the course of several days' discussion, "the ideological lines motivating the behaviour of the divergent groups were discovered,"[57] and there could no longer be any doubt about which had triumphed. As the Central Committee reported it, this clarification

> was the work of a group of comrades who have always kept themselves faithful to the interests of the masses, respecting collective values and fighting individualism and personal ambition that foment opportunism, comrades linked with the concrete reality and immersed in the realisation of the principal tasks of the struggle.
>
> Through criticism and self-criticism each one of us vowed to correct our conceptions and behaviour that do not conform to the exigencies of the Revolution.[58]

Clearly the revolutionary line had triumphed. Its triumph was certainly not inevitable, but it can now be seen to have been always in the ascendant. The Central Committee could not have been clearer on this point:

> We wish to stress that all these innovations are in fact a continuation; and that all of them are linked with the policy of our late President, Comrade Eduardo Mondlane, whose work is not only being continued, but is being taken to greater heights by the Movement. The unity he came to represent has now reached a higher stage: it is unity at the service of the Revolution.[59]

Little wonder, then, that the 1969 meeting of the Central Committee was thought to have "opened a new page in the history of our struggle for National Liberation" and to be "as important in the history of our organization as was the Second Congress."[60] Henceforth, official analyses of contradictions in FRELIMO would

always be placed in the context of the struggle between revolution and reaction and expressed in the language of class analysis. Similarly, all subsequent retrospective analyses would emphasize that "during the whole history of Frelimo, at every critical juncture, the correct line has triumphed."[61] No doubt some readers will find both of these modes of analysis objectionable—either because they seem merely rhetorical or self-serving or because they represent the genuine triumph of a revolutionary socialist ideology. The fact remains that these perceptions were part of a political reality born of a deep conviction that revolution is "a process of rejection and assimilation—rejection of reactionary ideas and practices and assimilation of revolutionary ideas and praxis."[62]

It should be emphasized, however, that no one in April 1969 entertained the belief that the struggle was over:

Of course, we are aware of the difficulties that lie ahead of us. This unity we have now achieved will have to be implemented each day, with all its difficult implications. We shall need all our attention and all our strength. We shall have setbacks, but we shall know how to learn from them, how to improve ourselves and our work. We do not deceive ourselves with false hopes of an easy path: because it is not a mechanical process, it needs our complete and active engagement, our constant efforts. Our experience has shown us that it takes an endless process of criticism and self-criticism to eliminate the residue of the colonial system that still persists in us, for us to place ourselves decisively on the right side of history, for us to discover and implement the *necessity* of the Revolution.[63]

THE TRANSITION TO A VANGUARD PARTY, 1970-1972

Looking back to this period, Machel declared in 1974 that the new phase into which FRELIMO had entered in 1970 was "the creation of an organized vanguard of the working masses and cleansing of our ranks of the ideas and values of the reactionary forces."[64] To be sure, this is what took place during the next seven years, and it was much more clearly carried out after 1972 than during the previous decade of struggle.

The playing out of these themes initially focused on the isolation of Simango as the leading representative of the counterrevolutionary forces that remained within FRELIMO's leadership. At the April 1969 meeting of the Central Committee, long simmering

suspicions about Simango's true political commitments seem to have come out into the open. During the troubled period of 1968-69, Simango had presented himself as a voice of moderation and had either defended or rationalized the actions of Gwenjere and Nkavandame, for which he was severely criticized at the April 1969 meeting.[65]

After the death of Mondlane, Simango had assumed "the functions of President" on February 11 by order of the executive committee "in conformity with the statutes of FRELIMO . . . until the next meeting of the Central Committee." But, as we have seen, Simango was called to task in April, and the Central Committee exercised its statutory right to determine how the presidency would be organized until the next meeting of the congress. It created "the Council of the Presidency, in which Uria Simango was controlled by two proven revolutionary comrades: Samora Moises Machel and Marcelino dos Santos."[66] Thus isolated, Simango was no longer able to straddle the ideological fence as he had done in the past. Simango made a final bid for power by presenting his case to forces external to FRELIMO. The publication of the pamphlet "Gloomy Situation in FRELIMO" openly revealed Simango's alliance with the most reactionary forces in FRELIMO over the previous several years and made apparent his unwillingness to work within the parameters of the political line and the structures of the movement.[67] On November 8, 1969, the executive committee of FRELIMO rejected Simango's desperate ploy and suspended him from the Council of the Presidency.[68] The process of *saneamento* (cleansing), by which contradictions are solved in the course of the struggle and "the revolution itself ensures the rejection of the impure load it carries," would continue and continues today, but the break with Simango had placed FRELIMO securely on the path toward the socialist transformation of Mozambique.[69]

It is worth noting here that in 1972 John Saul was less convinced than I am now of FRELIMO's commitment to socialism. At that time he observed that "the terms of the emerging ideology are still left somewhat undefined" and "any public hint that the movement has 'socialist' intentions is systematically avoided."[70] I have earlier in this article noted the editorial identification by FRELIMO of the idea of "revolution" with that of "socialism" in 1966 and to the increasing tendency over the years to emphasize the building of a new society based on "the end of exploitation of man by man." It seems to me that any lack of ideological definition during this period reflects FRELIMO's historical pragmatism more

than a lack of commitment to socialism—both in terms of the continuing need to mobilize the masses in Mozambique and in view of the recent experience of the successful revolutionary faction with comrades who professed one ideology and lived by another.

The significance of this experience for the ideological development of FRELIMO cannot be overestimated. Interviewed during the transitional period between the Lusaka Agreement of 7 September 1974 and independence on 25 June 1975, President Machel remarked that "the appearance of Uria Simango and Lazaro Nkavandame is a school for us, which teaches us that exploitation has no colour, has no race, that the enemy has no country, has no people and, besides, has no piety."[71]

In 1970 a booklet was produced which spoke directly to the need to define more precisely what it meant to be a member of FRELIMO. This publication—*The Qualities of a Member of the Central Committee*—is devoted primarily to defining the qualities of a FRELIMO militant, as contrasted to a FRELIMO supporter, because only a militant could become a member of the Central Committee. The five main sections deal with individual and collective responsibility, revolutionary practice and study, comradeship, unity, and the struggle against racism—all of which were conspicuously lacking in the Simango-Nkavandame-Gwenjere camp. Although socialism is not mentioned in defining the political line of FRELIMO, reference is made to FRELIMO's relationship to "the progressive forces of the entire world," while "the principle of democratic centralism" is invoked as a tenet of the organization. In the section on combatting racism an important distinction is made in defining who is the enemy which indicates FRELIMO's socialist progression:

> While it is true that most of the colonizers are white and the colonized are black in Mozambique, we must not lose sight of the fact that our struggle is not against the man in himself for being white, but against the system of colonization. What is responsible for the oppression that we suffer is not the colour of the man. What is responsible is the economic, social and political system, defended by the man against whom we are fighting.[72]

Thus, as is frequently the case, the goals of a political movement are clarified as much by defining the characteristics of the old order as the new.

This same line of argument runs through an important speech by Machel (named President by the Central Committee at the May 1970 meeting, with dos Santos assuming the vice-presidency) at the

second conference of the department of education and culture in September 1970. Here the system of exploitation is specifically named "capitalism" and its form of oppression identified as "bourgeois." Machel emphasizes the role of education in inculcating "the advanced, scientific, objective and collective ideology which enables us to progress in the revolutionary process," concluding that "Our chief strength, the primary cause of all we do is the people. In solving our problems we should rely first on them, following a mass line."[73] What was taking place from 1970 on, then, was the progressive definition of a socialist ideology which was historically specific to the national liberation struggle in Mozambique. FRELIMO's cautious pragmatism, especially its understanding of the need to prepare the ground before launching any form of struggle, made it more important to define specific objectives than to give them a name—socialism—which in its African context, at least, had been all too frequently abused.

It is sometimes overlooked that, while these ideological developments were taking place, FRELIMO was defeating the most important Portuguese counter-offensive of the entire war of liberation— Operation Gordian Knot, which lasted from May to November 1970. The armed struggle was necessarily the first priority until victory was gained; all other aspects of the struggle were subordinate.[74] But it had been recognized for many years that armed struggle was primarily a political process, not a military one, and the lessons learned in it were regularly being translated into general principles on which to build for the future. As Saul correctly remarked just before the coup in Portugal: "Practice is now being theorised and thus forged into an ever more effective instrument of progress."[75] I am suggesting that this process dates back to the beginnings of the armed struggle and was accelerated by the crisis of 1968-69.

The presidential message of 25 September 1971 shows how far toward a revolutionary socialist ideology FRELIMO had moved since 1969. Old themes are reiterated to emphasize that the enemy is the system of colonialism and exploitation of man by man rather than the Portuguese people. Other key themes are protracted struggle, the importance of unity between the masses and FRELIMO and its leadership, and internationalist solidarity. Ideological correctness is also stressed, as is the need for the people to transform revolutionary ideas into revolutionary practice. Machel goes on to say that "Cadres are decisive to the implementation of our political line, our ideology," and that "this can only be achieved through the method of always combining the practice of combat and production

with study, ensuring regular discussion, criticism and self-criticism, not allowing them to fall into a routine, ensuring study with practice." All of these themes are familiar, but to them a new element is added which shows the way to the future: "The seventh year [1970-71] was the point of departure of the conscious development of the nature of our organisation, of its development into a vanguard party of the working masses in our country, a vanguard party with a vanguard ideology." The new year must continue, he urged, "to make the fighters and above all the cadres living examples of the new mentality, active transformers of society, creators and promoters of our advanced, scientific, revolutionary ideology."[76]

If socialism was not yet a label to be assumed by FRELIMO in statements such as this one, internal and external actions indicated otherwise. In June 1971, for example, a FRELIMO delegation headed by the President visited the Soviet Union, Bulgaria, Romania, and the German Democratic Republic. According to the FRELIMO national bulletin:

> There were several reasons for this visit as decided upon by the Executive Committee of FRELIMO. First, the socialist countries are our natural allies; we form an alliance based on the fundamental fact that our aims are the same: to build a society where oppression and exploitation of man by man will no longer be possible, a society geared towards the well-being of the people and their political, economic, and social progress.

By contrast, the capitalist countries were seen to be the enemies of FRELIMO by virtue of their support for Portuguese fascism.

> This enmity has even deeper roots which lie in the contradiction between our ultimate aims on the one hand and the very nature of their society on the other. Thus capitalist society is characterised by the principle of exploitation of man by man: all the riches of the country are in the hands of big bosses, bankers and landowners, while the people, exploited, receiving only a small part of what they produce, must submit to an oppressive system designed merely to guarantee for the capitalists a continuance of such exploitation.[77]

The logic in FRELIMO's march toward socialism was finally made explicit at the long meeting of the Central Committee from 4-30 December 1972. "A general directive was laid down: to make a clear definition of the targets in each phase of the struggle, to

constantly explain the implications of enemy's strategies, to increase organisational work among the people, and to continue to implement FRELIMO's popular revolutionary line at every level." Here was not only a blueprint for action in the future, but an analysis of FRELIMO's method of procedure in the past several years. To this directive, in which "special importance was attached to the definition of who is the enemy," was added a major change in FRELIMO's definition of itself, antecedents of which can be found in the 1970 handbook on *Qualities of a Member of the Central Committee*:

> Also reaffirmed was the principle that FRELIMO is a Front, which ensures the participation of all genuinely anti-colonialist forces prepared to struggle for the total independence of Mozambique. Our experience, however, and more concretely the fact that at a certain historical moment there appeared within FRELIMO people who attempted to take power to continue to oppress and exploit the people, has led the CC to qualify this principle. Hence, the CC recognised that although we are a Front, this Front has as its point of departure the negation of the exploitation of man by man.

It should be noted that these decisions were taken in "absolute unanimity," which reflected a higher level of "ideological unity" than ever before as a result of "almost total cohesion within the movement."[78]

By the end of 1972, at the very latest, there can be little doubt that FRELIMO was well along the path to transforming itself into a socialist vanguard party with distinctly Marxist-Leninist underpinnings. By 1973 leaders of the movement were openly speaking of the need to create a party of revolution and were convinced that FRELIMO was moving in this direction.[79] In the years between this period and the Third Congress, which was held at Maputo from 3-7 February 1977, when FRELIMO transformed itself into a Marxist-Leninist Vanguard Party of the Working Class for the construction of socialism in Mozambique, there was an outpouring of important statements on both theory and practice from President Machel and the Central Committee in which FRELIMO's thinking can be vividly traced.[80] As had always been true of FRELIMO, progress toward this goal—like progress toward the creation of a socialist society in the People's Republic of Mozambique—was achieved as a result of a continuing dialectic between theory and practice rooted in a refusal to become rigidly dogmatic and a willingness to remain flexible in response to the realities of the historical context.[81]

ANGOLAN SOCIALISM

Kevin Brown

INTRODUCTION

When Angola became independent on November 11, 1975, the atmosphere in the capital city of Luanda was not one of joy and celebration, as one might have expected on such an occasion. On the contrary, a sense of foreboding overshadowed the ceremonies because everyone feared that the Frente Nacional de Libertacão de Angola (FNLA) and the União Nacional para a Independência Total de Angola (UNITA) would somehow keep their promise to disrupt them. The tension was so great that when shooting broke out, many of those attending the festivities dove to the ground until it was clear it came from guns of the friendly Movimiento Popular de Libertacão de Angola (MPLA). The impromptu fireworks continued throughout the night, filling the sky with tracer bullets in an eerie but oddly appropriate salute to the new People's Republic of Angola (RPA—Republica Popular de Angola).

These were not the only independence ceremonies in Angola that day. Earlier the Portuguese had refused to declare any of the three rival liberation movements the legitimate government and instead had granted independence to the Angolan people, maintaining that the collapse of the transition government left them no alternative. Yet another ceremony took place in the town of Nova Lisboa in the Central Highlands, where the FNLA and UNITA announced the formation of a coalition government. Such were the bizarre circumstances surrounding the beginning of the People's Republic, and although the MPLA eventually managed to rout its rivals on the battlefield with the help of the Cubans and Russians, the struggle for control of Angola is not over.

The civil war in Angola is essentially a struggle between the three major ethno-linguistic groups—the Mbundu, the Bakongo, and the Ovimbundu—each of which is the primary constituency of a liberation movement. The MPLA represents the approximately 1.5 million Mbundu living in the area surrounding Luanda; the FNLA, the one million Bakongo in the northeastern corner of Angola; and

UNITA, the more than two million Ovimbundu of the Central Highlands area. The rivalry between these groups dates from the slave trade era, and is so intense that even the goal of independence failed to unite them against their common enemy—the Portuguese. Indeed it can be argued that the civil war in Angola began with the outbreak of the liberation struggle in 1911: since then the movements have fought each other as much as the Portuguese.

The Portuguese exploited these ethnic rivalries in order to maintain control of the colony. By denying Angolans access to education and prohibiting interethnic associations of any type, they prevented the development of a larger "Angolan" identity and forced the fragmentation of nationalist sentiment along ethnic lines. The "success" of this policy created problems for the Portuguese when, in the aftermath of the April 1974 coup in Portugal, they sought to establish a transition government made up of representatives of the three movements to carry out orderly decolonization. No sooner had the transition government been inaugurated than it began to disintegrate, torn apart by the mutual distrust and suspicion of its participants.

In this context of an ongoing civil war, the MPLA is trying to implement the revolutionary doctrine known as "Angolan Socialism." In addition to the war, there are problems of economic dislocation, organizational inexperience, threats of foreign intervention, and internal dissension within the MPLA which hamper the radical transformation of Angolan society that the MPLA envisions. It is not too early to speak of Angolan Socialism, however, for the broad outlines of the new society have already been drawn and the fundamental orientation set. The purpose of this essay is to examine the theory and practice of Angolan Socialism and how domestic and foreign challenges have shaped its evolution.

THEORY AND PRACTICE OF ANGOLAN SOCIALISM

Angolan Socialism as defined by the MPLA has little in common with African Socialism. There are similarities in the aims of the two types of socialism—for example, the restructuring of former colonial societies into independent and egalitarian nations—but the MPLA leadership has repeatedly made clear its disdain for anything other than "scientific socialism." As Agostinho Neto, President of the RPA, states:

The so-called African Socialism doesn't take into account the universal character of the evolution of mankind. It does not take

into account the presence of social classes with opposing interests nor the implications of this. The so-called African Socialism . . . is based on a distorted conception of reality. . . . It exists generally in countries where a bourgeoisie flourished and which lives at the cost of the workers and peasants. . . . As for us, the only way to attain socialism is to abolish exploitation, to hand over the means of production to those who produce, and to insure the just distribution of the fruits of what they produce according to their work and according to their capacity.[1]

The Angolans are scornful of African Socialism because they consider the "socialism" of a Léopold Senghor or a Jomo Kenyatta to be little more than intellectual window-dressing that serves to legitimize essentially capitalist regimes. They believe that African Socialism, by emphasizing the uniqueness of the African personality, glosses over the problem of neo-colonialism and avoids confronting what should be the central issue: the radical transformation of African society. In their desire to distinguish themselves from those they regard as less serious socialists, the Angolans tend to ignore the similarities in their ideologies and therefore are probably guilty of exaggeration. Clearly, both forms of socialism represent to a greater or lesser degree adaptations of European socialism to African conditions; nevertheless, the Angolans insist that their conception is fundamentally different because it is rooted in "scientific socialism" rather than vague notions about African culture.

The Angolans feel that their experience of a long and bitter liberation struggle has been critical to the development of their more radical brand of socialism. In their view, the intransigence of Portuguese colonialism under Salazar's *Estado Novo* regime precluded the more evolutionary approach to independence that was possible in the French and English colonies, and dictated the adoption of a rigorous revolutionary theory that aimed at the elimination of all vestiges of colonialism. Along with many other observers of the third world, the Angolans believe that the evolutionary approach has led almost inevitably to the establishment of neocolonial societies dominated by a black instead of a white exploiting class. They are confident that by implementing "scientific socialism" they will prevent the emergence of neo-colonialism in Angola.

When they call themselves "scientific socialists," Angolans mean that they accept the Marxist-Leninist critique of the world order, according to which the capitalist exploiters are pitted against the proletarian exploited. They also subscribe to the idea that the working class should control the means of production and thereby

lay the foundation for the creation of a just society purged of the exploitation of man by man. But these ideas serve only to provide a fundamental orientation rather than as dogma. For example, it is possible for the MPLA to advocate a worker-controlled society and at the same time promise to preserve and protect private enterprise. Furthermore, although they accept the basic tenets of Marxism-Leninism and declare their solidarity with the socialist world, the Angolans vigorously assert their intention to pursue their revolution in their own way. ("Our revolution is not a carbon copy of any other revolution," states an MPLA pamphlet.) But what is most surprising about the MPLA ideology is that, for all its supposed radicalism, a careful examination reveals a program not dissimilar to European social-democratic thinking. The ideology is eclectic within a broad socialist framework, but the Angolan element is preponderant in it.

At the core of the MPLA ideology is the idea that the new socialist society to be founded in Angola will be dedicated to the conversion of the Angolan into a "new man." Thus the reconstruction of the country involves a far more fundamental process than economic reorganization. In President Neto's words:

> From our point of view, to construct a country does not mean simply to build houses or roads, but essentially to transform the mentality of the human being so that he considers himself a man of dignity, useful to society. Now our fundamental problem is that of the practical realization of the tasks of National Reconstruction, of the consolidation of our independence, of the transformation of a society, until now without possibilities of evolving, to a new, more just type of organization. Our fundamental task is that of transforming the tribalized man, full of racial and class complexes, into a truly free man.[2]

This "new man" will emerge from both the colonialist and tribalist mentalities, both of which represent cultural bondages that must be eradicated. In light of the deep ethnic cleavages in Angolan society, it is not surprising that Neto regards the tribal mentality as as much a hindrance to socialism as the petit-bourgeois mentality of the African colonial elite.

The process of transformation of political structures will be initiated through the installation of "people's power" (poder popular) at the local and national levels. Neighborhood committees, worker discussion groups, and government assemblies will be formed

to create a politically educated base upon which to build a democratic regime. The immediate aim is the

> gradual establishment of the organs of People's Power until we arrive at its highest expression, which is the Assembly of the People, the supreme organ of the State. We here in Angola are for Popular Democracy, which is the political objective of our State. It is for this reason we are laying the foundation so that the organs of People's Power can consolidate themselves, can function as state bodies.[3]

Ultimately, the working class, in alliance with the rural peasantry, is expected to emerge as the vanguard class of a socialist Angola. This worker-peasant alliance is an Angolan adaptation of orthodox Marxism-Leninism required by Angola's lack of an industrial base. As Neto explains:

> The working class constitutes a minority of the population. Although small in number, the working class has to be the directing class of the Angolan Revolution . . . because it has the ideology of the vanguard of scientific socialism, which is also called Marxism-Leninism. . . . Here in Angola, the workers by themselves or the peasants by themselves would not have been able to put an end to Portuguese colonialist domination. A very tight union of all patriots, led by the MPLA, was necessary to construct a force capable of ending colonialist domination and exploitation. . . . It was the rural population that suffered most from the colonialist reprisals. Also, in the urban areas, the capital, and other cities, patriots struggled, were jailed and thrown into concentration camps, tortured, and assassinated. It was through the struggle that the alliance between the workers and the peasants was forged —an alliance that was sealed with blood and suffering.[4]

By including the peasantry as well as the urban patriots who fought the Portuguese, the definition of the "working class" becomes sufficiently broad to embrace almost the entire population, thereby avoiding the problem of elites.

The most succinct expression of the goals of the MPLA can be found in the articles of the constitution adopted at the time of independence. The first article describes the fundamental objectives of the republic:

> The People's Republic of Angola is a sovereign, independent, and democratic state whose first objective is the total liberation of

the Angolan people from the vestiges of colonialism and the domination and aggression of imperialism, and the construction of a prosperous and democratic country, completely free from any form of man's exploitation by man, realizing the aspirations of the masses.[5]

The following sixteen articles establish a secular state separate from and respectful of all churches and religious institutions, guarantee private property, and promise to promote education and "just social relations in all sectors of production, stimulating and developing the public sector and increasing cooperative methods. The RPA will be particularly concerned with solving the land problem in the interest of the peasant masses."[6] They define the role of the MPLA as one of leadership in the political, economic, and social affairs of the nation, acting as the representative of the Angolan people, in whom all sovereignty resides. Although the masses are guaranteed "broad and effective participation in the exercise of political power," the Assembly of the People will not be formally installed until Angolan territory is totally liberated. In the meantime the Council of the Revolution, composed of members of the MPLA political bureau and the general staff of the armed forces, will exercise legislative and executive authority.

The MPLA leadership first came into contact with Marxist-Leninist thought as students in Lisbon, where the Partido Communista de Portugal organized study groups that brought together both overseas and metropolitan students interested in combatting fascism. Neto, for example, joined the Movimiento da Unita Democrata in 1949, along with Amílcar Cabral, Álvaro Cunhal, Mário Soares, Salgado Zenha, and Almeida Santos.* In the early 1950's, similar groups were formed in Luanda, more or less oriented by the PCP, although the extent of the connection is disputed. Mario Andrade, Viriato da Cruz, and other members of Luanda's literary circle mixed politics and literature with the publication of *Mensagem* [Message] in 1951—a journal shut down by the Portuguese after only two issues. Thereafter, numerous clandestine groups of limited effectiveness flourished and faded in rapid succession until the formation of the MPLA in 1956 coalesced the many fragments.[7]

---

*Cabral founded the Partido Africano da Independência da Guiné a Cabo Verde (PAIGC), and was its leader until his assassination in 1973; Cunhal heads the PCP; Soares is currently Prime Minister of Portugal; Zenha is head of the Socialist Party in Portugal; Santos has held various ministerial posts since 1974.

In 1961, following a period of intense repression of political activity, the MPLA was forced into exile, eventually choosing Brazzaville as its base of operations. Exile afforded the MPLA leaders contacts with the socialist countries of Europe, Africa, and Asia, and access to their wealth of intellectual and practical experience in fighting colonialism. They participated in the Afro-Asian Solidarity conferences sponsored by the Soviet Union and similar forums where socialism and liberation were the major themes. They studied the Algerian and Vietnamese liberation wars—the latter impressing them as being basically similar to their own. Lucio Lara, now the MPLA secretary and chief political organizer, recently remarked on the Vietnamese conflict:

> There was the same attempt to gain independence by peaceful means, by negotiation and explanations, and finally the conviction that the only way to really get independence was by armed struggle. The Vietnamese armed struggle was also very human, a blend of political and military action which became our model. In drawing up our MPLA program, we were strongly influenced by the Vietnamese experience. Obviously we also studied their military tactics, their concepts of people's war.[8]

However, the single most important influence on Angolan socialism is unquestionably the revolutionary theory of Amílcar Cabral, founder and leader of the PAIGC. Cabral's thinking shaped Neto's so profoundly that Angolan socialism can be characterized as a distillation of the Cape Verdian's more analytical and comprehensive writings. What is implicit in the MPLA ideology is explicit in the PAIGC ideology, which makes an understanding of the latter essential to an understanding of Angolan socialism.

Cabral's contribution to socialist theory is his innovative adaptation of Marxist-Leninist theory to the African colonial experience.[9] Whereas orthodox Marxism-Leninism posits the concepts of the class struggle and private ownership of property as central to the analysis of capitalist society, Cabral substitutes the concepts of cultural resistance and the Africanization of the means of production as more relevant to Guinea-Bissau's historical circumstances. He argues that although classes existed in colonial Africa, they were tangential to the fundamental dynamic of colonialism, which was the clash between European and African cultures. For Cabral, cultural oppression under the guise of a policy of assimilation was the cutting edge of the colonial experience—rather than the more obvious political and economic oppression. Yet because of the paradoxical nature

302

of assimilation—the denial of African culture, on the one hand, and the refusal to admit more than a token number of Africans into the ranks of the assimilated, on the other—cultural domination was never as complete as political and economic domination. Therefore it is not class but cultural interest and identification that should serve as the rallying point of resistance. By asserting their "Africanness" the people take the first step toward organizing an armed struggle.

Once the colony is successfully liberated, decisions must be made relating to the structure of society and the control of the means of production. Having already parted company with the orthodox Marxists over the role of the class struggle, Cabral moves one step further away by declaring that whether property is held collectively or privately is not the principal issue: what matters is that the colonizer be removed and the property Africanized. The issue of state versus private control of the means of production is secondary to the issue of African autonomy, and will be resolved democratically as circumstances warrant. Cabral's brand of socialism emphasizes "not the collectivization of property, but rather the collectivization of decision-making such that the increased participation of the people in the movement is facilitated."[10] Utilizing Marxist-Leninist theory as a method of analysis, Cabral succeeds in Africanizing European socialism.

Cuba's influence on Angolan socialism is particularly evident in the techniques of mass mobilization and organization currently being employed by the MPLA. With Cuban military and technical aid continuing at high levels, this influence is more likely to increase than diminish over the next few years. Cuba seems to have had an impact on the development of MPLA ideology as well. While it is not known whether the Angolans borrowed directly from the Cuban example, both ideologies express their visions of a transformed and transforming society in virtually the same terms. The Cuban *nuevo hombre* who will be purged of capitalist attitudes and transformed into a revolutionary socialist is the counterpart of the Angolan *novo homen* who will emerge shorn of his colonial and tribal mentality.*

Beyond sharing a commitment to the reconstruction of the individual in society, both socialisms emphasize the necessity of struggle for the achievement of their goals. The Angolan government

*The idea of the "new man" is of course found throughout socialist writings, but I suspect that the MPLA has used Cuban texts as models for its own ideological treatises.

bombards its citizens with the slogan "*A luta continua*" ("The struggle continues"). The "first war of liberation" against the Portuguese having ended, the "second war of liberation" against the internal "agents of imperialism" continues. The struggle is an integral part of the process of transformation; there can be no lasting change without struggle, which of itself promotes transformation. For both the Angolans and the Cubans, the millennium toward which the struggle aims—a society free of the exploitation of man by man—justifies the sacrifices of the present.

Given the similarities in the origins of the Cuban and Angolan revolutions, the methods employed to advance them, and the Latin cultural heritage, one might expect the Angolans to attempt a direct transplant of the Cuban experience to Angolan soil, but this will not happen for several reasons. First, Cuba in the 1950's was much more highly developed than Angola in the 1970's; statistically at least, Cuba compared favorably with European countries of that period. Second, Angola is ethnically very heterogeneous—a circumstance which threatens the republic's very existence. Third, Angola has an illiteracy rate of 90 percent, which, as a consequence of the mass exodus of Portuguese technicians, has resulted in a far more serious economic dislocation than Cuba faced when Castro came to power.[11] Finally, the Angolans have no intention of imitating another revolution; they will borrow whatever ideas, skills, money, etc., they need from any source provided they remain unrestricted in the pursuit of their own brand of socialism.

The translation of the MPLA's socialist ideals into practical reality is the task of a vast organizational effort that attempts to mobilize virtually the entire population into active participants in the process of national reconstruction. The transformation of society begins with the transformation of individuals, which begins with their participation in activities that promote socialist ideals. The immediate purpose of a particular activity might be to raise production in a factory, to teach literacy, to help with the sugar harvest, or to assist with any other pressing problem. But the ultimate purpose is the training of socialists. In their scope and number, these activities seem to reflect the conviction that constructive work is the first step toward the inculcation of correct values. What one observer noted about the philosophy of the Cuban revolution regarding participatory activity is equally pertinent to the Angolan revolution:

Such programs underline the elite's continuing emphasis on the inseparability of attitudinal, value, and behavioral changes. In this view, significant cultural shifts do not depend in linear fashion on changes in attitudes that in turn produce changes in behavior. Rather, the starting point of change is when more and more citizens take part in the right kinds of activities, activities that direct attention away from the self and toward the collectivity, activities that wordlessly but dramatically teach the lessons of development.[12]

The MPLA strives to mobilize all sectors of society through a variety of organizations, and despite elitist tendencies in some of them, generally there is something for everyone. For children, the Organization of Angolan Pioneers (OPA) operates as a politicized scout troop, offering training in military discipline as well as the fundamentals of ideology. During the civil war, many Pioneers took part in the fighting. For young adults, the Youth of the MPLA (JMPLA) is the principal training ground for future MPLA cadres. Since most of the members are students, its activities center around the secondary schools, and include student groups, volunteer work as literacy teachers, and the coaching of athletic teams. However, in response to accusations of elitist tendencies, the JMPLA is seeking to expand its membership into the factories and the countryside.

For women, the Organization of Angolan Women (OMA) symbolizes the Angolan revolution's commitment to their full equality with men. Founded in 1962 with the double objective of involving women in the liberation struggle against colonialism and of combatting the discrimination suffered by women in traditional society, OMA stresses education in hygiene and child care. There are hundreds of *guerrilheiras* in the armed forces, but day-care centers and schools for teaching sewing, literacy, and cultural history occupy OMA members more than military matters.

For factory workers, the National Union for Angolan Workers (UNTA) carries out the tasks of mobilization and political indoctrination. The union is a key instrument in the MPLA's campaign to revive an economy battered by the loss of most of its technical and managerial personnel. To date UNTA's approach has been educational—to convince the workers that higher wages must be earned by higher productivity. Most workers believed that getting rid of the Portuguese *patrao* (boss) would automatically bring the good life; when instead they saw inflation eroding their newly won wage increases, they reacted with strikes and work stoppages, fueling

further the inflationary spiral. It can be expected that once the economic situation stabilizes, UNTA will be less tolerant of disruptive worker discontent and will put muscle behind the slogan "There is no revolution without production."

Other mobilization units are the "action groups" whose purpose is to complement the political activity of the more formal organizations on a factory-to-factory or office-to-office basis. Activists from these groups conduct "enlightening sessions" to teach the MPLA ideology (or perhaps literacy). Though small, these groups offer militants an opportunity to display their zeal and initiative while they propagandize.

Once potential leaders have been identified in the various organizations, they may be sent to the recently (1977) founded party schools (escolas do partido) for political and ideological training. In Cuban-taught courses of two months' duration, the militants learn Marxist-Leninist theory and methodology, history, political economy, and philosophy. Upon graduation these cadres will be sent to the provinces for mobilization work. A sense of urgency permeates the entire operation of training cadres because the MPLA realizes that the countryside is where most of the people live and where the MPLA is weakest.

In the urban areas it would be difficult to escape participation in some activity of the neighborhood committee (comissao de bairro), whose wide-ranging responsibilities affect almost every aspect of neighborhood life. The committee is the centerpiece of the MPLA's mobilization effort—the basic institution through which the idea of poder popular is to be realized. The importance of the committees is indicated by their organizational structure, which parallels that of the MPLA itself. Typically a committee will include departments for (1) organization of the masses, (2) information and propaganda, (3) political orientation, (4) supply and provisions, and (5) coordination. Theoretically independent, the committee clearly functions as a mobilizing arm of the MPLA.

As the revolutionary institution most directly involved in the daily lives of Angolans, the committees promote a wide variety of activities, ranging from the management of cooperatives to the teaching of hygiene, literacy, and occasionally even English. While most activities include heavy doses of propaganda, their primary purpose is to provide badly needed social services to alleviate conditions in the urban areas. In the musseques (slums), sanitation, health, and nutrition are major areas of concern. The situation in the food cooperative of Sambizanga provides an example of the kinds of

problems the MPLA confronts in providing social services. Founded just before independence, the co-op's first task was to distribute essential foodstuffs—beans, rice, manioc flour, beer, and soft drinks —at fixed prices in order to undercut the speculation of the *cantineiros* (private food-store owners). As the war continued through 1976, food shortages became acute, placing severe strains on the administrative capacity of the co-op. Poor and sometimes corrupt management compounded distribution problems. (Some of the difficulties may have been the result of economic sabotage by MPLA dissidents who hoped to embarrass the Neto regime.) The erratic distribution of food was a source of discontent and unrest all over Luanda. Throughout 1976 and 1977 the *Jornal de Angola*, the principal government newspaper, carried the complaints of Luandans for whom obtaining food was the number one problem in their daily lives. Although the situation had eased by the end of 1977, the disruptions of the civil war continue to force reliance on imported foods.

The challenge confronting the MPLA in its efforts to implement the economic program of Angolan socialism is how to revive an economy crippled by the civil war and the flight of almost all of the Portuguese population. As many as 330,000 Portuguese (of a total population of 350,000) fled Angola before independence, taking with them their cars, their household possessions, and most important of all, their skills. They left behind an economic shambles— not so much the consequence of deliberate sabotage as of the rapidity of the exodus. (An international airlift evacuated more than 250,000 Portuguese refugees in the period June to October 1975.) A few statistics will indicate the depth of the economic paralysis. Production in the key export industries of coffee, diamonds, and iron ore dropped to almost nothing, and remains 80 percent below pre-independence levels. As of December 1976, only 3,000 of 28,000 trucks previously in operation were usable; the number of buses serving Luanda dropped from 600 to 30, and the number of taxis from 600 to 60; 120 bridges needed repair from damage suffered in the civil war; and there were only 119 stores—government and private—to distribute food to Luanda's remaining population of more than 100,000.* What kept the RPA from total economic

---

*As with all statistics from Angola, these should be treated with caution. The figure for the population of Luanda is my own minimum estimate. The official figure in 1970 was 350,000, but by the time of independence vast sections of the city were virtually empty—particularly the African sections. Presumably many people have returned, but there are no reliable figures.

collapse were the half billion dollars in revenues from Gulf Oil's Cabinda facility, which because of its distant location suffered little from the disturbances.

To revitalize the various sectors of the shattered economy, the MPLA embarked on an extensive program of nationalization of hundreds of firms, large and small. Ironically, this policy derived not from ideological dictates, as one might expect from a Marxist-Leninist regime, but from the necessity of coping with a lack of private initiative. As Lopo de Nascimento, the First Vice-President, put it:

> In fact we have no choice but to build socialism. Over 90% of the Portuguese fled the country abandoning their plantations and enterprises; they forced our hand. Some sectors—foreign trade for instance—we had not intended to nationalize, but the Portuguese who ran it pulled out. If the State does not handle it, who will? So we find ourselves taking it over along with many sectors that were not in our original plans.[13]

In its pre-independence economy program, the MPLA called for the establishment of a mixed economy of state, cooperative, and private enterprises. At that time it was expected that the state would control only the largest agricultural and industrial units. However, the experience of the civil war forced the MPLA to redefine the scope of state participation. The "Law on State Intervention in the National Economy" promulgated in February 1977, while reaffirming the basic goal of a mixed economy, stresses the role of government and also provides guidelines for joint state-worker management that guarantees worker participation at all levels.[14]

The new nationalization regulations affect all economic units —from beer companies and coffee and sugar plantations to textile firms and the fishing industry. Their impact will be felt only in time, however, for the government clearly lacks the capacity to furnish the required managerial cadres. In the area of coffee production, for example, the government has taken over 386 of 432 plantations in Uige province alone—far too many to manage effectively. Given the lack of technically trained Angolans, the RPA will be dependent upon foreign assistance to rebuild its economy for the foreseeable future. Foreign technicians (mainly Cuban) can now be found repairing bridges and broken machinery, reorganizing the civil administration, and training Angolans to be teachers, doctors, mechanics, and co-op managers. (Their presence is especially critical

in the area of medical services, where Cuban doctors are striving to fill the gap left by the departure of 530 of the 600 doctors in Angola prior to independence.)[15]

To minimize the economic dislocation, the MPLA has adopted a tolerant attitude toward foreign-owned enterprises as long as they respect Angolan interests. The long-term goal is to fully control the exploitation of Angola's natural resources, but for now the RPA will only nationalize foreign concerns when Angolans possess sufficient technological skills to manage them. Examples of this gradualist approach are recently negotiated contracts with Gulf Oil and Diamang (giants of the oil and diamond industries respectively), in which the Angolan government gains a majority share but no operating responsibility. Presumably this approach will be extended to the Benguela railroad and the Cassinga iron ore mines. For the time being, then, no change in the Western orientation of the export sector is contemplated.[16]

There are remarkably few ideological constraints controlling the radical transformation of the Angolan economy from a capitalist to a socialist framework. Because the MPLA applies socialism pragmatically, it retains flexibility to choose the most appropriate form of economic activity to achieve its goals without sacrificing idealism or nationalism. The changes in the MPLA's economic program occasioned by the civil war and the exodus of the Portuguese are changes in emphasis not substance; the guiding principle—that Angolan interests are paramount—remains the same. The heavy reliance on the state to stimulate the economy does not preclude the reemergence of the private sector should circumstances permit, and the dependence on foreign aid and investment does not compromise Angola's fundamental autonomy.

The MPLA's political mobilization campaign entered a new phase with the announcement in December 1977 that the movement would be transformed into a party. The decision, made twenty-one years after the founding of the movement, will be carried out according to guidelines set by a congress convened in Luanda. The change is seen as an essential and natural development in the process of implementing socialism:

> The party will emerge from the MPLA. The first cadres of the MPLA will constitute the first nucleus of the party. They will be the representatives of the workers, the peasants and laboring classes of our country, of progressive intellectuals capable of expressing the ideology of the proletariat. . . . The advance to socialism cannot be made unless the necessary conditions are at

hand, and one of the fundamental elements is the party. We have in the country a working class which, although small in relation to the whole of the laboring class, is capable of assuming the responsibilities of the nation. We have an economic structure that will serve as the base for people's power under the leadership of the working class. But without the party, without the politically disciplined people, all the optimal conditions for social advance will not be channelled for the socialist objective of the nation and the working class will not be an instrument adequate for the achievement of its most profound aspirations.[17]

As valid as the ideological arguments are, they do not fully explain the timing of the decision. There is certainly no theoretical necessity for the immediate creation of a party. Castro, for example, delayed forming a party in Cuba for several years after his takeover, and the Soviets, with their long experience in African politics, have modified their position many times concerning what organizational form is appropriate for conditions in Africa.[18]

The more likely explanation is that President Neto needs a tightly controlled, disciplined, and above all loyal organization to help him overcome internal opposition to his policies.* With cadres selected for their political reliability, Neto will be able to consolidate his control over the process of implementing Angolan socialism and reduce the confusion and instability caused by dissension within the movement. But the founding of the party may involve certain risks because it signifies an important shift in emphasis—perhaps even a radical departure—from the original philosophy of the MPLA. Whereas the MPLA began as a mass-based movement, it is now becoming a select organization of "true militants," which involves the risk of creating an elite in what is supposed to be an egalitarian society. Preliminary indications are that membership in the party will be determined by a combination of an individual's social class and militancy, and that all those who "do not live exclusively from the fruit of their labor" will be excluded.[19] Workers and soldiers will be required to wait only one year before being admitted; other aspirants will have to wait two years. It remains to be seen whether the working class origins of party members will prevent the emergence of elitist tendencies.

*Private communication from Gerald Bender, who visited Luanda in early 1978. Bender was told by Angolans that the purpose of the reconstitution of the MPLA into a party was not to institute orthodox Marxism-Leninism, but rather to cleanse the MPLA of Neto's opponents.

The MPLA leaders are aware of the potential difficulties in creating a party. As Lucio Lara commented:

> It is a very delicate question. The MPLA is a front designed to mobilize the maximum number of people who could be united in the national independence struggle. Within that front there is a nucleus of militants who act as party militants, but there are also many who joined for opportunistic reasons, especially when the prospects for independence became real. . . . Those who joined for opportunistic reasons must be purged if the movement is to be transformed into a party. We must proceed very slowly and cautiously on the question of forming a party in order to avoid splits and ruptures.[20]

The "purging" of the MPLA to form a party implies the installation of an increasingly authoritarian regime. It can also be expected that the expansion of *poder popular* at the local level will be curtailed until sufficient politically trained cadres are available to supervise the process. This trend toward the centralization of power around President Neto is certainly not a surprising development, but only the future will tell whether it solves more problems than it creates.

INTERNAL OPPOSITION

Of the major obstacles to the implementation of Angolan socialism—the civil war, the threat of hostile foreign intervention, dissension within the MPLA—the last is the most serious. The disunity afflicting the MPLA is rooted in the structure of Angolan society and therefore cannot be eliminated quickly by a decisive victory on a battlefield or a negotiated treaty. The source of this disunity is the resentment against the *mestico* community, which during the colonial period occupied an intermediate and often privileged position between the Portuguese and the Africans in the social hierarchy and was perceived by the Africans to be as exploitative as the whites. Those Africans who expected that independence would bring about profound changes in the social order were disillusioned by the sight of mesticos continuing to maintain their influential status. It is no consolation to black Angolans that the mesticos possess the talent and educational background to justify their prominence. But the MPLA is deeply committed to multiracialism, and since its inception has drawn heavily on the mestico intellectual elite for leadership and inspiration. It would be virtual

suicide for the MPLA to turn against the mesticos, but it must contend with the possibility that racial animosity will prove a graver threat to Angolan socialism than ethnic rivalries.

During its thirteen years in exile, there was little evidence of racial tensions within the MPLA. The two main challenges to Neto's leadership were based more on personal antagonisms than anything else. In 1974 a group of mestico intellectuals led by Mario Andrade and his brother Father Joaquim formed a faction known as the Revolta Activa to express their dissatisfaction with Neto. They accused him of ignoring the democratic principles of the MPLA and arrogating all authority to himself. Their opposition did not extend to ideological issues, however, and they remained within the fold, but this did not protect them from subsequent house arrest and imprisonment in Luanda. Another faction, known as the Revolta d'Este, was formed at the same time and attacked Neto for similar reasons. Its leader—Daniel Chipenda, an Ovimbundu and popular military commander—defected to the FNLA along with several hundred guerrillas. Neto survived both challenges.

Ideological opposition began to emerge after independence in clandestine groups such as the Organizacão Communista da Angola (OCA). These groups, which tended to espouse a "Maoist" line and to regard themselves as proponents of a more radical and purer Marxism, were dominated by students with little grasp of revolutionary theory. Such groups became a threat to the MPLA only because their ideological views were attractive to the racially motivated opposition: their attacks upon "bourgeois tendencies" could easily be construed as attacks upon the mestico community. The OCA even organized anti-mestico rallies that drew large crowds in Luanda. It became common knowledge that MPLA dissidents had participated in these rallies.

The most significant challenge to Neto came from a group of dissidents led by Nito Alves. Alves derived his main support from MPLA guerrillas who shared his resentment of the influence of mesticos (and some whites) in the new Angola. In their view, the mesticos had avoided the rigors of the liberation struggle by refusing to commit themselves to it or living in relatively comfortable exile, while they—the black guerrillas—bore the brunt of the suffering. This anti-mestico, black nationalist sentiment was first voiced by Alves and José Van Dunem at the 1974 MPLA congress in Lusaka when the question of Angolan citizenship was raised. They maintained that only those whites who had aided the MPLA directly should be eligible to become citizens, while mesticos should be

accorded the option of becoming Angolans, but not granted citizenship automatically. Neto refused to compromise his vision of a multi-
racial society and rejected the proposal, but the issue was by no
means dead.

When the MPLA returned from exile to Luanda in late 1974,
Alves quickly established himself as a rising star with his skill in
organizing the popular defense forces in the musseques. These forces
were a critical factor in the MPLA's successful *coup d'etat* against
the FNLA and UNITA in July 1975. Alves's reputation as a tough
guerrilla commander, his charismatic personality, and his large
popular following in Luanda guaranteed him a position of influence
in the MPLA power structure. He was rewarded with the post of
Minister of Interior in the first cabinet of the People's Republic,
where he supervised the civil administration. With the collaboration
of Van Dunem, a political commissar in the MPLA military, and
other friends throughout the government, Alves set up a clandestine
network that eventually appeared to include all the heads of the
provincial administrations, several members of the Army general
staff, and the Minister of Labor. He was thus in an excellent position
to orchestrate acts of economic sabotage to discredit the Neto
regime and foment discontent.

Apart from his black nationalism, Alves's ideological views are
difficult to define. Nowhere did he offer an exposition of his thinking more detailed than a vague espousal of a pro-Soviet stance and
the charge that Neto had betrayed the revolution. His "radicalism"
seemed to consist mainly of his ambition fueled by racism.* As for
Alves's relationship with the Soviets, the details are scanty, but it
is known that they actively promoted him—presumably because
they regarded him as a possible successor to Neto. Notwithstanding
their official support of Neto, the Soviets had reason to be displeased
with him because of his uncompromisingly nationalist stance which
has led him to persist in dealing with "imperialist" firms such as Gulf
Oil and Boeing and to refuse permission for Soviet military bases
on Angolan soil. They may have hoped for a more tractable client
in Alves. Another possible motive for Soviet interest in Alves might
have been their desire for a settlement of the civil war. It is rumored,
for example, that Alves had contacted Jonas Savimbi, founder of
UNITA, to discuss conditions for a possible reconciliation between

---

*Ironically, it appears that the true ideologues (if they can be termed that)
were the frustrated white Portuguese radicals who believed Angola offered more
fertile ground for revolution than Portugal and sought to impose a more rigorous
regime than Neto's non-doctrinaire and pragmatic conception.

UNITA and the MPLA.[21] Savimbi reportedly demanded the withdrawal of all Cuban and Russian personnel and the inclusion of the FNLA in any new government. Another rumor was that the Soviets talked with Savimbi directly, somewhere outside Angola.[22] These rumors, combined with a comment by Savimbi to *Washington Post* reporter Leon Dash to the effect that he felt closer ideologically to Alves than to Neto, suggest that if Alves had been in control of the MPLA, negotiations with UNITA might have been initiated.[23]

Months of mounting tension within the MPLA culminated in an abortive coup attempt in May 1977. At dawn on May 27, a group of dissidents led by Alves and Van Dunem, until very recently members of the MPLA Central Committee,* tried to seize the government palace and radio station. They failed because of poor planning, a lack of coordinated popular support, and the intervention of Cuban troops. The coup attempt was crushed within a few hours, but not before several members of Neto's inner circle of advisers had been assassinated. The most surprising aspect of the attempted coup was the number of old-line MPLA militants involved—many of them highly placed in the movement hierarchy and the government. Their participation showed how seriously divided the MPLA was over the issue of multiracialism.

Whatever the extent of the Soviet involvement in the coup—and it is unlikely that they participated directly—the suspicion of involvement implies a complicated relationship between Neto and his principal allies. Although the Angolans, Russians, and Cubans present a united front to the world, in reality there is a great deal of tension in their relations. The decisive Cuban intervention on Neto's side against the radical Alves suggests that the Cubans may act as a buffer between the Angolan leader and the Soviets, helping him to resist pressure to alter his internal and external policies. The idea that the Cubans may exert a moderating influence on the Soviets is apparently beyond the comprehension of U.S. policymakers, who continue to view the Cubans as Soviet surrogates and have made the withdrawal of Cuban

*Only a week earlier, the Central Committee had dismissed Alves and Van Dunem for factionalism and acts of economic sabotage. In his defense Alves accused the MPLA leadership of a long list of crimes against the Angolan people, including catering to petit-bourgeois tendencies, failing to uphold the revolution, giving preference to whites and mesticos in the government, not following a strict pro-Soviet line, and "factionalism": "If there is truly factionalism within the MPLA, it is among you, the present leadership, that you should look for it. Me, I embody the revolution. History has reserved for me the right to continue the process of this revolution" (*Afrique-Asie*, No. 139, 11-24 July 1977). Alves demanded the immediate resignation of the Central Committee and the formation of a new government. This was an extraordinary indictment, as much for its daring as for its content.)

troops a precondition of diplomatic recognition of Angola.[24] It remains to be seen whether this dogmatic position will give way to a more flexible policy that will take into account the complexity of the Angolan political scene.

The coup attempt demonstrates how much further the "mentalization" (*mentalizacão*) process must go before Angolans will be prepared for a socialist society. The intense racial antagonism among black Angolans that it exposed will not dissipate quickly. The coup conspirators were not just another power-seeking "faction," as the MPLA propaganda maintains, but a group of respected militants whose disenchantment with multiracialism reflects widespread popular sentiment. To most Angolans independence was a promise of a better life, free from colonial exploitation, and the ascendancy of the mestico community in the Luanda regime is a bitter reminder of how little things have changed. The MPLA will have to combine political indoctrination with concrete improvements in the economic well-being of Angolans if it is to overcome resistance to its program. This will not be easily accomplished: "The route will be difficult. We are making a Marxist-Leninist revolution. . . . We are moving step by step in taking account of the needs and possibilities of our people. Some have not yet understood that the Angolans are not yet decolonized in spirit."[25]

If Amílcar Cabral were alive today and were asked to comment on the Angolan revolution, he would probably argue that the divisions and instability of the Neto regime are the effects of insufficient politicization at the grass roots level. Despite fifteen years of fighting, cultural resistance was never far enough advanced among the major ethnic groups to organize a broadly based, unified armed struggle against the Portuguese. Consequently, the MPLA is in the position of imposing socialism from above, which inevitably leads to an emphasis on control at the expense of ideological consistency. *Poder popular*, supposedly the foundation of Angolan socialism, will not be implemented immediately because the MPLA leadership is unable to control its functioning at the local level.

Neto would undoubtedly agree with Cabral's analysis and add that if there is a gap between the rhetoric and the reality of the revolution, it is because of the extraordinary situation in Angola. Surrounded by hostile neighbors and challenged from within, Neto's priorities clearly must be order first and revolution second. This is not to say that ideology is unimportant; rather it means that Neto intends to achieve the transformation of Angolan society in his own way—guided but not ruled by ideological considerations.

Because Neto is so individualistic and nationalistic, he is more likely to be influenced by Castro than by any other socialist leader. Castro is an ideological eclectic, suspicious of bureaucratic and hierarchical organizations (including parties), and Neto shares with him an experimental approach to the problems of restructuring society. Neto lacks charisma, but like Castro he has a ruthless political will. Both men are supremely confident that their way is the best way, and the similarity of their personalities makes it likely that the Cuban influence will be marked throughout Angolan society.

FOREIGN INTERVENTION

Foreign powers have played a prominent role in the creation of the Angolan People's Republic. Without Soviet and Cuban aid, the republic probably would not exist today. By the same token, UNITA would not be as successful as it has been in its guerrilla struggle against the Luanda regime without aid from *its* foreign backers. But though they have been critical to the evolution of the Angolan civil war, foreign powers have not altered the fundamental character of the conflict nor been able to effect its resolution. The military stalemate that prevails between the MPLA and UNITA will likely continue regardless of the quality or quantity of support given to either side.

A variety of ideological and strategic considerations prompted foreign powers to attempt to take advantage of the power vacuum left by the departing Portuguese, who possessed neither the will nor the capacity to ensure an orderly transition to independence. For the Soviets, Angola presented an opportunity to bolster their revolutionary image as well as to expand their influence in southern Africa. They claim to have consistently supported the MPLA since 1961, but they neglect to mention cutting off aid to Neto when his effectiveness as a leader was called into question by the defection of Daniel Chipenda to the FNLA. Surprised both by the 1974 coup in Portugal and Neto's resiliency, the Soviets renewed their backing of Neto and poured materiel into Luanda in late 1974 and early 1975. Whether they intended merely to prevent the MPLA from being overwhelmed or committed themselves to an MPLA takeover has yet to be determined. What is clear is that their support of the MPLA was much stronger than the West's support of the FNLA and UNITA. If one views the Angolan civil war as an ideological battleground, then the Soviets have won an impressive victory. Not only did they refuse to buckle under to U.S. pressure over

detente, but more important they severely damaged the prestige of their chief rival in Africa—China. The Chinese, pursuing their consistent anti-Soviet policy, supported the FNLA and eventually found themselves in the awkward position of being allied with the United States.

The masterstroke of the Soviet intervention was the use of Cuban troops. By this maneuver they avoided the potentially volatile issue of sending "white" troops to Africa while at the same time giving Castro a chance to demonstrate his commitment to international socialist solidarity. Castro was no newcomer to the Angolan situation. In the early 1960's he learned about Angola when Cuban soldiers helped train PAIGC guerrillas fighting the Portuguese in Guinea-Bissau. Further contact resulted from a similar training mission in Congo-Brazzaville, where the MPLA maintained its headquarters. Precisely dating the time when the Cubans began to arrive in force in Angola is impossible, but the initial decision to send them must have been made in early 1975. By June 1975 there were at least several hundred advisers involved in training and logistical support (and perhaps some fighting). The Cubans claim that they intervened only in response to the invasion by South Africa in October, which may be true in the sense that the majority of Cuban troops landed after that. Eventually as many as twenty thousand Cubans engaged the South African expeditionary force, and approximately the same number continue to battle UNITA guerrillas.

For the South Africans, intervention in the Angolan civil war proved a costly gamble.[26] By failing in their objective of installing the FNLA/UNITA coalition in power, the South Africans suffered a psychological setback as well as a military defeat. The withdrawal from Angola heartened black nationalists in South Africa, who witnessed for the first time the vincibility of the much-vaunted South African army. It is no mere coincidence that the Soweto riots began in South Africa only months after the Angolan debacle.

In the United States, Congress saw no need for continued intervention in Angola because no vital American interests were threatened. Wary of foreign entanglements in the post-Vietnam era, Congress viewed a "Communist" Angola as an immediate threat only to Zaire and South Africa, and therefore of no strategic importance to the U.S. Furthermore, the principal American investor in Angola—Gulf Oil—had managed to continue operations throughout the fighting, protected by the Cubans. Gulf's success created an embarrassing situation for Secretary of State Kissinger: at the time his request for aid to the FNLA/UNITA coalition was being denied

by Congress, Gulf was depositing a quarterly revenue payment of $125 million in the MPLA-controlled Bank of Angola. Kissinger tried to hold up the revenue transfer, but after a number of weeks he relented.

It is interesting that both Kissinger and some of his liberal critics couched the debate on Angola in terms of a test of wills between the U.S. and the Soviet Union. In doing this they neglected the Sino-Soviet rivalry in Africa in general and in the former Portuguese colonies in particular. It is entirely possible that the Russians were more concerned with embarrassing the Chinese—their socialist "competition"—than with countering American influence.[27] In any event Congress ended the U.S. intervention and with it South Africa's hopes for support.

Zaire intervened in Angola both with troops and heavy logistical support of the FNLA, motivated by President Mobutu's desire for a friendly (i.e., non-Communist) neighbor to the south. Beset by widespread internal discontent triggered by the decline in world copper prices and a moribund economy, Mobutu sought to head off a threat to his shaky control of Zaire by backing the FNLA's bid for power in Angola. He felt vulnerable to a popular uprising should a hostile regime in Angola decide to unleash the ex-Katanga gendarmes against him. (His fears proved justified when the gendarmes invaded Shaba province, albeit unsuccessfully, in March 1977.) The possibility of gaining access to oil-rich Cabinda also influenced Mobutu's decision to intervene in Angola. Had the FNLA defeated the MPLA, Holden Roberto would have been under strong pressure to grant Mobutu—his benefactor and relative by marriage— concessions in Cabinda. His ambitions have been temporarily frustrated, but Mobutu continues to permit the FNLA to conduct border raids from bases in Zaire and, ever the opportunist, encourages Cabinda separatism. As a consequence, relations between Zaire and Angola remain very strained.

The MPLA has benefited most from foreign intervention, but it has been forced to defend itself against charges that it is a pawn of the Russians and Cubans. Not surprisingly, the MPLA categorically rejects this accusation and insists that it follows a policy of nonalignment. In the MPLA's view, their acceptance of Russian and Cuban aid does not imply their dependency; the Russians and Cubans are members of the international socialist community, and hence their motives for providing assistance are purely ideological:

We do not understand proletarian internationalism as a dependency. We socialists aid each other. . . . This does not mean that the receiver of aid must necessarily follow the giver of aid. We are therefore independent. . . . We make our own policy. . . . We reaffirm our complete commitment to the policy of nonalignment. We have not the slightest intention, not even if it were asked of us, of permitting the establishment of military bases.[28]

While this may not persuade critics of the MPLA concerned about the huge Cuban troops contingent, there can be no doubt of the nationalist conviction behind the nonaligned stance. To date the MPLA has refused to allow the Russians a base of any kind. Nor can there be any doubt about the idealism of the Cuban commitment. In a speech to Cuban soldiers and technicians in Angola, Castro summarized the ideological rationale for their presence there in these words:

I know the sacrifices that your work entails, separated from your families, far from your homes and those dear to you. Our cooperation with the Angolan people, in peace as in war, demands strains and sacrifices. Always raise high the flag of internationalism; and know how to remain modest. . . . Each victorious revolution is a contribution to the struggle of all people, and it is only by cooperation with one another that we will be able to defeat imperialism.[29]

THE CIVIL WAR AND THE FUTURE

On the basis of the admittedly scanty information available, it appears that anti-MPLA guerrilla activity in Angola is on the increase. With the exception of occasional border raids conducted by the badly disorganized FNLA and South African troops, this activity is internally based under the leadership of UNITA. If one accepts the findings of Leon Dash—the *Washington Post* reporter who recently spent seven months inside Angola with UNITA forces —one must conclude that UNITA has the capacity to harass, disrupt, and render the daily lives of the populace of the Central Highlands generally insecure, virtually at will. The arrival in Angola of five thousand additional Cuban troops in August 1977 would seem to confirm Dash's assessment. He describes a typical guerrilla campaign as follows: UNITA unhurriedly selects a target which it attacks with overwhelming numbers; then the MPLA and Cuban troops

retaliate by burning the villages of suspected UNITA collaborators. Caught in the middle are the people who cannot escape the terrorist tactics of either side.[30] The result is an exceedingly nasty, hit-and-run war that shows no sign of ending.

UNITA possesses some important advantages in its struggle against the MPLA. Ably led by Savimbi, UNITA is well-supplied with American and South African arms (left over from the 1975-76 campaign) and operates inside its ethnic home base. The MPLA, on the other hand, even with the latest Cuban reinforcements, can hardly be more effective in containing UNITA than it has been to date, given the vast area that must be patrolled. It should be remembered that the Portuguese, with sixty thousand troops, never entirely eliminated the guerrilla threat of the liberation movements. In addition, time works in UNITA's favor. Because the Central Highlands area is the population and agricultural center of Angola, prolonged disorder and turmoil there would deal a serious blow to the MPLA's plans for economic recovery, which aim toward self-sufficiency in foodstuffs.

The present military stalemate and Savimbi's claim that he desires only his rightful share of a government of unity (to include the FNLA) would seem to provide grounds for compromise, but the personalities of the leaders are likely to prevent it. Of the three leaders, only Savimbi has ever displayed a willingness to share power with his rivals. Since the transition government, in which he played the role of mediator between the two arch-enemies Neto and Roberto, Savimbi has consistently advocated a division of power as the only possible solution to the civil war. But both Neto and Roberto have refused to dilute their personal authority even within their own movements. Furthermore, Neto, having fought for so many years to overcome so many obstacles, is not likely to give in now that he has the advantage of Cuban troop support. In the unlikely event that Neto were to negotiate a settlement, he would do so only when he felt confident of his control over the dissidents within the MPLA. Thus barring some dramatic development such as the death of Savimbi or the withdrawal of Cuban troops, the civil war seems destined to continue for several years. The future is not entirely bleak, however. Neto's dependence on the Cubans raises the possibility that they might encourage Neto to negotiate with Savimbi. The Cuban experience in Ethiopia, where they have decided not to engage in the civil war with the Eritreans (presumably because that war is unwinnable), suggests that they might react similarly to the Angolan situation. Cuban military strategists can hardly fail to

320

realize that the war with UNITA is also unwinnable, given UNITA's advantages in terrain and popular support, and they may eventually come to believe that the best hope for a socialist regime in Angola lies in a negotiated settlement rather than a military victory.

A long, drawn-out civil war will inevitably have a deleterious effect on the implementation of Angolan socialism. How serious the drain on human and material resources will be depends on how actively the MPLA works toward eliminating the causes of unrest. Clearly a lasting solution will come only when the MPLA transcends its ethnic identification and establishes Angolan socialism as a national ideology encompassing all ethnic groups. The MPLA must recognize that in ethnic terms the majority of Angolans are in opposition to them, and that the aspirations of the majority must be accommodated. However, the MPLA's capacity to integrate the country, militarily or otherwise, is conditioned by its capacity to cope with dissension within its own ranks. The opposition to multiracialism from the MPLA's anti-mestico, black nationalist wing represents a power struggle within a power struggle, and the resolution of one will necessarily affect the other. The confidence and determination of the MPLA leadership that its vision of Angola will prevail is expressed in the slogan "The struggle continues, but the victory is certain" (*A luta continua, mas a vitória é certa*). Let us hope that the "victory" is for all Angolans, and that out of the present turmoil and suffering a united Angolan nation emerges.

SOCIALIST-ORIENTED DEVELOPMENT IN GUINEA-BISSAU

Lars Rudebeck

I. INTRODUCTION

In September 1956, Amílcar Cabral and a small group of comrades founded the Partido Africano da Independencia da Guiné e Cabo Verde (PAIGC) in Bissau, then the capital of Portuguese Guinea—a small and backward West African colony. In September 1973 the first elected National Assembly of the People met in Boé to proclaim the de jure existence of the sovereign state of Guinea-Bissau. Through political and military struggle, the PAIGC had by then freed about two-thirds of Guinean territory from the Portuguese colonial system. One year later, in September 1974, after the fall of the fascist regime in Lisbon, Portugal formally recognized the Republic of Guinea-Bissau. More than five hundred years of colonialism in West Africa had come to an end.

At present the PAIGC controls the state of Guinea-Bissau and directs the development of the country.* My purpose here is to use the experience of Guinea-Bissau to highlight some of the possibilities and difficulties of what is sometimes called "non-capitalist," sometimes "socialist," and sometimes "socialist-oriented" development in

---

*The PAIGC is also in power in the Republic of Cape Verde (independent since July 1975), which consists of ten small islands off the coast of West Africa with about 300,000 inhabitants. It is rare indeed to find one political party controlling the governments of two different sovereign states.

This report is based upon knowledge and information gained during research visits to Guinea-Bissau in 1976 and 1977, including information obtained through interviews with party and government officials as well as direct observation which is not documented in the footnotes. Documentation for some of this material is provided in my book *Guinea-Bissau. Folket, partiet och staten. Om den fredliga kampen för utveckling* [The people, the party, and the state: On the peaceful struggle for development] (Uppsala: Scandinavian Institute of African Studies, 1977). It is a continuation of my earlier studies of the new society under construction in the liberated areas of the country while the struggle against the Portuguese colonial army was still going on (see Rudebeck, *Guinea-Bissau: A Study of Political Mobilization*, 1974).

the third world. (My own preference is for the latter term.) I shall begin by looking at the general background—the geographical, economic, demographic, and political conditions under which the PAIGC and the government of Guinea-Bissau are leading the struggle for development in their country.

The next step will be to take a brief look at the ideology and political strategy of the PAIGC. The development strategy of Guinea-Bissau has emerged in the interaction of given physical and historic conditions with political ideology and action throughout seven years of political preparations, eleven years of armed struggle, and a brief period of complete state sovereignty (since 1974), and it was reconfirmed at the 1977 party congress of the PAIGC.

The relationship of this development strategy to the international economic system and the internal class structure of Guinea-Bissau will then be examined in terms of (1) the problem of external dependence, (2) the organization and social basis of state power, and (3) the major policies of the development strategy.

In a concluding section, I shall comment briefly on what we may be able to learn—both specifically about Guinea-Bissau and in a more general and theoretical sense—from studying given conditions and actual political practice in this way.

II. GENERAL BACKGROUND

Guinea-Bissau is a small country, fairly densely populated for West African conditions: approximately 900,000 inhabitants in a territory of 36,125 square kilometers. Its small size may be an advantage at its present stage of development, but in the long run it will not be possible to contain economic development within such narrow geographical limits. New forms of cooperation and integration in West Africa will become necessary, and differences in development strategies between the various countries may then create problems. The main source of wealth in Guinea-Bissau, both now and in the foreseeable future, is agriculture. It has hardly any industry and a very poor infrastructure, but there is some mineral wealth—mainly bauxite.

In Guinea-Bissau there is no one ethnic group dominant over all the others, but rather a kind of balance between four main groups— the Balante, the Mandjaque, the Fula, and the Mandinga—and several smaller ones. The number of white settlers has always been very small, and the few who remain in Guinea-Bissau do not pose a serious political problem. The general educational level of the people is very low.

A long war of national liberation was imposed upon Guinea-Bissau by Portugal. When the Portuguese colonial power finally withdrew in 1974, it left the country's treasury almost empty. The lack of financial resources has created dependence upon foreign aid and credits, which cannot be made up through foreign trade because the balance of trade for Guinea-Bissau has been very negative during the first few years of its independence. Portugal continues to play a special and important role in relation to Guinea-Bissau—not least as its dominant foreign trade partner. Apart from Portugal, the most important points in the network of international relations for Guinea-Bissau during the first years of independence have been (in alphabetical order) Algeria, Cuba, the Soviet Union, Sweden, and the UN, but a number of other organizations and countries—both capitalist and socialist, industrialized and third world—have become involved as well.

While Guinea-Bissau is of little or no economic importance as a challenge to the international capitalist system, it has political importance as a challenge to imperialism and as an example of independent and progressive development in Africa. This relates to its role during its first years of independence as a member of the strongly anti-imperialist group within the Organization of African Unity (OAU). To cite just one example, Guinean troops fought alongside the MPLA and Cuban troops during the second war of liberation in Angola (1975-76) to stop the two-pronged invasion of Angola from South Africa and Zaire.

Guinea-Bissau's immediate geographical neighbors are Senegal and Guinea-Conakry—two countries that were politically and economically opposed until their reconciliation in 1978. Guinea-Conakry gave the PAIGC decisive support during the war of liberation; as a consequence there are special ties of political solidarity between the two Guineas. During recent years, however, a great deal of practical cooperation has developed between Guinea-Bissau and Senegal, while relations with Conakry have been limited largely to political declarations of mutual goodwill.

The peasantry is a strong political force in Guinea-Bissau because the main political strength of the PAIGC is in the countryside—especially in the two-thirds of the country that had been liberated from colonialism before the surrender of the Portuguese and where a new society had been under construction for a long time before 1974. Among the urban population, on the other hand, the attitudes and ideals of the dominant petit-bourgeois groups are not always consistent with the developmental goals of the PAIGC

and the government. The working class, though still very small, provides support for the regime.

In summary, then, Guinea-Bissau is a small, economically underdeveloped agricultural country lacking in financial resources, but with a strong, ideologically radical political organization (built up during eleven years of armed struggle for national liberation) with firm support in the major part of the countryside. While its main foreign policy principle is nonalignment, for historical reasons Guinea-Bissau has generally developed closer political ties with industrialized socialist countries and the anti-imperialist third world countries than with capitalist countries. Since the years of the liberation struggle, Guinea-Bissau has received military equipment and training from the Soviet Union, but it remains unaligned with either of the great power blocs. The foreign policy of the PAIGC by no means excludes close economic and political ties with some of the smaller capitalist countries—in particular, Sweden, whose cooperation with the PAIGC dates back to 1969[1]—and there is increasing cooperation with the rest of the capitalist world. Guinea-Bissau is, for instance, an associate member of the European Economic Community through the Lomé Convention, and plans are being made for extended cooperation with Brazil.

III. THE IDEOLOGY AND POLITICAL STRATEGY OF THE PAIGC

The PAIGC was founded in 1956 as a national liberation movement. Its immediate goal until 1974 was to achieve political independence from the Portuguese colonial power by any means possible, including armed struggle. However, political independence was never the ultimate goal of the PAIGC: it was merely a necessary station along the road to a better future. This point was always very clear in the party program and in the various writings of Amilcar Cabral—the main sources for written presentations of basic PAIGC ideology.[2] The long-term, overriding goal of the PAIGC has always been the socialist ideal of ending—once and for all—"the exploitation of man by man."

Despite this long-term goal, clearly reaffirmed at the 1977 party congress,[3] the word "socialism" appears very rarely in authoritative declarations of PAIGC ideology. It is not found in the original party program or in the various documents of the 1977 congress. The reason for this is that Cabral was always careful to make a clear distinction between the concrete goals attainable by a society in the historical situation of Guinea-Bissau and the theoretical potential

of such a society. According to Cabral, whose views are still the party's official views, the achievement of a socialist society in Guinea-Bissau is very far in the future because Guinea-Bissau is an economically and technologically undeveloped agricultural country which has become *under*-developed through the mechanisms of colonial dependency. However, the social and political analysis of the situation of Guinea-Bissau can and should be socialist in the sense of using Marxist points of departure and viewing socialism as a natural and desirable goal for the development of society. From this perspective, socialism is synonymous with human emancipation and liberation from exploitation.*

The basic PAIGC ideology concerning the struggle for national independence is coherent and well-elaborated.[4] It includes an anti-imperialist ideology and a socialist class analysis, implying *inter alia* that the peoples of the third world will have to rely primarily upon their own forces to achieve liberation and national development in their own interest. But the application of this ideology to the peaceful struggle for development—after the attainment of political independence—has remained quite general. One reason for this is probably that Cabral—the only theoretical innovator of the PAIGC so far—was murdered by agents of the Portuguese colonial regime in January 1973, on the eve of final victory in the struggle for independence.

According to the basic tenets of PAIGC ideology, the people must be brought to see for themselves the connection between the goals of material and social improvement and the means necessary to achieve them. The focal point of the political mobilization process is the formulation of concrete goals in close connection with the experiences of the people and the recognition of the obstacles that must be overcome to attain them. The following oft-quoted passage

---

*At a meeting in London in October 1971 the question of the relevance of Marxism to the struggle for national liberation in Guinea-Bissau was put to Cabral. Among other things, Cabral answered: "Is Marxism a religion? I am a freedom fighter in my country. You must judge from what I do in practice. If you decide that it's Marxism, tell everyone that it is Marxism. If you decide it's not Marxism, tell them it's not Marxism. But the labels are your affair; we don't like those kinds of labels. People here are very preoccupied with the questions: Are you Marxist or not Marxist? Are you Marxist-Leninist? Just ask me, please, whether we are doing well in the field. Are we really liberating our people, the human beings in our country, from all forms of oppression? Ask me simply this, and draw your own conclusions." (Quoted from Amilcar Cabral, *Our People Are Our Mountains* [London: Committee for Freedom in Mozambique, Angola, and Guiné, 1971], pp. 21f.)

from the PAIGC guidelines, written by Cabral at the beginning of the liberation struggle, illustrates how clearly the basic problem of political mobilization has always been posed within the party:

> Always remember that the people do not fight for ideas, for things that exist only in the heads of individuals. The people fight and they accept the necessary sacrifices. But they do it in order to gain material advantages, to live in peace and to improve their lives, to experience progress, and to be able to guarantee a future for their children. National liberation, the struggle against colonialism, working for peace and progress, independence—all these will be empty words without significance for the people, unless they are translated into real improvements of the conditions of life. It is useless to liberate a region if the people of that region are then left without the elementary necessities of life.[5]

Here Cabral emphasizes the necessary material basis of political work. Not beautiful words, but concrete improvements in the lives of the people give meaning to politics; in order to have such improvements, the people need power; in order to have power, they need to organize.

We may define *political mobilization* as the process through which the people's interest in social transformation is converted into organized political action in interaction with leaders in whom the people have confidence and over whom they have a measure of control. The people's control arises from the leaders' dependence upon them for support to achieve the goals the leaders have stimulated them to pursue. Political mobilization may involve some compulsion, but it differs from oligarchy and dictatorship in two important respects: (1) the starting point is the people's self-interest in social transformation, and (2) the leaders depend upon the people's support. When the participation of the masses in politics is controlled from above through manipulation and violence, the result is *fictitious* political mobilization.

Clearly, political mobilization is not the only way to initiate developmental efforts to benefit the broad majorities of the people in third world countries. Harsh dictatorship is another possibility. In the short run, this may appear to be an easier way—at least in the eyes of political leaders. But in the longer run, the risk is great that the means will pervert the end. And it is not easy to make a dictatorship function efficiently. In any case, the situation

in Guinea-Bissau after liberation quite clearly favored the political mobilization approach.

The Third Congress of the PAIGC. The Party Congress, which is the highest organ of the PAIGC, has met three times. The first congress was convened in 1964 at Cassaca in the southern part of Guinea after a year and a half of armed struggle against the Portuguese. The second congress met in the summer of 1973, half a year after the murder of Cabral. The third congress was the first to be held in time of peace and complete political independence, but in terms of stocktaking and looking ahead it was as important as the two previous ones. Its function was to sum up the experiences of the armed struggle and the first few years of independence and to cast the political and ideological foundations of "the second phase of the struggle"—i.e., the peaceful struggle for continued development. The congress met in Bissau on November 15-20, 1977, a little over three years after the last Portuguese soldier had left the capital. In attendance were 305 party delegates—200 from Guinea and 105 from Cape Verde. The three main themes were *Independence*, *Unity*, and *Development*.[6]

Under the theme of *Independence* the necessity to consolidate the political independence of Guinea-Bissau and Cape Verde and to struggle for economic independence was stressed, as well as anti-imperialism and nonalignment in foreign policy.

Under the theme of *Unity*, the need for national unity within each of the two countries was emphasized, but the primary emphasis was on the future goal of uniting Guinea-Bissau and Cape Verde into some kind of federated state. Besides the old historical ties between the two countries—ever since Portuguese navigators first sighted the green and swampy coast of Guinea (probably in 1446) and arrived at Cape Verde some fifteen years later—Guineans and Cape Verdeans had struggled together against Portuguese colonialism. Their common liberation and future union was always an important point in the program of the PAIGC, and many Cape Verdeans had important functions within the liberated areas of Guinea during the war with Portugal. Without a military victory on the mainland, it would not have been possible to force the Portuguese from the islands. However, there are important differences between the two countries with regard to economic and social structure; these make it essential that any future union be prepared carefully and thoroughly. The two economies must be made to function complementarily. The union was strongly reaffirmed as a political goal by the third con-

gress, but it is probably a long-term project. For the time being, the PAIGC remains the political party of two sovereign but closely cooperating countries.

The third theme of the congress—*Development*—needs little elaboration here. To the PAIGC, development is material and social progress for the broad masses of the people based upon their own work. With regard to general developmental goals, the congress did not make any important additions to the existing doctrine. The point was stressed that agriculture is the basis of the economy of Guinea and will have to play a central role in the development of Cape Verde, despite the limited land and water supplies on the islands. The initial surplus needed to finance the national development and industrialization of Guinea-Bissau will have to come from the productive work of the peasants. This surplus will be used to finance export industries based upon the raw materials of the fields and forest, as well as industrial production of consumer goods for the home market, which is expected to grow as production in agriculture rises from present low levels. For the time being, however, international aid will remain important since the initiation of industrial activities cannot await the creation of a large internal surplus.

These ideas concerning economic and social development, as well as policies already underway within the fields of commerce, education, health, and justice, are dealt with in concrete details in the congress documents—particularly in the main report from the Conselho Superior da Luta (Highest Council of the Struggle), which is the PAIGC's ninety-member equivalent of a central committee.

Party Organization. During the struggle for national liberation, the PAIGC was more or less a mass movement open to all anti-colonialists prepared to support the struggle. There was never any system of membership cards or files of registered members. However, the backbone of the organization—i.e., all members with special responsibilities and tasks from the local committees upward—were often referred to as "the party within the party." This core of committed and trained cadres also provided the administrative and judicial structure of the new society emerging in the liberated areas. It was both a *party* and a *state* at the same time.

With political independence the situation changed. A need was felt for a separation of functions between the party and the state, and discussions about whether the new party should be an

open mass organization or some kind of *avant-garde* party for the most dedicated and politically conscious—"the best children of the people"—were begun. The 1977 congress decided in favor of the *avant-garde* party, which surprised no one, since the idea of such a party had been advanced in the proposed party statutes distributed for discussion throughout Guinea and Cape Verde in preparation for the congress.

The PAIGC differs from the Frelimo of Mozambique and MPLA of Angola in not defining itself as a Marxist-Leninist party.* Instead the concept "national liberation movement holding power" (*movimento de libertacao no poder*) has been advanced as defining the present character of the PAIGC. This concept embodies the view that political independence is only a stepping-stone on the path toward national liberation from underdevelopment and dependence.

As we have seen, the overriding goal is to end the exploitation of man by man. But the road is long and difficult. In order to proceed, it is necessary to analyze the class forces at work in the societies of Guinea and Cape Verde. Is there any class able to lead the struggle against underdevelopment? According to the PAIGC, the answer is No. The working class is too small and undeveloped; the farmers are the primary producers (particularly in Guinea), but they cannot lead a development program that will have to include industrialization; the bourgeois/petit-bourgeois cannot be trusted to promote the interests of the masses without strong popular control. Thus the peasants, workers, and all others who accept the goal of national development in the interest of the masses will have to join forces under the leadership of the PAIGC—"the leading political force of society."

For this purpose a new, stricter party organization is thought to be required. To become a full member of the PAIGC, it will now be necessary to spend at least one year as a candidate in a local committee of the party and then be recommended by two members of at least three years' standing. Only those who dedicate themselves wholeheartedly to party work can expect to become and remain members. It is hoped that the party will be able to function with free and open internal discussion, with contact between the party and the people maintained through local village and neighborhood committees, as well as through unions and women's and youth organizations.

A new eight-member Comissão Permanente (Permanent Commission) is substituted for the previous four-member Permanent

*The Frelimo and the MPLA defined themselves as Marxist-Leninist parties at their congresses held in February and December 1977 respectively.

Secretariat as the highest permanent organ of the party. This commission includes, among others, the President of Cape Verde (and secretary-general of the PAIGC), Aristides Pereira, and the President of Guinea-Bissau (and deputy secretary-general of the PAIGC), Luiz Cabral. Between the two Permanent Commissions and the previously mentioned Conselho Superior da Luta, there remains the twenty-six member Comité Executivo da Luta (Executive Committee of the Struggle), which carries considerable political weight. Thus the organizational structure of the PAIGC remains intact at the top level. Since there are no important changes of personalities, the top leadership is still firmly in the hands of those who led the liberation struggle.

IV. EXTERNAL DEPENDENCE VERSUS INTERNAL POLITICAL STRENGTH

The concept of *dependence* has an important place in the debate on development in third world countries. Historically, the underdevelopment of third world societies is seen as due to the exploitation of their natural resources and labor forces in the interests of those countries that now make up the "industrialized West." The resulting unequal dependence upon the international capitalistic system is now a great hindrance to most efforts to begin development in the interests of the masses of people of the third world—even though they have political independence. Guinea-Bissau illustrates this problem with great clarity.

Tables 1-3 indicate the basic economic situation of Guinea-Bissau during its first years of independence. The tables speak more or less for themselves. They show that (1) despite a clear improvement in 1977, substantial credits and aid are needed to balance the country's foreign trade deficit and (2) it is necessary for Guinea to diversify its exports—both with regard to products and receiving countries. In 1975 and 1976, Swedish aid alone [Sweden is the largest supplier of foreign aid to Guinea-Bissau] was greater than Guinea's total export earnings.* Still more is needed, which will

*Guinea-Bissau received totals of $42.8 million in gifts and $23.1 million in loans in 1976, of which Sweden provided $9.1 million in gifts and the Soviet Union $10.5 million in loans. The totals for 1977 were $36.1 million in gifts and $22.5 million in loans, of which Sweden provided $13.7 million in gifts and the Soviet Union $11 million in loans. Other major donors and lenders were the United Nations, Portugal, the Netherlands, Arab states acting jointly, and the EEC (International Monetary Fund, *Guinea-Bissau, Economic Situation, FM/77/199*, August 10, 1977).

LARS RUDEBECK

Table 1

APPROXIMATE VALUE OF GUINEA-BISSAU'S EXPORTS AND IMPORTS:
1974-1977

(*In U.S. dollars*)

Time Period	Exports	Imports	Exports as Percentage of Imports
July-December 1974	$ 1,100,000	$16,000,000	7%
1975	4,900,000	29,800,000	16
1976	5,000,000	34,000,000	15
1977	13,116,000	37,889,000	35

Sources: *Boletim Mensal de Comercio Externo* (Bissau: Planning Ministry), July 1975, tables 1, 2; December 1976, t. 1, 2; April-June 1977, p. 15, t. 1; *Anuário Estatístico, 1977* (Bissau: Planning Ministry), p. 46.

Table 2

PORTUGAL'S SHARE OF GUINEA-BISSAU'S FOREIGN TRADE
AS PERCENTAGE OF TOTAL VALUE

Time Period	Share of Exports	Share of Imports
1968[a]	78%	69%
January-July 1975	74	56
1976	77	45
1977	59	40

Sources: *Boletim Mensal de Comercio Externo*, July 1975, t. 5, 6; December 1976, t. 11; *Anuário Estatístico, 1977*, p. 48. Figures for 1968 are from *Anuário Estatístico, Provincias Ultramarinas, 1969*, vol. 2 (Lisbon: National Institute of Statistics, 1971), pp. 142, 146.

[a]The colony of Portuguese Guinea.

Table 3

VALUE OF PRINCIPAL EXPORT GOODS OF GUINEA-BISSAU
AS PERCENTAGE OF TOTAL EXPORT EARNINGS: 1976-1977

Export[a]	1976	1977
Groundnuts		
[Portugal, Egypt]	59%	60 %
Palmnut-seeds		
[Portugal, France, Netherlands]	11	12
Fish and shrimps		
[Senegal, Nigeria, Liberia, Algeria, Portugal, Spain, Soviet Union]	9	19
Sawed timber and timber products		
[Cape Verde, Portugal, Algeria, Spain, Gambia, Senegal]	8	2.5
Cashew nuts		
[India, Italy, China, France]	1	2.5
Total	88	96

Sources: Boletim Mensal de Comercio Externo, December 1976, t. 3, 6; Anuário Estatístico, 1977, t. 5.2 (annex).

[a]Receiving countries indicated in brackets.

necessarily create problems of dependence in the long run. What can be done to counteract this difficult situation? The counterbalance is to be found in productive work creating a surplus for investments and exports, which (as we shall see below) requires the strong political organization of the country.

Self-Sufficiency in Rice. The great majority of the working people of Guinea are mainly subsistence farmers living in villages. The surplus required to finance Guinea's development will have to come from the productive work of these peasants if its dependence upon the outside world is not to become even greater than it is now. At least to begin with, the surplus to be sold on the world market will have to come from groundnuts. But the first goal of economic

development in Guinea is to get the peasants to produce enough rice to feed both themselves and the urban population of the country.

Rice is the basic food of the people of Guinea. Previous to the war of national liberation, production was about 120,000 tons of raw rice per year. This was enough to cover internal consumption—estimated to be about 60,000 tons of shelled rice (equivalent to about 90,000 tons of raw rice)—and to leave a certain surplus for export. During the first six months of 1975, rice constituted 23 percent of the country's imports. Thus the agricultural country of Guinea-Bissau was forced to spend almost one quarter of its import funds just to provide the people with their daily rice. This situation improved considerably, however, during the two following years: in 1976 the share of rice in the total value of imports was only 7 percent, and in 1977 it was 8 percent. The Guinea-Bissau authorities had hoped to equal the prewar level of production in 1977, but as can be seen in Table 4, they did not succeed, and rice imports had to be continued during 1977. Because the drought of the West African Sahel reached as far south as Guinea-Bissau in 1977, import needs for 1978 soared well above the previous high of 1974. This was a severe setback for the Guinean development strategy, but in 1978 the harvest returned to normal.

Table 4

IMPORTS OF SHELLED RICE INTO GUINEA-BISSAU:
1974-1977

(*In tons*)

Year	Amount
1974	30,000
1975[a]	14,314
1976	10,891
1977	13,082

Sources: Interviews with officials of the People's Stores and *Anuário Estatístico, 1977*, t. 4.2 (annex).

[a]First full year of PAIGC control of the country.

In working toward the developmental goal of self-sufficiency in rice, the connection between politics and agricultural production is clearly shown. Political work in the rice-producing areas of Guinea-Bissau is to a great extent directed at mobilizing the peasants to reach this goal. It is particularly important to construct dikes to keep the salty water of the tide away from the flat coastal lands, and thus make it possible to expand the acreage of rice cultivation. Everywhere in the villages, the political commissars and agricultural technicians must assemble the people to explain how the peasants themselves will gain from the construction of such dikes.

The Creation of a National Currency. On February 28, 1976, the government of Guinea-Bissau announced the nationalization of the Guinea operations of the Portuguese Banco Nacional Ultramarino. Up to then the BNU had been in charge of issuing the Portuguese/Guinean *escudo* in circulation in Guinea-Bissau, but now the National Bank of Guinea-Bissau was given the task of issuing a new national currency—the *peso*—non-convertible, but initially at par with the Portuguese escudo. This step was taken after negotiations with the Portuguese government had come to a complete impasse with regard to the public debt of the former colony of Portuguese Guinea. The Portuguese government wanted the government of independent Guinea-Bissau to assume the debt, but this was unacceptable to the Guineans. The best solution appeared to be a clean break with the Portuguese currency system, giving Guinea-Bissau complete control of its foreign exchange operations. The Portuguese government retaliated by freezing all Guinean assets in Portuguese banks, but Guinea-Bissau stood firm, and in the fall of 1976 the problem was resolved to the satisfaction of the Guineans.[7]

It is unlikely that the government of Guinea-Bissau would have dared challenge the Portuguese in this way had it not been for its strong political position at home. Breaking with the Portuguese currency system initially led to shortages and some hardship for the Guinean population (particularly in the urban sectors), but through the state and party structures it was possible to explain the long-term necessity of this step and have it applauded by the majority of the people.

V. THE ORGANIZATION AND SOCIAL BASIS OF STATE POWER

The people of Guinea-Bissau are brought most directly into contact with the organized political structure of their country through

the local committees (*comité de base*)—popularly elected five-member committees that the PAIGC attempts to establish in all villages and urban neighborhoods. According to party rules, at least two of the five members must be women. No official figure on the number of such committees has been published, but my rough estimate is that there are over one thousand of them spread throughout the country. In the rural areas there are—on the average—perhaps five hundred inhabitants (including children) per committee.

The local committees are grouped in *sections* of about five to ten committees each, and a number of sections make up a *sector*, of which there are thirty-six in the entire country. The largest administrative and political division below the national level is the *region*, of which there are eight: Bissau, Cacheu, Oio, Bafatá, Gabu, Tombali, Buba, and Bolama. (The capital city of Bissau forms an "autonomous sector" of its own, besides the other regions and sectors.)

The local committee is the only elected element in this political and administrative structure below the regional level. All administrators at the section level, as well as the members of the sector and regional committees, are appointed. The president of the regional committee is both administrative governor and head of the regional party committee.

Above the regional level are the central organs of party and government, which are closely interrelated in the sense that the same leaders have key posts in both types of organs. The President and his councillors are elected for four-year terms by the Assembleia Nacional Popular (National Assembly of the People), which meets annually for sessions of a few weeks. The members of the Assembly are elected by and from the members of Regional Councils, who have been elected in nationwide regional elections. The first such elections were held in the liberated areas in 1972; the second elections were held in December 1976, when the people in each region were asked to vote for or against single lists of PAIGC candidates for Regional Councils. Altogether, 81 percent of the votes were for the PAIGC lists, with approximately one half of the potential electorate of citizens eighteen years or older voting.[8]

In the National Assembly, laws are passed, debates are carried on, and announcements are made, but it is in the politico-administrative structure, beginning with the local committees and ending with the national party/government, that permanent contact is maintained between the national leadership and the rural villages. This structure, which developed in the liberated areas during the struggle for independence, is not merely an adaptation of the colo-

nial state (as is the case in many other African countries), but a break with the colonial state.

Prior to 1974, a radically new judicial system, based upon an evolving synthesis of customary law and the ideological principles of the PAIGC, developed in the liberated areas of Guinea-Bissau, completely replacing the legal system of the colonial regime.[9] The situation is somewhat different in independent Guinea-Bissau, where portions of the colonial system of civil law remain in force, for practical reasons, as long as they are not clearly contrary to the principles of the PAIGC; however, much work is being done within the State Commissariat of Justice to extend the system of elected People's Courts (*Tribunais do Povo*) to the entire country.

The major social basis of state power in Guinea-Bissau is the peasantry, politically mobilized by the PAIGC during the liberation struggle. Since independence, this basis has been mixed with some of the petit-bourgeois elements of the colonial state's social basis, and conflicts have begun to emerge. In general, however, the state is still much more closely connected with the rural masses than in most other African countries.

What about the working class? *Ideologically*, the PAIGC represents all the working people—i.e., the masses of peasants and workers—as well as all others committed to the goal of national liberation and progress. *In theory*, this assigns the working class a major role in a long-term perspective, but *in practice* the working class of Guinea-Bissau is too small to play such a role for many years to come. There are very few workers directly engaged in industrial production in Guinea-Bissau—less than two thousand in 1977.[10] The PAIGC is attempting to rally these workers, as well as the approximately 23,000 other wage and salaried employees in the country, behind the party and the regime through the União Nacional dos Trabalhadores da Guiné. Relations of trust between the regime and the members of the unions are clearly essential to the success of the socialist-oriented PAIGC policies.

While the working class of Guinea provides social support for the PAIGC regime, the same cannot be said of the urban petite-bourgeoisie. The petit-bourgeois strata are dominant in the towns (particularly in Bissau), and they offer little support for PAIGC policies, which tend to favor the countryside over the urban areas. This problematic political situation is reflected in the frequent calls for vitalization of party activities in Bissau. However, this may be a less serious problem for the regime than it first appears, since the urban petite bourgeoisie neither control the party and ma-

jor policies nor are the producers of the country's economic surplus. The key posts of the party and the government are held by leaders of the liberation struggle, and by far the major part of all production is carried out by the peasants. On the other hand, the conflicts between the interests of the working people and those of the petite-bourgeoisie must be dealt with in the long run.

The contradictions inherent in the social basis of state power are becoming visible in conflicting tendencies in PAIGC development policies. These conflicting tendencies concern such things as large-scale commercial export agriculture versus production of food for the people, luxury consumption for the elite versus raised living standards for the masses, elite-oriented training in the schools versus broad political orientation and participation in productive work. In these and related areas there is an ongoing class struggle in Guinea-Bissau, and the balance of power between social forces established through this struggle determines, in a continuous process, the development orientation of the regime.

VI. THE CONCRETE DEVELOPMENT STRATEGY OF GUINEA-BISSAU

The best indicator of the class character of a regime is what it actually does, in political and economic practice. In the case of Guinea-Bissau, in the absence (up to now) of an elaborated development plan, the concrete policies within various fields together provide a fairly good picture of the development strategy of the country.[11]

A. Agriculture. It is clearly essential for the national economy that the first goal of economic development—self-sufficiency in rice—be reached. Only when the country's dependence on loans and gifts for the basic support of the people has ended will it be possible to speak seriously of autonomous development in the interest of the masses.

The PAIGC government promotes the goal of self-sufficiency in food through the use of agricultural technicians and party cadres working hand-in-hand with peasants at the village and section levels, as well as through such measures as raising the prices paid to the peasants for their products. During the last years of the colonial regime, the peasants received a little over 25 percent of the price paid by the consumer for the most common variety of shelled rice, but during the harvesting seasons of 1975 and 1976, they received a little over 40 percent of the consumer price.[12] In addition, a great

338

deal of the difference now goes to the state-run People's Stores organization rather than to private traders.

Agricultural land in Guinea-Bissau is communally held by the people of the villages. (In a juridical sense it is the property of the nation, according to a law of nationalization passed by the National Assembly in 1975).[13] It is usually cultivated by families, with privately owned tools. The long-term goal of the PAIGC is to transform this communal system of landholding and cultivation into a system where all land is held and cultivated by producers' cooperatives. The plan is to proceed slowly—not forcing the peasants to adopt measures they do not accept or understand. The first step will usually be a buying cooperative, where a number of peasants pool their resources to buy seed, fertilizer, or perhaps a machine, then a sales cooperative, and finally a producers' cooperative to invest the returns from sales.

Little has been achieved so far with respect to the creation of producers' cooperatives, but there are many plans and projects.* It is obvious that the process of moving from traditional village agriculture to modern producers' cooperatives will be long and difficult, with many obstacles and with potential conflicts between different strata of the peasants as well as between the peasantry and the party/state. The peasants have to be convinced of the need to transform age-old habits in order to improve their lives. There are three possible outcomes of the process now set in motion in the Guinean countryside:

1. Continuation for a long time to come of traditional agriculture, with stagnating production and consequent failure to produce enough food to achieve self-sufficiency. This could occur under the cover of an organizational framework of modern cooperatives.

2. "Kulakization"—i.e., stratification between relatively wealthy private agricultural producers and an increasing number of small peasants who cannot support themselves on the land. (All land is nationalized in Guinea-Bissau, but rights of cultivation could be granted to individuals.) A variant of this would

---

*In Contuboel, one such project has had a promising start. There a group of internationally (including U.S.) supported Guinean agricultural technicians have developed locally suitable varieties of rice and introduced irrigation, while encouraging the peasants to join in a cooperative to make better use of the new production possibilities. During the first year of the project, with 112 families associated with the project, yields per hectare increased up to eight times (to four tons).

be the development of pilot cooperatives into "elite" farms with incomes and productivity well above average.

3. Development along the lines desired by the party and the state—i.e., toward collectively organized modern agriculture with the traditional community as its point of departure.

Whether the third possibility is realized will depend upon the ability of the PAIGC to maintain the confidence of the peasantry while developing further its revolutionary line in ideology and political action. The task is not an easy one. There are few signs of progress so far, but it is clearly too early to judge the outcome.

B. Industrial Development. The industrialization of Guinea-Bissau must begin almost from scratch. Only two industrial plants of some size (both in Bissau) were inherited from the colonial period. One is a highly automatized beer and soft drink factory built in 1974, employing 70 people and with a productive capacity to supply an army of approximately 40,000 men. The other is a groundnut oil factory completed in 1959 and employing some 140 people; its processing capacity is well below the groundnut production capacity of the country. Apart from these two plants, at the time of independence there were only a few small rice and groundnut shellers, a number of small saws, a few carpentry and furniture shops, one seamstress shop with twenty-seven sewing machines, etc.

The industrial projects initiated under the independent regime reflect the PAIGC development strategy already outlined: the promotion of export industries based upon semi-processed or processed local raw materials combined with some import-substitution industries for the local market. One such project is the state-owned SOCOTRAM (Sociedade de Comercializacão e Transformacão de Madeiras [Society for the sale and processing of lumber]), inaugurated in December 1976. SOCOTRAM operates a factory producing wooden tiles (primarily for export) as well as a number of saw mills and carpentry shops throughout the country. There is also a factory for the production of fruit juices and other preserves from local fruits which began to operate in March 1977. An import-substitution factory to produce plastic foam mattresses has been started, and plans are being made for textile industries based upon locally cultivated cotton and small-scale metal industries using scrap iron salvaged from the war of liberation. A major industrial project is underway at the mouth of the river Geba, where a plant to husk both rice and groundnuts is being installed. The husks are to be burned to produce heat for a power station, which will provide part

of the energy for a groundnut oil and a soap factory. There is also a project for cultivation of sugar cane on a state plantation in the interior of the country. The bauxite deposits in the southeastern part of Guinea-Bissau are to be exploited only as part of an integrated regional development plan that will combine the mining of bauxite with the construction of dams on the river Corubal and a railroad to a new port on the coast. An agreement for the prospecting of bauxite and for general geological investigations was signed with the Soviet Union in February 1977.[14]

The PAIGC regime favors state and cooperative ownership of major industries, but does not exclude the idea of joint ventures with foreign private capital, provided that the state retains major control. However, the PAIGC prefers agreements with governments and international organizations to arrangements with private companies. Complete independence of the surrounding world (autarchy) is neither possible nor desirable in the long run for any country—least of all for a small country like Guinea-Bissau—and that is not what is meant by independent or autonomous economic development of third world countries. These terms usually refer to development policies aimed at achieving control of one's own resources, ending dependence for the bare necessities of life, and reducing other forms of dependence on the outside world. One means of avoiding excessive dependence on outside interests is to accept aid from as many different donors as possible—in both capitalist and socialist countries. It is too early to tell how all this will succeed in Guinea-Bissau. In any case, the creation of an internal surplus remains a basic prerequisite.

C. Commerce and Distribution. The prices of essential consumer goods are strictly controlled in Guinea-Bissau, with low maximum prices set for the five basic necessities of rice, flour, cooking oil, sugar, and soap. These five basic necessities, as well as many other goods, are sold mainly through the system of People's Stores (*Armazens do Povo*). The first People's Store of the liberated areas was established in 1964; within four years there were fifteen, and a few more were added later. The function of the People's Stores during the struggle was to provide the inhabitants of liberated Guinea with an outlet for their surplus production and a means of supplying themselves with necessary consumer goods without relying upon the Portuguese. After the complete liberation of the country in 1974, the number of People's Stores grew rapidly. In August 1975 there were 72 stores, and in February 1976 the number was

110. In 1978 there were still many private stores—mainly in Bissau, but also in a few other urban centers.

The People's Stores have a legal import monopoly on the five basic necessities, and this monopoly will probably be extended to include all goods in the future. A step in this direction was taken in December 1975, when the People's Stores took over all the commercial and trading activities of the Gouveia, one of the two great colonial companies operating in Guinea-Bissau. (A groundnut oil factory in Bissau is still owned and operated directly by Gouveia.) The other colonial company is the Ultramarina; it still maintains its commerce in Guinea-Bissau, but 80 percent of the company's shares were taken over by the Guinea government in June 1976.

Thus the PAIGC policies in commerce and distribution are indicators of the regime's intention to favor the masses of the people. These policies constitute a break with capitalist principles of determining what goods should be made available to whom at what prices. They do not affect the system of production, however.

D. Education. It would be hard to find a national development plan in the third world that does not stress the importance of education for development—at least on an abstract level. Education is seen by the PAIGC both as an essential part of the struggle against the cultural degradation of colonialism and as an instrument for the concrete material improvement of the people's situation. The two go hand-in-hand in practice; it is only analytically that they can be separated. This ideological-strategic perspective gives consistency to the daily work carried on in the many village schools.

There has been a dramatic expansion of educational facilities in the country during the first two years of complete independence. Now more than 10 percent of the total population of the country attend school[*]—not counting ten thousand persons in adult education and various extra courses of training. This is a very high percentage for Africa. There is a bottleneck in the transition from primary to secondary school, however, and one urgent goal is to make secondary education available in at least the eight regional capitals. Another problem is a lack of teachers.

[*]Adult education is an essential part of the educational program of the PAIGC. Important gains were made during the literacy campaign through which the soldiers of the liberation army were organized. In the countryside, there have been difficulties, however, caused in particular by the people's very limited knowledge of the official language, Portuguese, which is the only written language in the country.

E. Health and Medical Services. During the struggle for independence, a system of health and medical care was built up in the liberated areas with country hospitals, sanitary posts, mobile health brigades, and the member of each village committee in charge of health and social affairs as its organizational foundation. The basic principles of this system have been carried over into the post-independence period. According to a plan established in 1975 for the seven regions outside Bissau (to be fully implemented by about 1980), there are to be seven fully equipped regional hospitals and twenty smaller hospitals at the sector level. Of these, there were five regional hospitals (besides two in Bissau) in operation in early 1977—and probably four sector hospitals. The regions that do not yet have a good regional hospital have at least a small hospital and a regional doctor.

There is a severe lack of trained personnel at all levels of Guinean medical services. In early 1977 there were only sixty-six fully trained medical doctors in the country, twenty-nine of whom worked in Bissau.[16] Only eleven of these were Guineans; the rest had come mostly from Cuba, the Soviet Union, and China. Further training is a top priority in health planning.

VII. SOCIALIST ORIENTATION AND POLITICAL STRUGGLE

In principle, economic development can be financed in two ways: (1) with foreign investments, credits, and aid or (2) with an internally generated surplus resulting from the people's productive work. These two types of sources—external and internal—can also be combined in varying proportions. Control can be exercised by the foreign interests that have provided the capital, by local minorities unrestrained by any type of popular control, or by local regimes sensitive to the interests of the broad majority of peasants and workers.

We have seen that the point of departure of the development strategy of Guinea-Bissau is the fact that agriculture dominates the country's economy. The only autonomous base for surplus generation with which to initiate broad economic and social development is the peasants and their land. This fits well with the political situation at the end of the armed struggle for national liberation—i.e., a politically mobilized peasantry constructing a new society under the leadership of the PAIGC. On the other hand, the state is heavily dependent upon external financing, which in the long run is hardly conducive to extended popular influence over development policies.

The PAIGC regime is thus involved in a race against time. The objective situation of the country, the history of national liberation, the present political basis of the regime, and the declared intentions of the leadership—all indicate a strategy of development emphasizing the internal generation of a surplus, the use of which is controlled by a party and a state deriving strength from popular participation and support. Such a strategy can be called socialist-oriented—both in terms of the tendencies it seeks to encourage and in terms of the structural preconditions of its success. These preconditions include control of the state (and thus of external inflows of capital) by a revolutionary party supported by the broad masses of the people, increasing production in agriculture, and gradual industrialization in interaction with agricultural development.[17]

In the case of Guinea-Bissau there is still the possibility of such a socialist orientation of the country's development, but there is no historical determinism guaranteeing it. On the contrary, the future orientation of development policies will be an expression of the evolving class character of the society. In other words, it will depend upon the outcome of the ongoing social and political struggle in Guinea, which in turn will be influenced by international economic and political developments.

SOCIALIST POLITICS IN REVOLUTIONARY ETHIOPIA

John W. Harbeson

For more than four years, the Provisional Military Government (PMG) of Ethiopia has struggled to maintain control of the revolution it launched against the regime of Emperor Haile Selassie I (1930-74). During this period the military insurgents have imprisoned the emperor, arrested or executed dozens of notables of the old order, detained or shot several hundred less powerful individuals whom it found to be subverting the revolution, mobilized over forty thousand students and teachers to bring the message of socialism and revolution to millions of rural Ethiopians mired deeply in poverty and isolation, nationalized all major industrial and commercial firms, and promulgated far-reaching urban and rural land reform programs as revolutionary as any ever undertaken. Two years after embarking on its revolutionary course, the PMG or *derg* ("committee" in Amharic) promulgated a new National Democratic Revolutionary Program (NDRP) to rest on the foundations established by the earlier reforms and to set forth the country's future political direction. Particularly important in this new socialist program was the establishment of a political bureau to mobilize the masses behind the revolution. The NDRP was the ideological culmination of a revolutionary movement that stated its goals very cautiously at first and only gradually became explicitly socialist.

The fundamental problem for the revolutionary military regime has been the definition and legitimization of the PMG's own role in the revolution. The derg originated as a committee more or less representing and coordinating units of the armed forces in the gradual dismantling of the old regime, which began to collapse under the weight of demands placed upon it by drought and inflation conditions. The derg made few overt attempts to broaden its political base until long after the "coup" deposing Haile Selassie.[1] Not until three months after the military seized power did the derg make its first, very general commitment to socialism. The PMG did not turn

An earlier version of this paper was presented at the American Political Science Association annual meeting, Chicago, September 1976.

to the task of building a grass roots political movement to spearhead the revolution until after it had promulgated socialist policies of far-reaching importance: nationalization of businesses and industries and urban and rural land reform charters. Since the derg thereby seized responsibility for defining the direction of the revolution rather than simply removing the traditional political and socioeconomic obstacles to its emergence, the belated commencement of a revolutionary mass-based political movement has appeared to critics on both the Ethiopian left and right to be aimed at consolidating the derg's power rather than the reforms of the revolution.[2] By leaving its role and purposes in the revolution ambiguous, the derg has alienated those constituencies most sympathetic to the socioeconomic reforms already instituted—even those civilian groups that initially cooperated with the derg on the NDRP. Consequently, the derg's only political resource (and the only skill to which its members have been socialized) has been the employment of physical force. Because its own legitimacy has not been established, the derg's use of force has also been considered illegitimate by many Ethiopians committed to socialism, and its internal military position, therefore, appears to be very troubled. The more the derg has used force to secure control of the revolution, the more it has alienated its natural and badly needed constituency.

The character of the revolution and the travails of the PMG should be viewed against the background of a pre-revolutionary context that was unique among African countries. Ethiopia is perhaps the only country in Africa whose political order has not been transformed and disrupted by the intrusions of Western imperialism, notwithstanding the Muslim jihad of the sixteenth century and the Italian occupation during World War II. Westernization under Haile Selassie and his predecessors did not destroy host traditions, but was in effect grafted onto them.[3] The derg's revolutionary struggle has been directed not only against imperialism, but also against the long-standing institutions, policies, and styles of government of Ethiopia's own past, and indigenous patterns of change as well. The revolutionary socialist opposition to the Provisional Military Government (which claims the socialist ideological mantle itself) has been based upon the PMG's allegedly pre-revolutionary political style—not the policies and programs the derg has enunciated.[4] The very superficiality of Ethiopia's Westernization under the last emperors has perhaps helped to undermine a revolutionary movement determined to eradicate the *ancien regime*.

Political change in pre-revolutionary Ethiopia cannot be ana-

lyzed in the same terms as in other African countries. Modernization and Westernization have continued to be largely indistinguishable in the literature on the developing nations, with the result that change has been viewed as the consequence of alien civilizations intruding on host cultures.[5] In Ethiopia, by contrast, "modernization" as it is often understood in the West has been a feature of Ethiopia's own traditions rather than a by-product of their devastation by the forces of colonialism.[6] In the Ethiopian context, therefore, "modernization" was not the same as "Westernization." The heart of the difference is between ends and means.* Ethiopia sought modernization without becoming the captive of the means offered by the West. The argument of this paper will be that, like the regime it replaced, the derg in seeking to institute socialism continues to emphasize modernization objectives by uniquely Ethiopian means.

I

Since the sixteenth century the task of maintaining rudimentary political integration in Ethiopia has been interwoven with preserving a basis of national political identity through the medium of the Ethiopian Orthodox faith, in the context of territorial pressures by foreign powers representing alien religions.[7] Portugal became interested in Ethiopia as part of its strategy to circumvent Moslem domination of Middle Eastern trade routes and because of the reported adherence of the country's rulers to the Christian faith, and it was instrumental in helping Ethiopia survive the Muslim jihad launched by Adal, an Ottoman Turkish client state. Portuguese clerics remained in Ethiopia, creating controversy and divisiveness by attempting to convert Ethiopia to Roman Catholicism. Emperors who apostasized to the Roman faith were forced to abdicate, and the country's religious and military battles left it vulnerable to attack by the Galla (or Oromo) peoples to the south. A Galla insurgency, motivated largely by internal pressures for land and a warrior ethic, resulted in the further diminution of Ethiopian unity as Galla chief-

---

*The primary indicators of modernization have in general been urbanization, participation, industrialization, commercialization, literacy, and per capita income (Phillips Cutright, "National Political Development: Measurement and Analysis," *American Sociological Review* 28 [April 1963]: 253-64). Assumed without argument is the relationship between these indicators and the basic characteristics of modernization such as specialization, development of political identity, political integration, political capability. It is this assumption that is contradicted by the Ethiopian experience.

tains became increasingly powerful in the country.[8] Between the mid-eighteenth and mid-nineteenth centuries, Ethiopia scarcely knew central government, lapsing into what has become known as the "Era of the Princes."[9]

The rebirth of the Ethiopian nation began with the regime of Tewodros (1855-69), who combined militant attachment to the Ethiopian Orthodox church with a commitment to nationalism that brooked no opposition from either priest or landlord.[10] Lacking royal pedigree, Tewodros achieved the throne because of his skills as a warrior. Though interested in reforming his country and restoring its past greatness, his preoccupation with military solutions to persistent rebellions against the renewed central authority under his leadership contributed significantly to his downfall.* The parallels with the present regime's attempt to reform and maintain the unity of the country deserve consideration. Johannes IV (1868-86) may have been as fanatical in his attachment to the Ethiopian Orthodox church, and he labored throughout his reign against threats to the country's newly asserted territorial integrity posed by Egypt and Italy, in which Great Britain played no insignificant role, but he wisely employed diplomacy rather than costly internecine warfare in controlling his chief vassals.[11]

The expansion of Ethiopia's territorial boundaries to the south and east under Menelik II (1889-1916) brought millions of Muslim subjects into the empire and caused the Amhara Christian population to be a minority in what had historically been "their" country.[12] The importance of Menelik's conquests lies not only in the fact that they represented the culmination of the dreams of Ethiopian emperors since European medieval times, but also in the complication of Ethiopia's sense of political identity, which had historically centered around the Orthodox Church in an overwhelmingly Christian area.[13] Unlike their predecessors, both Menelik and Haile Selassie were obliged not so much to defend their country's religious-based political identity and territorial integrity as to assimilate the conquered infidel to the political culture of the ancient kingdom, and both focused upon the coopting of elites rather than upon transforming the cultures of conquered peoples. The Orthodox

*Sven Rubenson and Donald Crummey differ somewhat on the causes for Tewodros's fall. Crummey argues that the heart of the problem was Tewodros's disaffection for "habits of insubordination and decentralization" that had become entrenched during the era of princes; Rubenson places more weight on Tewodros having attacked the church for its alleged uncooperativeness. (For sources, see note 10.)

Church made relatively little effort to convert the rank-and-file in the conquered areas. Conquered land was awarded partially to elites of the conquering regime and partially to civil servants and peasants from overcrowded regions of the traditional kingdom. Some land was returned to cooperating local elites—some of whom were made officials on the lowest rung of the Ethiopian government. Local elites gained land and political importance not only by accepting conquest but by adopting the civilization of the conquerors: the Orthodox faith and the Amharic language. Different regions in southern and eastern Ethiopia were brought into the empire on terms which varied according to the degree and length of resistance they offered Menelik's armies and Menelik's disposition. With the expansion of the empire the common link between Ethiopia's diverse peoples became not so much the church as patron-client relationships based on land, reinforced to some degree by the shared experience of resisting the Italian invaders.[14]

The changing basis of political identity as a consequence of the expansion and consolidation of the empire was accompanied by Menelik's interest in introducing Western skills and technologies. Even before Menelik became emperor—when he was only king of Shewa province—he evinced great interest in developing the reciprocal relationship between expansion of the empire and trade with Europe.[15] Conquest brought him wealth with which to purchase arms for further conquest. Western arms were instrumental in the political modernization of the traditional Ethiopian state, but not in its transformation. Western inventions and craftsmen were imported primarily to enhance the quality of life in the imperial court, radiating outward secondarily to the imperial city, and only very indirectly to the countryside as a whole.[16] The tools of Westernization were coopted for the reinforcement of the traditional power structure as it expanded its scope.

Under Haile Selassie considerable Westernization occurred which, like his predecessors, he deployed to strengthen the Ethiopian state more than to transform the lives of his subjects, concentrating it similarly on the capital city to a far greater extent than upon the countryside. Haile Selassie encouraged the development of an internal airline network and an Ethiopian highway system, and telephone and electric power facilities were greatly expanded, but all these improvements centered upon the capital city (Addis Ababa). The road system, for example, emphasized the country's export markets and the dependence of the capital upon foreign imports rather than the need of Ethiopia's myriad of small farmers for

improved access roads to local markets. The emperor took advantage of the dislocation attendant upon the Italian invasion to introduce Western-type taxation and administrative systems, but he used the increasingly centralized authority resulting from these changes to reinforce traditional patron-client relationships. He granted tracts of land to patriots and exiles to reward them for their loyalty and ensure support for his renewed rule. Though some landless and unemployed persons were among those receiving land, as much as 80 percent of the land grants went to representatives of the armed forces and to civil servants. He allocated a significant proportion to those who already held privileged economic or political positions in the empire.[17] Even a modest land tax reform attempted in 1966 may have had the effect of sharpening distinctions between land-holding elites beholden to the Crown and peasants made technically landless by this "reform."

In the last twenty years of his reign, the emperor's government made the first attempts to induce economic development in the vastnesses of rural Ethiopia. But these undertakings were isolated and compartmentalized, both geographically and technologically, from the surrounding communities. In the 1960's the Swedish government financed and constructed the Chilalo Agricultural Development Unit featuring comprehensive measures to stimulate agricultural development and social change in a single southern district. On a reduced scale, other area-specific development projects were launched at Ada, Wolamo, and Setit-Humera. The Awash Valley Authority was chartered in 1962 to oversee the development of a rich eastern lowland region previously invaded by plantation interests—foreign and domestic—and jointly administered. Each of these projects increased the productivity of rural Ethiopia, generating export crops, import-substitution crops, and tax revenue to the state, but very little of this revenue redounded to the benefit of the pastoralists in the Awash Valley displaced by the plantations.[18] The level of mechanization in the schemes prevented peasants in surrounding areas from imitating the project innovations, and the heavy investment they required made replication financially prohibitive.

Similar developments occurred in the fields of education and urbanization. Haile Selassie was committed to educational development, and during his reign a substantial number of schools were opened at all levels. Haile Selassie I University opened on the grounds of a former imperial palace, and he personally sponsored advanced education abroad for numbers of his subjects. But the sluggish

expansion of the economy prevented the embryonic educational system from keeping pace with growing numbers of school-age children.[19] Access to primary education was far from universal and, as in other developing countries, the percentage of primary school graduates attending secondary school and later the university was microscopic. In 1973 about one Ethiopian in 150 entering primary school could expect to attend Haile Selassie I University twelve years later.[20] Access to school facilities was very unequally distributed throughout the country, and the governates of Shoa and Eritrea plus the city of Addis Ababa nearly monopolized places in the university.

Along with the Eritrean city of Asmara, Addis Ababa appropriated a greatly disproportionate share of Ethiopia's investment in Western amenities. The important point is not that the urban-rural gap was perhaps more pronounced than in other African countries, but rather that it represented a continuing pattern in the evolution of Ethiopia since the mid-nineteenth century. Then, as on the eve of the revolution, the importation of Western skills and technology served the interest of the state as defined by the monarch, and the people participated in the improvements in roughly direct proportion to their geographic and political proximity to the palace. On the eve of the revolution, over 50 percent of the country's doctors were resident in Addis Ababa, while the country as a whole had but one doctor for about every seventy-five thousand subjects. The city displayed an unusually unrepresentative air of socioeconomic Westernization and prosperity for a country whose per capita income hovered around $85 per capita. But even within the capital there remained great inequalities: a substantial proportion of the city's real estate was controlled by a very small number of urban landlords,* and those urban Ethiopians who had risen above the status of domestic gardener, petty clerk, or street hawker to become wage laborers in the country's fledgling, state-dominated industrial economy were frustrated by a union movement hampered by governmental attempts to manipulate and coopt its leadership. Such industrial and commercial growth as occurred prior to the revolution was only rarely accompanied by corresponding improvements in wages and benefits. Inflationary pressures struck urban labor particularly hard—notably the trans-

---

*A highly classified but widely reported study of land ownership in Addis Ababa was conducted by the Imperial Ethiopian Government about 1970. The study is reported to have shown that land ownership in the cities was concentrated in the hands of a very few families.

portation workers, who played an important role in the initial stage of the revolution. Meanwhile, soaring land values enhanced the incomes of the relatively small class of urban landlords.

A highly significant dimension of Ethiopia's pattern of elite Westernization was that the Western governments and industrial interests investing in the country became partners of the traditional order rather than agents of its transformation. There is evidence that one of the consequences of this partnership was the net export of capital from the country, weakening its capacity for economic growth.[21] More fundamentally, the symbiosis of Westernization and the defense of the traditional order caused elites critical of the old regime to view both Westernization and the old regime as antithetical to many aspects of modernization. Ethiopian emperors began to experiment with Westernization in order to defend the integrity of their country and to restore what they believed to be its traditional borders, but the education, urbanization, commercialization, expansion of the cash crop and export economy, and even the structures of political participation seemed to hinder rather than enhance structural differentiation, political capacity, political identity, and participation in the political and economic life of the country. Markakis has demonstrated that the overwhelming tendency of the system was "to dissolve specialized modern into the vague, all-encompassing role of administrator," the blurring of roles serving "to maintain the primacy of traditional criteria."[22] Westernization of the economy did not enhance popular participation, and the crypto-Westminster parliamentary structures inaugurated in 1955 (the year of the emperor's jubilee) provided landed and provincial elites a new theater in which to assert their interests while stimulating low and declining citizen electoral participation. In a world influenced by Western values, the trappings of constitutional monarchy gave the old order the appearance of legitimacy rather than set the stage for genuine political change.

II

How did the revolution come to pass in the singular circumstances of twentieth-century Ethiopia? How did a species of socialism emerge as the general objective of a revolutionary military cadre? The principal hypotheses of this paper are (1) that the collapse of the old regime preceded the emergence of rebels committed to destroying and replacing the *ancien regime*, (2) that a group within the revolutionary military cadre having socialist inclinations pro-

duced a socialist blueprint in the first instance out of a need to consolidate its position as the liberators of Ethiopia from the old order and the architects of the new one, and (3) that the military regime has pursued its socialist ideal by promoting change in a manner paradoxically reminiscent of Ethiopia's former emperors.

The old regime began to collapse in 1973 and 1974 because the drought and subsequent famine of 1972 and 1973 combined with rampant inflation to demonstrate the incapacity of Haile Selassie's regime to serve the needs of its subjects.[23] Westernization under Haile Selassie created an apparent but not a real institutional capability to cope with the severe demands imposed upon the regime by the extreme suffering of great masses of the emperor's subjects. The prevalence of traditional values in the civil service perpetuated *inter alia* the dependence of governmental functionaries upon imperial favor for their positions rather than their capacity to exert initiative in meeting the needs of the imperial subjects. The demands placed upon the regime by famine and inflation were structurally distinct from those the old regime had dealt with in the course of its development, and their potential for political trouble was not recognized because they were not presented in the familiar form of localized military resistance under the banner of a disgruntled provincial chieftain. They called for rational economic planning, efficient and timely distribution of goods and services, and informed analysis of the nature and seriousness of the problems. These capabilities were not among those enhanced by the emperor in his Westernization of the country. Foreign inquiries about the drought and famine struck a deeply traditional and responsive chord in Ethiopian political circles, however. In a few instances Ethiopian officials reacted harshly to such inquiries, dubbing them offensive foreign meddling in Ethiopia's internal affairs.[24] While the emperor and high officials practiced limited and largely symbolic charity, the drought and famine called for a massive rehabilitation of ordinary Ethiopians' standard of living.[25] Nothing in what is known of Ethiopia's political culture embraced such ideas.*

Famine and drought had not led to political revolt on other occasions in Ethiopian history. That they did so in 1974 may be partly explained by the fact that they were accompanied by inflation, reflecting Ethiopia's involvement in world economic patterns in contrast to its relative isolation during the nineteenth century and before. Like Ethiopia's pattern of Westernization under Haile

*The author had planned and received funding for such a study when the outbreak of the revolution made implementation impossible.

Selassie, inflation combined with drought to accentuate inequalities, both urban and rural. Drought-stricken rural Ethiopians were obliged to sell land to pay increasingly high prices for increasingly scarce food. Poorer landholders who sold out to larger and wealthier ones were in no position to insist on inflated prices for their land.[26] In the urban areas, food prices and rents exhibited strong inflationary tendencies while wages generally remained low. Civil servants, armed forces personnel, ministers, and parliamentarians affected by the inflation were accommodated by pay increases, but ordinary folk were not so favored.

The revolution began when the transportation workers struck because the emperor's government refused to permit fare and wage increases to compensate for an attempted 50 percent increase in the price of fuel.[27] The increase was ostensibly the result of the Arab oil boycott, but parliamentarians forced a cabinet minister to admit that it was posted because of inefficient management of Ethiopia's government-controlled oil refinery at Assab. The government retreated to a 30 percent increase, but by this time students and teachers had joined the fray over a new education policy that teachers saw as threatening to their economic interests and students considered hostile to the needs of the peasantry.[28] The government withdrew this policy, but the armed forces were now threatening the regime by mutinying in support of wage increases for themselves. Professing to be dissatisfied with the wage increases offered them by the emperor, the military units added general calls for greater political freedom, free education, land reform, price controls, and trials for corrupt government officials to their immediate economic demands.* Fearing the portent of continued discontent in the military units and hounded by worker and student demonstrations in the capital, the cabinet of Prime Minister Aklilu Habte Wold tendered its resignation.

The resignation of the Aklilu government signaled the visible beginning of the collapse of Emperor Haile Selassie's forty-four-year-old regime. This action demonstrated how the importation of Western ways had been melded with the defense of tradition to corrode the foundations of the regime, rendering it incapable of meeting the demands placed upon it by those experiencing drought, famine,

---

*The early weeks of the revolution were referred to as the "day of the pamphlet." Literally dozens of position papers were surreptitiously distributed around the city, dropped from helicopters, or distributed unofficially in some other way. From these pamphlets the early ideological drift of the revolution can be discerned.

and inflation. Referring the demands of insurgent military forces to the emperor reflected the continuing application of the traditional theory that the emperor was the fount of all political power and that his officials lacked independent delegated power—even his own cabinet, notwithstanding proclamations in 1955 and 1966.[29] They appear to have hoped and assumed that responsibility for policy outcomes would also be placed upon the emperor; in this they misjudged the intentions of the military mutineers. The resignation of the cabinet, familiar in Western countries under such circumstances, was unprecedented in Ethiopia, as traditionalists in the Council of Ministers sharply pointed out.[30] In reality, however, the Aklilu cabinet used a familiar Western procedure implicit in Ethiopia's embryonic Westminster constitutional structures to dramatize its traditional powerlessness in relation to the emperor on matters of vital importance. But in thus emphasizing tradition, the cabinet set in motion the dissolution of that tradition by breaking the bonds of personal, client-like allegiance to the emperor. The waves of strikes that followed in the next few months may be viewed as imitation of superiors—another hallowed Ethiopian tradition—in dissolving (at least in the urban areas) traditional bonds of allegiance. The strikers thus destroyed the old as they asserted the new—already implicit in the tacit acceptance of Western-style trade unions.

The government of Endalkachew Makonnen (February-July 1974) represented a futile attempt to institute long-needed reforms and to strengthen the constitutional democratic institutions already superficially functioning. In seeking Western-style reforms, this new regime collapsed under the weight of the demands placed upon it from all organized quarters—demands that may have been fueled by evidence that Westernization had corroded traditional bonds of political obligation. The Confederation of Ethiopian Labor Unions struck successfully, and a wide variety of individual employee organizations struck on their own more than once during the first six months of 1974. The demands engulfed the Endalkachew government, drowning its efforts to launch reforms that were too modest in design and too late.* A military coordinating committee emerged more or less officially representing all units, with the exception of field grade officers. This committee arrested the members of the Aklilu cabinet who had resigned, reorganized itself after Endal-

*Unpublished draft proclamations were prepared to effect (1) a land reform that would limit the size of holdings and (2) institute a revised and *somewhat* more democratic constitution. (The latter contained a long section detailing the rights of imperial succession.)

kachew tried to coopt its leaders to quell air force unrest, and then proceeded to arrest dozens of high military, judicial, civil service, parliamentary, and even clerical figures. Almost all of these surrendered voluntarily at the bidding of the coordinating committee, greatly underestimating the fundamental nature of the change in process and probably expecting that all the blame would be put on the emperor. Even parliament, dominated as it was by provincial elites, contributed to the destruction of the old order by summarily rejecting the emperor's plan for a commission of inquiry to investigate wrongdoing under the Aklilu government, substituting its own version: a commission elected by organized interests that would investigate not merely legal infractions but all acts of corruption, gross negligence, and/or self-aggrandizement.[31]

By the summer of 1974 it was clear to all observers that the ultimate target of the military coordinating committee was the emperor himself and that the question had become *when* rather than *whether* he would be deposed. The persons being arrested were closer and closer politically and personally to Haile Selassie. In August the committee shut down the emperor's *chilot* (court), wherein he played his traditional role as the final arbiter of justice, and made arrests within the palace organization itself. In the same month Endalkachew himself was arrested, and General Aman Andom emerged as Minister for Defense. A distinguished war leader from his campaigns against Somalia, an Eritrean by birth, and neither Orthodox nor Muslim but Lutheran by religion, General Aman became titular head of state when the emperor, almost anticlimactically, was deposed on September 12—a role he served in for only about two months. Because he sought to be more than a titular head of state, insisted on regular trials for those arrested, and demanded diplomatic rather than military efforts to quell Eritrean liberation groups, Aman was forced from office and executed on November 22. Nearly sixty other officials of the old regime were also executed. This move was widely believed to have been calculated to justify the "coup-within-a-coup" as a suppression of reactionary forces bent on undermining the revolutionary movement. From these dramatic events the current leader of the revolutionary government emerged—Lt. Col. Mengistu Haile Mariam.* The

---

*Mengistu was virtually unknown prior to the executions. He surfaced shortly beforehand for the first time when he took public credit for the idea of the *zemecha* (see p. 362 below), which paradoxically may have originated with the university students who initially opposed it when mandated by the derg.

major reform policies described above and the official proclamation of Ethiopia's socialist ideological course have been followed since.

The reasons the military played such a decisive role in advancing and defining the socialist ideological thrust of the Ethiopian revolution are not easy to ascertain—in part because so little has been written about the armed forces in Ethiopia.[32] A plausible hypothesis is that the military units became revolutionary because of (1) supportive traditions, (2) the symbiosis between Westernization and Ethiopian tradition that affected other sectors of Ethiopian society, (3) the mobilizational effects of entry into the armed forces at the level of the rank-and-file soldiers, (4) the resources at hand for political insurgence, and (5) the military's sense of its indispensability. Ethiopia has a long tradition of "citizen" armies mobilized by emperors and regional chieftains for internecine struggles over political power, which is distinguished from warfare in much of pre-colonial Africa by its focus on more centralized, more clearly articulated political institutions.[33] Westernization affected the armed forces in much the same way it affected Ethiopian society at large. Training facilities were established, and technical assistance and advanced equipment were provided by the United States for more than twenty years preceding the revolution, but the professionalized military did not become detached from traditional Ethiopian society. Officers were rewarded with imperial land grants roughly in proportion to their rank, and senior field grade officers were incorporated into the aristocracy—thereby preserving the traditional diffusion of military and civilian roles. Only on the eve of the revolution did Haile Selassie seek to rationalize the armed forces' rank and salary structures, betraying thereby clear evidence that imperial favor as much as competence and the responsibilities of rank determined salaries and advancement.[34] A crucial effect of Westernization upon the military was the exposure of middle- and low-ranking officers as well as the rank-and-file to significant social change. The income and benefits paid rank-and-file military men substantially exceeded those of most Ethiopians, and a great many were drawn directly from among the citizenry rather than being isolated from them by long years of education or urban residence.[35] They also acquired in varying degrees skills that in themselves were less amenable to political corruption than those of a civil servant (as distinct from the uses to which such skills might be put). As a well-trained, large, and well-financed establishment by African standards, the military possessed resources to play a substantial political role.[36] Finally, the military—both in fact and

in its perception of itself—appears to have become increasingly indispensable to the maintenance of Ethiopian national unity and the power of the emperor during the fifteen years preceding the revolution. The beginning of a prolonged conflict with Eritrean liberation groups, the persistent Somalia threat, and the use of the military in other local rebellions appear to have contributed to this result by demonstrating the inability of the Endalkachew regime to control rebellions against the central government authority.[37] This, combined with a famine relief operation necessitated by the government's previous lethargy, and competing with the army's need for transport equipment, convinced middle-range officers and men that the army would be required to replace a collapsing imperial regime.

The military coordinating committee that engineered the liquidation of the old regime's leadership cadre apparently turned to socialism for a variety of reasons, pragmatic as well as ideological. A younger generation of Ethiopians, born after World War II, took advantage of somewhat expanded educational facilities to become familiar with ideological currents diametrically opposed to the bases of Haile Selassie's regime. Censorship practiced periodically with regard to books and magazines did not extend to the Haile Selassie I University's collections of the works of Marx and his followers. Particularly after the abortive coup attempt of 1960, brands of Marxism were religiously espoused by university students. The prevalence of traditional values in the civil service and the military and the emperor's personal support for higher education did not prevent these ideas from percolating into the minds of young Ethiopians. Among African leaders, the university students were particularly attracted to the writings and practices of Tanzania's Julius Nyerere.[38] However, there is little to suggest that the new generation of Ethiopians were inspired to mount the revolution by specific socialist movements or governments abroad.

The military coordinating committee's first position papers gave little indication that after the removal of the emperor militant socialism would become the masthead of the revolution.[39] The July 1974 manifesto emphasized the idea of "Ethiopia Tikdem" (Ethiopia First)—i.e., it emphasized social and economic reform within a framework of strengthened national unity.[40] A reasonable hypothesis is that the military coordinating committee was reacting in particular to the breakdown of central government authority witnessed during Endalkachew's brief tenure as prime minister. The first clear espousal of socialism came in December 1974 after Mengistu had assumed de facto leadership of the derg.[41] Having

executed General Aman, the derg was in great need of legitimization, particularly in the minds of university and high school students whom it proposed to send on a *zemecha* (campaign) to hundreds of rural communities to preach the gospel of "Ethiopia Tikdem" and explain the revolution. At the same time, Mengistu and his associates felt the need to confirm the liquidation of the old order, having attacked Aman for insisting on fair trials for the arrested officials of the old order and for attempting to consolidate in his own hands some of the power once exercised by the emperor. The announcement that "Ethiopia Tikdem" meant "Ethiopian Socialism" was an act of creation of the design for a new order to replace the one that had been decapitated during the previous year: "Having demolished the old order it is necessary to show what political and social order takes its place. An act of demolition should immediately be followed by an act of creation. It is an unfinished job which starts with the former and shies away from the latter."[42]

The first socialist statement was very general in its formulations and moderate in its tone. It postulated as general goals the achievement of non-discrimination on the basis of sex, religion, or nationality; the creation of equality; discarding the "limitless idolatry of private gain which has chained our people to poverty and which has so humiliated our country in the eyes of the world"; "restoration" of local self-governance to the country's many communities (taken from them presumably by the centralizing proclivities of Haile Selassie); emphasis upon the dignity of work as essential to collective welfare; self-reliance; and "above all, the unity of Ethiopia as [a] sacred faith of all our people."[43] These were to be the parameters for the establishment of a political philosophy that would "spring from the culture and soil of Ethiopia . . . emanating from the aspirations of the majority of the population."[44] Anticipated results of adhering to these principles were the solution of the country's endemic problems, including the familiar triumvirate of poverty, ignorance, and disease.

The principles enunciated in the *Declaration of Economic Policy of Socialist Ethiopia*, issued shortly after the first declaration of socialist intentions, closely resemble those expressed in other African socialist manifestos. The *Declaration* concentrates on the alleviation of poverty and its underlying causes: underdevelopment of productive resources and exploitation attendant upon private ownership of property. Economic activities are classified in three categories: (1) those requiring government proprietorship, (2) those reserved to private entrepreneurs, and (3) those in which joint

enterprise would be fostered. The policy justifies nationalization of "the commanding heights" as the most appropriate technique for mobilizing popular participation in development, rationally allocating scarce economic assets, directing resources to meet the needs of the ordinary citizens rather than to satisfy the appetites of well-to-do urban elites, eliminating exploitation, and providing for workers' control of economic enterprises. More unique is the justification of nationalization as the appropriate means of guarding Ethiopia against the "vicissitudes of the capitalist economy, which cannot help but go through periodic cycles of booms and depressions with the resultant wastes."[45] The intriguing assumption of this argument is that some regimes are intrinsically better adapted to shielding constituents from hazards of the global economy than others.

This design for the creation of a socialist Ethiopia from among the ruins of the *ancien regime* subtly but clearly reflected the underlying motivations and concerns of the young revolutionary regime. Clearly troubled by Ethiopia's image as a nation isolated by its backwardness from other African and third world states, the PMG seemed anxious to bridge the gap by establishing ideological linkages with other socialist states expressed through the pursuit of common objectives by similar means. Implicit particularly in the first socialist statement is the classic tension between a focus on class and a focus on national unity as the basis for a new regime. This tension was to be more sharply defined in the April 1976 manifesto outlining the National Democratic Revolutionary Program and in subsequent events.[46] Persistent regional stirrings, never far below the surface under Haile Selassie despite his attempts to consolidate centralized authority, had become open and hostile even as the PMG attempted to stress the brotherhood of shared poverty and past oppression cross-cutting these diverse regional loyalties.* Finally, these manifestos are singularly apolitical—perhaps pre-political. They suggest the logical and temporal primacy not of politics but of ideological and socioeconomic reform, and in this create a new basis for Ethiopia's uniqueness among African and third world nations, both socialist and non-socialist. The most important domestic consequence of this revolutionary strategy has been the inability of the derg to explain and legitimize its role as the first architect of the revolution as distinct from its role as the deliverer of the country from the chains of the old order.

*Nationalist uprisings have occurred not only in the Ogaden and in Eritrea, but in several of the other provinces of the country as well. The nationalist aspect of the struggle in the Ogaden has probably been underplayed by the press.

During 1975 the derg decreed both the nationalization of major industrial and commercial firms and comprehensive rural and urban land reform measures.[47] The land reforms were more egalitarian and comprehensive than anything anticipated by the earlier policy statements on Ethiopian socialism. They created a blueprint specifying a socioeconomic transformation arguably more fundamental than any attempted elsewhere in Africa—perhaps comparing favorably in this regard even with China. In the rural areas private ownership of land was to be abolished, with usufructuary holdings limited to a maximum of ten hectares. Disposition of land was apparently to be vested in thousands of small peasant associations. The incipient agricultural proletariat was to be virtually liquidated by requiring each family to cultivate its own holdings, though in practice families were to be permitted (even encouraged) to cooperate with each other at various points in the agricultural cycle. Initial ambiguity concerning the locus of real authority for the governance of rural land has been somewhat resolved by subsequent proclamations giving increasing financial, legal, and developmental responsibility to peasant associations. These peasant associations are to participate as collectivities in larger cooperative societies.[48]

The urban land reform proclamation unambiguously stated that urban land belongs to the government.[49] Rents were to be lowered by fixed percentages, greater reductions being mandated for lower rent properties. Individuals were to be allowed ownership of a single house. The urban rentier class was to be eliminated by provisions mandating sale of "extra" houses to the government, payment of rents on expensive landholdings directly to the government, and payment of rents on cheaper properties to urban housing cooperatives. The urban housing cooperatives (*kebelles*) were to assign housing in their respective neighborhoods and to use rental incomes for neighborhood improvements in roads, schools, and other services. Land transfers of any nature other than usufructuary inheritance were proscribed under both reforms. But the two reforms did not remove all vestiges of urban-rural inequality and disparity in opportunity. Rural landlords have been granted a high priority on the acquisition of rural usufructuary rights, while the urban land reform specifies no priorities. Urban landlords were to be compensated for properties seized from them while their rural counterparts are not.[50]

The institution of the land reforms cannot be considered in isolation from the political structure of the revolutionary regime

in which they were launched.* While seeking to liberate rural and urban masses from their previous oppression through these reforms, the derg has been attempting simultaneously to establish its own political legitimacy and generate a political constituency to sustain its enterprises on behalf of the revolution. The preliminary indications have been that the derg has been far more successful in selling the reforms themselves than in building a political base for itself on the foundation of their popularity. Crucial to the implementation of the rural land reform proclamation was the launching of the zemecha—the campaign of more than forty thousand students and teachers to explain and implement the reforms as well as stimulate revolutionary consciousness throughout rural Ethiopia. The zemecha campaigners often were involved in a three-way struggle for power in the local communities where they worked —competing not only with local landlords but frequently with the local officials of the central government as well. The destruction of the old regime by arresting and in some cases executing its high officials did not automatically result in the disarming of local and provincial elites, and these continued to resist the new regime. Moreover, the loyalties of the local governmental officials were often in question because some were themselves landholders and identified in other ways with local elite groups.

The results of this struggle varied from locale to locale, though in general the response to land reform was more positive in the southern regions brought into the empire by Menelik's conquests than in the northern areas of the ancient kingdom.[51] However, in a number of instances the derg stood with the local officials against the zemecha students' rush to collectivize landholding.[52] In opting for stability over revolutionary change, the derg alienated many of the students who were loyal to the Ethiopian Peoples Revolutionary Party (EPRP), which opposed the derg from the left. Since the peasant associations came into existence in 1976 and 1977, the derg appears to have made numerous attempts to coopt the loyalties of the associations' elected officials; in so doing, it has in many instances apparently weakened these officials' standing in their own communities.[53] The fledgling peasant associations, already burdened with heavy responsibilities for implementing land reform and instigating local development efforts, have thereby been further strained by the PMG's attempt to marshal their support

*Analyses of the land reforms so far have per force been legal and policy-focused. A full political analysis of the reforms' implementation awaits calmer times in the country.

for the revolutionary political movement it seeks to build. Furthermore, in rural areas there have been persistent reports that alleged saboteurs of the revolution have been arrested or shot summarily, instilling an environment of fear that has undermined local leadership initiatives in implementing land and related rural reforms. Finally, there are indications that in yielding to peasant pressures for arms to combat counterrevolutionary activities of former landlords, the derg may have begun to lose control over the rural revolution. With their own defense committees, peasant associations have been enabled to control passage through their territories and resist the government as well as the remaining provincial elites. With varying degrees of success, the PMG has sought to use peasant associations and urban associations as draft boards for its Eritrean and Somali wars. In short, the derg appears to have generated considerable grass roots support for its land reforms while experiencing great difficulty in building political support for its nominally transitional leadership of the revolution.

In its struggle to build a political constituency, the derg has fared little better in the cities. Urban land reform has been implemented in Addis Ababa, for example, by the creation of a great many kebelles, which have taken responsibility for allocating rental properties. This program has not enabled the derg to quell the very potent opposition to its rule in the cities. The EPRP has been particularly strong in the cities and towns, partly because of alienated students returning there from zemecha assignments, but working-class support for the PMG has not been forthcoming because the workers have perceived only small economic gains from the revolution. Urban workers have received nothing to compare with increased land tenure security gained by the peasants. On more than one occasion, strikes have been forcibly suppressed, and there has been considerable bloodshed in the cities resulting from the derg's attempts to suppress the EPRP, which has alienated middle class and professional groups. Even the specter of residual royalist opposition under the banner of the Ethiopian Democratic Union (EDU) has not been sufficient to rally support for the derg from students and working-class groups that are the traditional constituency of socialist movements.

The National Democratic Revolutionary Program (NDRP), promulgated by the derg in April 1976, represented a major offensive to set in motion processes that would result in the emergence of viable political leadership for the revolution.[54] The essence of the program was not the creation of the political movement

itself, but the specification of guidelines within which the movement was to develop. The NDRP called upon the masses to unite in opposition to enemy forces: feudalism, imperialism, and bureaucratic capitalism.[55] Mengistu conceived feudalism to be the absence of political unity, signified by internecine warfare, and accompanied by socioeconomic stagnation, with little or no popular political participation. He emphasized the symbiosis of imperialism and feudalism, particularly in post-World War II Ethiopia; together they resulted in "a social order based on classes of exploiters and exploited." Bureaucratic capitalists corrupted the emperor's state capitalism, forming a class that was "an integral part of the ruling class and control[ed] the means of production to satisfy its exploitative appetite as an exploiting class."[56] The emphasis on bureaucratic capitalism is of considerable significance to the meaning of socialist politics in Ethiopia. Whereas Marx argued that the proletariat is a creation of capitalism, and other African socialist writers have stressed the creation of exploitation under colonialism, Mengistu seems to believe that the Ethiopian masses had made little or no progress since European medieval times. Imperialism and bureaucratic capitalism only intensified exploitation of very long standing. Where other African socialist writers have sought to restore traditions shattered by colonialism, Mengistu finds few customs deserving of rehabilitation to be employed as building blocks for a new political order. Only the masses per se—not their customs—appear worthy of the new era. The reference in the December 1974 manifesto to the restoration of local traditions of self-governance was not repeated in the NDRP.

A major premise of the NDRP is that religious, nationality, and sex discrimination practiced in pre-revolutionary times are secondary problems soluble by forming a united front to attack the primary problems of bureaucratic capitalism, feudalism, and imperialism.[57] In this regard the NDRP perhaps constituted a desperate diplomatic overture to nationalist and/or secessionist groups in the various provinces, most notably Eritrea. The NDRP proposes that peoples united by opposition to the primary enemies can permit constituent communities a considerable measure of autonomy. The derg has consistently sought to appeal to the Eritrean people over the heads of Eritrean Liberation Front cadres on just these grounds. But Eritrea has not been the only source of separatist nationalism within the country: Afar pastoralists, located along the crucial highway link between Addis Ababa and the post of Assab, were never content under Haile Selassie's regime, and have formed their own liberation

group since the revolution, inspired in part by the forcing of their sultan into exile.[58] In 1977 competition between Somalia and Ethiopia flared into military combat for control of the Ogaden desert, sparsely populated by pastoralists of Somali origin. Nationalist outcroppings have been reported in a number of other provinces as well.

In late 1978 it was not clear that the derg's attempt to rally the masses against common class enemies would finally prevail over these resurgent separatist tendencies, because socioeconomic change did not proceed far enough under Haile Selassie for class consciousness to counteract rooted parochial ethnic allegiances. Nevertheless, the NDRP promised the "right of nationalities for local autonomy to be implemented in a democratic way."[59] Moreover, the NDRP promised special consideration for the political, social, and economic needs of "small nationalities scattered along the border areas"—surely a reference to the Afar, the Somali, and perhaps the Nilotic groups on the frequently troubled Sudanese border. The NDRP also guaranteed that strategies would be formulated "on a priority basis so that these nationalities [will become] equal participants in the political, economic, and social processes prevailing among other nationalities."[60] Left to conjecture has been the bearing of these undertakings on land tenure relationships. The Afar, for example, have long sought recognition of their traditional sultanate as the proprietor of the pastoral and delta land within their sphere of influence.[61] The NDRP and subsequent statements have failed to clarify whether the derg intends to recognize this claim, notwithstanding the presence within this area of major plantations upon which Ethiopia's economy is dependent.[62] The rural land reform offered pastoralists only "possessory rights" over their grazing lands, and the legal strength of such rights remains dubious.[63]

The NDRP relied upon the full implementation of its announced reforms to mobilize the peoples of Ethiopia for the political phase of the revolution. It was assumed that the urban and rural land reforms, along with the nationalization of industries, would release previously stifled creative energies by eliminating the prerevolutionary superstructure identified as imperial, feudal, and bureaucratic capitalist. Upon the validity of this assumption depended not only the mobilization of popular support for the revolution's political phase, but also the possibility of a general rise in the standard of living:

Since the raising of the standard of living of the broad masses and the country's progress as a whole depends on the struggle and determination of the masses, people must be mobilized from one end of the country to the other to work hard and increase production.[64]

Particularly noteworthy is the NDRP's approach to education for socialist Ethiopia. The program provides for free education both for the benefit of the people and the furtherance of the political revolution. Education is to serve "all the children of the broad masses" and to "spark off the flame of the struggle against feudalism, bureaucratic capitalism and imperialism," it is to be both practical and theoretical, and it is to prevent "imperialist inroads and reactionary tampering" with Ethiopian cultures whose vitality is of great importance: "No effort will be spared in developing and enriching these cultures along modern lines."[65] The NDRP honors rather than attacks cultural diversity. In the last days of Haile Selassie's regime, his government endorsed an educational reform program calling for a slowdown in the rate of increasing access to higher education in favor of practical education for the masses.[66] This new policy appeared to be an attack on the students and teachers for their opposition to Haile Selassie's regime, as well as a means of encouraging acceptance of the rural political and economic status quo. The NDRP proposes to do more than restore the balance between elite and mass education: it appears to call for universal education—cultural and political, as well as practical.

The architects of Ethiopian socialism have experienced a set of contradictions arising from their wish both to adhere to their understanding of orthodox Marxism and to reconcile this ideological rigor with the realities of their country's present circumstances. Nowhere is this problem more evident than in the NDRP's specification that the new political order shall be "under proletarian leadership in close collaboration [with] farmers and the support of the petit-bourgeois, anti-feudalist, and anti-imperialist forces."[67] The NDRP encourages the formation of political parties that are eventually to be united under a popular revolutionary front.[68] While the proletariat is assigned the primary responsibility for revolutionary political leadership, recognition is also given to revolutionary parties mobilizing other progressive classes and democratic parties opposed to the principal enemies of pre-revolutionary origin. Thus the NDRP refers to the masses in two senses: one undifferentiated and egalitarian, the other differentiated and hierarchical. Though frequent references are made to turning the economic and political

control of the country over to the "broad masses," at the same time it is proposed to create a hierarchy of classes within the revolution. The assignment of revolutionary leadership to the "working class," as distinct from the peasantry and other groups, suggests the continued political primacy of urban Ethiopia over the vastly larger rural sector, notwithstanding the assertion in the NDRP that agricultural development will command top priority in the allocation of financial and manpower resources.[69] (The gap between the standard of living in urban and rural areas was a significant aspect of the general and deplorable inequality characterizing pre-revolutionary Ethiopia.) Working-class political preeminence fits uneasily with the derg's apparent wish to recognize large measures of autonomy for constituent nationalities, because these nationalities are by no means equally distributed throughout the country's urban centers and among the working-class personnel. Similarly, there is a tension between the specification of a leadership cadre and the NDRP's commitment to a revolution that is democratic in character, one that "aims at crushing feudalism and bureaucratic capitalism in order to transfer ownership of land and other vital means of production to the broad masses as well as giving them democratic rights—freedom of the press, speech, assembly, and organization, etc."[70]

The derg appears to have aimed the revolution's social and economic reforms more directly at the peasantry than at the urban working class. The wage increases achieved by the workers in the general strike in early 1974 have been less significant economically than the increased control over land gained by the peasants. The derg has been more restrictive of labor's right to strike than was the previous regime, which accepted (albeit grudgingly) occasional strikes. The size and geographical scope of the working class have been restricted by the abolition of hired agricultural labor under the rural land reform. On the other hand, the urban land reform proclamation has benefitted the urban working classes by reducing residential rents and establishing neighborhood control of rental property. But these benefits, while important, may not compare favorably in an economic sense with the gains of the peasants under the rural land reform. The labor union confederation, reorganized more than once under the derg's leadership, provides a possible organizational basis for the generation of a revolutionary political party, but it is not clear that the new leadership of union confederation has been any more free of attempted manipulation by the derg (with comparable negative effects on the union's legitimacy)

than the peasant associations in the rural areas. In short, the Ethiopian proletariat does not appear to have acquired an economic stake in the revolution corresponding to its assigned ideological importance; consequently, its willingness to be the political sponsor of the revolution as designed by the derg has remained in doubt.

Perhaps the most crucial feature of the NDRP is the process proposed for creating the revolutionary political movement, because it touches for the first time on the derg's role. First, the program assigns the armed forces a dual role: (1) guardian of the revolution against domestic and foreign enemies and (2) catalyst in the processes of generating social and economic change in line with the planned reforms.[71] Members of the armed forces are to be trained for the latter purpose. During 1977 the domestic role of the military focused less on spearheading the land reforms, for example, than on assisting in the formation of peasant association defense committees. There is some reason to believe that the derg may have contemplated blurring the distinction between professional soldiers and peasant militia by assigning small cadres of trained soldiers on a regular basis to these defense leagues. If that occurs the peasant associations will be subject to yet another claim on their limited administrative resources: defense of the realm will compete for the energies of the peasants with organizing primary education facilities, political mobilization, administration of land tenure arrangements, adjudication of land disputes, and formation of cooperative societies for economic development.

Second, the NDRP anticipates that with the formation of the People's Revolutionary Front the provisional military leadership of the revolution will come to an end.[72] To facilitate the eventual "transfer of power," the NDRP establishes a People's Organizing Provisional Office (POPO) to liaise between the derg and the embryonic political movement. Among its responsibilities are to be political education, analysis of current developments, ideological instruction, catalyzing political organization, and training revolutionary cadres. POPO branches are to be organized in all the country's administrative subdivisions. This "politburo" is charged with preparing directives "in accordance with which democratic rights can be enforced," supervising the Democratic Rights Proclamation (forthcoming), and overseeing generally the implementation of the NDRP, including its translation.

The POPO appears to be of critical importance in the PMG's political strategy for creating a socialist Ethiopia. POPO is to be the instrument by which Ethiopians are instructed in the authoritative

allocation of social values within a framework of revolutionary reforms previously established, and the posited objective of a working class-led People's Democratic Republic. At the same time POPO is to be the means by which the PMG hopes to establish its own political legitimacy for the duration of its transitional regime. The creation of POPO indeed clearly casts the PMG in a role of transitional leadership for the first time, anticipating the military's future roles as guardian of the revolution against counterrevolutionaries and external enemies and catalyst in processes of socialist economic development and social change.

Since the creation of POPO, the derg's attempts to build a political movement have been extremely troubled. The principal parties seeking to cooperate with the derg in organizing the revolution's political dimension—Meison and then Revolutionary Flame—have fallen out of favor with the derg. Many of Meison's members joined the opposition being led by the EPRP. Even a military-based movement such as Revolutionary Flame has been unable to work effectively with Mengistu, so great has been the level of distrust. The derg in 1977 and 1978, while fighting wars in the Ogaden and in Eritrea, has worked directly to coopt the leadership groups of the urban *kebelles* and the rural peasant associations, trained and indoctrinated new administrative cadres through the Yekatit 66 school, propagandized, terrorized, "rehabilitated," and imprisoned or executed emerging grass roots leadership cadres in a momentous struggle to build a foundation for the revolution and/or the derg's leadership. During 1978 the terror dimension has been less in evidence, in part because Mengistu appears to have consolidated his power within the derg in relation to most of his known challengers—particularly Atnafu Abate, his former lieutenant, who was executed in November 1977.

III

Ethiopian socialism is clearly a singular concept within the family of socialist ventures. It embraces social and economic reforms as fundamental and comprehensive as any attempted elsewhere on the African continent, but its real distinctiveness is in its political dimensions. Ethiopian socialism seeks socioeconomic equality and a political regime directly derived from the collective power of the people. In this, Ethiopian socialism is at one with other socialist movements. In its assertion of working-class leadership within the political movement of revolutionary Ethiopian classes, Ethiopian

socialism is more problematically orthodox than most other African socialist movements. In the creation of thousands of urban coopera- tives and rural peasant associations, Ethiopian socialism follows the Chinese pattern more closely than other African socialist ideologies, with the possible exceptions of Tanzania and Guinea. In the creation of the zemecha, the derg harnessed the energies of its educated youth more fully than contemplated elsewhere in Africa other than in Somalia and Tanzania.

The basic political strategy of the Ethiopian socialist revolution has few parallels in the annals of socialist and/or revolutionary politics. First, political change has followed rather than preceded the inauguration of socioeconomic changes, so that it has focused more on consolidation of reforms than on promising them, placing the derg itself in an ambiguous political position as a nominally "provisional" regime. Second, military socialism itself has few paral- lels. In the merging of defense and developmental roles contemplated in the NDRP, indicated by recent developments in the country and in the use of military force as a surrogate for political processes both domestically and within the Horn of Africa, the derg has dramatically raised an important problem for socialist movements: the reconciliation of socioeconomic and political idealism with the practical problem of maintaining and exercising the power to imple- ment such ideals. Third, the military has assigned itself the role of "tutor" in the political phase of the Ethiopian revolution. In this, Ethiopian socialism raises on the African continent a fundamental, original issue of socialism first posed by Lenin's revolution: the legitimation of a transitional regime standing between the unwanted past and the promised land and coping with practical problems of political power not examined in the original blueprint.

The political strategy of the Ethiopian revolution, in addition to its other uniquenesses, represents an entirely novel approach to political modernization within the Ethiopian framework. (1) The creation of effective specialized institutions for the conduct of political decision-making and the training of political cadres in post- revolutionary Ethiopia will be without precedent, if realized. Left unanswered to date has been the question whether political roles and institutions will be differentiated or diffuse, coopted to lending political legitimacy to a transitional military regime just as embryon- ic pre-revolutionary institutions were captured by the old order. (2) The political strategy of the Ethiopian revolution embraces a radically different approach to the building of political capability, another generally accepted tenet of modernization. In pre-revolu-

tionary Ethiopia, the emphasis was upon building such capacity through territorial expansion and centralization of political authority. The theory of the NDRP is that political capacity should be founded upon the mobilization of the masses rather than their subordination by conquest, upon decentralization of decision-making to constituent nationalities rather than their acquiescence to the strengthened power of the central government. (3) Where the "masses" remained spectators to political life concentrated on a very small stage around the imperial office, the PMG in its land reforms and subsequent proclamations has emphasized the self-governance of the masses at the local level more than the creation of a central government responsive to their needs. Perhaps in pragmatic recognition of its limited resources, the PMG has to some degree attempted to finesse the need to formulate processes for input of demand and for output generation, one consequence of which is the lack of processes for the generation of political support for the derg's own measures. It remains to be seen whether the derg will be able to refrain from relying upon the old regime's means of generating political capability as it fights to prevent nationalist stirrings in Eritrea, the Ogaden, and elsewhere from resulting in secession and the dismemberment of Ethiopia. In seeking to create a basis for political identity common to the country as a whole (another facet of modernization), the derg proposes its blueprint for Ethiopian socialism.

In contrast to other socialist plans in Africa, Ethiopian socialism is perhaps less avowedly secular than multi-religious in design. The derg has not attempted to undermine the Orthodox Church, although the Orthodox patriarch was replaced. Indeed Mengistu himself and most of the derg are practicing church members. But the NDRP contemplates the recognition of Islam on an equal footing with Christianity and the coexistence of religions under a regime dedicated to socialist principles. Indeed the promulgation of an Ethiopian socialist ideology represents perhaps the first occasion in Ethiopian history when socioeconomic and political institutions have been subjected to an explicitly stated set of guidelines. However, it remains unclear whether and how Ethiopian socialism is to gain legitimacy and institutionalization, given the distractions of military and political struggle in Ethiopia and the Horn.

By late 1977 the whole future of the Ethiopian socialist revolutionary experiment under military auspices was in question. The integrity of the long-heralded and apparently popular socioeconomic reforms is in doubt because the reforms appear to have been founded upon shifting political sands. In seeking to remove pre-revolutionary

elites and imperial structures from Ethiopian political life, the derg may have unleashed parochial nationalist sentiments that were submerged but not extinguished by the regimes of Menelik and Haile Selassie. The reforms of the derg, especially the rural land reform and the zemeche campaign undertaken in the name of Ethiopian socialism, may have stimulated local nationalism instead. The recognition of such sentiments in the NDRP, justified by sentiments of socialist tolerance and the derg's own precarious political position, may presage less rather than more national unity, contrary to the derg's hope and belief. The serious challenges to the country's unity posed by the Eritrean and Somalia secessionist struggles in particular may indicate more than the temporary diversion of resources from reform to defense of the state against "foreign" attack. As occurred under the reigns of Tewodros, Johannes IV, and Menelik II, the Ethiopian nation state may again require rebuilding by military means as a precondition for the mobilization of political resources in the cause of social and economic progress.

On the other hand, the possibility exists that, despite the limitations of the pre-revolutionary regime and the strategic difficulties of the MPG's tenure, the roots of Ethiopian nationhood are deeper than one might assume them to be. Perhaps the peoples of Ethiopia have absorbed and refined common traditions over generations of imperial rule so that they stand independently of their origins in the military struggles of Ethiopian princes. What appear to be fissiparous political tendencies may augur not the dismemberment of the country but simply the twilight of the revolution's first phase and perhaps the rule of this particular provisional military regime. Out of the interplay of nationalisms, founded on interwoven political traditions and the shared inspiration of socialist vision, may yet emerge an integrating political movement that will be able to build according to the specifications of contemporary blueprints for Ethiopian socialism.

NOTES

Ann Seidman: African Socialism and the World System

1. A. Seidman, "Old Motives, New Methods: Foreign Enterprise in Africa Today?" in *African Perspectives*, eds. R.W. Johnson and C.H. Allen (Cambridge: Cambridge University Press, 1970).

2. T. Szentes, "Nature and Effects of the Unfolding Crisis Phenomena in International Capitalism, *Acta Oeconomica* 14 (1974): 335-54; see also D. Babatunde Thomas, *Importing Technology into Africa* (New York: Praeger, 1976).

3. For discussion, see A. Seidman, *Planning for Development in Subsaharan Africa* (New York: Praeger, 1974), ch. 2. For annual earnings for these commodities, see International Monetary Fund, *International Financial Statistics*, by country.

4. For discussion of the historical development of this competition, see S. Amin, *Accumulation on a World Scale: A Critique of the Theory of Underdevelopment* (New York: Monthly Review, 1974).

5. E.g., U.S. Department of Commerce, *Current Survey of Business*, August 1975.

6. R. Barnett and R.E. Muller, *Global Reach: The Power of the Multinational Corporations* (New York: Simon and Schuster, 1974), esp. pp. 239-45, 141-42.

7. A. Seidman, *Planning for Development*, ch. 2; for specific discussion of transnational copper companies, see A. Seidman, ed., *National Resources and National Welfare: The Case of Copper* (New York: Praeger, 1976).

8. *Ibid.*

9. Detailed in A. Seidman, "Import-Substitution Industrialization: The Zambian Case," *Journal of Modern African Studies* 13, 4.

10. This is often reinforced by foreign funding agencies; e.g., see World Bank International Development Association, *Annual Report, 1970*.

11. See M. Lofchie, "Political and Economic Origins of African Hunger," *Journal of Modern African Studies* 13 (1975): 551, and N. Ball, "Understanding the Causes of African Famine," *ibid.* 14 (1976): 517.

12. R. Sklar refers to them as the "managerial bourgeoisie" (*Corporate Power in an African State: The Political Impact of Multinational Mining Companies in Zambia* [Los Angeles: University of California Press, 1975], p. 199).

13. *New York Times*, April 19, 1977.

14. E.g., A. Seidman, "The 'Have—Have-Not' Gap in Zambia" (Lusaka: University of Zambia, 1974; mimeo).

15. South African Reserve Bank, *Second Census of Foreign Transactions and Liabilities, December 31, 1973* (Pretoria: Government Printers, 1976). See also United Nations, Economic and Social Council, Commission on Transnational Corporations, "Activities of Transnational Corporations in Southern Africa and the Extent of Their Collaboration with the Illegal Regimes in the Area" (E/C.10/26, 6 April 1977), and A. and N. Seidman,

Southern Africa and U.S. Multinationals (Westport, Conn.: Lawrence Hill, 1977; Dar es Salaam: Tanzania Publishing House, 1977).

16. All data relating to U.S. corporate investment in South Africa, unless otherwise identified, are from the U.S. Department of Commerce, *Survey of Current Business*, August 1976.

17. For data, see International Monetary Fund, *Annual Reports*; for general discussion, see A. Seidman, *Planning for Development*, ch. 2; for examples of copper producing countries, see A. Seidman, ed., *Natural Resources and National Welfare.*

18. P.A. Wellons, *Borrowing by Developing Countries on the Euro-Currency Market* (Paris: Development Centre of the Organization for Economic Cooperation and Development, 1977).

19. M. Odjagov, "Transnational Banking" (paper prepared for the Development Centre of Organization for Economic Cooperation and Development, 1977; mimeo).

20. Wellons, *Borrowing by Developing Countries*, p. 117.

21. *New York Times*, May 15, 1977, and C.F. Bergsten, G. Berthoin, and K. Mushakaj, "The Reform of International Institutions," *The Triangle Papers* (New York: Trilateral Commission, May 9-11, 1976).

22. See A. Cabral, *Revolution in Guinea*, and *African People's Struggle* (London, 1969).

23. R. Sandbrook and R. Cohen, *The Development of an African Working Class: Studies in Class Formation and Action* (Toronto: University of Toronto Press, 1975).

24. See A. Seidman, *Planning for Development*, passim.

25. K. Levine, "The TANU Ten-House Cell System," in *Socialism in Tanzania: An Interdisciplinary Reader*, Vol. 1: *Politics*, eds. L. Cliffe and J.S. Saul (Nairobi: East African Publishing House, 1972). The problems of ten-house cell leaders are also discussed in K.K.S. Musoke, "The Establishment of Ujamaa Villages in Bukoba Rigazi (Nyerere) Village: A Case Study" (March 1970), in *A Collection of Essays on Ujamaa Villages* (Dar es Salaam: University of Dar es Salaam, Political Science Department, March 1971), and A. Nimtz, "Ten-House Cell Leaders as an Index of Political Change: The Case of Bagamoyo"; J.F. O'Barr, "TANU Cells and Their Leaders: The Pare Case"; and J. Samoff, "Agents of Change-Cell Leaders in an Urban Setting" —papers presented to African Studies Association, 14th annual meeting, November 3-6, 1971, Denver, Colorado.

26. See I.G. Shivji, *The Silent Class Struggle* (Dar es Salaam: Tanzania Publishing House, 1973).

27. *The Arusha Declaration* (Dar es Salaam, 1967).

28. R.B. Seidman, *The State, Law and Development* (London: Croom Helm, 1978), ch. 16.

29. J. Rweyemamu, *Underdevelopment and Industrialization in Tanzania: A Study of Perverse Industrial Development* (Nairobi: Oxford University Press, 1973), p. 138.

30. B. Mramba and B. Mwansasu, "Management for Socialist Development in Tanzania," *African Review* 37 (1972): 33.

31. *Ibid.*, p. 38.

32. *Ibid.*, pp. 38-39.

33. See T. Szentes, *Economic Policy and Implementation Problems in Tanzania: A Case Study* (Budapest, 1970), p. 14.

34. Presidential Circular, No. 1 (Dar es Salaam), 1970; K.F. Ileti, "Post-Mwongozo Workers' Disputes in Tanzania: The Case Studies," *East African Law Journal* 7 (1974): 157.

35. Mramba and Mwansasu, "Management for Socialist Development in Tanzania," and Ileti: "Post-Mwongozo Workers' Disputes" and "Labour Unrest and the Result for Workers' Control in Tanzania: Three Case Studies," *East African Law Journal* 7 (1974).

36. J. Loxley and J.S. Saul, "The Political Economy of the Parastatals," *East African Law Review* 9 (1972): 12-13.

37. K.E. Svendsen, "Decision-Making in the National Development Corporation," *Economic Research Bureau (Restricted) Paper 68.4* (Dar es Salaam: University College, 1968); reprinted in L. Cliffe and J. Saul, eds., *Socialism in Tanzania*, pp. 89, 90; see also Rweyemamu, *Underdevelopment and Industrialization in Tanzania*.

38. Tanzania, *Second Five Year Plan for Economic and Social Development (1969-1974)* (Dar es Salaam: Government Printer, 1972).

39. This goal was laid down in the early stage of the National Development Corporation creation (*Tanzania Industrial Development Corporation, 1964*), and was reiterated by the President in the late 1960's; see Svendsen, "Decision-Making in the NDC."

40. E. Penrose, "Some Problems of Policy in the Management of the Parastatal Sector in Tanzania: A Comment," *African Review* 1 (1972): 50.

41. International Bank for Reconstruction and Development, *Economic Development in Tanganyika* (Dar es Salaam: Government Printer, 1960).

42. International Monetary Fund, *International Financial Statistics* (Washington, August 1977), pp. 342-43.

43. When the IMF provides credit to a given country, it may also require that it pursue policies considered essential to restore its balance-of-payments equilibrium (see C. Payer, *The Debt Trap: The IMF and the Third World* [Penguin, 1974]).

44. A. Seidman, *Ghana's Development Experience, 1955-1965* (Nairobi: East African Publishing House—forthcoming).

45. Ghana, *Economic Survey, 1966* (Accra: Government Printing Office, 1966).

46. K. Amoako-Atta, *Budget Speech, 1966*; reported in *Ghana Daily Gazette*, February 23, 1966.

47. A. Seidman, *Planning for Development*, contrasts their experiences and policies.

48. See Nkrumah's retrospective analyses in his *Dark Days in Ghana* and *Class Struggle in Africa*.

49. M. Missiaen, *Algeria's Agricultural Economy in Brief* (Economic Research Service, U.S. Department of Agriculture, Foreign Region Analysis Division, May 1970). See also A. Krieger, *Les premices d'une reforme agraire en Algérie*, summarized in International Institute for Labour Studies, International Educational Materials Exchange, FSAF IV/July, 1966; and Secretariat Social d'Algér, *Information Rapide, Dossier sur l'enterprise agricole autoger* (Algiers, November-December 1964).

50. République Algeriénne Démocratique et Populaire, *Plan Quadriennal 1970-1973—Rapport Général* (Algiers, 1970); and *Plan Quadriennal 1974-1977—Rapport Général* (Algiers, 1974).

51. For Algeria's foreign liabilities, see International Monetary Fund, *International Financial Statistics* (Washington, D.C., August 1977), pp. 40-41; see also Economist Intelligence Unit, *Quarterly Economic Review of Algeria*, 2nd Quarter 1977, p. 17.

52. See République Algeriénne Démocratique et Populaire, *Plan Quadriennal, 1974-1977—Rapport General*, for discussion of current strategy.

53. See Economist Intelligence Unit, *Quarterly Economic Review of Angola, Mozambique*, 1st Quarter 1977, for survey of current situation.

54. *New York Times*, December 5, 1977: "Angola Moves Towards Marxist Rule."

55. S. Machel, *The Tasks Ahead; Selected Speeches of Samora Moises Machel*, ed. by Afro-American Information Services (New York, 1975); see also S. Machel, *Establacer poder para servir as masses* (Lisboa: Publicacoes Nova Aurora, 1974).

56. *The Times* (London), February 9, 1977; see also *News Agencies*, February 7, 1977 (reported in *Africa Research Bulletin* 14, 2 (March 15, 1977); Economist Intelligence Unit, *Quarterly Economic Review: Angola and Mozambique*, 1st Quarter 1977, p. 13.

57. M.T. Kaufman, "Relic of Colonialism Still in Mozambique," *New York Times*, November 20, 1977; see also P. Pringle, "Mozambique's Task," *New York Times*, December 1, 1977. These measures are outlined in Frelimo, *III Congresso da Frelimo-Directivas Economicas e Sociais* (Maputo: Cento de Documentacao e Informacao do Banco de Mocambique, 1977).

58. *Africa Diary* 16, 23 (June 3-9, 1976) and *Africa Diary* 16, 41 (October 7-13, 1976). A number of large agricultural companies have been nationalized, however, and the workers are involved in their management (*Africa Diary* 16, 30 [July 22-28, 1976]).

59. Economist Intelligence Unit, *Quarterly Economic Review* 4 (1977): 13-14.

60. United Nations, Economic and Social Council, Commission on Transnational Corporations, "Activities of Transnational Corporations in Southern Africa"; see also Seidman and Seidman, *Southern Africa and U.S. Multinationals*.

61. *Ibid.*

62. *Africa Magazine*, No. 67, March 1977.

63. "U.S. Corporate Interests in South Africa" (Subcommittee on African Affairs, Committee on Foreign Relations, United States Senate [Washington, D.C., 1977]).

64. "Black Nations Urge UN to Adopt Economic Curbs on South Africa," *New York Times*, November 15, 1977.

65. *South African Financial Mail*, November 2, 1976.

Dean E. McHenry, Jr.: The Struggle for Rural Socialism in Tanzania

1. Julius K. Nyerere, *The Arusha Declaration: Ten Years After* (Dar es Salaam: Government Printer, 1977), p. 1.

2. J.K. Nyerere, "Ujamaa—The Basis of African Socialism," in Nyerere, *Freedom and Unity* (London: Oxford University Press, 1966), pp. 162-71.

3. *Ibid.*, p. 170.

4. Fred G. Burke, "Tanganyika: The Search for Ujamaa," in *African Socialism*, eds. William H. Friedland and Carl Rosberg, Jr. (Stanford: Stanford University Press, 1964), p. 207.

5. Cranford Pratt, *The Critical Phase in Tanzania 1945-1968: Nyerere and the Emergence of a Socialist Strategy* (Cambridge: Cambridge University Press, 1976), p. 229—a definitive study.

6. J.K. Nyerere, "The Arusha Declaration," in Nyerere, *Freedom and Socialism* (Dar es Salaam: Oxford University Press, 1968), pp. 231-50.

7. Issa G. Shivji, *Class Struggles in Tanzania* (Dar es Salaam: TPH, 1975), p. 79.

8. Pratt, p. 242.

9. *Ibid.*, pp. 239-42.

10. J.K. Nyerere, "Socialism and Rural Development," in Nyerere, *Freedom and Socialism*, pp. 337-66.

11. *Daily News* (Dar es Salaam), 24 January 1975, p. 4, and Ralph Ibbott, "The Disbanding of the Ruvuma Development Association in Tanzania," November 1969 [mimeo].

12. Nyerere, "Socialism and Rural Development," p. 357.

13. Nikos Georgulas, "Settlement Patterns and Rural Development in Tanganyika," *Occasional Paper No. 29*, Program of Eastern African Studies (Syracuse, May 1967), p. 28.

14. J.K. Nyerere, "President's Inaugural Address," in Nyerere, *Freedom and Unity*, p. 184.

15. Nyerere, "Socialism and Rural Development," p. 357.

16. J.K. Nyerere, "Presidential Circular No. 1 of 1969," in *Rural Cooperation in Tanzania*, eds. Lionel Cliffe et al. (Dar es Salaam: TPH, 1975), p. 29.

17. Total rural population figures are from Tanzania, *Quarterly Statistical Bulletin*, Vol. XXVI, No. 1 (June 1975), Table 1, and projections based on those figures. Figures for the population in government-recognized villages (identified as Ujamaa villages until 1975) are from the following sources: Estimate(s) for early 1969: A.O. Ellman, "Progress and Prospects in Ujamaa Development in Tanzania," paper given at East African Agricultural Economic Society Conference, Dar es Salaam, 31 March to 4 April 1970, p. 4; for end of 1969: *Nationalist* (Dar es Salaam), 8 May 1971, p. 4; for 1970-74: Sehemu ya Mipango na Utafiti Kikundi cha Takwimu, ofisi ya Waziri Mkuu na Makamu wa Pili wa Rais, *Maendeleo ya Vijiji vya Ujamaa* (Dar es Salaam: National Printing Company, 1974), Table 2.1; for 1975: Francis Fanvel Lyimo, "Problems and Prospects of Ujamaa Development in Moshi District" (M.A. thesis, University of Dar es Salaam), p. 11; for 1976: *Daily News*, 29 December 1976, p. 1.

18. Nyerere, "Presidential Circular No. 1 of 1969," p. 27.

19. Pius Msekwa, "Towards Party Supremacy: The Changing Pattern of Relationship between the National Assembly and the National Executive Committee of TANU Before and After 1965" (M.A. thesis, University of Dar es Salaam, 1974), p. 60.

20. J.K. Nyerere, "Hotuba ya Rais wa Chama Kwenye Mkutano Mkuu wa TANU wa 16," in TANU, *Maendeleo ni Kazi* (Dar es Salaam, 1973), p. 23.

21. Press Release A/2944/73, 6 November 1973.

22. *Uhuru* (Dar es Salaam), 8 November 1973, p. 6. Emphasis in original.

23. *Daily News* (Dar es Salaam), 5 December 1975, p. 5.

24. Nyerere, *The Arusha Declaration: Ten Years After*, p. 43.

25. Based on estimate of twenty such villages in late 1960's cited in Roger Lewin and Griffiths L. Cunningham, "The Prospects for Ujamaa Villages," in *Self-Reliant Tanzania*, eds. K.E. Svendsen and M. Teisen (Dar es Salaam: TPH, 1969), p. 277, and government estimate of about 200 total villages.

26. "Maendeleo ya Vijiji vya Ujamaa" (District Cooperative Office [Kondoa]: RD/KD/VVV/G, n.d.).

27. "Hatua za Kuendeleza Vijiji vya Ujamaa Mkoa wa Iringa," (DCO [Iringa], n.d.).

28. Substantial diversity of interpretation was similarly found by Burke, pp. 195-204.

29. Tanzania, *The Economic Survey and Annual Plan, 1970-71* (Dar es Salaam: Government Printer, 1970), p. 24.

30. Tanzania, *Villages and Ujamaa Villages (Registration, Designation and Administration) Act*, 1975 (No. 21 of 1975).

31. Government Notice No. 168, published 22 August 1975, sec. 4.

32. Tanzania, *Villages . . . Act*, Sec. 16.

33. *Nationalist* (Dar es Salaam), 28 October 1971, p. 3.

34. *Daily News* (Dar es Salaam), 24 September 1975, p. 1.

35. *Ibid.*, 17 February 1976, p. 1.

36. *Ibid.*, 18 February 1976, p. 1, and 20 February 1976, p. 1.

37. *Ibid.*, 20 May 1976, p. 1.

38. *Sunday News* (Dar es Salaam), 23 May 1976, p. 1.

39. Student reports on visits to Ujamaa villages during 1972 and 1973 for the Institute of Adult Education, University of Dar es Salaam, confirm both the variations and similarities.

40. Shivji, pp. 63-91.

41. Hill's contention that "the party's main role is as a forum for Nyerere within the national levels of the party-state" is perhaps overdrawn. See Frances Hill, "Ujamaa: African Socialist Productionism in Tanzania," in *Socialism in the Third World*, eds. Helen Desfosses and Jacques Levesque (New York: Praeger, 1975), p. 229.

42. Phil Raikes, "Ujamaa and Rural Socialism," *Review of African Political Economy* 3 (May-October 1975): 51.

43. The Tanzanian reaction was bitter; see the editorial in *Sunday News* (Dar es Salaam), 22 December 1974, p. 6.

44. Shivji, p. 104.

45. Case No. 212 (Saidi *Mwamwindi* v. *R.*) Crim. Sess. 37-Iringa-72, 2 October 1972.

46. Raikes, p. 45.

47. Shivji, p. 108.

48. D.E. McHenry, Jr., "Peasant Participation in Communal Farming: The Tanzanian Experience," *African Studies Reivew* 20, 3 (December 1977): 43-63.

49. *Daily News* (Dar es Salaam), 8 October 1975, p. 4.

50. Nyerere, *The Arusha Declaration: Ten Years After*, p. 28.

51. See McHenry, "The Ujamaa Village in Tanzania: A Comparison with Chinese, Soviet, and Mexican Experiences in Collectivization," *Comparative Studies in Society and History* 18, 3 (July 1976): 347-70.

Ladipo Adamolekun: The Socialist Experience in Guinea

1. Ahmed Sékou Touré, "Le Leader politique, considéré comme le représentant d'une culture," *Presénce Africaine* 24-25 (February-May 1959): 169. [Unless otherwise indicated, all translations are mine—L. A.]

2. Touré, *La Lutte du Parti Démocratique de Guinée pour l'émancipation africaine: La Planification économique* [V] (Conakry, 1969), p. 281.

3. *Ibid.*, p. 285. Emphasis in original.

4. *Ibid.*, p. 309.

5. *Ibid.*, p. 311. Emphasis in original.

6. Touré, *Huitième Congrès National du Parti Démocratique de Guinée* (Conakry, 1967), p. 14.

7. *Horoya* (Conakry, PDG daily), 31 August 1978.

8. For an independent account of this plot, see *Le Monde*, 6/7 March 1966.

9. *La RDA-PDG* (PDG periodic journal), 41 (August 1970): 93.

10. *Horoya*, 10 March 1969.

11. Touré, *Le Pouvoir populaire* [XVI] (Conakry, 1968), p. 45.

12. Touré, *La Technique de la révolution* [XVIII] (Conakry, 1972), p. 69.

13. *Bulletin d'information du BPN* (Bureau Politique National of the PDG) (Conakry) 94 (1970): 98.

14. Special title given to *La RDA-PDG* 41.

15. Touré, *Extraits du discours tenu lors de la première conférence nationale de Labé* (Conakry, 1961), p. 17; mimeo.

16. Touré, *La Lutte du Parti Démocratique de Guinée pour l'emancipation africaine* [IV] (Conakry, 1959), p. 60.

17. Touré, *Concevoir, analyser, réaliser* [XII] (Conakry, 1966), p. 35. Emphasis in original.

18. *Ibid.*, p. 58.

19. Touré, *La Lutte du Parti . . .* [IV], p. 60.

20. *Ibid.*, p. 63.

21. Touré, *Le Pouvoir populaire*, p. 223.

22. For an eyewitness account of this invasion, see Ladipo Adamolekun, "L'Aggression du 22 novembre: Faits et commentaires," *Revue Francaise d'Études Politiques Africaines* (Paris), June 1975: 79-114.

23. On the Chinese experience, see F. Schurmann, *Ideology and Organization in Communist China* (Berkeley, 1968), esp. pp. 163-67 and 170-72.

24. *Horoya-hebdo* (PDG weekly), No. 88, 26 September-2 October 1970.

25. Touré, *L'Action politique du Parti Démocratique de Guinée pour l'émancipation africaine* [III] (Conakry, 1959), p. 312.

26. Quoted in *Afrique Nouvelle* (Dakar), 27 April 1960, p. 2.

27. Touré, *Concevoir, analyser, réaliser*, pp. 24-25.

28. *Horoya* (Conakry), 18 December 1962.

29. Touré, *Concevoir, analyser, réaliser*, p. 56.

30. Touré, *Huitième Congrès*, p. 14.

31. *Horoya*, 21 March 1972.

32. *La RDA-PDG* 41 (August 1970): 101-2.

33. For an attempt at an analysis of the emerging social stratification in Guinea, see Claude Rivière, "Dynamique de la stratification sociale en Guinée" (Doctoral thesis, University of Sorbonne, 1975).

34. For more details on this point, see Adamolekun, "L'Aggression du 22 Novembre," passim.

35. According to the French scholar Alain Cournanel, there has been a relative decline in the material well-being of the Guinean working class between 1958 and 1976; see his "Le Capitalisme d'etat en Afrique: Le Cas guinéen," *Revue Francaise d'Études Politiques Africaines* 123 (March 1976): 18-51.

36. Touré, *Plan septennial, 1964-71*, p. 96.

37. Touré, *La Lutte du Parti* . . . [V], p. 309.

38. On the Soviet experience, see M. Fainsod, "Bureaucracy and Modernization: The Russian and Soviet Case," in *Bureaucracy and Political Development*, ed. J. LaPalombara (Princeton, 1963).

39. Touré, *La Lutte du Parti* . . . [V], p. 95.

40. Adamolekun, *Sékou Touré's Guinea: An Experiment in Nation Building* (London: Methuen, 1976), p. 33.

41. For details of the impressive achievements of the Touré regime in this sector, see *ibid.*, pp. 97-110.

42. See C. Rivière, "Bourgeoisie du tracteur," *Revue Francaise d'Études Politiques Africaines* (March 1976): 74-101.

43. See Adamolekun, *Sékou Touré's Guinea*, pp. 84-85.

44. Touré, *Concevoir, analyser, réaliser*, p. 44. Touré asserts further that "contrary to what happened in the old established monarchies, in Guinea it was not the organization of a nation which created the state, but a nation which had to be built on to the framework of a state" (*idem*).

45. For example, C. Morse has described Touré as "the most avowedly Marxist of the African leaders" (see C. Morse, "The Economics of African Socialism," in *African Socialism*, eds. W. H. Friedland and C. G. Rosberg [Stanford, 1964], p. 36). For an opposite viewpoint, see Alpha Condé, *Guinée: l'Albanie de l'Afrique ou néo-colonie américaine* (Paris, 1972), passim.

46. See Touré, *Premier Congrès Islamique National*, special issue of the *RDA* No. 100 (Conakry, November 1976).

47. See *RDA*, 103 (Conakry, August 1977).

48. See Adamolekun, *Sékou Touré's Guinea*, pp. 162-75.

49. W. Derman, *Serfs, Peasants and Socialists* (Berkeley: University of California Press, 1973), p. 251.

50. Quoted in N. Mackenzie, *Socialism: A Short History* (rev. ed.; London: Hutchinson, 1966).

Stephen A. Quick: Socialism in One Sector: Rural Development in Zambia

1. On the nature of socialist society, see Alfred Meyer, *Marxism: The Unity of Theory and Practice* (Ann Arbor, 1966), pp. 74-90; Michael Harrington,

Socialism (New York: Bantam, 1970), pp. 41-90; Gajo Petrovic, *Marx in the Mid-Twentieth Century* (New York: Doubleday, 1967), pp. 135-71.

2. Paul Sweezy and Charles Bettleheim, *On the Transition to Socialism* (New York: Monthly Review, 1970), pp. 31-32. For a theoretical view on the dialectic between base and superstructure, see Louis Althusser, *Lenin and Philosophy* (New York: Monthly Review, 1971), pp. 127-86.

3. The importance of transforming the relations of production using non-material incentives has been stressed most thoroughly in the Cuban and Chinese experiments; see E. L. Wheelwright and Bruce McFarlane, *The Chinese Road to Socialism* (New York: Monthly Review, 1970), pp. 143-60, and Robert Bernardo, *The Theory of Moral Incentives in Cuba* (University of Alabama Press, 1971).

4. The problem of linking town and country in the course of socialist development is one of the most underanalyzed aspects of the socialist model; see Aidan Foster-Carter, "Neo-Marxist Approaches to Development and Underdevelopment," in *Sociology and Development*, eds. E. DeKadt and G. Williams (London: Tavistock, 1974), pp. 67-105.

5. For a critical review of Marx's thoughts on the peasantry, see David Mitrany, *Marx Against the Peasant* (Chapel Hill: University of North Carolina Press, 1951), pp. 36-40.

6. Paul Baran, *The Political Economy of Growth* (New York: Monthly Review, 1957), pp. 267-68. For an analysis of the specific problems encountered by the Soviet Union with the peasants under the New Economic Policy, see Moshe Lewin, *Russian Peasants and Soviet Power* (New York: Norton, 1975), pp. 172-97.

7. Charles Wilber, "The Role of Agriculture in Soviet Economic Development," *Land Economics* 45, 1 (February 1969): 87-96; Wheelwright and McFarlane, pp. 49-52.

8. This is the phenomenon of the "fetishism of commodities"; for analyses see Paul Sweezy, *The Theory of Capitalist Development* (New York: Monthly Review, 1942), pp. 34-40, and Karl Korsch, *Karl Marx* (New York: Russell and Russell, 1963), pp. 129-37.

9. On the administrative problems of "war communism," see Maurice Dobb, *Soviet Economic Development Since 1917* (New York: International Publishers, 1968), pp. 97-124, and E. H. Carr, *The Bolshevik Revolution*, vol. 2 (Harmondsworth: Penguin, 1966), pp. 151-267.

10. Immanuel Wallerstein, "Dependence in an Interdependent World: The Limited Possibilities of Transformation within the Capitalist World Economy," *African Studies Review* 17, 1 (April 1974): 1-23.

11. The most obvious example of this is, of course, Chile; see James Petras and Morris Morley, *The United States and Chile* (New York: Monthly Review, 1975).

12. Peter Evans, "National Autonomy and Economic Development: Critical Perspectives on Multinational Corporations in Poor Countries," *International Organization* 35, 3 (1971): 689; John Loxley and John Saul, "Multinationals, Workers and Parastatals in Tanzania," *Review of African Political Economy* 2 (January-April 1975): 82.

13. Issa Shivji, "Capitalism Unlimited: Public Corporations in Partnership with Multinational Corporations," *African Review* 3, 3 (1973): 359-81; Ingemund Hegg, *Some State-Controlled Industrial Companies in Tanzania: A Case Study* (Uppsala: Scandinavian Institute for African Studies, 1971).

14. This argument has been developed most fully by Hamza Alavi, "The State in Post-Colonial Societies: Pakistan and Bangladesh," *New Left Review* 74 (July-August 1972): 59-81; John Saul, "The State in Post-Colonial Societies: Tanzania," in *The Socialist Register, 1974*, eds. R. Miliband and J. Saville (London, 1974), pp. 349-72. For a critique see Colin Leys, "The Overdeveloped Post-Colonial State: A Re-evaluation," *Review of African Political Economy* 5 (January-April 1976): 39-48.

15. On the importance of this kind of penetration, see Franz Schurmann, *Ideology and Organization in Communist China* (Berkeley: University of California Press, 1970), pp. 366-80, 409-25.

16. On Tanzania, see Cranford Pratt, *The Critical Phase in Tanzania* (Cambridge: Cambridge University Press, 1976), pp. 232-48.

17. For arguments of this type, see Elliott Berg, "Socialism and Economic Development in Tropical Africa," *Quarterly Journal of Economics* 78, 4 (November 1964): 549-73; Gerald Helleiner, "Socialism and Economic Development in Tanzania," *Journal of Development Studies* 8, 2 (January 1972): 183-204; Michael Lofchie, "Agrarian Socialism in the Third World: The Tanzanian Case," *Comparative Politics* 8, 4 (April 1976): 479-99.

18. For details of the debate, see Robert Daniels, *The Conscience of the Revolution* (New York: Simon and Schuster, 1969), pp. 242-52, and Herbert Marcuse, *Soviet Marxism* (New York: Random House, 1961), pp. 77-84.

19. For background material on Zambian politics, see Richard Hall, *Zambia* (New York: Praeger, 1965), and David Mulford, *Zambia: The Politics of Independence* (Nairobi: Oxford University Press, 1967).

20. On the nature of Zambian Humanism see Henry S. Meebelo, *Main Currents of Zambian Humanist Thought* (Lusaka: Oxford University Press, 1973).

21. Robert Molteno, "Zambian Humanism: The Way Ahead," *African Review* 3, 4 (1973): 546-48.

22. K. Quinn, "Industrial Relations in Zambia, 1935-69," in *Constraints on the Economic Development of Zambia*, ed. Charles Elliott (Nairobi: Oxford University Press, 1971), pp. 57-70.

23. Michael Burawoy, "Another Look at the Mineworker," *African Social Research* 14 (December 1972): 266-80.

24. Richard Jolly, "The Skilled Manpower Constraint," in Elliott, ed., p. 21.

25. For a general evaluation of the Zambian planning process, see William Tordoff, "Government and Administration," in *Politics in Zambia*, eds. William Tordoff and Robert Molteno (Berkeley: University of California Press, 1974), pp. 274-89.

26. Charles Harvey, "The Fiscal System," in Elliott, ed., p. 155.

27. For a discussion of these reforms, see Baastian DeGaay Fortman, ed., *After Mulungushi: The Economics of Zambian Humanism* (Nairobi: East African Publishing House, 1969).

28. Richard Sklar, *Corporate Power in an African State: The Political Impact of Multinational Mining Companies in Zambia* (Berkeley: University of California Press, 1975), p. 200; P. Semonian, "Nationalizations and Management in Zambia," *Maji Maji* 1 (January 1971): 34; Rukudzo Murapa, "Nationalization of the Zambian Mining Industry," *Review of Black Political Economy* 7, 1 (Fall 1976): 52.

29. Molteno, pp. 541-57; Timothy Shaw, "Zambia: Dependence and Underdevelopment," *Canadian Journal of African Studies* 10, 1 (1976): 16-18.

30. William Tordoff and Ian Scott, "Political Parties," in Tordoff and Molteno, eds., p. 132.

31. Jan Pettman, "Zambia's Second Republic: The Establishment of a One-Party State," *Journal of Modern African Studies* 12, 2 (1974): 242; Sklar, p. 207; N. Sefelino Mulenga, "Humanism and the Logic of Self-Sufficiency," *Zambia Daily Mail*, January 30-31, 1974.

32. John Hellen, *Rural Economic Development in Zambia, 1890-1964* (Munich: Weltforum, 1968), pp. 139-64.

33. David Mulford, *The Northern Rhodesian General Election of 1962* (Nairobi: Oxford University Press, 1964), p. 60.

34. Mulford, *Zambia*, p. 233.

35. Meebelo, p. 83.

36. In August 1963 Kaunda unsuccessfully pressed the UNIP National Council to launch a pilot program of cooperative development (see Thomas Melady, ed., *Profiles of African Leaders* [New York: Macmillan, 1961], p. 217). In early 1964 he again urged similar action by the party and was ignored (see Colin Legum, ed., *Independence and Beyond: The Speeches of Kenneth Kaunda* [London: Nelson, 1966], p. 158).

37. Kenneth Kaunda, "Speech at Chifubu Rally, 17 January 1965," Zambia Information Services, Press Background 3/65.

38. For a detailed analysis of the organizational problems of the Department of Cooperatives, see Paul Wiffin, "The Staffing and Organization of the Department of Cooperative Societies " (Ministry of Finance, Staff Inspection Unit, 1970; mimeo).

39. This general confusion of policy is discussed in International Bank for Reconstruction and Development, General Agricultural Division, Eastern Africa Regional Office, *Republic of Zambia: Agricultural and Rural Sector Survey*, vol. 1 (October 1975), p. 3.

40. For a comparative analysis of the Soviet and Chinese programs, see Thomas Bernstein, "Leadership and Mass Mobilization in the Soviet and Chinese Collectivization Campaigns of 1929-30 and 1955-56: A Comparison," *China Quarterly* 31 (July-September 1967): 1-45.

41. Wiffin, p. 17.

42. For explicit statements putting pressure on the department, see the speeches of the MP for Zambezi, *Zambia National Hansard*, 28 July 1965, p. 44; the MP for Kasempa, *ibid.*, 23 July 1965, p. 309; and the MP for Serenje, *ibid.*, 5 August 1966, p. 588.

43. On the effects of the market see Norman Long, *Social Change and the Individual* (Manchester: Manchester University Press, 1968), pp. 80-98; on the impact of colonial administration see W. H. Rangeley, "Notes on Chewa Tribal Law," *Nyasaland Journal* 1, 3 (1948): 53.

44. See "Minutes of the Provincial Cooperative Officer's Conference, 16 March 1966" (Department of Cooperatives, Lusaka, File 9/1).

45. Rene Dumont, "The Principal Problems of Agricultural Development in Independent Zambia" (unpublished report to the Government of the Republic of Zambia, April 1967). See also "Dr. Dumont's Diagnosis," *Business and Economy of Central and East Africa*, May 1967, pp. 26-29.

46. J. B. Knight, "Wages and Zambia's Economic Development," in Elliott, ed., pp. 100-101.

47. For information on the productivity drive, see the remarks of the Minister of Finance in *Zambia National Hansard*, 25 January 1968, p. 42. See also Zambia Information Services, Press Background no. 6/68, 13 January 1968, and Press Releases nos. 485/68 and 493/68, 15 March 1968.

48. For a discussion of these reforms, see Sheridan Johns, "State Capitalism in Zambia: The Evolution of the Parastatal Sector" (paper presented to the 18th meeting of the African Studies Association, San Francisco, October 1975).

49. See the various discussions in Parliament: *Zambia National Hansard*, 21 September 1966, pp. 2355-56; 23 June 1967, p. 440; 20 February 1968, p. 464; 26 March 1968, p. 1447.

50. See especially International Labour Organization, *Report to the Government of Zambia on Cooperative Education and Training and the Financing of Cooperatives* (Geneva: ILO, 1966); International Labour Organization, *Report to the Government of Zambia on Cooperative Management and Administration* (Geneva: ILO, 1968). See also the report written by the expatriate-dominated National Institute of Public Administration: "Report on the Cooperative Movement in Zambia" (Lusaka: NIPA, December 1967; mimeo).

51. Kenneth Kaunda, speech to delegates in Zambia, *National Convention on Rural Development, Incomes, Wages and Prices in Zambia, 2nd, Kitwe, 12-16 December 1969* (Lusaka: Government Printer, 1970), p. 29.

52. Kenneth Kaunda, *Humanism in Zambia and a Guide to Its Implementation* (Lusaka: Government Printer, 1968), p. 37.

53. See "Address by the Director of Cooperative Societies to the Eastern Province Cooperative Officers Conference, 22-23 September 1969 (Department of Cooperatives, Eastern Province, File 9/1).

54. R. C. E. Kapteyn and C. R. Emery, *Research Project on Administration for Rural Development*, Vol. 3: *Cooperatives: General* (Lusaka: National Institute for Public Administration, April 1972), p. 19.

55. See *Annual Report* of the Ministry of Rural Development for 1972 (Lusaka: Government Printer, 1974).

56. The main reason for this criticism was a fear that the COZ was undermining the "credit morality" of the African population; see Charles Harvey, "The Control of Credit in Zambia," *Journal of Modern African Studies* 11, 3 (1973): 389.

57. This impression is derived from numerous interviews by the author with expatriate economic advisors, including some whose task it was specifically to advise the Department of Cooperatives.

58. Stephen Quick, "Bureaucracy and Rural Socialism in Zambia," *Journal of Modern African Studies* 15, 3 (1977): 379-400.

59. Beveridge, pp. 477-90.

60. Issa Shivji, *Class Struggles in Tanzania* (London: Heinemann, 1975), is undoubtedly the most important of these writings. See also K. Nsari, "Tanzania: Neo-Colonialism and the Struggle for National Liberation," *Review of African Political Economy* 4 (November 1975): 109-18; Helleiner, pp. 183-204; Lofchie, pp. 479-99; P. Neerso, "Tanzania's Policies on Private Foreign Investment," *African Review* 4, 1 (1974): 61-78.

Thomas M. Callaghy: The Difficulties of Implementing Socialist Strategies of Development in Africa: The "First Wave"

1. Merle Fainsod, *Smolensk Under Soviet Rule* (Cambridge, Mass.: Harvard University Press, 1958).

2. Quoted in *From Underdevelopment to Affluence: Western, Soviet and Chinese Views*, ed. Harry Shaffer (New York: Appleton-Century-Crofts, 1968), p. 54; emphasis added. See also Arthur J. Klinghoffer, *Soviet Perspectives on African Socialism* (Cranbury, N. J.: Fairleigh Dickinson University Press, 1969); I. I. Poteklin, "On African Socialism: A Soviet View," in *African Socialism*, eds. W. H. Friedland and C. G. Rosberg (Stanford: Stanford University Press, 1964), pp. 97-112; and A. Nove, "The Soviet Model and Underdeveloped Countries," *International Affairs* 37, 1 (1961).

3. See A. Etzioni: *A Comparative Analysis of Complex Organizations* (New York: Holt, Rinehart and Winston, 1961), ch. 1, and "Power and Alienation in a Comparative Perspective," in *Comparative Perspectives: Theories and Methods*, eds. A. Etzioni and F. L. Dubow (Boston: Little, Brown, 1970), pp. 137-61.

4. Kenneth Jowitt, *Revolutionary Breakthroughs and National Development: The Case of Romania 1944-1965* (Berkeley: University of California Press, 1971), p. 7. (This section of my article is a slightly modified version of Jowitt's argument in this outstanding book.)

5. Frances Hill, "Ujamaa: African Socialist Productionism in Tanzania," in *Socialism in the Third World*, eds. H. Desfosses and S. Levesque (New York: Praeger, 1975), p. 238; emphasis added.

6. *Ibid.*, p. 241; emphasis added.

7. See esp. A. Zolberg, *Creating Political Order: The Party-States of West Africa* (Chicago: Rand McNally, 1966); see also S. E. Finer, "One-Party Systems in Africa: Reconsiderations," *Government and Opposition* 2, 4 (July-October 1967): 491-509; S. Rothman, "One-Party Regimes: A Comparative Analysis," *Social Research* 34, 4 (Winter 1967): 675-702; I. Wallerstein, "The Decline of the Party in Single-Party African States," in *Political Parties and Political Development*, eds. J. LaPalombara and M. Weiner (Princeton, N. J.: Princeton University Press, 1966); S. Ryan, "The C. P. P. Re-examined," *Canadian Journal of African Studies* 4 (Spring 1970); Henry Bienen, "Policital Parties and Political Machnies in Africa," in *The State of the Nations*, ed. M. Lofchie (Berkeley: University of California Press, 1973), pp. 195-213.

8. See A. Zolberg's excellent article on "The Structure of Political Conflict in the New States of Tropical Africa," *American Political Science Review* 62, 1 (March 1968): 70-87.

9. *Ibid.*

10. See Reinhard Bendix, *Max Weber* (New York: Doubleday, 1962), p. 344.

11. See Robert M. Price, "Military Officers and Political Leadership: The Ghanaian Case," *Comparative Politics* 3, 3 (April 1971): 361-79; A. Zolberg, "Military Rule and Political Development in Tropical Africa," in *Military Profession and Military Regimes*, ed. J. Van Doorn (The Hague: Mouton, 1969), pp. 175-202; E. Feit, "Military Coups and Political Development: Some Lessons from Ghana and Nigeria," *World Politics* 20, 2 (January 1968): 179-93.

12. See the article by Samuel Decalo in this volume; for the notion of "forensic ideology," see A. Zolberg, *Creating Political Order*, p. 59 and *passim*.

13. For general treatments of the ideology of African socialism, see Friedland and Rosberg, eds., *African Socialism*; David E. Apter, *Politics of Modernization* (Chicago: University of Chicago Press, 1965), pp. 172, 308, 335-40; L. V. Thomas, *Le socialisme et l'Afrique*, 2 vols. (Paris: Le Livre Africain, 1966), esp. vol. 2, pp. 201-3; Marion Mushkat, "African Socialism Reappraised and Reconsidered," *Africa* 27, 2: 151-76; Father Bede Onuoha, *The Elements of African Socialism* (Andre Deutsch, 1965); Ian C. Parker, "Ideological and Economic Development in Tanzania," *African Studies Review* 15, 1 (April 1972): 43-78; Kenneth W. Grundy, "Nkrumah's Theory of Underdevelopment," *World Politics* 15, 3 (April 1963): 438-54; D. G. Folson, "The Development of Socialist Ideology in Ghana," *Ghana Social Science Journal* 1, 2 (November 1971): 1-20; J. L. Hymans, "The Origins of Léopold Senghor's African Road to Socialism," *Gèneve-Afrique* 6, 1 (1967): 33-48; W. Skurnik, "Léopold Sedar Senghor and African Socialism," *Journal of Modern African Studies* 3, (1965): 349-69; Ahmed Mohiddin, "Socialism in Two Countries: The Arusha Declaration of Tanzania and the African Socialism of Kenya," *African Quarterly* 12, 4 (January-March 1963): 332-57.

14. On traditional "African socialism," see Igor Kopytoff, "Socialism and Traditional African Societies," in Friedland and Rosberg, eds., pp. 53-62; Ahmed Mohiddin, "The Basic Unit of African Ideal Society in Nyerere's Thought," *Africa* (Milan) 25,1 (March 1970): 3-24; Ehud Spinzak, "African Traditional Socialism—A Semantic Analysis of Political Ideology," *Journal of Modern African Studies* 11, 4 (1973): 629-47; Julius K. Nyerere: *Ujamaa: Essays on Socialism* (Oxford, 1968), *passim*, and "The Arusha Declaration Ten Years After" (United Republic of Tanzania, January 1977).

15. Nyerere, *Ujamaa*, pp. 89, 131; Hill "Ujamaa," p. 220.

16. See G. Arrighi and J. Saul, "Socialism and Economic Development in Tropical Africa," *Journal of Modern African Studies* 6, 2 (1968): 167 and *passim*.

17. General references consulted for this section include: Jon Kraus, "Socialism and Political Economy in Ghana," in Desfosses and Levesque, eds.; Dennis Austin, *Politics in Ghana* (Oxford, 1964); David Apter, "Nkrumah, Charisma, and the Coup," *Daedalus* 97 (Summer 1968): 757-92; Eliot Berg,

"Structural Transformation Versus Gradualism: Recent Economic Development in Ghana and the Ivory Coast," and Reginald Green, "Reflections on Economic Strategy, Structure, Implementation, and Necessity: Ghana and the Ivory Coast, 1957-1967"—both in *Ghana and the Ivory Coast*, eds. P. Foster and A. Zolberg (Chicago: University of Chicago Press, 1971); Samir Amin, *Trois expériences africaines de développement: Le Mali, la Guinée, et le Ghana* (Paris, 1965).

18. Kraus, pp. 197-201.

19. *Ibid.*, pp. 200-204.

20. Sources used in this section include: Helen Desfosses and J. Dirck Stryker, "Socialist Development in Africa: The Case of Keita's Mali," in *Socialism in the Third World*, eds. Desfosses and Levesque, pp. 167-79; Francis G. Snyder: "The Political Thought of Modibo Keita," *Journal of Modern African Studies* 5, 1 (1967): 79-106; "An Era Ends in Mali," *Africa Report*, March-April 1969, pp. 16-22; and *One-Party Government in Mali: Transition Toward Control* (New Haven: Yale University Press, 1965); William I. Jones: "Economics of the Coup," *Africa Report*, March-April 1969, pp. 23-26, 51-53; *Planning and Economic Policy: Socialist Mali and Her Neighbors* (Washington: Three Continents Press, 1976); and "The Mise and Demise of Socialist Institutions in Rural Mali," *Gèneve-Afrique* 40, 2 (1972); Guy Martin, "Socialism, Economic Development and Planning in Mali, 1960-1968," *Canadian Journal of African Studies* 10, 1 (1976): 23-47; Nicholas S. Hopkins, "Socialism and Social Change in Rural Mali," *Journal of Modern African Studies* 7, 3 (1969): 457-67; Kenneth W. Grundy, "Mali: The Prospects of 'Planned Socialism,'" in *African Socialism*, eds. Friedland and Rosberg. See also: Samir Amin, *Trois expériences africaines de développement: Le Mali, la Guineé, et le Ghana*; Nicholas S. Hopkins, *Popular Government in an African Town* (Chicago: University of Chicago Press, 1972); Claude Meillassoux, "A Class Analysis of the Bureaucratic Process in Mali," *Journal of Development Studies* 6, 2 (January 1970): 99-105; Horeya T. Megahed, *Socialism and Nation-Building in Africa: The Case of Mali (1960-1968)* (Budapest: Center for Afro-Asian Research, 1970); Thomas Hodkin and Ruth Schacter Morgenthau, "Mali," in *Political Parties and National Integration in Tropical Africa*, eds. James S. Coleman and Carl G. Rosberg (Berkeley: University of California Press, 1966); Ruth Schacter Morgenthau, *Political Parties in French-Speaking West Africa* (Oxford: Clarendon Press, 1964).

21. *Plan quinquennial, 1961-1966* (Bamako).

22. The brief argument in this section is elaborated in an unpublished paper by the author entitled "Historical Configurations and the Political Economy of State Formation: Seventeenth-Century French Mercantilism and Twentieth-Century African Neomercantilism"; see also my dissertation—"State Formation and Absolutism in Comparative Perspective: Seventeenth-Century France and Mobutu Sese Seko's Zaire" (forthcoming). Among the works on mercantilism consulted were the following: Jacob Viner, "Economic Thought: Mercantilist Thought," in *International Encyclopedia of the Social Sciences*; Walter E. Minchinton, ed., *Mercantilism: System or Expediency?* (New York: Heath and Co., 1969); Philip W. Buck, *The Politics of Mercantilism* (New York: Henry Holt and Co., 1942); J. W. Horrocks, *A*

Short History of Mercantilism (New York: Brentano's Publishers, n. d.); Max Weber, *General Economic History* (London: Allen and Unwin), pp. 347-51; Joseph Schumpeter, *History of Economic Analysis* (Oxford: Oxford University Press, 1954), esp. pt. II, ch. 7; Joseph J. Spengler, "Mercantilist and Physiocratic Growth Theory," in *Theories of Economic Growth*, ed. B. Hoselitz (Glencoe, 1960); Shepard B. Clough, *European Economic History* (New York: McGraw-Hill, 1968); D. C. Coleman, "Editor's Introduction" and "Eli Heckscher and the Idea of Mercantilism"—both in Coleman, ed. *Revisions in Mercantilism* (London: Methuen, 1969); Jacob Van Klaveren, "Fiscalism, Mercantilism and Corruption," in Coleman, ed.; Herbert Heaton, "Heckscher on Mercantilism," *Journal of Political Economy* 45 (1937): 370-93; Lionel Rothkrug, *Opposition to Louis XIV* (Princeton: Princeton University Press, 1965).

23. See Eli Heckscher, *Mercantilism* (London: Allen and Unwin, 1935) vol. 1, p. 21, vol. 2, p. 17; Charles W. Cole, *Colbert and a Century of French Mercantilism* 2 vols. (Hamden, Conn.: Archon Books, 1964), esp. vol. 1, p. 25.

24. On the development of early modern European states, see Charles Tilly, ed., *The Formation of National States in Western Europe* (Princeton: Princeton University Press, 1975); Felix Gilbert, ed., *The Historical Essays of Otto Hintze* (Oxford: Oxford University Press, 1975); Max Beloff, *The Age of Absolutism* (New York: Hutchinson, 1967); Perry Anderson, *Lineages of the Absolutist State* (London, 1974); I. Wallerstein, *The Modern World-System* (New York: Academic Press, 1974); Aston Trevor, ed., *Crisis in Europe, 1560-1660* (New York: Basic Books, 1965); David Maland, *Europe in the Seventeenth Century* (London: Macmillan/St. Martin's, 1967); R. Hatton, *Europe in the Age of Louis XIV* (London: Thames and Hudson, 1969); Joseph Strayer, *On the Medieval Origins of the Modern State* (Princeton, 1970); Alexis de Tocqueville, *The Old Regime and the French Revolution* (New York: Anchor Books, 1955); Robert Mandrou, *La France aux XVIIe et XVIIIe siècles* (Paris: Nouvelle Clio, 1967); Jean Meuvret, "The Condition of France, 1688-1715," in *New Cambridge Modern History*, vol. 6, (Oxford, 1957); Roland Mousnier, *Etat et société en France aux XVIIe et XVIIIe siècles* (Paris: Centre de Documentation Universitaire, 1969); Pierre Goubert, *The Old Regime* (New York: Harper and Row, 1973).

25. Weber makes this distinction in the *Protestant Ethic and the Spirit of Capitalism* (New York: Scribner's, 1958), pp. 13-27; see also *Economy and Society* (Totowa, N. J.: Bedminster Press, 1968), vol 3, pp. 1096-1104.

26. See Maurice Dobb, *Studies in the Development of Capitalism* (New York: International Publishers, 1963), pp. 199, 215, and Robert L. Heilbroner, *The Making of Economic Society* (Englewood Cliffs: Prentice-Hall, 1968), p. 67.

27. Eli Heckscher, "Mercantilism," in *Encyclopedia of the Social Sciences* (New York: 1937), vol. 9, p. 339.

Kenneth Jowitt: Scientific Socialist Regimes in Africa: Political Differentiation, Avoidance, and Unawareness

1. "Address on U. S. Policy Toward Africa"; quoted in *New York Times*, June 21, 1978.

2. Conor Cruise O'Brien, "Report from Southern Africa," *New York Review of Books*, 25, 3 (March 9, 1978), p. 27.

3. R. W. Johnson, "Sékou Touré and the Guinean Revolution," *African Affairs* 69 (October 1970): 360.

4. Samuel Decalo, *Coups and Army Rule in Africa* (New Haven and London: Yale University Press, 1976), p. 155.

5. This appears to be the thrust of Thomas H. Henriksen's "People's War in Angola, Mozambique, and Guinea-Bissau," *Journal of Modern African Studies* 14, 3 (1976): 377-79.

6. In this connection see David E. Albright, "The USSR and Africa: Soviet Policy," *Problems of Communism* 27 (January-February 1978): 27.

7. For this composite "view," I have drawn on the arguments of Elliot J. Berg, "Socialist and Economic Development in Tropical Africa," *Quarterly Journal of Economics* 78, 4 (November 1964): 549-73; Immanuel Wallerstein, "The Range of Choice: Constraints on the Policies of Governments of Contemporary African Independent States," in *The State of the Nations: Constraints on Development in Independent Africa*, ed. Michael F. Lofchie (Berkeley: University of California Press, 1971), pp. 19-37; and Giovanni Arrighi and John S. Saul, *Essays on the Political Economy of Africa* (New York: Monthly Review Press, 1973), passim.

8. O'Brien suggests this in "Report from Southern Africa," as does David Laitin in "Somalia's Military Government and Scientific Socialism," in this volume.

9. See A. James Gregor, "African Socialism, Socialism, and Fascism: An Appraisal," *Review of Politics* 29, 3 (July 1967): 336.

10. Arnold Hughes and Martin Kolinsky, "'Paradigmatic Fascism' and Modernization: A Critique," *Political Studies* 24, 4 (December 1976): 371-96.

11. Igor Kopytoff, "Socialism and Traditional African Societies," in *African Socialism*, eds. William H. Friedland and Carl G. Rosberg, Jr. (Stanford: Stanford University Press, 1964), p. 55.

12. See Owen Lattimore, *Nationalism and Revolution in Mongolia* (New York: Oxford University Press, 1955).

13. On the voting of Italians in Rhode Island, see Duane Lockard, *New England State Politics* (Princeton, N. J.: Princeton University Press, 1959), pp. 196-203, 312-13.

14. Perry Anderson, *Passages from Antiquity to Feudalism* (London: NLB, 1974), p. 118. Emphasis added.

15. Decalo, p. 84.

16. The notion of an "established" elite is Ralf Dahrendorf's; see his *Society and Democracy in Germany* (Garden City, N. Y.: Anchor Books, 1967), pp. 218, 258-60.

17. Decalo, p. 158.

18. See "Revolution in Ethiopia," *Monthly Review* 29 (July-August 1977): 52-53; written by "An Observer."

19. See R. W. Johnson's excellent piece—"The Parti Democratique de Guinée and the Mamou 'Deviation'"—in *African Perspectives*, eds. Christopher Allen and R. W. Johnson (Cambridge: Cambridge University Press, 1970), pp. 347-69.

20. See chapter on Dahomey (now Benin) in Decalo.

21. Joseph Stalin, *Dialectical and Historical Materialism* (New York: International Publishers, 1970), p. 27.

22. Enver Hoxha, "It Is in the Party-People-State Power Unity that Our Strength Lies" (Tirana: The "Naim Frasheri" Publishing House, 1970), p. 35.

23. J. B. Bury, *The Invasion of Europe by the Barbarians* (New York: W. W. Norton, 1967), p. 46. See the related discussion by H. St. L.B. Moss, *The Birth of the Middle Ages 395-814* (New York: Oxford University Press, 1964), pp. 71-75.

24. For a contemporary instance of a group favoring one religion over another because of its greater congruence with existing self-conceptions and practices, see Elliott P. Skinner, "Christianity and Islam among the Mossi," in *Gods and Rituals*, ed. John Middleton (Austin: University of Texas Press, 1967), pp. 353-77. In this instance the Moslem religion was more readily appropriated because of its greater congruence with Mossi institutions while Catholicism was resisted due to the number of ways in which it threatened basic Mossi institutions.

25. See David Laitin's essay on Somalia in this volume. While information on Ethiopia must be treated cautiously, some is provided in Jan Valdelin, "Ethiopia 1974-77: From Anti-feudal Revolution to Consolidation of the Bourgeois State," *Race and Class* 19, 4 (Spring 1978): 379-99. On Guinea, see Johnson, "The Parti Democratique de Guinée and the Mamou 'Deviation.'"

26. For a discussion of the Turkish case, see Richard Lowenthal, *Model or Ally? The Communist Powers and the Developing Countries* (New York: Oxford University Press, 1977), p. 73. For a fuller account of the Turkish-Soviet connection, see P. Dumont, "L'axe Moscou-Ankara. Les relations turco-sovietiques de 1919 à 1922," *Cahiers du Monde Russe et Sovietique* 18, 3 (July-September 1977): 165-95.

27. On Egypt see Anouar Abdel-Malek, *Egypt: Military Society* (New York: Vintage Books, 1968), pp. 96, 123, 127, 290, 307; the Iraqi's actions are discussed in *New York Times*, July 30, 1978.

28. The Somali case is illustrative. As populists the Somali leaders are likely to attack religious elites but not institutions (see "Somalia Trying to Live by Both the Koran and Das Kapital," *New York Times*, October 11, 1977).

29. Iliya Harik, "The Single Party as a Subordinate Movement: The Case of Egypt," *World Politics* 26, 1 (October 1973): 80-106.

30. Quoted in Alexander Erlich, *The Soviet Industrialization Debate, 1924-1928* (Cambridge, Mass.: Harvard University Press, 1960), p. 162.

31. Aristide R. Zolberg, "The Dakar Colloquium: The Search for a Doctrine," in Friedland and Rosberg, eds., pp. 118-19.

32. Stanislav Andreski, *The African Predicament* (New York: Atherton Press, 1968), p. 88.

33. Sheldon Gellar quite appropriately emphasizes this distinction in "State-Building and Nation-Building in West Africa," *International Development Research Center* (Bloomington, Indiana: Indiana University Press, 1972).

34. P. Erny, "Parole et travail chez les jeunes d'Afrique centrale," *Project* (September-October 1966); cited in Decalo, p. 145.

35. See Henry Roberts, "Politics in a Small State: The Balkan Example," in *Eastern Europe: Politics, Revolution and Diplomacy*, ed. H. Roberts (New York: Alfred A. Knopf, 1970), pp. 178-204.

36. Weber's statement is quoted in Alvin W. Gouldner, *The Dialectic of Ideology and Technology* (New York: Seabury Press, 1976); for Bendix's observation see his *Max Weber: An Intellectual Portrait* (Berkeley: University of California Press, 1977), p. 46.

37. For an abstract of P. I. Manchkha, "Communists, Revolutionary Democrats and the Noncapitalist Path of Development in African Countries" (*Voprosy Istorii KPSS*), see *Current Digest of the Soviet Press*, 27, 51 (January 21, 1976), pp. 4-5; published by American Association for the Advancement of Slavic Studies.

38. *Idem.*

39. See, for example, Cabral's statement on the "absolute necessity of creating a party" in "Brief Analysis of the Social Structure in Guinea . . . ," in *Revolution in Guinea: Selected Texts by Amilcar Cabral*, trans. and ed. Richard Handyside (New York: Monthly Review Press, 1969), p. 65.

40. Amilcar Cabral, "The Weapon of Theory" (address delivered in Havana, 1966), p. 110. It is ironic that in a talk about theory the emphasis should be on the leader's ethical qualities, not the party's programmatic features.

41. *Idem.*

42. Julius K. Nyerere, *Ujamaa: Essays on Socialism* (New York: Oxford University Press, 1968), p. 6.

43. See Cabral, "Brief Analysis of the Social Structure in Guinea . . . ," pp. 56-76, and Nyerere, "Varied Paths to Socialism," in *Ujamaa*, p. 79.

44. Anwar Sadat's statements and actions in the Summer of 1978 provide a clear example of avoidance behavior; see *New York Times*, July 23 and August 1, 1978. My colleague Robert Price informs me that Nkrumah's behavior exemplifies this equally well.

45. Cabral, "Brief Analysis . . . ," p. 14.

46. *Ibid.*, pp. 68, 102.

47. *Ibid.*, p. 141.

48. See the recent article by the Yugoslav Milan Bekic attacking the arguments presented in the Soviet book *Proletarian, Socialist Internationalism* that, according to Bekic, denounce "theories of 'various types of Marxism' and 'inventions' about various 'models' of socialism" (*Radio Free Europe Research* 3, 21 [24-31 May 1978]).

49. Nyerere, *Ujamaa*, p. 78.

50. *Idem.*

51. Robert C. Tucker, *The Marxian Revolutionary Idea* (New York: W. W. Norton, 1969), pp. 126-29.

52. For an analysis of Leninist and reformist strategies, see K. Jowitt, *The Leninist Response to National Dependency* (Berkeley: Institute of International Studies, 1978), and *Revolutionary Breakthroughs and National Development* (Berkeley: University of California Press, 1971). Franz Schurmann's *Ideology and Organization in Communist China* (Berkeley: University of California Press, 1966), and Zbigniew Brzezinski, *The Soviet Bloc* (Cambridge, Mass.: Harvard University Press, 1967), provide very valuable analyses of *Leninist* strategies in the Chinese and East European contexts.

53. Karl Marx and Friedrich Engels, "Manifesto of the Communist Party," in *Marx and Engels: Basic Writings on Politics and Philosophy*, ed. Lewis S. Feuer (Garden City, N. Y.: Anchor Books, 1959), p. 33.

54. Benjamin I. Schwartz, *Chinese Communism and the Rise of Mao* (New York: Harper & Row, 1967), p. 35; emphasis added.

55. See R. W. Johnson on Touré's Leninism (note 3 above). For a "Blanquist" interpretation of Lenin that practically sterilizes the sociocultural dimensions of Leninist organization, see Samuel P. Huntington, *Political Order in Changing Societies* (New Haven: Yale University Press, 1968), pp. 334-43.

56. Harik, pp. 88, 92, 97, and passim.

57. V. I. Lenin, *"Left-Wing" Communism—An Infantile Disorder*, in *Collected Works*, 31 (Moscow: Progress Publishers, 1966), p. 21.

58. See Max Weber, *General Economic History* (Glencoe, Ill.: The Free Press, 1950); G. R. Elton, *Reformation Europe 1517-1559* (New York: Harper & Row, 1963), p. 323; Immanuel Wallerstein, *The Modern World-System*, passim.

59. See Cecil A. Gibb, "Leadership," in *The Handbook of Social Psychology*, 4, eds. Gardner Lindzey and Elliot Aronson (Reading, Mass.: Addison-Wesley, 1969), pp. 205-83, esp. 258-65.

60. See C. R. Bawden, *The Modern History of Mongolia* (London: Weidenfeld & Nicolson, 1968), pp. 290-381.

61. Gibb, p. 263.

62. See Karl W. Deutsch et al., *Political Community and the North Atlantic Area* (Princeton: Princeton University Press, 1957), pp. 137-39.

63. See R. W. Johnson: "Sékou Touré and the Guinean Revolution," *African Affairs* 69 (October 1970): 352, 359-60, 364; "Guinea," in *West African States: Failure and Promise*, ed. John Dunn (London: Cambridge University Press, 1978), pp. 49, 62-65. On the Teachers' Plot, see Johnson, "The Parti Democratique de Guinée and the Mamou 'Deviation,'" pp. 365-68. The characterization of Touré's position on social transformation as resting on the "radicalisation of language" is from Lansine Kaba, "Guinean Politics: A Critical Historical Overview," *Journal of Modern African Studies* 15, 1 (1977): 45.

64. The competing Communist images of how the "socialist camp" should be organized are analyzed in K. Jowitt, "The Romanian Communist Party and the World Socialist System: A Redefinition of Unity," *World Politics* 22, 1 (October 1970): 38-61.

65. See Elizabeth Kridl Valkenier, "Soviet Economic Relations with the Developing Nations," in *The Soviet Union and the Developing Nations*, ed. Roger E. Kanet (Baltimore: Johns Hopkins University Press, 1974), pp. 215-36, and Richard Lowenthal, "Soviet 'Counterimperialism,'" *Problems of Communism* 25, 6 (November-December 1976): 52-64.

66. For Edgar Snow's impressions of the October Revolution's impact and Chinese perception of the Soviet Union, see *Red Star over China* (New York: Grove Press, 1961) pp. 148-56, 404-10; see also Benjamin Schwartz, pp. 13-27, and Bernard B. Fall, ed., *Ho Chi Minh on Revolution: Selected Writings, 1920-1966* (New York: Frederick A. Praeger, 1967), pp. 291-304 and passim.

67. For an excellent discussion of pure and practical ideology, see Franz Schurmann, *Ideology and Organization in Communist China*, pp. 20-24.

68. O'Brien, p. 27.

69. Laitin, passim.

70. Philip Selznick, *Leadership in Administration* (New York: Harper & Row, 1957), pp. 82, 87. Selznick's later discussion on "organizational opportunism" speaks directly to the condition of most contemporary African regimes (pp. 142-49).

71. On Castro's political shifts, see Edward Gonzalez, "Complexities of Cuban Foreign Policy," *Problems of Communism* 26, 6 (November-December 1977): 1-16. For his clear alignment with the Soviet Union, see his speech at the conference of non-aligned nations in Algiers, September 1973 (*Granma*, Ano 9, No. 213, September 8, 1973).

72. Richard Pipes, *The Formation of the Soviet Union: Communism and Nationalism 1917-1923* (Cambridge, Mass.: Harvard University Press, 1964), p. 169.

73. *Ibid.*, pp. 261-62. The first quotation is from Pipes; the second, from Sultan-Galiev.

74. *Ibid.*, p. 262.

75. See note 71.

David D. Laitin: *Somalia's Military Government and Scientific Socialism*

1. Maxamed Siyaad Barre, *My Country and My People*. Three volumes have been published, covering speeches from 1969-74. Subsequent references will be to "Siyaad," with date of the speech.

2. Siyaad, July 29, 1972.

3. See Julius K. Nyerere, *Freedom and Socialism* (London: Oxford University Press, 1968), esp. the Arusha Declaration.

4. Interview with A.A. Castagno, *Africa Report*, December 1971, p. 24.

5. Siyaad, September 28, 1971.

6. *Africa* (London), November 1973.

7. Siyaad, April 3, 1973.

8. Brian Crozier, "The Soviet Presence in Somalia," *Conflict Studies* 54 (February 1975): 6.

9. In Part I of my *Politics, Language and Thought* (Chicago: University of Chicago Press, 1977) the political implications of language choice in Somalia are discussed.

10. Lewis's study of Somalia is appropriately entitled *A Pastoral Democracy* (London: Oxford University Press, 1961).

11. Some of what follows overlaps my discussion in "The Political Economy of Military Rule in Somalia," *Journal of Modern African Studies*, September 1976.

12. Siyaad, October 21, 1973.

13. *New Era* (Muqdisho), 36 (August 1976), p. 12.

14. See Paoli Contini, *The Somali Republic: An Experiment in Legal Integration* (London: Frank Cass, 1969).

15. *Ololaha Horumarinta Reer-Miyaga* [Rural development campaign] (Muqdisho, October 1975), p. 12.

16. *Maxaynu Hantiwadaag U Qaadanay* [Why we choose scientific socialism] (Muqdisho, October 1975), p. 30.

17. Siyaad, December 18, 1970, and December 4, 1971.

18. Siyaad, July 29, 1972 [slightly modified].

19. Ministry of Information and National Guidance, "The Role of Our Socialist Women" (Muqdisho, June 1974), p. 8.

20. "On African Women's Equality, Role in National Liberation, Development and Peace," *Report and Proceedings of the Regional Seminar for Africa*, Muqdisho, April 3-5, 1975 (October 1975), p. 44.

21. "The Role of Our Socialist Women," p. 17.

22. See, e.g., Basil Davidson, "Somalia in 1975: Some Notes and Impressions," *Issue*, Spring 1975.

23. Ministry of Information and National Guidance, "Agriculture in the Service of the Nation" (Muqdisho, June 1974), p. 1.

24. See Mark Karp, *The Economics of Trusteeship in Somalia* (Boston: Boston University Press, 1960) for a description of the constricting effects of the Italian monopsony on the economy of Somalia.

25. "Agriculture in the Service of the Nation," pp. 21-22.

26. See Saadia Touval, "Somalia and Its Neighbors," in *Conflict in World Politics*, eds. Steven Spiegel and Kenneth Waltz (Cambridge: Winthrop, 1974), pp. 329-30, and Laitin, "Somalia's Territorial Claims in International Perspective," *Africa Today*, June 1976.

27. Ministry of Information and National Guidance, "Our Foreign Relations" (Muqdisho, 1974): Introduction.

28. *Africa Confidential* 17, 6 (March 19, 1976), p. 8.

29. U.S. Congress, Senate, Committee on the Armed Services, "Soviet Military Capability in Berbera, Somalia" [Report of Senator Bartlett], July 1975.

30. United Nations, Economic Commission for Africa, *Summaries of Economic Data, Somalia*, M75-169, No. 9 (January 1975), p. 16.

31. "Our Foreign Relations," p. 46.

32. "Agriculture in the Service of the Nation," p. 1.

33. Interview with Siyaad, *U.S. News and World Report*, July 21, 1975, p. 32, and interview with A.A. Castagno, p. 24.

34. Siyaad, May 1, 1971.

35. Siyaad, October 22, 1970.

36. The most recent assessments are in *Socialism in the Third World*, eds. Helen Desfosses and Jacques Levesque (New York: Praeger, 1975). From a reading of the essays by Jon Kraus (Ghana), Frances Hill (Tanzania), and Helen Desfosses and J.D. Stryker (Mali), one begins to wonder what socialism can possibly achieve with the innumerable bureaucratic, international, economic, and political constraints working against it. See also J. Mittleman, *Ideology and Politics in Uganda* (Ithaca: Cornell University Press, 1975).

37. Joseph Stalin, *Marxism and the National Question* (New York: International Publishers, 1942).

38. These terms were suggested by Clifford Geertz, *The Interpretation of Cultures* (New York: Basic Books, 1973), pp. 234-54.

39. *Dawn* (Muqdisho), October 22, 1972.

40. E.J. Hobsbawm, *The Age of Revolution* (New York: Mentor, 1962), p. 17, and Raymond Williams, *Culture and Society 1780-1950* (New York: Harper and Row, 1958), p. xiii.

41. Karl Marx, "On the Jewish Question," in *Karl Marx: Early Writings*, ed. T.B. Bottomore (New York: McGraw-Hill, 1964).

42. Karl Mannheim, *Ideology and Utopia* (New York: Harcourt, Brace, 1936), ch. 4—esp. pp. 256ff.

43. See Xusen Adam, "Language and Cultural Development in Somalia" (paper presented to the Frantz Fanon Research and Development Center, Port of Spain, Trinidad, 1978).

44. Siyaad, January 30, 1972.

45. Interview with Castagno, p. 25.

46. Siyaad, February 17, 1970.

47. See Maxime Rodinson, *Islam and Capitalism* (New York: Pantheon, 1973), trans. from the French by Brian Pearce; and Fazlur Rahman, "The Sources and Meaning of Islamic Socialism," in *Religion and Political Modernization: Comparative Perspectives*, ed. Donald E. Smith (New Haven: Yale University Press, 1974).

48. *New Era* (Muqdisho), February 1973, p.31.

49. Lest I be considered naive, I recognize that Geertz's only attempt to show how ideology works as symbol is fraught with the same problems as any analysis of socialism as program (see his "Ideology as a Cultural System," in *Interpretation of Cultures*, pp. 220-29, esp. p. 228).

50. Immanuel Wallerstein, "The Rise and Future Demise of the World Capitalist System: Concepts for Comparative Analysis," *Comparative Studies of Society and History*, September 1974, pp. 415, 402.

51. Immanuel Wallerstein, *The Modern World-System* (New York: Academic Press, 1974).

52. For a different view, see Ruth Collier, "Parties, Coups and Authoritarian Rule: Patterns of Political Change in Tropical Africa," *Comparative Political Studies*, Spring 1978.

53. Wallerstein, "The Rise and Future Demise . . .," p. 406. The essays in Desfosses and Levesque (especially those by Hill and Kraus); Elliot Berg, "Structural Transformation Versus Gradualism," in *Ghana and Ivory Coast*, eds. A. Zolberg and P. Foster (Chicago: University of Chicago Press, 1971), and T. Callaghy, "Implementation of Socialist Strategies of Development: State Power, Conflict, and Uncertainty" (paper delivered at the APSA annual convention, Chicago, 1976), focus much of their attention on domestic variables to explain the failure of socialism in Africa.

James A. McCain: Ideology and Leadership in Post-Nkrumah Ghana

1. See Kenneth Grundy, "The Political Ideology of Kwame Nkrumah," in *African Political Thought* ed. W. A. E. Skurnik (Denver: International University Booksellers, Inc., 1968), pp. 66-100.

2. Kwame Nkrumah, "African Socialism Revisited," in *The Africa Reader: Independent Africa*, eds. W. Cartey and M. Kilson (Vintage Books; New York: Random House, 1970), p. 201.

3. *Ibid.*, p. 207.

4. K. E. deGraft Johnson; as quoted in "African Roundtable," *Africa Report* 17, 5 (May 1963): 20.

5. Aristide R. Zolberg, *Creating Political Order* (Chicago: Rand McNally, 1966), pp. 152-53.

6. See James A. McCain, "Ideology in Africa: Some Perceptual Types," *African Studies Review* 18, 1 (April 1975): 61-87.

7. Karl W. Deutsch, "Social Mobilization and Political Development," *American Political Science Review* 55 (September 1961): 497-98.

8. James S. Coleman, "Conclusion: The Political Systems of the Developing Areas," in *The Politics of the Developing Areas*, eds. Gabriel A. Almond and James S. Coleman (Princeton: Princeton University Press, 1960), pp. 535-36.

9. William John Hanna, "Students," in *Political Parties and National Integration*, eds. James S. Coleman and Carl G. Rosberg, Jr. (Berkeley: University of California Press, 1964), p. 413.

10. Fred M. Hayward, "A Reassessment of Conventional Wisdom About the Informed Public: National Political Information in Ghana," *American Political Science Review* 70, 2 (June 1976): 433-51.

11. Edited version of statement made by President David Dacko of the Central African Republic at the congress of the Mouvement d'Emancipation Sociale de l' Afrique Noire (MESAN), Bambari, July 26, 1962; as cited in *Africa Report*, May 1963, p. 20.

12. Léopold Senghor, "Dakar Colloquium," *Africa Report*, April 1963, p. 20.

13. Edited version of a statement by Léopold Senghor cited in Irving L. Markovitz, *Léopold Sedar Senghor and the Politics of Negritude* (New York: Atheneum Publishers, 1969), p. 157.

14. Edited version of a statement from Frantz Fanon, *The Wretched of the Earth* (New York: Grove Press, 1963), p. 139.

15. *Final Report of the Commission of Enquiry on Bribery and Corruption* (Tema: Government Printer, 1975), p. 45. See also Victor LeVine, *Political Corruption: The Ghana Case* (Stanford: Hoover Institution, 1975), and Maxwell Owusu, *Uses and Abuses of Political Power* (Chicago: University of Chicago Press, 1970).

16. Based upon statement in George Padmore, "A Guide to Pan-African Socialism," in *African Socialism*, eds. William H. Friedland and Carl G. Rosberg, Jr. (Stanford: Stanford University Press, 1964), p. 230.

17. Based upon a statement in Kwame Nkrumah, *Consciencism* (London: Heinemann, 1964), p. 74.

18. Based upon a statement published in *The Spark*; cited in K. A. Busia, *Africa in Search of Democracy* (New York: Praeger, 1967), p. 79.

19. Cited in Cartey and Kilson, p. 202.

20. Based upon a statement by Nkrumah cited in Friedland and Rosberg, eds., p. 263.

21. Léopold Senghor, "West Africa in Evolution," *Foreign Affairs* 39 (1960-61): 243.

22. Ali Mazrui, *Towards a Pax Africana* (Chicago: University of Chicago Press, 1967), p. 100.

23. Julius Nyerere; cited in Friedland and Rosberg, eds., p. 104.

24. Based upon a statement in Kenneth Kaunda, *Zambia: Independence and Beyond* (London: Nelson, 1966), p. 148.

25. Ezekiel Mphalele, *The African Image* (New York: Praeger, 1962), pp. 19-20.

26. Julius Nyerere; cited in Friedland and Rosberg, eds., p. 246.

27. Based upon statements by Nyerere in Friedland and Rosberg, eds., pp. 240-42.

28. *Ibid.*, p. 240. (Emphasis added.)

29. Similar to a statement by Tom Mboya in Friedland and Rosberg, eds., p. 252.

30. Similar to a statement by Modibo Keita cited in Francis G. Snyder, "The Political Thought of Modibo Keita," *Journal of Modern African Studies* 5 (May 1967): 79-106.

31. Mphalele, p. 66.

32. See the comments of Murray Edelman, *The Symbolic Uses of Politics* (Urbana, Illinois: University of Illinois Press, 1967), p. 6.

Samuel Decalo: Ideological Rhetoric and Scientific Socialism in Benin and Congo/Brazzaville

1. See Samuel Decalo: "The Politics of Instability in Dahomey," *Geneva-Africa* 7 (1968); "Full Circle in Dahomey," *African Studies Review*, December 1970; and "Regionalism, Politics and Military Rule in Dahomey," *Journal of Developing Areas*, April 1973; see also Dov Ronen, *Dahomey* (Ithaca: Cornell University Press, 1975).

2. For an excellent analysis of the pre-independence political array of power, see Martin Staniland, "The Three Party System in Dahomey," *Journal of African History* 14, 2 and 3 (1973); for the origin of political parties, see F. M. Oké, "Des comités electoraux aux partis dahoméens," *Revue Francaise d'Etudes Politiques Africaines*, August 1969.

3. See S. Decalo, "The Army in a Praetorian State: Dahomey," in Decalo, *Coups and Army Rule in Africa* (New Haven: Yale University Press, 1976).

4. *West Africa*, November 20, 1972.

5. See Banque Centrale des Etats de l'Afrique de l'Ouest, "Indicateurs economiques beninois," *Indicateurs Économiques* 255 (November 1977) and Table 2-3 in Decalo, *Coups and Army Rule in Africa*, p. 45; for the Benin budgets see Table 2-4 in *ibid.* (p. 46) or the quarterly issues on Benin of the BCEAO.

6. See Samir Amin, *L'Afrique de l'Ouest Bloquée* (Paris: Editions Minuit, 1971), pp. 134-50, 235-38.

7. For a recent review of the Beninois economy, see "Benin's Balance-Sheet," *West Africa*, February 16, 1976.

8. For details on these and other parties, see S. Decalo, *Historical Dictionary of Dahomey* (Metuchen, N. J.: The Scarecrow Press, 1976).

9. See the very detailed study by Maurice A. Glélé: *Naissance d'un état noire: l'Evolution politique et constitutionelle du Dahomey* (Paris: R. Pichon et R. Durand Auzias, 1969).

10. For a schematic diagram of some of these, see Oké, "Des comités electoraux aux partis dahoméens."

11. Decalo, "Full Circle in Dahomey"; for the 1970 results, see *Afrique Contemporaine*, May-June 1970, p. 7.

12. For their biographies and roles in Dahomean politics see Decalo, *Historical Dictionary of Dahomey*.

13. See Decalo, *Coups and Army Rule in Africa.*

14. *Africa Research Bulletin*, Political Series, July 1973. A committee had been appointed to "recommend" which of these was appropriate for Dahomey; see *Africa Contemporary Record*, 1972-73, p. B581.

15. *Africa Research Bulletin*, Economic Series, December 1974.

16. According to Kerekou: "The only historic and just way of development is socialism. . . . The basis and guide of our revolutionary movement is Marxism-Leninism. Some . . . say that Marxism-Leninism is not an authentic Dahomeyan doctrine. Such people are only deceiving themselves" (as cited in *West Africa*, December 16, 1974).

17. From an interview in Cotonou, July 1973.

18. *Africa Research Bulletin*, Political Series, January 1975, and *Africa Research Bulletin*, Economic Series, December 1974.

19. See "Benin—La loi fondamentale," *Afrique Contemporaine* 93 (September-October 1977): 23-35.

20. *West Africa*, January 1, 1973.

21. See *Le Monde*, March 3, 1973; *West Africa*, April 23, 1973; and *Africa Report*, May-June 1973.

22. See the evaluation of the regime's first year in office in *Africa Contemporary Record, 1973-74* (London: Rex Collings, 1974). See also *Afrique-Asie* 33 (25 June 1973), in which Kerekou stressed that a drive for "authenticity" was the prime target of the Revolution.

23. *Marchés Tropicaux et Méditerranéens*, June 27, 1975.

24. For a listing of some of these organizations, see *West Africa*, September 29, 1975, and October 4, 1976.

25. The best example is the takeover from a French company of the cotton industry, which promptly collapsed under state control (see *Le Monde*, December 1, 1976).

26. For a recent analysis, see "Benin's Balance-Sheet," *West Africa*, February 16, 1976.

27. See *Africa Contemporary Record, 1974-75*, p. B629.

28. *Africa Research Bulletin*, Political Series, December 1973.

29. *Ibid.*

30. *Marchés Tropicaux et Méditerranéens*, September 5, 1975.

31. *Africa Research Bulletin*, Political Series, April 1974.

32. *West Africa*, November 12, 1973.

33. *Africa Contemporary Record, 1974-75*, p. B625.

34. See Michael Wolfers, "Letter from Cotonou," *West Africa*, December 19, 1974.

35. *Africa Contemporary Record, 1975-76*, p. B675.

36. *West Africa*, August 4, 1975.

37. *The New Nigerian* (Kaduna), September 3, 1973; as cited in *Africa Contemporary Record, 1973-74*, p. B632.

38. See *West Africa*, September 29, 1975.

39. For the coup attempt and subsequent trials, see *West Africa*, March 31, 1975; *Le Soleil* (Dakar), March 8, 1975, and March 19, 1975; and *Jeune Afrique*, April 18, 1975.

40. For details, see Decalo, *Historical Dictionary of Dahomey*, p. 80.

41. *Africa Contemporary Record, 1975-76*, p. B652.

42. See *West Africa*, June 30, 1975, and July 28, 1975.

43. See, for example, *Africa Research Bulletin*, Political Series, February 1977.

44. *West Africa*, August 4, 1975, and September 15, 1975.

45. Cited in *Africa Contemporary Record, 1975-76*, p. B672.

46. *West Africa*, October 27, 1975.

47. *Africa Contemporary Record, 1972-73* (London: Rex Collings, 1973), p. B580.

48. "Benin: Raid on Cotonou," *West Africa*, January 27, 1977, p. 141.

49. *Africa Contemporary Record, 1974-75*, p. B631.

50. Raoul Crabbe, "Du Dahomey à la République Populaire du Benin," *Eurafrica*, April-June 1976, p. 77.

51. For an analysis that argues that Kerekou's nationalizations were unintended, see Gerard Malivot, "Le Dahomey, sortira-t-il un jour du marasme actuel?," *Eurafrica*, July-August 1975, pp. 19-22.

52. *Ibid.*, p. 21.

53. *Ibid.*, p. 22.

54. See *New York Times*, February 4, 1977, and the recent defense of Benin's claim of an imperialist attack in N. K. Bentsi-Enchill, "Remember Benin," *West Africa*, January 16, 1978, pp. 92-93.

55. "Benin—Mercenaries and Machiavelli," *West Africa*, January 31, 1977.

56. Emmanuel Terray, "Les Révolutions congolaise et dahoméenne," *Revue Francaise de Science Politique*, October 1964; F. Constantin, "Fulbert Youlou 1917-1972," *Revue Francaise d'Etudes Politiques Africaines*, June 1972; John Ballard, "Four Equatorial States," in *National Unity and Regionalism in Eight African States*, ed. G. Carter (Ithaca, N. Y.: Cornell University Press, 1966).

57. *Africa Contemporary Record, 1970-71*, p. B305.

58. *Africa Contemporary Record, 1969-70*, p. B419.

59. Ngouabi's description as cited in *West Africa*, April 9, 1973.

60. *Africa Research Bulletin*, Economic Series, November 1977.

61. See, *inter alia*, Georges Balandier, *The Sociology of Black Africa: Social Dynamics in Central Africa* (New York: Praeger, 1970); Samir Amin and Catherine Coquery-Vidrovitch, *Histoire économique du Congo 1880-1968* (Paris: Editions Anthropos, 1969); Catherine Coquery-Vidrovitch, *Le Congo au temps du grandes compagnies concessionaires* (Paris: Mouton, 1974), and Pierre Philippe Rey, *Colonialisme, neo-colonialisme et transition au capitalisme: Example de la 'comilog' au Congo-Brazzaville* (Paris: Maspero, 1971).

62. See Roland Devauges, *Le chomage à Brazzaville: Etude sociologique* (Paris: ORSTOM, 1959).

63. J. M. Wagret, *Histoire et sociologie politiques de la République du Congo Brazzaville* (Paris: R. Pichon and R. Durand-Auzias, 1964).

64. *Le Monde*, November 11, 1969; cited in J. M. Lee, "Clan Loyalties and Socialist Doctrine in the People's Republic of the Congo," *The World Today*, January 1971, p. 46.

65. See Decalo, *Coups and Army Rule in Africa*, pp. 135-36, 141-43.

66. From interviews in Kinshasa, June 1972.

67. For basic analyses of the Congolese economy, see "Congo" in International Monetary Fund, *Surveys of African Economies* (Washington, D. C., 1972), and "Congo," *Marchés Tropicaux et Méditerranéens*, April 19, 1969.

68. From data in United States, *Area Handbook for People's Republic of Congo* (Washington, D.C., 1971), pp. 159-210, and United Nations, *Statistical Yearbook 1965* and *1970*, and *Africa Research Bulletin*, Economic Series, September 1974.

69. *Africa Contemporary Record, 1969-70*, p. B427.

70. *Le Monde*, November 11, 1969; see also Gilbert Comte, "Le Socialisme de la parole," *Le Monde Hebdomadaire*, March 26-April 1, 1970.

71. Title of the Congo Information Agency's August 10, 1966, editorial celebrating the Third Anniversary of the Revolution; see *African Research Bulletin*, Political Series, September 1966.

72. See Martial Sinda, *Le Messianisme congolaise* (Paris: Payot, 1972), and E. Andersson, *Messianic Popular Movements in the Lower Congo* (New York: W. S. Heinemann, 1958).

73. Pierre Bonnafé, "Une classe d'age politique: La J. M. N. R. de la République du Congo-Brazzaville" *Cahiers d'Etudes Africaines* 31, 3 (1968).

74. P. Erny, "Parole et travail chez les jeunes d'Afrique Centrale," *Projet*, September-October 1966.

75. The "wild man of the Congo Revolution" according to V. Thompson and R. Adloff, *Historical Dictionary of the People's Republic of Congo* (Metuchen, N.J.: The Scarecrow Press, 1973). Hombessa ultimately was downgraded to the Ministry of Information (1968); later that same year he was imprisoned for resisting Ngouabi's takeover by organizing youthful holdouts in "Camp Biafra."

76. *Afrique Nouvelle*, April 26, 1967.

77. Thompson and Adloff, p. 16.

78. See "Revolutionary Rhetoric and Army Cliques in Congo/Brazzaville," in Decalo, *Coups and Army Rule in Africa*.

79. "Brazzaville: Ten Years of Revolution," *West Africa*, August 20, 1973.

80. *Vers la construction d'une société socialiste en Afrique* (Paris: Presence Africaine, 1975).

81. *West Africa*, March 28, 1977.

82. For a discussion of the problem of using such terminology in an African context, see Immanuel Wallerstein, "Left and Right in Africa," *Journal of Modern African Studies*, May 1971, and "Left, Right and Centre," *West Africa*, December 12, 1977.

83. *Afrique Nouvelle*, March 25, 1971.

84. *Le Monde*, October 30, 1973.

85. *Le Monde*, December 18, 1971; see also *New York Times*, July 17, 1972.

86. *Africa Contemporary Record, 1969-70*, p. B424.

87. *Le Moniteur Africain du Commerce et de l'Industrie*, August 10, 1972.

88. *Africa Contemporary Record, 1969-70*, p. B419.

89. *Le Monde*, April 27, 1971.

90. Cited in Ngouabi, "Pour un programme du Parti Congolais du Travail" (Brazzaville, December 1972), p. 2. For some of the program's main themes in the English language, see Sol Dubula, "The Congo on the Road to Socialism," *African Communist* 64 (1976): 43-51.

91. Ngouabi, *Vers la construction*.

92. *Le Monde*, April 30, 1975.

93. *West Africa*, January 13, 1975.

94. For some details, see *Marchés Tropicaux et Méditerranéens*, March 14, 1975.

95. *Africa Contemporary Record, 1975-76*, p. B477.

96. "Congo—Oil Not Enough," *West Africa*, April 19, 1976.

97. *West Africa*, March 1, 1976.

98. *Africa Contemporary Record, 1970-71*, p. B307.

99. *West Africa*, July 29, 1974.

100. *West Africa*, April 2 and 16, 1973.

101. *West Africa*, January 2, 1978.

102. *Africa Contemporary Record, 1975-76*, p. B472.

103. *Ibid.*, p. B471, and *West Africa*, December 15, 1975.

104. *West Africa*, November 17, 1975.

105. *West Africa*, March 28, 1977.

106. *West Africa*, October 11, 1976.

107. *West Africa*, December 20, 1977.

108. *West Africa*, March 28, 1977.

109. *West Africa*, February 14, 1977.

110. For a detailed look at these problems, see *Marchés Tropicaux et Méditerranéens*, January 7, 1977.

111. *West Africa*, April 11, 1977, and November 14, 1977.

112. *Africa Research Bulletin*, Economic Series, May 1977; see also *West Africa*, May 9, 1977.

113. For a summary, see "Self-criticism in Congo," *West Africa*, November 14, 1977.

Edward A. Alpers: The Struggle for Socialism in Mozambique, 1960-1972

1. Deposition of Alberto Joaquim Chipande (then Deputy Chief Commander of the Mozambican People's Armed Forces and member of the Central Committee of FRELIMO) in *Mozambique Revolution*, official organ of FRELIMO (hereafter *MR*) 43 (April-June 1970): 12; interview with Marcelino dos Santos in Joao Reis and Armando Pedro Muiuane, comps., *Datas e documentos da história da FRELIMO* (2d ed., rev.; Lourenco Marques: Imprensa Nacional, 1975), p. 38. Mondlane, *The Struggle for Mozambique* (Baltimore: Penguin, 1966), p. 119, gives 1961 as the date of MANU's foundation and notes the primacy within it of the Mozambique Makonde Union, but in this case I think Chipande's more direct testimony is to be preferred. (In general throughout this essay I have attempted to use contemporary evidence wherever possible, rather than relying exclusively on more recent FRELIMO assessments of its history.)

2. Editorial, *MR* 51 (April-June 1972): 1.

3. Reis and Muiuane, comps., p. 39.

4. "FRELIMO Faces the Future"—an interview with Marcelino dos Santos by Joe Slovo in *African Communist* 55 (1973): 32, 35-36.

5. Mondlane, "The Crystallization of a Struggle for Freedom," Appendix 2 in *Eduardo Mondlane* (London: Panaf, 1972) [Panaf Great Lives], pp. 156-57.

6. These can be found in Ronald H. Chilcote, *Emerging Nationalism in Portuguese Africa—Documents* (Stanford: Hoover Institution, 1972), pp. 429-35, 458-59, and 463-64.

7. Ronald H. Chilcote, *Portuguese Africa* (Englewood Cliffs: Prentice-Hall, 1967), pp. 120-21; for Gwambe's position in early 1963, see Chilcote, *Documents*, pp. 465-75.

8. The figures are from Mondlane, "Crystallization," p. 158.

9. Samora Machel, *Mozambique: Revolution or Reaction?* (Richmond, B.C.: LSM Press, 1975), p. 23.

10. Dos Santos, "FRELIMO Faces the Future," p. 47.

11. *Afrique-Asie*, Spécial Mozambique, 109 (17-30 May 1976), p. 4.

12. For a glimpse of the dimensions of this problem, see Allen F. Isaacman, *A Luta Continua: Creating a New Society in Mozambique* [Southern Africa Pamphlets, No. 1] (Binghamton, N.Y.: Fernand Braudel Center for the Study of Economics, Historical Systems, and Civilizations, 1978), pp. 85-87, and "U.S. Press Smears Mozambique," *Southern Africa*, August 1977, pp. 6-9.

13. Walter C. Opello, Jr., "Pluralism and Elite Conflict in an Independence Movement: FRELIMO in the 1960s," *Journal of Southern African Studies* 2, 1 (1975): 66-82. Cf. the excellent earlier accounts of this developing class conflict by John S. Saul, "FRELIMO and the Mozambique Revolution," in G. Arrighi and J.S. Saul, *Essays on the Political Economy of Africa* (New York and London: Monthly Review Press, 1973), pp. 378-405; Iain Christie, "Le temps des epreuves," *Afrique-Asie*, Special Mozambique, pp. 22-25; and Isaacman, *A Luta Continua*, pp. 16-23.

14. Dos Santos, "FRELIMO Faces the Future," pp. 36-38; Chipande as quoted in Mondlane, *Struggle*, pp. 135-36.

15. Mondlane, *Struggle*, pp. 130-33. See Chilcote, *Documents*, pp. 479-86, for examples of the kinds of documents produced by the ephemeral groups constituted by these opportunists.

16. Boubakr Adjali, *FRELIMO: Interview with Marcelino dos Santos* (Richmond, B.C.: LSM Press, 1971), p. 3.

17. Barbara Cornwall, *The Bush Rebels* (New York: Holt, Rinehart and Winston, 1972), pp. 30-31.

18. Quoted in *ibid.*, p. 57.

19. *Ibid.*, pp. 33-34.

20. John Paul, *Mozambique: Memoirs of a Revolution* (Harmondsworth: Penguin, 1975), p. 140.

21. Mondlane, *Struggle*, pp. 147-48.

22. *A Voz da Revolucao* (hereafter *VR*), April 1966, pp. 2-4. (This passage is translated differently in *MR*, 24 (March-May 1966), p. 10, where the word

revolution is inserted, though it does not appear at this point in the Portuguese text.)

23. Machel, *Revolution or Reaction?*, p. 24.

24. *VR*, November 1965, pp. 3-5.

25. *VR*, April 1966, pp. 5-7.

26. Editorial, *MR* 25 (June-July 1966): 1-3.

27. *MR* 24 (March-May 1966): 2. The wording of this editorial and its date make it apparent that it was written in reaction to the overthrow of Kwame Nkrumah in March 1966.

28. *Ibid.*, p. 3.

29. *VR*, 25 September 1966, p. 3.

30. *MR* 27 (October-December 1966): 1.

31. *Ibid.*, p. 2. For the progress made by Mozambican women in succeeding years, see *The Mozambican Woman in the Revolution* (Richmond, B.C.: LSM Press, January 1974); Mondlane, *Struggle*, pp. 185-87; Michele Manceaux, *Les Femmes du Mozambique* (Paris: Mercure de France, 1975). The problems of tribalism and regionalism were attacked in "We Must Fight United within FRELIMO," translated in *MR* 28 (May 1967): 9-10, and "Mozambican Tribes and Ethnic Groups: Their Significance in the Struggle for National Liberation," *MR* 36 (October-December 1968): 20-23. Originally unattributed, the second statement was written by Mondlane.

32. See, e.g., the special issue of *MR* commemorating the first three years of armed struggle (25 September 1967).

33. Editorial, *MR* 38 (March-April 1969): 1.

34. The best account of Gwenjere's activities is Christie, pp. 22-23; see also Saul, "FRELIMO and the Mozambique Revolution," p. 389, and Opello, pp. 74-75.

35. Cornwall, p. 37.

36. *MR* 34 (April-May 1968): 5-6, and editorial, *MR* 36 (October-December 1968): 4.

37. Editorial, *MR* 38 (March-April 1969): 2; on Nkavandame, see Mondlane, *Struggle*, pp. 104, 116-17, and Saul, "FRELIMO," pp. 389-90.

38. *MR*, Special Issue, 25 September 1967, p. 35.

39. Quoted in Cornwall, pp. 68-69. For examples of Portuguese economic policies elsewhere in northern Mozambique at this time, see Paul, pp. 64, 73-75. Cf. Mondlane, *Struggle*, pp. 85-86.

40. Editorial, *MR* 38 (March-April 1968): 2.

41. *MR* 34 (April-May 1968): 6 and 9; see also *Eduardo Mondlane*, p. 104.

42. Opello, p. 76; Machel, *Revolution or Reaction?*, pp. 24-25. The outsiders organized a meeting at Mtwara (Tanzania) in early August, but the results were the same (see Basil Davidson, *In the Eye of the Storm: Angola's People* [Garden City, N.Y.: Anchor Books, 1973], pp. 230-31).

43. FRELIMO, *Estatutos e programa* (Lourenco Marques: Imprensa Nacional, 1975).

44. Mondlane, *Struggle*, p. 171.

45. Christie, p. 24.

46. FRELIMO, *Estatutos e programa*, p. 9.

47. *Ibid.*, p. 14.

48. *Ibid.*, pp. 18-19, 20; Mondlane, *Struggle*, pp. 190, 194.

49. *Ibid.*, p. 195.

50. Machel, *Revolution or Reaction?*, p. 25.

51. Mondlane, undated letter to the present writer.

52. "Press Statement on Lazaro Nkavandame," *MR* 38 (March-April 1969): 10.

53. The best account of the police work involved in identifying the assassins is David Martin, "Interpol Solves a Guerilla Whodunit," *The Observer*, 6 February 1972.

54. Machel, *Revolution or Reaction?*, p. 25.

55. *MR* 40 (25 September 1969): 20.

56. *Ibid.*, p. 21.

57. Editorial, *MR* 38 (March-April 1969): 2.

58. *Ibid.*, p. 3.

59. *Ibid.*

60. *Ibid.*; *MR* 40 (25 September 1969): 20.

61. Adjali, *FRELIMO*, p. 1.

62. *Ibid.*, p. 5.

63. Editorial, *MR* 38 (March-April 1969): 3.

64. Machel, *Revolution or Reaction?*, p. 25.

65. Editorials, *MR* 43 (April-June 1970): 9-10, and *MR* 41 (October-December 1969): 3.

66. "Communique of the Executive Committee," *MR* 37 (January-February 1969): 5; Reis and Muiuane, comps., pp. 122-23.

67. Saul, "FRELIMO," pp. 391-96.

68. "Communique of the Executive Committee," *MR* 41 (October-December 1969): 5-6. Simango was expelled from FRELIMO in May 1970 (see editorial, *MR* 43 [April-June 1970]: 10-11).

69. Citation is from editorial, *MR* 41 (October-December 1969): 4.

70. Saul, "FRELIMO," p. 397.

71. Quoted in AJMA, *25 de Setembro—Dia da Revolucao Mocambicana* (Lisbon: Revolucao Proletária, 1975), p. 47.

72. FRELIMO, *As qualidades de um membro do Comité Central* (Lourenco Marques: Edicoes SIPEAAM, 25 April 1975).

73. Machel, *Mozambique: Sowing the Seeds of Revolution* (London: MAGIC, n.d. [1974]), pp. 38, 39, 43.

74. This point was driven home in an interview with dos Santos on 21 August 1976. For a brief account of Operation Gordian Knot, see Reis and Muiuane, comps., p. 153.

75. Saul, "Introduction" to Machel, *Sowing*, p. 4.

76. *MR* 48 (July-September 1971): 1-4.

77. "Alliance against Imperialism," *MR* 48 (July-September 1971): 5-6.

78. Editorial: "Central Committee Reviews the War," *MR* 53 (October-December 1972): 1-2.

79. Dos Santos, "FRELIMO Faces the Future," pp. 49-50. Some evidence that the leadership was beginning to think of FRELIMO as a party as early as 1971 can be found in *MR* 47 (May-June 1971): 8.

80. Among the most important are speeches by Machel in *A Nossa Luta*, pp. 69-254; *Revolution or Reaction?*; "The People's Republic of Mozambique: The Struggle Continues," *Review of African Political Economy* 4 (1975): 14-25; *A nossa luta é uma revolucao: nacionalizcoes—Mocambique* (Lisbon: CIDA-C, 1976), pp. 9-70; and *A classe trabalhadora deve conquistar e exercer o poder na frente da ciencia e da cultura* (Lisbon: Cadernos Ulmeiro, No. 9, n.d.). See also FRELIMO, *Comités do partido* (Lourenco Marques: Imprensa Nacional, 1974). The documents of the Third Congress are published in *Tempo*, 333 (20 February 1977), pp. 18-55. Of particular interest is the report of the Central Committee to the Third Congress, which traces the development of the struggle, its theory and its practice, and the reasoning behind the creation of a Marxist-Leninist Working Class Vanguard Party; see *Tempo*, 331 (6 February 1977), pp. 17-52, and *Tempo*, 332 (13 February 1977), pp. 18-40.

81. See, e.g., interview with Machel in *Afrique-Asie*, Special Mozambique, p. 9.

Kevin Brown: Angolan Socialism

1. *Guardian* (New York), December 24, 1976. This leftist weekly is an important source of information on Angola; one of its correspondents reports regularly from Luanda.

2. MPLA pamphlet, 1974 (1975?).

3. *Jornal de Angola*, January 2, 1977. The *Jornal* is the principal government-owned newspaper in Angola.

4. *Ibid.*

5. *Tricontinental* (Havana), X, 1975.

6. *Ibid.*

7. For the best description of this complicated period, see John Marcum, *The Angolan Revolution*, vol. I (Cambridge, Mass.: MIT Press, 1969).

8. *Guardian*, September 6, 1976.

9. I have relied heavily on Michael S. Morgado, "Amilcar Cabral's Theory of Cultural Revolution," *Black Images* 3, 2, pp. 3-16. See also *Return to the*

Source: Selected Speeches of Amilcar Cabral (New York: Monthly Review Press, 1973).

10. Morgado, p. 13.

11. Richard R. Fagen, The Transformation of Political Culture in Cuba (Stanford: Stanford University Press, 1969), p. 24. Fagen argues that Castro seized power in a relatively advanced country. I have used his points as a basis for my comparison with Angola.

12. Ibid., pp. 149-50.

13. Guardian, March 24, 1977.

14. Ibid., March 17, 1977. This issue contains an extensive commentary on the Law on State Intervention.

15. Afrique-Asie, No. 144, 19 September - 2 October 1977, p. 23.

16. Colin Legum and Tony Hodges, After Angola: The War Over Southern Africa (New York: Africana Publishing Co., 1976), p. 60.

17. Guardian, November 24, 1976.

18. Helen Desfosses, Soviet Policy Toward Black Africa (New York: Praeger, 1972), pp. 159-62.

19. Afrique-Asie, No. 150, 12-25 December 1977, p. 33.

20. Guardian, September 6, 1976.

21. Personal communication from Bruce Porter, Foreign Service Officer and former Consul in Luanda in 1975.

22. L'Express, No. 1369, 3-9 October 1977.

23. Personal communication from Leon Dash.

24. Charles K. Ebinger argues that the Cubans "balance" Soviet influence and asserts that Kissinger's insistence on Cuban withdrawal "borders on the absurd" ("External Intervention in Internal War: The Politics of the Angolan Civil War," Orbis, Fall 1976, p. 698).

25. Jeune Afrique, No. 863, 22 July 1977.

26. For an "official" account of the South African intervention, see John Barratt, "Southern Africa: A South African View," Foreign Affairs 55 (October 1976): 147-68.

27. Legum and Hodges, After Angola, p. 26. This is the best account of the extremely complex series of foreign interventions in the Angolan civil war.

28. Jornal de Angola, January 2, 1977.

29. Afrique-Asie, No. 144, 19 September - 2 October 1977, p. 23.

30. Personal communication.

Lars Rudebeck: Socialist-Oriented Development in Guinea-Bissau

1. In the main report delivered to the third Party congress of the PAIGC by the Secretary-General, only three countries are mentioned by name for having given substantial support to the PAIGC during the struggle for

national liberation: the Soviet Union, Cuba, and Sweden. See *Relatório do Conselho Superior da Luta, apresentado ao Congresso pelo Secretário-Geral do PAIGC, camarada Aristides Pereira* [Report from the Highest Council of the Struggle, presented to the congress by the Secretary-General of the PAIGC, comrade Aristides Pereira] (Bissau, 1977), pp. 192f.

2. See Lars Rudebeck, *Guinea-Bissau: A Study of Political Mobilization* (Uppsala: Scandinavian Institute of African Studies, 1974), pp. 71-104, for a summary and analysis of the PAIGC ideology.

3. The affirmation of this goal is the first point made in the *Resolucão Geral do III Congresso* [General resolution of the third congress], published in *No Pintcha*, no. 402, November 24, 1977. *No Pintcha* ["Forward" in Guinean creole, a language mixing African and Portuguese elements] is the official newspaper of the PAIGC regime, appearing three days a week in Bissau. During the congress week of 1977, it appeared daily.

4. The most important source is Cabral's address to the first Tri-Continental Conference of the Peoples of Asia, Africa, and Latin America in Havana in January 1966. This text has been published in a number of versions in several different languages. The most complete printed version is in English; it is entitled "The Weapon of Theory" and is included in Cabral, *Revolution in Guinea: An African People's Struggle* (London: Stage 1, 1969).

5. *Palavras de ordem gerais do camarada Amílcar Cabral aos responsáveis do partido. Novembro de 1965* (PAIGC, 1969), p. 23. [New edition (Bolama: National Printing Office of Guinea-Bissau, n.d.), p. 31.]

6. In addition to the main report (see note 1 above) and the final resolution (see note 3), there are two other important Congress documents: *Teses para o III Congresso do PAIGC, Cadernos para o III Congresso, n.º 5, 21 de Outubro de 1977* and *Ante-Projecto dos Estatutos do PAIGC, Cadernos ..., n.º 4, 7 de Outubro de 1977*, both published by the Information and Propaganda Services of the General Secretariat of the PAIGC. The first document contains six general theses that were later approved by the Congress; the second document contains proposed new party statutes that were also later approved by the Congress. Both texts were first widely discussed at meetings in local neighborhoods and places of work all over Guinea-Bissau and Cape Verde.

7. Confirmed by the Minister of Planning, Vasco Cabral, in *No Pintcha*, no. 251, November 18, 1976.

8. Documentation on the election of 1976 can be found in *No Pintcha*, nos. 257-266, December 4-28, 1976. The official results are in no. 266.

9. In Rudebeck, *Guinea-Bissau: A Study of Political Mobilization*, pp. 137-43, this judicial system is described in detail.

10. The number of persons engaged in extractive and processing industries in December 1977 was 1,833, according to *Classificacão das Actividades Económicas* (Planning Ministry, December 1977), pp. 32, 50.

11. Rudebeck, *Guinea-Bissau. Folket, partiet och staten*, gives a more thorough presentation.

12. The prices are found in the *Boletim Oficial*, no. 4 (January 25, 1975), p. 41, and no. 51 (December 20, 1975), p. 540.

13. Law No. 4/75, *Boletim Oficial*, no. 19 (May 10, 1975), p. 214.

14. *No Pintcha*, no. 287, February 17, 1977.

15. Based upon figures given in an interview by the Minister of Education, Mario Cabral, to the Portuguese newspaper *Diário de Lisboa*; reprinted in *No Pintcha*, no. 317, April 28, 1977.

16. *Boletim Trimestral de Estatística*, January-March 1977.

17. My thinking on these matters has been influenced by an essay by the Danish social anthropologist Peter Aaby: *The State of Guinea-Bissau: African Socialism or Socialism in Africa?*, Research Report 45 (Uppsala: Scandinavian Institute of African Studies, 1978).

John W. Harbeson: Socialist Politics in Revolutionary Ethiopia

1. Whether the changes in Ethiopia constituted a revolution is a question which will take some time to answer. The issue arose, for example, at the Wingspread Conference discussed in my "Perspectives on the Ethiopian Revolution," *Ethiopianist Notes* 1 (Fall 1977): 1-9.

2. See, for example, "The Ethiopian Peoples Revolutionary Party Program" (Addis Ababa, August 1975), and "The Political Economy of Ethiopia" (working paper presented at the 24th Congress of ESUNA by the Wisconsin chapter of ESUNA, August 1976).

3. See discussion in John Markakis, *Ethiopia: Anatomy of a Traditional Polity* (Oxford: Clarendon Press, 1974).

4. "Ethiopian Peoples Revolutionary Party Program."

5. Note, for example, the seven-volume series *Studies in Political Development*, published by Princeton University Press. The last of these—*Crises and Sequences in Political Development*, edited by Leonard Binder—appeared in 1974.

6. See, for example, the standard works on Ethiopian political history, such as A.M. Jones and E. Monroe, *A History of Ethiopia* (London: Oxford University Press, 1955), and Sven Rubenson, *The Survival of Ethiopian Independence* (London: Heinemann, 1976).

7. Jones and Monroe.

8. *Ibid.*

9. The central study of this period is Mordecai Abir, *Ethiopia: The Era of the Princes* (London: Longmans and Green, 1968).

10. Rubenson, *Survival of Ethiopian Independence*; Rubenson, *King of Kings: Tewodros of Ethiopia* (Addis Ababa: Oxford University Press, 1966); Donald Crummey, "Tewodros as Reformer and Modernizer," *Journal of African History* 10, 3 (1969): 457-69.

11. Rubenson, *Survival of Ethiopian Independence*; Zewde Gebre Selassie, *Johannes IV of Ethiopia* (Oxford: Clarendon Press, 1975).

413

12. See H. Marcus, *The Life and Times of Menelik II* (Oxford: Clarendon Press, 1974), and R.H. Kofi Darkwah, *Shewa, Menelik and the Ethiopian Empire, 1813-1889* (London: Heinemann, 1975).

13. Discussions of Ethiopian political identity are very limited. See D. Levine: *Greater Ethiopia: The Evolution of a Multi-Ethnic Society* (Chicago: University of Chicago Press, 1974), and "Ethiopia: Identity, Authority, and Realism," in *Political Culture and Political Development*, eds. Lucian Pye and Sidney Verba (Princeton: Princeton University Press, 1965), pp. 245-82.

14. See Levine, *Greater Ethiopia*.

15. Darkwah.

16. Bahru Zewde, "An Historical Outline of Famine in Ethiopia," in *Drought and Famine in Ethiopia*, ed. Abdul Mejid Hussein [African Environment Special Report 2] (London: International African Institute, 1976).

17. H. Westerhall, "Government Land in Ethiopia" (Ministry of Land Reform and Administration, 1972).

18. John W. Harbeson, "Afar Pastoralists and Ethiopian Rural Development," *Rural Africana* 28 (Fall 1975): 71-87; Lars Bondestam, "People and Capitalism in the North-Eastern Lowlands of Ethiopia," *Journal of Modern African Studies* 12 (1974): 423-39.

19. M. Abir, "Education and National Unity in Ethiopia," *Ethiopian Observer* 59, 27 (1970): 44-59.

20. Imperial Ethiopian Government, *Education Sector Review*, 1973.

21. Bondestam.

22. Markakis, p. 190.

23. John W. Harbeson, "Politics and Reform in Revolutionary Ethiopia" (paper presented to 18th Annual Meeting of the African Studies Association, San Francisco, 1976).

24. Interviews with senior ministers of the Endalkachew government.

25. Hussein, ed.; Karl Johan Lundstrom, *Northeastern Ethiopia: Society in Famine* (Uppsala: Scandinavian Institute of African Studies, 1976).

26. Hussein, ed.; Lundstrom.

27. Harbeson, "Politics and Reform"; Peter Koehn, "Ethiopian Politics: Military Intervention and Prospects for Further Change," *Africa Today* 20 (1975): 7-21; W.A.E. Skurnik, "Revolution and Change in Ethiopia," *Current History* 68, 405 (1975): 206ff.

28. *Education Sector Review*.

29. Darkwah is one of the more explicit defenders of the unwritten "Ethiopian Imperial Constitutional" theory; see his *Shewa, Menelik* . . . .

30. "Ethiopia: Crisis Diary," *Africa*, May 1974, pp. 21ff. The diary is believed to have been that of Asrata Kassa, chairman of the Emperor's Crown Council, a close advisor to the emperor, sometimes regarded as a potential opponent because of his royal blood, and one of those executed in November 1974.

31. Harbeson, "Politics and Reform."

32. See Donald Levine, "The Military in Ethiopian Politics," in *The Military Intervenes*, ed. H. Bienen (New York: Russell Sage Foundation, 1968); Richard Pankhurst, "The Ethiopian Army of Former Times," *Ethiopian Observer* 7, 2 (1964): 118-42; R. Caulk, "The Pre-Modern Army and Ethiopian Society: 1850-1935" (unpublished paper).

33. See, for example, Pankhurst.

34. *Administration of the Armed Forces Order, 1973*; Order No. 81 of 1973.

35. Levine.

36. U.S. Arms Control and Disarmament Agency, *World Military Expenditures*, 1971 (Washington, 1972).

37. Peter Schwab, "Haile Selassie: Leadership in Ethiopia," *Plural Societies* 6, 2 (1975).

38. Impressions gained from classroom discussions and informal talks with Ethiopian students at Haile Selassie I University, 1973-75.

39. Based on reading of ephemeral pamphlets circulated during the first weeks of the revolution, 1974 (see note on p. 354 above).

40. *Ethiopian Mirror*, July 1974, pp. 20ff.

41. *Ethiopian Herald*, December 13, 1974.

42. *Ibid.*

43. *Ibid.*

44. Provisional Military Government of Ethiopia, *Declaration of Economic Policy for Socialist Ethiopia* (Addis Ababa, February 1975).

45. *Ibid.*, pp. 3-4.

46. *National Democratic Revolutionary Program (NDRP)* (Addis Ababa, 1976). The *Program* was initially published in the *Ethiopian Herald*, April 21, 1976, along with an introduction by Lt. Col. Mengistu and a description of the role of the Peoples Organizing Provisional Office. A later version was published by Artistic Printers in Addis Ababa. Quotations in this paper are from the original version.

47. Proclamation 31 of 1975, *Public Ownership of Rural Lands*, May 1975, and Proclamation 47 of 1975, *Government Ownership of Urban Lands and Extra Houses*, August 1975. There have been a number of commentaries on these proclamations; see particularly John M. Cohen and Peter H. Koehn, "Rural and Urban Land Reform in Ethiopia," *African Law Studies* 14 (1977): 3-59.

48. Proclamation 31.

49. Proclamation 47, Article 3.1.

50. *Ibid.*

51. Allan Hoben, "Perspectives on Land Reform in Ethiopia: The Political Role of the Peasantry," *Rural Africana* 28 (Fall 1975): 55-71.

52. M. Ottaway, "Land Reform and Peasant Associations: A Preliminary Analysis," *Rural Africana* 28 (Fall 1975): 39-55.

53. Based on interviews with field officials of the Ministry of Agriculture, June and July 1977.

54. *NDRP.*

55. *Ethiopian Herald*, April 21, 1976.

56. *Ibid.*

57. *NDRP*: Introduction.

58. For background, see Bondestam; Harbeson, "Afar Pastoralists"; and Harbeson, "Territorial and Developmental Politics on the Horn of Africa: The Afar of the Awash Valley" (paper presented to the International Political Science Association meetings, Edinburgh, Scotland, August 1976; scheduled for publication in *African Affairs*).

59. *NDRP*, Section 2.5.

60. *Ibid.*

61. Harbeson, "Territorial and Developmental Politics."

62. *Ibid.*

63. J. Bruce, "Legal Considerations—Nomadic Lands" (Ministry of Land Reform and Administration, May 1970).

64. *NDRP*, Section 2.4.

65. *Ibid.*, Section 2.4a.

66. *Education Sector Review.*

67. *NDRP*, Section 1.2.

68. *Ibid.*, Section 3.2.

69. *Ibid.*, Section 2.3.

70. Mengistu speech accompanying release of *NDRP*; cited in *Ethiopian Herald*, April 21, 1976.

71. *NDRP*, Section 2.7.

72. *Ibid.*, Introduction and Section 4.

A SELECTED BIBLIOGRAPHY: 1964-1978

A major problem was faced by the editors in their selection of works to be included in this bibliography. In a sense, every study of government and public policy in the African states that have been labeled "socialist"—from Nkrumah's Ghana to the "new wave" of people's republics—is relevant to an assessment of the evolution of African socialism as an ideology and its practical implementation. To include all such references in the bibliography to this volume would be impossible. In order to limit the bibliography to manageable proportions, the editors have confined their selection to (1) primary statements on the content of African socialism and (2) secondary works that seek to relate the policies pursued by African socialist governments to the ideologies they articulate. Works concerned primarily with the technicalities of implementation of economic and social policies pursued by African socialist states have not been included. A selection of material published before 1964 is provided in the bibliography in William H. Friedland and Carl G. Rosberg, eds., *African Socialism* (Stanford: Stanford University Press, 1964), pp. 301-6. For additional material, readers are referred to the excellent bibliography "Current Africana" compiled by Chris Allen and published in the *Review of African Political Economy*.

BIBLIOGRAPHY

Adamolekun, L. *Sékou Touré's Guinea*. London: Methuen, 1976.

_____. "Politics and Administration in West Africa: The Guinean Model." *Journal of Administration Overseas* 8, 4 (October 1969): 235-42.

Adotevi, Stanislas Spero K. *Négritude et négrologies*. Paris: Union Générale d'Editions, 1972.

Ameillon, B. *La Guinée, bilan d'une indépendance*. Paris: F. Maspero, 1964.

Apter, David. "Nkrumah, Charisma and the Coup." *Daedalus* 97 (Summer 1968): 757-92.

Arnault, Jacques. *Du colonialisme au socialisme*. Paris: Editions Sociales, 1966.

Arrighi, Giovanni, and Saul, John S. *Essays on the Political Economy of Africa*. New York: Monthly Review Press, 1973.

_____. "Socialism and Economic Development in Tropical Africa." *Journal of Modern African Studies* 1, 2 (August 1968): 141-69.

Auma-Osolo, A., and Osolo-Nasubo, N. "Democratic African Socialism: An Account of African Communal Philosophy." *African Studies Review* 14, 2 (September 1971): 265-72.

The editors wish to express their gratitude to John Ravenhill for his assistance in the preparation of this bibliography.

Barker, Jonathan S. "Ujamaa in Cash-Crop Areas of Tanzania: Some Problems and Reflections." *Journal of African Studies* 1, 4 (Winter 1974): 441-63.

Bartels, C. M. J. *Senghor y el socialisme africano*. Algorta: Editions Zero, 1970.

Bénot, Yves. *Idéologie des indépendances africaines*. Paris: Maspero, 1969.

_____. *Indépendances africaines: Idéologies et réalités*. 2 vols. Paris: Maspero, 1975.

_____. "Idéologies, nation et structures sociales en Afrique." *Tiers-Monde* 57 (January-March 1974): 135-70.

Berg, Elliot. "Socialism and Economic Development in Tropical Africa." *Quarterly Journal of Economics* 78, 4 (November 1964): 549-73.

_____. "Structural Transformation versus Gradualism: Recent Economic Developments in Ghana and the Ivory Coast." In *Ghana and the Ivory Coast*, eds. P. Foster and A. Zolberg. Chicago, 1971.

Bienen, Henry. "An Ideology for Africa." *Foreign Affairs* 47, 3 (April 1969): 545-59.

_____. "State and Revolution: The Work of Amilcar Cabral." *Journal of Modern African Studies* 15, 4 (1977): 555-68.

Bing, Geoffrey. *Reap the Whirlwind: An Account of Kwame Nkrumah's Ghana from 1950 to 1966*. London: MacGibbon & Kee, 1968.

Blackey, Robert. "Fanon and Cabral: A Contrast in Theories of Revolution for Africa." *Journal of Modern African Studies* 12, 2 (June 1974): 191-210.

Boesen, Jannik, Madsen, Birgit Storgard, and Moody, Tony. *Ujamaa—Socialism from Above*. Uppsala, Sweden: Scandinavian Institute of African Studies, 1977.

Cabral, Amilcar. *Revolution in Guinea: Selected Texts*. New York: Monthly Review Press, 1969.

_____. *Return to the Source: Selected Speeches*. New York: Monthly Review Press, 1973.

_____. *Unité et lutte*. Vol. 1. *L'Armie de la théorie*; Vol. 2. *La Pratique révolutionnaire*. Paris: Maspero, 1975.

Charles, Bernard. "Le Socialisme africain: Mythes et réalités." *Revue Francaise de Science Politique* 15, 5 (October 1965): 856-84.

Chauleur, P. "Un dictateur aux abois: M. Sékou Touré." *Etudes* (Paris), May 1971, pp. 659-73.

Chilcote, Ronald H. "Amílcar Cabral: A Bio-Bibliography of His Life and Thought 1925-73." *Africana Journal* 4 (Winter 1974-75): 289-307.

Clark, E. "Socialist Development in Tanzania." *World Development* 3, 4 (1975): 223-28.

Cliffe, Lionel. "Planning Rural Development." *Development and Change* 3, 3 (1971-72): 77-98.

_____. "Tanzania: Socialist Transformation and Party Development." *African Review* 1, 1 (March 1971): 119-35.

_____. "Underdevelopment or Socialism? A Comparative Analysis of Kenya and Tanzania." In *The Political Economy of Africa*, ed. Richard Harris. Cambridge, Mass.: Schenkman Publishing Co. 1975.

A SELECTED BIBLIOGRAPHY: 1964-1978

Cliffe, Lionel et al., eds. *Rural Cooperation in Tanzania*. Dar es Salaam: Tanzania Publishing House, 1975.

Cliffe, Lionel, and Saul, John S., eds. *Socialism in Tanzania*. Vol. 1. *Politics*; Vol. 2. *Policies*. Dar es Salaam: East African Publishing House, 1972; 1973.

Cohen, Dennis L. "The Convention People's Party of Ghana: Representational or Solidarity Party?," *Canadian Journal of African Studies* 4, 2 (Spring 1970): 173-94.

Cox, Idris. *Socialist Ideas in Africa*. London: Lawrence & Wishart, 1966.

Davidson, Basil. "Somalia: Towards Socialism." *Race and Class* 17, 1 (Summer 1975): 19-37.

Decraene, P. "Spécifités somaliennes." *Revue Francaise d'Etudes Politiques Africaines* 115 (July 1975): 29-40.

_____. "Scientific Socialism: African Style." *Africa Report* 20, 3 (March 1975): 46-51.

Derman, B. "Mali's Socialist Years Reconsidered." *Africa Today* 14, 4 (1977): 83-87.

Desfosses, Helen, and Levesque, Jacques, eds. *Socialism in the Third World*. New York: Praeger, 1975.

Desfosses, Helen, and Stryker, J. Dirck. "Socialist Development in Africa: The Case of Keita's Mali." In *Socialism in the Third World*, eds. H. Desfosses and J. Levesque. New York, 1975.

Dumont, René, and Mazoyer, Marcel. *Développement et socialismes*. Paris: Seuil, 1969.

Durand-Reville, L. "Le Socialisme africain." *Revue des Travaux de l'Académie des Sciences Morales et Politiques* 122, 2 (1969): 119-30.

Emmert, Kirk. "African Socialism and Western Liberalism." *Africa Quarterly* 15, 1 and 2 (April-June and July-September 1975): 5-21.

Eshag, Eprime, and Richards, P. J. "A Comparison of Economic Developments in Ghana and the Ivory Coast Since 1960." *Bulletin of the Oxford University Institute of Economics and Statistics* 29, 4 (November 1967): 353-72.

Esseks, John D. "Political Independence and Economic Decolonization: The Case of Ghana under Nkrumah." *Western Political Quarterly* 24, 1 (March 1971): 59-64.

Feldman, David. "The Economics of Ideology: Some Problems of Achieving Rural Socialism in Tanzania." In *Politics and Change in Developing Countries*, ed. Colin Leys. Cambridge, 1969.

Feldman, Rayah. "Rural Social Differentiation and Political Goals in Tanzania." In *Beyond the Sociology of Development*, eds. Ivor Oxaal et al. London, 1975.

Fitch, Bob, and Oppenheimer, Mary. *Ghana: End of an Illusion*. New York: Monthly Review Press, 1966.

Folson, D. G. "The Development of Socialist Ideology in Ghana." *Ghana Social Science Journal* 1, 2 (November 1971): 1-20.

Fortman, Bastiaan de Gaay, ed. *After Mulungushi: The Economics of Zambian Humanism*. Nairobi: East African Publishing House, 1969.

Foster, Philip, and Zolberg, Aristide, eds. *Ghana and the Ivory Coast*. Chicago: University of Chicago Press, 1971.

A SELECTED BIBLIOGRAPHY: 1964-1978

Genoud, Roger. *Nationalism and Economic Development in Ghana*. New York: Praeger, 1969.

Gershenberg, Irving. "Slouching Towards Socialism: Obote's Uganda." *African Studies Review* 25, 1 (April 1972): 79-95.

Green, Reginald H. "Reflections on Economic Strategy, Structure, Implementation and Necessity: Ghana and the Ivory Coast 1957-1967." In *Ghana and the Ivory Coast*, eds. P. Foster and A. Zolberg. Chicago, 1971.

Gregor, A. James. "African Socialism and Fascism: An Appraisal." *Review of Politics* 29, 3 (July 1967): 324-53.

Grundy, Kenneth W., and Falchi, J. P. "The United States and Socialism in Africa." *Journal of Asian and African Studies* 4, 4 (October 1969): 300-14.

Gupta, A. "Kwame Nkrumah: A Reassessment." *International Studies* 12, 2 (April-June 1973): 207-21.

Harbeson, John. "Socialism, Traditions and Revolutionary Politics in Contemporary Ethiopia." *Canadian Journal of African Studies* 11, 2 (1977): 217-34.

Hazard, John N. "Mali's Socialism and the Soviet Legal Model." *Yale Law Journal* 77, 1 (November 1967): 28-69.

_____. "Marxian Socialism in Africa." *Comparative Politics* 2, 1 (October 1969): 1-15.

_____. "Négritude, Socialism and the Law." *Columbia Law Review* 65, 5 (May 1965): 778-809.

Helleiner, G. K. "Socialism and Economic Development in Tanzania." *Journal of Development Studies* 8, 2 (January 1972): 183-204.

Henriksen, Thomas H. "Marxism and Mozambique." *African Affairs* 77, 309 (October 1978): 441-62.

_____. "The Revolutionary Thought of Eduardo Mondlane." *Genève-Afrique* 12, 1 (1973): 37-52.

Hill, Frances. "Experiments with a Public Sector Peasantry: Agricultural Schemes and Class Formation in Africa." *African Studies Review* 20, 3 (December 1977): 25-42.

_____. "Ujamaa: African Socialist Productionism in Tanzania." In *Socialism in the Third World*, eds. H. Desfosses and P. Levesque. New York, 1975.

_____. *Ujamaa: Mobilization and Participation in Tanzania*. London: Frank Cass, 1978.

Hiwet, Addis. *Ethiopia: From Autocracy to Revolution*. London: Review of African Political Economy, Occasional Paper no. 1, 1975.

Holas, Bohumil Theophile. *La Pénsee africaine: Textes choisis 1949-1969*. Paris: Greuthner, 1972.

Hopkins, N. S. "Socialism and Social Change in Rural Mali." *Journal of Modern African Studies* 7, 3 (October 1969): 457-67.

Hughes, Arnold, and Kolinsky, Martin. "'Paradigmatic Fascism' and Modernization: A Critique." *Political Studies* 24, 4 (December 1976): 371-96.

Hughes, Glyn. "Preconditions of Socialist Development in Africa." *Monthly Review* 22, 1 (May 1970): 11-30.

Hymans, Jacques L. "The Origins of Léopold Senghor's African Road to Socialism." *Genève-Afrique* 6, 1 (1967): 33-48.

Hyden, Goran. "Can Coups Make It in Africa?" *Africa Report* 15, 12 (December 1970): 12-15.

Inukai, I. "African Socialism and Agricultural Development Strategy: A Comparative Study of Kenya and Tanzania." *Developing Economies* 12, 1 (March 1974): 3-22.

Isaacman, Allen. "A Luta Continua: Creating a New Society in Mozambique." Binghamton, N.Y.: Southern Africa Pamphlet Series, Fernand Braudel Center, S.U.N.Y., 1978.

Janke, Peter. *Marxist Statecraft in Africa: What Future?* London: Institute for the Study of Conflict, 1978. [Conflict Studies No. 95]

Jeffries, Richard. "Political Radicalism in Africa: The Second Independence." *African Affairs* 77, 308 (July 1978): 335-46.

Jinadu, L. Adele. "Ideology, Political Religion and Modernization: Some Theoretical and Empirical Explorations." *African Studies Review* 19, 1 (April 1976): 119-37.

Johnson, R. W. "Sékou Touré and the Guinean Revolution." *African Affairs* 69, 277 (October 1970): 350-65.

_____. "The Parti Democratique de Guinée and the Mamou 'Deviation.'" In *African Perspectives*, eds. C. Allen and R. W. Johnson. Cambridge, 1970.

_____. "Guinea." In *West African States: Failure and Promise: A Study in Comparative Politics*, ed. J. Dunn. Cambridge, 1978.

Jones, T. *Ghana's First Republic, 1960-66: Pursuit of the Political Kingdom*. London: Methuen, 1976.

Jones, William. "The Mise and Demise of Socialist Institutions in Rural Mali." *Genève-Afrique* 11, 2 (1972): 19-44.

Kaba, Lansiné. "Cultural Revolution, Artistic Creativity, and Freedom of Expression in Guinea." *Journal of Modern African Studies* 14, 2 (June 1976): 201-18.

_____. "Guinean Politics: A Critical Historical Overview." *Journal of Modern African Studies* 15, 1 (March 1977): 25-46.

Karioke, James. "Socialism in Africa: The Tanzanian Experience." *Civilisations* 23, 1-2 (1973-74): 31-47.

_____. "Tanzania and the Resurrection of Pan-Africanism." *Review of Black Political Economy* 4, 4 (Summer 1974): 1-26.

Kaunda, Kenneth D. *A Humanist in Africa*. London: Longmans, 1966.

_____. *Humanism in Africa and a Guide to Its Implementation*. Lusaka: Zambian Information Services, 1968.

Kaushal, Indra. *Political Ideologies in Africa*. Delhi: Sunindu Publishers, 1972.

Kjekshus, Helgo. "The Tanzanian Villagization Policy: Implementational Lessons and Ecological Dimensions." *Canadian Journal of African Studies* 11, 2 (1977): 269-82.

Klinghoffer, Arthur J. *Soviet Perspectives on African Socialism*. Rutherford, N. J.: Fairleigh Dickinson University Press, 1969.

Kraus, Jon. "A Marxist in Ghana." *Problems of Communism* 16, 3 (May-June 1967): 42-49.

_____. "Socialism and Political Economy in Ghana." In *Socialism in the Third World*, eds. H. Desfosses and J. Levesque. New York, 1975.

Laitin, David D. "The Political Economy of Military Rule in Somalia." *Journal of Modern African Studies* 14, 3 (September 1976): 449-68.

Lofchie, Michael. "Agrarian Socialism in the Third World: The Tanzanian Case." *Comparative Politics* 8, 4 (July 1976): 474-99.

Machel, Samora. "Independence Message." *Marxism Today* 19, 4 (April 1975): 102-9.

_____. "The People's Republic of Mozambique: The Struggle Continues." *Review of African Political Economy* 4 (November 1975): 14-25.

Markowitz, Irving Leonard. *Senghor and the Politics of Negritude*. London: Heinemann, 1970.

Martin, Guy. "Socialism, Economic Development and Planning in Mali 1960-68." *Canadian Journal of African Studies* 10, 1 (1976): 23-46.

Martin, Robert. *Personal Freedom and the Law in Tanzania: A Study of Socialist State Administration*. Nairobi: Oxford University Press, 1974.

Mazrui, Ali A. "Socialism and Neo-McCarthyism in Uganda." *Venture* 23, 3 (March 1971): 16-19.

_____, and Engholm, George. "Rousseau and Intellectualized Populism in Africa." *Review of Politics* 30, 1 (January 1968): 19-32.

Mboya, Tom. "Sessional Paper No. 10: It Is African and It Is Socialism." *East Africa Journal* 6, 5 (May 1969): 15-22.

McCain, James A. "Ideology in Africa: Some Perceptual Types." *African Studies Review* 18, 1 (April 1975): 61-87.

McHenry, Dean E., Jr. "Peasant Participation in Communal Farming: The Tanzanian Experience." *African Studies Review* 20, 3 (December 1977): 43-64.

_____. "The Ujamaa Village in Tanzania: Comparison with Chinese, Soviet and Mexican Experiences in Collectivisation." *Comparative Studies in Society and History* 18, 3 (July 1976): 347-70.

Meebelo, Henry S. *Main Currents of Zambian Humanist Thought*. Lusaka: Oxford University Press, 1973.

Mittelman, James H. *Ideology and Politics in Uganda: From Obote to Amin*. Ithaca: Cornell University Press, 1975.

Mohan, J. "Varieties of African Socialism." In *The Socialist Register*, eds. R. Miliband and J. Saville. London, 1966.

Mohiddin, Ahmed. "Reflections on Socialist Tanzania." *East Africa Journal* 9, 11 (November 1972): 26-37.

_____. "Socialism in Two Countries: The Arusha Declaration of Tanzania and the African Socialism of Kenya." *Africa Quarterly* 12, 4 (January-March 1973): 332-57.

_____. "Socialism or Capitalism? Sessional Paper No. 10 Revised." *East Africa Journal* 6, 3 (March 1969): 7-16.

_____. "The Basic Unit of African Ideal Society in Nyerere's Thought." *Africa* (Milan) 25, 1 (March 1976): 3-24.

_____. "Ujamaa: A Commentary on President Nyerere's Vision of Tanzanian Society." *African Affairs* 67, 267 (April 1968): 130-43.

Mondlane, Eduardo. *The Struggle for Mozambique*. Baltimore: Penguin Books, 1969.

Morrison, Lionel. "Ujamaa Villages—Tanzania's Rural Revolution." *Africa and the World* 6, 61 (July 1970): 14-16.

Murray, Roger. "Second Thoughts on Ghana." *New Left Review* 42 (March-April 1967): 25-39.

Mushkat, Marion. "African Socialism Reappraised and Reconsidered." *Africa* (Rome) 27, 2 (June 1972): 151-78.

Mutiso, Cyrus Gideon, and Rohio, S. W., eds. *Readings in African Political Thought*. London: Heinemann Educational, 1973.

Ncube, Patrick D. *African Socialism, Imperialism, and Reconsidering of Trotsky's Theory of Permanent Revolution*. Oslo: Instituttet for Sociologi, Universitetet 1 Oslo, 1975.

Neuberger, Benjamin. "Classless Society and One-Party State Ideology in Africa." *African Studies Review* 14, 2 (September 1971): 287-92.

Nkrumah, Kwame. "African Socialism Revisited." *The African Reader*. Vol. II. *Independent Africa*, eds. W. Cartey and M. Kilson. New York, 1970.

_____. *Class Struggles in Africa*. London: Panaf Books, 1970.

_____. *Dark Days in Ghana*. London: Panaf Books, 1967.

_____. *Revolutionary Path*. London: Panaf Books, 1973.

Nyerere, Julius K. *The Arusha Declaration Ten Years After*. Dar es Salaam: Government Printer, 1977.

_____. *Freedom and Unity/Uhuru Na Umoja*. Dar es Salaam: Oxford University Press, 1965.

_____. *Freedom and Socialism/Uhuru Na Ujamaa*. Dar es Salaam: Oxford University Press, 1968.

_____. *Ujamaa: Essays on African Socialism*. Dar es Salaam: Oxford University Press, 1968.

_____. *Freedom and Development/Uhuru Na Maendeleo*. Dar es Salaam: Oxford University Press, 1973.

_____. *Man and Development*. Dar es Salaam: Oxford University Press, 1973.

Obote, Apollo Milton. *Myths and Realities*. Kampala: African Publishers, 1970.

O'Connor, Michael. "Guinea and the Ivory Coast—Contrasts in Economic Development." *Journal of Modern African Studies* 10, 3 (October 1972): 409-26.

Onuoha, Bede. *The Elements of African Socialism*. London: Andre Deutsch, 1965.

Ottaway, Marian. "Social Classes and Corporate Interests in the Ethiopian Revolution." *Journal of Modern African Studies* 14, 3 (September 1976): 469-80.

A SELECTED BIBLIOGRAPHY: 1964-1978

_____. "Land Reform in Ethiopia, 1974-77." *African Studies Review* 20, 3 (December 1977): 79-90.

_____, and Ottaway, David. *Ethiopia: Empire in Revolution*. New York: Africana Publishing Company, 1978.

Owusu, Maxwell. *Uses and Abuses of Political Power: A Case Study of Continuity and Change in the Politics of Ghana*. Chicago: University of Chicago Press, 1970.

Parker, Ian C. "Ideological and Economic Development in Tanzania." *African Studies Review* 15, 1 (April 1972): 43-78.

Person, Y. "Le Socialisme en Afrique noir et les socialismes africains." *Revue Francaise d'Etudes Politiques Africaines* 27 (July 1976): 15-68.

Pratt, Cranford. "Foreign Policy Issues and the Emergence of Socialism in Tanzania 1961-68." *International Journal* 30, 3 (Summer 1975): 445-70.

_____. *The Critical Phase in Tanzania, 1945-68: Nyerere and the Emergence of a Socialist Strategy*. Cambridge: Cambridge University Press, 1976.

_____. "Nyerere on the Transition to Socialism in Tanzania." *African Review* 5, 1 (1975): 63-76.

Quick, Stephen A. "Bureaucracy and Rural Socialism in Zambia." *Journal of Modern African Studies* 15, 3 (September 1977): 379-400.

Raikes, P. L. "Ujamaa and Rural Socialism." *Review of African Political Economy* 3 (May-October 1975): 33-52.

Rich, P. "African Socialism." *Black Sash* 18, 4 (February 1976): 14-16.

Rodney, Walter. "Tanzanian Ujamaa and Scientific Socialism." *African Review* 1, 4 (April 1972): 61-76.

Rweyemamu, Anthony H., and Mwansasu, B. *Planning in Tanzania: Background to Decentralization*. Nairobi: East Africa Literature Bureau, 1974.

Rweyemamu, J. F., "Planning Socialism and Industrialization: The Economic Challenge." *Development and Change* 3, 3 (1971-72): 26-42.

Ryan, Selwyn D. "Economic Nationalism and Socialism in Uganda." *Journal of Commonwealth Political Studies* 11, 2 (July 1973): 140-58.

_____. "The Theory and Practice of African One-Partyism: The C.P.P. Re-examined." *Canadian Journal of African Studies* 4, 2 (Spring 1970): 145-72.

Sane, P. A. "Réflexions sur le socialisme africain." *Revue Libanaise des Sciences Politiques* 1 (January-June 1970): 75-94.

Sathyamurthy, T. V. "Idéologies politiques au Kenya, en Tanzanie et en Ouganda." *Revue Francaise d'Etudes Politiques Africaines* 116 (August 1975): 83-111.

Saul, John S. "African Socialism in One Country: Tanzania." In *Essays on the Political Economy of Africa*, eds. G. Arrighi and J. Saul. New York, 1973.

_____. "Frelimo and the Mozambique Revolution." In *Essays on the Political Economy of Africa*, eds. G. Arrighi and J. Saul. New York, 1973.

_____. "On African Populism." In *Populism: Its Meaning and National Characteristics*, eds. G. Ionescu and E. Gellner. London, 1969.

A SELECTED BIBLIOGRAPHY: 1964-1978

_____. "Tanzania's Transition to Socialism." *Canadian Journal of African Studies* 11, 2 (1977): 313-39.

_____. "Planning for Socialism in Tanzania: The Socio-Political Context." *Development and Change* 3, 3 (1971-72): 3-25.

Schumacher, Edward J. *Politics, Bureaucracy and Rural Development in Senegal.* Berkeley: University of California Press, 1974.

Senghor, Léopold Sédar. *On African Socialism.* New York: Praeger, 1964.

_____. *Liberté I: Négritude et humanisme.* Paris: Editions du Seuil, 1964.

_____. *Liberté II: Nation et voie africaine du socialisme.* Paris: Editions du Seuil, 1971.

Shivji, Issa G. *Class Struggles in Tanzania.* London: Heinemann, 1975.

_____, ed. *Tourism and Socialist Development.* Dar es Salaam: Tanzania Publishing House, 1973.

Silveira, Onerimo. *Africa South of the Sahara: Party Systems and Ideologies of Socialism.* Uppsala: Political Science Association Publication No. 71, 1976.

Skurnik, W. "Léopold Sédar Senghor and African Socialism." *Journal of Modern African Studies* 3, 3 (October 1965): 349-69.

Snyder, Frank G. *One-Party Government in Mali: Transition Toward Control.* New Haven: Yale University Press, 1965.

_____. "The Political Thought of Modibo Keita." *Journal of Modern African Studies* 1 (May 1967): 79-106.

The Spark (Accra), eds. *Some Essential Features of Nkrumaism.* London: Panaf Books, 1970.

Sprinzak, Ehud. "African Traditional Socialism—A Semantic Analysis of Political Ideology." *Journal of Modern African Studies* 11, 4 (December 1973): 629-47.

Suret-Canale, Jean. *La Republique de Guinée.* Paris: Editions Sociales, 1970.

Thiam, Habib. "The African Road to Socialism." *Review of International Affairs* 16 (December 1965): 12-15.

Thomar, L. V. *Le Socialisme et l'Afrique.* Paris: Le Livre Africain, 1966.

Thukral, K. B. "Tanzanian Socialism with Special Reference to 'Arusha Declaration.'" *Journal of African and Asian Studies* 2, 1 (Autumn 1968): 53-68.

Touré, Sékou. *L'Afrique et la révolution.* Switzerland, 1966.

_____. *Apprendre, savoir, pouvoir.* Conakry, 1965.

_____. *Concevoir, analyser, réaliser.* Conakry, 1966.

_____. *Défendre la révolution.* 2d ed. Conakry, 1969.

_____. *Plan Septennial, 1964-1971.* Conakry, 1967.

_____. *Le Pouvoir populaire.* Conakry, 1968.

_____. *La Révolution culturelle.* Conakry, 1969.

_____. *La Révolution guinéenne et le progrès social.* 4th ed. Conakry, 1967.

_____. *Stratégie et tactique de la révolution.* Conakry, 1977.

A SELECTED BIBLIOGRAPHY: 1964-1978

_____. *La Technique de la révolution*. Conakry, 1972.

Uganda. *The Common Man's Charter*. Entebbe: Government Printer, 1969.

Valdelin, Jan. "Ethiopia 1974-77: From Anti-Feudal Revolution to Consolidation of the Bourgeois State." *Race and Class* 19, 4 (Spring 1978): 379-99.

Varga, I. "Present Problems of the Realisation of Socialism in Tanzania." *Vierteljahresberichte* 48 (June 1972): 175-85.

Wallerstein, Immanuel. "Left and Right in Africa." *Journal of Modern African Studies* 9, 1 (May 1971): 1-10.

_____. "The Range of Choice: Constraints on the Policies of Governments of Contemporary African Independent States." In *The State of Nations: Constraints on Development in Independent Africa*, ed. Michael F. Lofchie. Berkeley, 1971.

Wright, R. "Machel's Marxist Mozambique." *Munger Africana Library Notes*, No. 34, 1976.

INSTITUTE OF INTERNATIONAL STUDIES
UNIVERSITY OF CALIFORNIA, BERKELEY

CARL G. ROSBERG,
Director

Monographs published by the Institute include:

RESEARCH SERIES

1. *The Chinese Anarchist Movement*, by Robert A. Scalapino and George T. Yu ($1.00)
3. *Land Tenure and Taxation in Nepal*, Volume I, *The State as Landlord: Raikar Tenure*, by Mahesh C. Regmi. ($8.75; unbound photocopy)
4. *Land Tenure and Taxation in Nepal*, Volume II, *The Land Grant System: Birta Tenure*, by Mahesh C. Regmi. ($2.50)
6. *Local Taxation in Tanganyika*, by Eugene C. Lee. ($1.00)
7. *Birth Rates in Latin America: New Estimates of Historical Trends*, by O. Andrew Collver. ($2.50)
8. *Land Tenure and Taxation in Nepal*, Volume III, *The Jagir, Rakam, and Kipat Tenure Systems*, by Mahesh C. Regmi ($2.50)
9. *Ecology and Economic Development in Tropical Africa*, edited by David Brokensha. ($8.25; unbound photocopy)
12. *Land Tenure and Taxation in Nepal*, Volume IV, *Religious and Charitable Land Endowments: Guthi Tenure*, by Mahesh C. Regmi ($2.75)
13. *The Pink Yo-Yo: Occupational Mobility in Belgrade, ca 1915-1965*, by Eugene A. Hammel. ($2.00)
14. *Community Development in Israel and the Netherlands: A Comparative Analysis*, by Ralph M. Kramer. ($2.50)
* 15. *Central American Economic Integration: The Politics of Unequal Benefits*, by Stuart I. Fagan. ($2.00)
16. *The International Imperatives of Technology: Technological Development and the International Political System*, by Eugene B. Skolnikoff. ($2.95)
* 17. *Autonomy or Dependence as Regional Integration Outcomes: Central America*, by Philippe C. Schmitter. ($1.75)
18. *Framework for a General Theory of Cognition and Choice*, by R.M. Axelrod. ($1.50)
19. *Entry of New Competitors in Yugoslav Market Socialism*, by S.R. Sacks. ($2.50)
* 20. *Political Integration in French-Speaking Africa*, by Abdul A. Jalloh. ($3.50)
21. *The Desert and the Sown: Nomads in the Wider Society*, ed. by Cynthia Nelson. ($3.50)
22. *U.S.-Japanese Competition in International Markets: A Study of the Trade-Investment Cycle in Modern Capitalism*, by John E. Roemer. ($3.95)
23. *Political Disaffection Among British University Students: Concepts, Measurement, and Causes*, by Jack Citrin and David J. Elkins. ($2.00)
24. *Urban Inequality and Housing Policy in Tanzania: The Problem of Squatting*, by Richard E. Stren. ($2.50)
* 25. *The Obsolescence of Regional Integration Theory*, by Ernst B. Haas. ($2.95)
26. *The Voluntary Service Agency in Israel*, by Ralph M. Kramer. ($2.00)
27. *The SOCSIM Demographic-Sociological Microsimulation Program: Operating Manual*, by Eugene A. Hammel *et al.* ($4.50)
28. *Authoritarian Politics in Communist Europe: Uniformity & Diversity in One-Party States*, edited by Andrew C. Janos. ($3.75)

*International Integration Series

29. *The Anglo-Icelandic Cod War of 1972-1973: A Case Study of a Fishery Dispute*, by Jeffrey A. Hart. ($2.00)
30. *Plural Societies and New States: A Conceptual Analysis*, by Robert Jackson. ($2.00)
31. *The Politics of Crude Oil Pricing in the Middle East, 1970-1975: A Study in International Bargaining*, by Richard Chadbourn Weisberg. ($3.50)
32. *Agricultural Policy and Performance in Zambia: History, Prospects, and Proposals for Change*, by Doris Jansen Dodge. ($4.95)
33. *Five Classy Programs: Computer Procedures for the Classification of Households*, by E.A. Hammel and R.Z. Deuel. ($3.75)
34. *Housing the Urban Poor in Africa: Policy, Politics, and Bureaucracy in Mombasa*, by Richard E. Stren ($5.95)
35. *The Russian New Right: Right-Wing Ideologies in the Contemporary USSR*, by Alexander Yanov. ($3.95)
36. *Social Change in Romania, 1860-1940: A Debate on Development in a European Nation*, ed. by Kenneth Jowitt. ($4.50)
37. *The Leninist Response to National Dependency*, by Kenneth Jowitt ($2.50)
38. *Socialism in Sub-Saharan Africa: A New Assessment*, ed. by Carl G. Rosberg and Thomas M. Callaghy. ($8.50)

POLITICS OF MODERNIZATION SERIES

1. *Spanish Bureaucratic-Patrimonialism in America*, by Magali Sarfatti ($2.00)
2. *Civil-Military Relations in Argentina, Chile, and Peru*, by Liisa North. ($2.00)
3. *Notes on the Process of Industrialization in Argentina, Chile, and Peru*, by Alcira Leiserson. ($1.75)
4. *Chilean Christian Democracy: Politics and Social Forces*, by James Petras ($1.50)
5. *Social Stratification in Peru*, by Magali S. Larson and Arlene E. Bergman. ($4.95)
6. *Modernization and Coercion*, by Mario Barrera. ($1.50)
7. *Latin America: The Hegemonic Crisis and the Military Coup*, by José Nun. ($2.00)
8. *Development Processes in Chilean Local Government*, by Peter S. Cleaves. ($1.50)
9. *Modernization and Bureaucratic-Authoritarianism: Studies in South American Politics*, by Guillermo A. O'Donnell. ($3.50)

POLICY PAPERS IN INTERNATIONAL AFFAIRS

1. *Images of Detente and the Soviet Political Order*, by Kenneth Jowitt. ($1.00)
2. *Detente After Brezhnev: The Domestic Roots of Soviet Foreign Policy*, by Alexander Yanov. ($3.00)
3. *The Mature Neighbor Policy: A New United States Economic Policy for Latin America*, by Albert Fishlow. ($2.00)
4. *Five Images of the Soviet Future: A Critical Review and Synthesis*, by George W. Breslauer. ($2.50)
5. *Global Evangelism Rides Again: How to Protect Human Rights Without Really Trying*, by Ernst B. Haas. ($2.00)
6. *Israel and Jordan: The Implications of an Adversarial Partnership*, by Ian Lustick. ($2.00)
7. *Political Syncretism in Italy: Historical Coalition Strategies and the Present Crisis*, by Giuseppe Di Palma. ($2.00)
8. *U.S. Foreign Policy in Sub-Saharan Africa: National Interest and Global Strategy*, by Robert M. Price. ($2.25).
9. *East-West Technology Transfer in Perspective*, by R. J. Carrick. ($2.75)

Address correspondence to:

Institute of International Studies
215 Moses Hall
University of California
Berkeley, California 94720

SOCIALISM IN

SUB-SAHARAN AFRICA